THE MEANING OF

ANXIETY

By

ROLLO MAY, Ph.D.

ASSOCIATE IN UNIVERSITY SEMINARS
COLUMBIA UNIVERSITY

THE RONALD PRESS COMPANY ⚹ NEW YORK

Library of Congress Catalog Card Number: 50-6600

PRINTED IN THE UNITED STATES OF AMERICA

I SAW that all the things I feared and which feared me had nothing good or bad in them save in so far as the mind was affected by them.—Spinoza, *Treatise on the Correction of the Understanding.*

I WOULD SAY that learning to know anxiety is an adventure which every man has to affront if he would not go to perdition either by not having known anxiety or by sinking under it. He therefore who has learned rightly to be anxious has learned the most important thing.—Kierkegaard, *The Concept of Dread.*

. . . ONE THING is certain, that the problem of anxiety is a nodal point, linking up all kinds of most important questions; a riddle, of which the solution must cast a flood of light upon our whole mental life.—Freud, *General Introduction to Psychoanalysis.*

PREFACE

This book is the result of several years of exploration, research, and thought on one of the most urgent problems of our day. Clinical experience has proved to psychologists and psychiatrists generally that the central problem in psychotherapy is the nature of anxiety. To the extent that we have been able to solve that problem, we have made a beginning in understanding the causes of integration and disintegration of personality.

But if anxiety were merely a phenomenon of maladjustment, it might well be consigned to the consulting room and the clinic and this book to the professional library. The evidence is overwhelming, however, that men and women of today live in an "age of anxiety." If one penetrates below the surface of political, economic, business, professional, or domestic crises to discover their psychological causes, or if one seeks to understand modern art or poetry or philosophy or religion, one runs athwart the problem of anxiety at almost every turn. There is reason to believe that the ordinary stresses and strains of life in the changing world of today are such that few if any escape the need to confront anxiety and to deal with it in some manner.

For the past hundred years, for reasons which will appear in the following chapters, psychologists, philosophers, social historians, and other students of humanity have been increasingly preoccupied with this nameless and formless uneasiness that has dogged the footsteps of modern man. Yet in all that time, to the present writer's knowledge, only two attempts have been made in book form—one essay by Kierkegaard and one by Freud—to present an objective picture of anxiety and to indicate constructive methods of dealing with it.

This study seeks to bring together in one volume the theories of anxiety offered by modern explorers in different areas of our culture, to discover the common elements in these theories, and to formulate these concepts so that we shall have some common ground for further inquiry. If the synthesis of anxiety theory presented here serves the purpose of producing some coherence and order in this field, a good part of the writer's goal will have been achieved.

It is of course clear that anxiety is not merely an abstract theoretical concept, any more than swimming is to a person whose boat has capsized a mile from shore. A discussion of anxiety that was not geared to immediate human problems would not be worth either writing or reading. Hence the theoretical synthesis has been tested by investigation of actual anxiety situations and selected case studies to discover what concrete evidence there may be to support the author's conclusions as to what anxiety means and what purpose it serves in human experience.

In order to keep this study within manageable limits, the author has restricted its scope to the observations of men who are our contemporaries in all important respects, and even within these limits only the most significant figures have been treated extensively. These are men who represent Western civilization as we experience it, whether they are philosophers like Kierkegaard, psychotherapists like Freud, novelists, poets, economists, social historians, or others with keen insight into human problems. These restrictions in time and space serve to bring the problem of anxiety into sharp focus, but they should not be taken to imply that anxiety is exclusively a modern problem or solely a Western one. The writer hopes that this book will stimulate similar surveys in other parts of the field.

Because of the vital general interest in the subject of anxiety, the author has stated his findings so that they will be clear not only to professional readers but also to students of psychology and psychiatry, to social scientists, and to general readers who seek a psychological understanding of modern problems. The book is in fact pertinent to the concerns of any intelligent citizen who feels on his own pulse the tensions and anxiety-creating conflicts of our day and who has asked himself what the meaning and causes of this anxiety may be and how the anxiety can be dealt with.

For those interested in a comparative survey of modern schools of psychotherapy, this volume should serve as a convenient textbook, presenting as it does the views of a dozen leaders in this field. There is no better way to understand these various schools than to compare their theories of anxiety.

During the years the author was working on this study, his ideas on anxiety were sharpened and broadened by discussions with many professional colleagues and friends, too numerous, unfortunately, to be mentioned here. But he does not wish to forego the pleasure of specifically expressing appreciation to Dr. O. H. Mowrer, Dr. Kurt Goldstein, Dr. Paul Tillich, and Dr. P. M. Symonds, who read the manuscript at its various stages and who discussed with the author at many different times and through many stimulating hours the approach to the problem of anxiety in the fields they represent. The author is also indebted for direct and indirect help in this study to Dr. Erich Fromm and other colleagues in the William Alanson White Institute of Psychiatry. As is to be expected, however, the particular approach to the problem of anxiety and the synthesis of anxiety theory in this study are not to be identified with any of the above persons; the author himself takes responsibility for the manner of approach and the conclusions. The author wishes also to express gratitude to his wife, Florence DeFrees May, for innumerable constructive reactions to the ideas in this study, and for making the index. A final word of appreciation is directed to the psychiatrist and the social workers at the institution in which the case studies of unmarried mothers were made. These colleagues gave expert help in the understanding of the cases; though for obvious reasons they must remain anonymous, the author wishes at least to acknowledge their cooperation.

ROLLO MAY

New York, N. Y.
February, 1950

ACKNOWLEDGMENTS

The author wishes to acknowledge the courtesy of the following authors and publishers in permitting quotations from their publications:

American Book Company, for excerpts from Kurt Goldstein, *The Organism: A Holistic Approach to Biology,* copyright 1939 by American Book Company, pages 292, 293, 295, 303, and 306, in Chapter 3.

Mr. W. H. Auden, for excerpts from *The Age of Anxiety: A Baroque Eclogue,* copyright 1947 by W. H. Auden, and published by Randont House, Inc., pages 8, 42, 44, 45, 134, in Chapters 1, 5, and 8.

The Blakiston Company, for an excerpt from R. R. Grinker and S. P. Spiegel, *Men Under Stress,* copyright 1945 by The Blakiston Company, page 144, in Chapter 3.

Clark University Press, for an excerpt from R. R. Willoughby, "Magic and Cognate Phenomena: An Hypothesis," in Carl Murchison, editor, *A Handbook of Social Psychology,* copyright 1935 by Clark University, page 466, in Chapter 3.

Columbia University Press, for excerpts from Helen Flanders Dunbar, *Emotions and Bodily Changes,* revised edition, copyright, 1935, 1938 by Columbia University Press, pages xxx, 128, 145, and 155, in Chapter 3; and from Abram Kardiner, *The Psychological Frontiers of Society,* copyright 1945 by Columbia University Press, pages 264, 411, and 445, in Chapter 5.

Mr. Erich Fromm, for excerpts from *Escape from Freedom,* copyright 1941 by Erich Fromm, and published by Rinehart & Co., Inc., pages 14, 29, 48, 62, 105, 152, and 186, in Chapter 5; also for excerpts from *Man for Himself,* copyright 1947 by Erich Fromm, and published by Rinehart & Co., Inc.

Harcourt, Brace and Company, Inc., for excerpts from Karl Mannheim, *Man and Society in an Age of Reconstruction,* copyright 1941 by Harcourt, Brace and Company, Inc., pages 117, 128, and 130, in Chapter 5; and from R. H. Tawney, *The Acquisitive Society,* copyright 1920 by Harcourt, Brace and Company, Inc., page 72, in Chapter 5.

Harvard University Press, for excerpts from Kurt Goldstein, *Human Nature in the Light of Psychopathology,* copyright 1940 by Harvard University Press, pages 115 and 117, in Chapter 3.

Henry Holt & Company, Inc., for excerpts from Herman Hesse, *Steppenwolf*, translated by Basil Creighton, copyright 1947 by Henry Holt & Company, Inc., pages 26-28, in Chapter 1.

Journal of the History of Ideas and Mr. Paul Tillich, the author, for an excerpt from "Existential Philosophy," *Journal of the History of Ideas*, copyright 1944 by Journal of the History of Ideas, V, 66-67, in Chapter 2.

Alfred A. Knopf, Inc., for excerpts from Otto Rank, *Will Therapy*, copyright 1936 by Alfred A. Knopf, Inc., pages 172 and 175, in Chapter 4.

Mr. Howard S. Liddell, for excerpts from a paper read before the American Psychopathological Association at its meeting of June 4, 1949.

Liveright Publishing Corporation and Sigmund Freud Copyrights, Ltd., for excerpts from Sigmund Freud, *A General Introduction to Psychoanalysis*, published by Liveright, New York; copyright renewed 1948; pages 341-344, 350, 353, and 355, in Chapter 4.

Mr. O. H. Mowrer, for excerpts from various articles and addresses, published and unpublished, in Chapter 4.

W. W. Norton & Company, Inc., for excerpts from Walter B. Cannon, *The Wisdom of the Body*, revised and enlarged edition, copyright 1939 by Walter B. Cannon, pages 253-254, in Chapter 3; from Karen Horney, *New Ways in Psychoanalysis*, copyright 1939 by W. W. Norton & Company, Inc., pages 76, 78, 82, and 83; also *The Neurotic Personality of Our Time*, copyright 1937 by W. W. Norton & Company, Inc., pages 71, 199, and 289, and *Our Inner Conflicts*, copyright 1945 by W. W. Norton & Company, Inc., page 12, in Chapter 4; from Sigmund Freud, *New Introductory Lectures in Psychoanalysis*, copyright 1933, by Sigmund Freud, pages 113, 119, and 120, in Chapters 4 and 6, and *The Problem of Anxiety*, copyright 1936 by The Psychoanalytic Quarterly Press, pages 22, 51-52, 75, 80, 86, 98-100, 112, and 152, in Chapter 4.

The Peter Pauper Press, for excerpts from *Pascal's Pensées*, edited and translated by G. B. Rawlings, pages 7 and 36, in Chapter 2.

Princeton University Press, for eleven illustrative extracts from Søren Kierkegaard, *The Concept of Dread*, translated by Walter Lowrie, copyright 1944 by Princeton University Press, from page xii to page 144, and one excerpt from *Sickness Unto Death* by the same author and translator, copyright 1941 by Princeton University Press, page 52, all in Chapter 2 except for one at the front of the book and one in Chapter 4.

Rinehart & Company, Inc., for excerpts from C. Landis and W. A. Hunt, *The Startle Pattern*, copyright 1939 by Carney Landis and William A. Hunt, pages 21, 136, 141, and 153, in Chapter 3.

The Ronald Press Company, for excerpts from Leon J. Saul, "Physiological Effects of Emotional Tension," in J. McV. Hunt, editor, *Personality and the Behavior Disorders,* copyright 1944 by The Ronald Press Company, pages 269, 276, 277, in Chapter 3.

University of Chicago Press, for excerpts from Paul Tillich, *The Protestant Era,* copyright 1947 by University of Chicago Press, pages 245-246, in Chapters 1 and 2.

The Viking Press, Inc., for an excerpt from Norman Cousins, *Modern Man Is Obsolete,* copyright 1945 by Norman Cousins, page 10, in Chapter 1.

Yale University Press, for excerpts from Ernst Cassirer, *An Essay on Man,* copyright 1944 by Yale University Press, page 21, in Chapter 1, and Carl Jung, *Psychology and Religion,* copyright 1938 by Yale University Press, pages 18 and 120, in Chapter 4.

CONTENTS

PART I

Modern Interpretations of Anxiety

PART II

Clinical Analysis of Anxiety

APPENDIX

PART I

MODERN INTERPRETATIONS OF ANXIETY

Chapter 1

INTRODUCTION

Now there are times when a whole generation is caught . . .
between two ages, two modes of life, with the consequence that
it loses all power to understand itself and has no standards, no
security, no simple acquiescence.—Herman Hesse, *Steppenwolf.*

1. CENTRALITY OF THE PROBLEM OF ANXIETY IN OUR DAY

Every alert citizen of our society realizes, on the basis of his
own experience as well as his observation of his fellow-men, that
anxiety is a pervasive and profound phenomenon in the middle
of the twentieth century. The alert citizen, we may assume,
would be aware not only of the more obvious anxiety-creating
situations in our day, such as the threats of war, of the uncon-
trolled atom bomb, and of radical political and economic upheaval; but also of the less obvious, deeper, and more personal
sources of anxiety in himself as well as in his fellow-men—
namely the inner confusion, psychological disorientation, and
uncertainty with respect to values and acceptable standards of
conduct. Hence to endeavor to "prove" the pervasiveness of
anxiety in our day is as unnecessary as the proverbial carrying
of coals to Newcastle.

Since the implicit sources of anxiety in our society are generally recognized, our task in this introductory chapter is somewhat more specific. We shall point out how anxiety has
emerged, and has to some slight extent been defined, as an *explicit* problem in many different areas in our culture. It is as
though in the present decade the explorations and investigations
in such diverse fields as poetry and science, or religion and
politics, were converging on this central problem, anxiety.
Whereas the period of two decades ago might have been termed

3

the "age of covert anxiety"—as we hope to demonstrate later in this chapter—the present phase of our century may well be called, as Auden and Camus call it, the "age of overt anxiety." This emergence of anxiety from an implicit to an explicit problem in our society, this change from anxiety as a matter of "mood" to a recognition that it is an urgent issue which we must at all costs try to define and clarify, are, in the judgment of the present writer, the significant phenomena at the moment. Not only in the understanding and treatment of emotional disturbances and behavioral disorders has anxiety become recognized as the "nodal problem," in Freud's words; but it is now seen likewise to be nodal in such different areas as literature, sociology, political and economic thought, education, religion, and philosophy. We shall cite examples of testimony from these fields, beginning with the more general and proceeding to the more specific concern with anxiety as a scientific problem.

In Literature.—If one were to inquire into anxiety as exhibited in the American literature, say, of 1920 or 1930, one would be forced in all probability to occupy oneself with symptoms of anxiety rather than overt anxiety itself. But though signs of open, manifest anxiety were not plentiful in that period, certainly the student could find plenty of symptomatic indications of underlying anxiety. *Vide,* for example, the pronounced sense of loneliness, the quality of persistent searching—frantically and compulsively pursued but always frustrated—in the writings of a novelist like Thomas Wolfe.[1]

---

[1] See especially *Look homeward angel* (New York, 1929) and *You can't go home again* (New York, 1934), and the later *Of time and the river* (New York, 1935). It is exceedingly interesting that the central psychological theme of Wolfe's writings, the relation of the individual to his mother and the conflicts stemming from that relationship, is one of the central problems in any discussion of the origins of anxiety, and is in fact discussed at some length in following chapters of the present study. In the cases demonstrating anxiety in Part II, below, it will be observed that anxiety frequently, and in many cases basically, hinged on the issue symbolically expressed in Wolfe's title, *You can't go home again.* We shall observe in these cases that neurotic anxiety occurred because these patients were unable to accept the psychological meaning of not going home again, namely psychological autonomy. One could wonder (realizing that literary artists symbolically express, often with remarkable fidelity, the unconscious assumptions and conflicts of their culture) whether these symbols in Wolfe's writing could be taken to mean that many people in the late 1920's and early 1930's were beginning to realize that one cannot go home again, e.g., that it was impossible to depend for

In 1950, however, our inquiry is simpler because anxiety has now emerged into overt statement in contemporaneous literature. W. H. Auden has entitled his latest poem with the phrase which he believes most accurately characterizes our period, namely, *The Age of Anxiety*.[2] Though Auden's profound interpretation of the inner experience of the four persons in this poem is set in the time of war—when "necessity is associated with horror and freedom with boredom" [3]—he makes it very clear that the underlying causes of the anxiety of his characters, as well as of others of this age, must be sought on deeper levels than merely the occasion of war. The four characters in the poem, though different in temperament and in background, have in common certain characteristics of our times: loneliness, the feeling of not being of value as persons, and the experience of not being able to love and be loved, despite the common need, the common effort, and the common but temporary respite provided by alcohol. The sources of the anxiety are to be found in certain basic trends in our culture, one of which, for Auden, is the pressure toward conformity which occurs in a world where commercial and mechanical values are apotheosized:

> We move on
> As the wheel wills; one revolution
> Registers all things, the rise and fall
> In pay and prices. . . .[4]

> . . . this stupid world where
> Gadgets are gods and we go on talking,
> Many about much, but remain alone,
> Alive but alone, belonging—where?—
> Unattached as tumbleweed.[5]

security on past economic, social, and ethical criteria, and that the upshot of this realization would be the increasing emergence of overt anxiety as a conscious problem, along with a feeling of "homelessness." This conjecture is, to be sure, an oversimplification, but if we take it as speculation about the central symbols of the home and the mother, it may usefully raise a problem that we shall be confronting, in much more specific form, time and again in this study of anxiety.

2 W. H. Auden, *The age of anxiety* (New York, 1947).
3 *Ibid.*, p. 3.
4 *Ibid.*, p. 45.
5 *Ibid.*, p. 44.

And the possibility facing these persons is that they too may be drawn into the mechanical routine of meaninglessness:

> . . . The fears we know
> Are of not knowing. Will nightfall bring us
> Some awful order—Keep a hardware store
> In a small town. . . . Teach science for life to
> Progressive girls—? It is getting late.
> Shall we ever be asked for? Are we simply
> Not wanted at all? [6]

What has been lost is the capacity to experience and have faith in one's self as a worthy and unique being, and at the same time the capacity for faith in, and meaningful communication with, other selves, namely one's fellow-men.[7]

The French author, Albert Camus, in a phrase parallel to Auden's, designates this age as "the century of fear," in comparison with the seventeenth century as the age of mathematics, the eighteenth as the age of the physical sciences, and the nineteenth as that of biology. Camus realizes that these characterizations are not logically parallel, that fear is not a science, but "science must be somewhat involved, since its latest theoretical advances have brought it to the point of negating itself while its perfected technology threatens the globe itself with destruction. Moreover, although fear itself cannot be considered a science, it is certainly a technique." [8]

Another writer who graphically expresses the anxiety and anxiety-like states of people in our period is Franz Kafka. The remarkable surge of interest in the 1940's in the writings of Kafka is important for our purposes here because of what it shows in the changing temper of our time; the fact that increasing numbers of people are finding that Kafka speaks significantly to them must indicate that he is expressing some profound aspects

---

[6] *Ibid.*, p. 42.

[7] The present writer was excited to discover, during the preparation of this manuscript, that Leonard Bernstein has composed a symphony, which had its premiere in 1949, entitled *Age of anxiety*. On the basis of his conviction that Auden's poem truly presents the "state of our age" in general, as well as speaking for the particular individual members of that age like himself, Bernstein has translated the poem into the symbols of instrumental music.

[8] Quoted in the *New York Times*, December 21, 1947, Sec. 7, p. 2.

of the prevailing experience of many members of our society. In Kafka's novel *The Castle*,[9] the chief character devotes his life to a frantic and desperate endeavor to communicate with the authorities in the castle who control all aspects of the life of the village, and who have the power to tell him his vocation and give some meaning to his life. Kafka's hero is driven "by a need for the most primitive requisites of life, the need to be rooted in a home and a calling, and to become a member of a community." [10] But the authorities in the castle remain inscrutable and inaccessible, and Kafka's character is as a result without direction and unity in his own life and remains isolated from his fellows. What the castle specifically symbolizes could be debated at length, but since the authorities in the castle are represented as the epitome of a bureaucratic efficiency which exercises such power that it quenches both individual autonomy and meaningful interpersonal relations, it may confidently be assumed that Kafka is in general writing of those aspects of his bourgeois culture of the late nineteenth and early twentieth centuries which so elevated technical efficiency that personal values were largely destroyed.

Herman Hesse, writing less in literary symbols than Kafka, is more explicit about the sources of modern man's anxiety. He presents the story of Haller, his chief character in the novel *Steppenwolf*, as a parable of our period.[11] Hesse holds that Haller's—and his contemporaries'—isolation and anxiety arise from the fact that the bourgeois culture in the late nineteenth and early twentieth centuries emphasized mechanical, rationalistic "balance" at the price of the suppression of the dynamic, irrational elements in experience. Haller tries to overcome his isolation and loneliness by giving free rein to his previously suppressed sensuous and irrational urges (the "wolf"), but this reactive method yields only a temporary relief. Indeed, Hesse

9 Franz Kafka, *The castle* (New York, 1930).
10 Max Brod, in Appendix to Kafka's *The castle*, p. 329.
11 Herman Hesse, *Steppenwolf*, trans. Basil Creighton (New York, 1947); originally published in German in 1927. The awareness of traumatic social change in the twentieth century occurred in Europe before it did in America; thus what Hesse wrote is much more relevant to conscious problems in this country in the 1940's than in 1927. Belatedly, Hesse received the Nobel prize for literature in 1946.

presents no thoroughgoing solution to the problem of the anxiety of contemporaneous Western man, for he believes the present period to be one of those "times when a whole generation is caught . . . between two ages." That is to say, bourgeois standards and controls have broken down, but there are as yet no social standards to take their place. Hesse sees Haller's record "as a document of the times, for Haller's sickness of the soul, as I now know, is not the eccentricity of a single individual, but the sickness of the times themselves, the neurosis of that generation to which Haller belongs . . . a sickness which attacks . . . precisely those who are strongest in spirit and richest in gifts." [12]

In Sociological Studies.—The emergence of awareness of anxiety as an overt sociological problem in an American community during the third and fourth decades of our century is seen when we compare the Lynds' two studies of Middletown.[13] In the first study, made in the 1920's, anxiety is not an overt problem to the people of Middletown, and the topic does not appear in the Lynds' volume in any of its explicit forms. But anyone reading this study from a psychological viewpoint would suspect that much of the behavior of the citizens of Middletown was symptomatic of *covert anxiety*—for example, the compulsive work ("businessmen and workingmen seem to be running for dear life" in the endeavor to make money [14]), the pervasive struggle to conform, the compulsive gregariousness, (*vide* the great emphasis on "joining" clubs), and the frantic endeavors of the people in the community to keep their leisure time crammed with activity (such as "motoring"), however purposeless this activity might be in itself.[15] But only one citizen—whom the Lynds describe as a "perspicacious" observer—looked below these symptoms and sensed the presence of covert apprehension:

---

[12] *Ibid.*, p. 28.

[13] R. S. Lynd and H. M. Lynd, *Middletown* (New York, 1929), and *Middletown in transition* (New York, 1937).

[14] *Middletown*, p. 87.

[15] On a Sunday afternoon the regular practice of many people was to get in their ears, drive fifty miles, and then drive back again. One is reminded of Pascal's description of some symptoms of covert anxiety: the constant endeavor of people to divert themselves, to escape ennui, to avoid being alone, until "agitation" becomes an end in itself. (See next chapter.)

of his fellow townsmen he observed, "These people are all afraid of something; what is it?" [16]

But the later study of the same community made in the 1930's presents a very different picture: *overt anxiety is now present.* "One thing everybody in Middletown has in common," the Lynds observe, "is insecurity in the face of a complicated world." [17] To be sure, the immediate, outward occasion of anxiety was the economic depression; but it would be an error to conclude that the inclusive *cause* of the emerging anxiety was economic insecurity. The Lynds accurately relate this insecurity in Middletown to the *confusion of role* which the individual was then experiencing; the citizen of Middletown, they write, "is caught in a chaos of conflicting patterns, none of them wholly condemned, but no one of them clearly approved and free from confusion; or, where the group sanctions are clear in demanding a certain role of a man or woman, the individual encounters cultural requirements with no immediate means of meeting them." [18] This "chaos of conflicting patterns" in Middletown is one expression of the pervasive social changes occurring in our culture, which the present writer will show in a later chapter to be intimately connected with the widespread anxiety of our times. [19] The Lynds observe that, since "most people are incapable of tolerating change and uncertainty in all sectors of life at once," [20] the tendency in Middletown was toward a retrenchment into more rigid and conservative economic and social ideologies. This ominous development as a symptom of, and defense against, anxiety points toward the discussion of the relation between anxiety and political authoritarianism in the next section.

In the Political Scene.—Turning to the political scene, we again find pronounced anxiety evidenced both in symptomatic and in overt forms. Without going into the complex determinants of fascism, we wish to note that it is born and gains its

---

[16] *Op. cit.,* p. 493.
[17] *Middletown in transition,* p. 315.
[18] *Ibid.,* p. 177.
[19] This problem is discussed in some detail in Chapter 5, where we endeavor to demonstrate the relation between cultural change and anxiety.
[20] *Op. cit.,* p. 315.

power in periods of widespread anxiety. Tillich describes the situation in Europe in the 1930's out of which German fascism developed:

> First of all a feeling of *fear* or, more exactly, of indefinite anxiety was prevailing. Not only the economic and political, but also the cultural and religious, security seemed to be lost. There was nothing on which one could build; everything was without foundation. A catastrophic breakdown was expected every moment. Consequently, a longing for security was growing in everybody. A freedom that leads to fear and anxiety has lost its value; better authority with security than freedom with fear! [21]

In such periods, people grasp at political authoritarianism in the desperate need to be relieved of anxiety. Totalitarianism in this sense may be viewed as serving a purpose on a cultural scale parallel to that in which a neurotic symptom protects an individual from a situation of unbearable anxiety.[22] With some very significant differences, communistic totalitarianism fulfills a similar function.[23] As we shall endeavor to indicate later in this study, fascism and communism are not only economic phenomena, but are also the product of the spiritual, ethical, and psychological vacuum which characterized the breakdown of the bourgeois tradition in Western Europe.[24] As Martin Ebon phrases it, communism is a product of "the desperate wish to find a purpose in what seems confusion and emptiness." [25] In this confusion and emptiness one thing did exist, namely anxiety; and we are submitting that totalitarianism gains its foothold to a considerable extent because, like a symptom, it "binds" and provides some relief from the anxiety.[26]

---

[21] Paul Tillich, *The Protestant era* (Chicago, 1947), p. 245.

[22] Cf. Goldstein, p. 57, below. Also, Herbert L. Matthews, observer of Italian and Spanish fascism, writes: "Fascism was like a jail where the individual had a certain amount of security, shelter, and daily food."—*The education of a correspondent* (New York, 1946).

[23] Arthur M. Schlesinger, Jr.: "[Communism] has filled the 'vacuum of faith' caused by the waning of established religion; it provides a sense of purpose which heals internal agonies of anxiety and doubt."—*New York Times,* February 1, 1948.

[24] See also Erich Fromm, *Escape from freedom* (New York, 1941), discussed with respect to this point on pages 169-76, below.

[25] *World communism today* (New York, 1948).

[26] A task which awaits doing on the part of students of anxiety is the detailed study of dictatorship as an anxiety phenomenon. To some extent, it might be said,

In addition to anxiety in the above symptomatic forms, *unsystematized* anxiety has been increasingly evident in the sociopolitical scene in the past decade. The frequent references to Roosevelt's sentence in his first inaugural, "The only thing we have to fear is fear itself," testify to the fact that large numbers of people have become increasingly aware of "fear of fear," or more accurately, anxiety, in the face of the radical sociopolitical changes in our day. The emergence of the atom bomb brought the previously inchoate and "free-floating" anxiety of many people into sharp focus. The stark possibilities of modern man's situation are stated in an impassioned expression of the crystallization of anxiety at that moment by Norman Cousins:

> The beginning of the Atomic Age has brought less hope than fear. It is a primitive fear, the fear of the unknown, the fear of forces man can neither channel nor comprehend. This fear is not new; in its classical form it is the fear of irrational death. But overnight it has become intensified, magnified. It has burst out of the subconscious into the conscious, filling the mind with primordial apprehensions. . . . Where man can find no answer, he will find fear.[27]

Even if we should escape being confronted with actual death in a shooting and atomic war, the anxiety inhering in our portentous world situation would still be with us. The historian Arnold Toynbee has stated his belief that overt warfare on a world scale is not probable in our lifetime, but that we shall remain in a "cold" war for a generation, which will mean a perpetual condition of tension and worry. To live in a state of anxiety for a generation is, indeed, a horrendous prospect! But the picture is not inevitably black: Toynbee holds that the tension in the persistent cold war can be used constructively as

dictatorships are born and come to power in periods of cultural anxiety; once in power they live in anxiety—e.g., many of the acts of the dictating group are motivated by its own anxiety; and the dictatorship perpetuates its power by capitalizing upon and engendering anxiety in its own people as well as in its rival nations. Just how completely, however, such statements can be made awaits a good deal of investigation; the present writer, for one, believes such a study would be very fruitful.

[27] *Modern man is obsolete* (New York, 1945), p. 1. First printed as an editorial in *The Saturday Review of Literature* and then published in book form.

our motivation for bettering our own socioeconomic standards in the West. The present writer agrees with Toynbee that our political and social survival depends both on our capacity for tolerating the anxiety inherent in the threatening world situation (and thus not irrationally precipitating war as a way out of the painful uncertainty) and also on our capacity for turning this anxiety to constructive uses.[28]

In Philosophy and Religion.—The fact that anxiety has emerged as a central problem in contemporaneous philosophy and religion is not only a general, but also a specific indication of the prevalence of anxiety in our culture. It is a specific indication in the respect that anxiety has become most prominent in the thought of those theologians, like R. Niebuhr, who are most intimately concerned with the economic and political issues of our day; and in those philosophers, like Tillich and M. Heidegger, who have experienced in their own lives the cultural crises and upheavals of Western society in the past three decades.[29]

Tillich describes anxiety as man's reaction to the threat of *nonbeing.* Man is the creature who has self-conscious awareness of his being, but he is also aware that at any moment he might cease to exist.[30] Thus in philosophical terms anxiety

---

28 Arnold Toynbee, How to turn the tables on Russia, *Woman's Home Companion,* August, 1949, 30 ff. Toynbee gives an analogy which is such a vivid parable of the constructive uses of anxiety that we summarize it here. The fishermen bringing in their herring from the North Sea were faced with the problem of the fish becoming sluggish in their tanks and thus losing some of their market value for freshness. Then one fisherman conceived the idea of placing a couple of catfish in the herring tanks. Because of the threat of death in the presence of these catfish, the herring not only did not grow sluggish but became even more active and flourishing. Of course, whether the reaction of the Western world to the catfish (Russia) will be constructive or not is another question; in other words, whether we *shall* use the anxiety in our world situation predominantly for constructive purposes remains largely to be seen. There are some momentously constructive signs, e.g., the Marshall Plan; psychologically, this experiment has, in the present writer's opinion, the expansive, cooperative, courageous characteristics of a typically constructive approach to anxiety. But on the other hand there are the ominous tendencies in the "spy scares," "witch hunts," etc., which, again speaking in psychological analogy, look very much like the retrenchments and phobic withdrawals which classically characterize the neurotic approach to anxiety.

29 In the light of Nietzsche's idea that the philosopher is a "physician of culture," the thought of these writers is to be regarded not as the product of ivorytower speculation, but is a diagnosis and articulation of one phase of the condition of our culture.

30 This concept of Tillich's was of course formulated before the emergence of the atom bomb, but the bomb is undoubtedly a symbol by which many more people are able to comprehend the immediate threat of nonbeing.

arises as the individual is aware of being as over against the ever present possibility of nonbeing.[31] "Nonbeing" does not mean simply the threat of physical death—though probably death is the most common form and symbol of this anxiety. The threat of nonbeing lies in the psychological and spiritual realms as well, namely the threat of *meaninglessness* in one's existence.[32] Generally the threat of meaninglessness is experienced negatively as a threat to the existence of the self (the experience of the "dissolution of the self" in Goldstein's term). But when this form of anxiety is confronted affirmatively—when the individual both realizes the threat of meaninglessness and takes a stand against the threat—the result is a strengthening of the individual's feeling of being a self, a strengthening of his perception of himself as distinct from the world of nonbeing, of objects.

Niebuhr makes anxiety the central concept of his theological doctrine of man. To Niebuhr every act of man, creative or destructive, involves some element of anxiety. Anxiety has its source in the fact that man is on one hand finite, involved like the animals in the contingencies and necessities of nature; but on the other hand man has freedom. Unlike "the animals he sees this situation [of contingency] and anticipates its perils," and to this extent man transcends his finiteness. "In short, man, being both bound and free, both limited and limitless, is anxious. Anxiety is the inevitable concomitant of the paradox of freedom and finiteness in which man is involved." [33] Much will be said later in the present study about anxiety as the precondition of neurosis; it is significant that Niebuhr, in parallel theological terms, makes anxiety "the internal precondition of sin. . . . Anxiety is the internal description of the state of temptation." [34]

In Psychology.—"Anxiety is the most prominent mental characteristic of Occidental civilization," R. R. Willoughby asserts. He then presents statistical evidence for this assertion

---

[31] Cf. Kierkegaard's description of anxiety as the "fear of nothingness."

[32] References to Tillich's explanation of the causes of the prevalence of meaninglessness in our culture will be made in later Sections. (See Chapters 2 and 5.)

[33] Reinhold Niebuhr, *The nature and destiny of man* (New York, 1941), p. 182.

[34] *Ibid.*

in the form of the rising incidences in three fields of social path-
ology which he believes may reasonably be understood as reactions to anxiety, namely *suicide, the functional forms of mental
disorder,* and *divorce.*[35] Suicide rates for the last 75 to 100
years show a steady increase in the majority of the countries of
continental Europe. With regard to the functional forms of
mental illness, Willoughby holds, "it seems probable . . . that
there is a real rise in incidence of mental disease even when the
greatest reasonable allowance is made for increasing facilities for
hospitalization and insight in diagnosis." [36] The divorce rates
for every country except Japan have shown a steady upward
trend in the twentieth century. Willoughby believes the incidence of divorce is a measure of the inability of the members
of the culture to tolerate the additional stress of the critical
marital adjustment, and the higher incidence must presuppose a
considerable load of anxiety in the culture.[37]

We would not question Willoughby's purpose in introducing
these statistics, namely, to substantiate the "commonsense
proposition that there is in our civilization a large and increasing
incidence of anxiety." But there might rightly be considerable
question as to whether the relation between these statistical evidences and anxiety is as direct as he holds. Suicide can be due
to other motivations than anxiety—revenge is one example.
And the rising incidence of divorce would seem to be due to
changing social attitudes toward divorce as well as to the prevalence of anxiety. But certainly the three groups of statistics
Willoughby presents indicate radical social upheavals in our
society which involve psychological and emotional trauma. To
the present writer it seems more logical to regard rising divorce,
suicide, and mental disease rates as symptoms and products of
the traumatically changing state of our culture, and to regard
anxiety also as a symptom and product of that cultural state.

---

[35] R. R. Willoughby, *Magic and cognate phenomena: an hypothesis,* in Carl
Murchinson (ed.), *Handbook of social psychology* (Worcester, Mass., 1935), p. 498.
   [36] *Ibid.,* p. 500.
   [37] An important fact in America is that divorces for "cruelty" are "solely
responsible for the increase, all other causes steadily declining." Willoughby interprets "cruelty" as a matter of increase of anxiety—"if the conduct of the spouse
is such as to exacerbate anxiety, it is 'cruel.' "—(*Op. cit.*)

And certainly a culture described by these statistics would be a culture which generates much anxiety.

Since in subsequent chapters we are concerned in detail with the study of anxiety in the various fields of psychology, we shall here only cite, in line with our introductory purpose, that anxiety has gradually come to be seen as a central problem in learning theory, in dynamic psychology, and specifically in psychoanalysis and other forms of psychotherapy. While it long has been recognized that apprehensions and fears, particularly those related to approval or punishment from parents and teachers, exerted much power over the child in school, not until recently have there been scientific recognitions of the innumerable subtle expressions and influences of anxiety permeating the child's educational and classroom experience. For this appreciation of anxiety as a focal problem in learning theory, and the scientific formulation thereof, we are indebted to such learning psychologists as Mowrer, Miller, and Dollard.[38]

More than three decades ago, Freud singled out anxiety as the crucial problem of emotional and behavioral disorders. Further development of psychoanalysis has only substantiated his proposition, until it is now recognized on all sides that anxiety is the "fundamental phenomenon of neurosis," or in Horney's term, the "dynamic center of neuroses." But not only in psychopathology; in the actions of "normal" people as well as "abnormal," it is now recognized that anxiety is much more prevalent than was suspected several decades ago. From the viewpoint of dynamic psychology, Symonds accurately notes that "it would surprise most persons to realize how much of their behavior is motivated by a desire to escape anxiety by either reducing it or disguising it in one way or another." [39] Whether we are concerned with "normal" or pathological behavior, Freud was correct in saying that the solution to the "riddle" of anxiety "must cast a flood of light upon our whole mental life." [40]

---

38 Discussed in Chapter 4.
39 P. M. Symonds, *The dynamics of human adjustment* (New York, 1946), p. 138.
40 Sigmund Freud, *General introduction to psychoanalysis* (American ed.; New York, 1920), p. 341.

2. Purpose of This Study

Despite the fact that anxiety has become a central problem in so many diverse areas in our culture, the attack on the problem has been handicapped by the fact that the various theories and studies of anxiety have, to date, been uncoordinated. Freud's description of the state of the problem in the opening paragraph of his chapter on anxiety published in 1933 is still largely accurate: "You will not be surprised to hear that I have a great deal of new information to give you about our hypotheses on the subject of anxiety . . . and also that none of this information claims to provide a final solution of these doubtful problems." What is necessary at the present stage of the understanding of anxiety is "the introduction of the right abstract ideas, and of their application to the raw material of observation so as to bring order and lucidity into it." [41]

The purpose of the present study is to bring, so far as we are able, some "order and lucidity" into the presently uncoordinated field of anxiety theory. We propose to bring together the various theories of anxiety and to view them in their cultural and historical as well as their biological and psychological dimensions. We shall then seek the basic common denominators in these theories, assess the points of disagreement, and, so far as possible, synthesize the various viewpoints into a *comprehensive theory of anxiety.* The case studies (in Part II) of this book are presented for the purpose of testing anxiety theory clinically; that is, for illustrating and demonstrating, or questioning, various aspects of a comprehensive, contemporary theory of anxiety.

---

[41] Sigmund Freud, *New introductory lectures in psychoanalysis* (New York, 1933), p. 113.

Chapter 2

PHILOSOPHICAL PREDECESSORS TO MODERN
THEORIES OF ANXIETY

> I have no desire to speak in strong terms about this age as a
> whole, but he who has observed the contemporary generation will
> surely not deny that the incongruity in it and the reason for its
> anxiety and restlessness is this, that in one direction truth in-
> creases in extent, in mass, partly also in abstract clarity, whereas
> certitude steadily decreases.—Søren Kierkegaard, *The Concept of
> Dread.*

Until the advent of Freud and the other depth psychologists,
the problem of anxiety lay in the provinces of philosophy, especially in its branch of ethics, and religion. The particular philosophers who dealt most explicitly with anxiety and fear were
those whose primary concern was not with the formation of
abstract intellectual systems, but rather with the existential conflicts and crises of immediate human beings. It is thus no historical accident that the most penetrating insights into anxiety
and its related problems should have come from those thinkers
whose interests were both religious and philosophical, such as
Pascal, Spinoza, and Kierkegaard.

An inquiry into the philosophical backgrounds of the problem of anxiety is of help in understanding contemporaneous
anxiety in two respects. The first and most obvious help is in
the actual insights into the meaning of anxiety to be found in the
writings of some philosophers, insights which, as seen in Kierkegaard, not only often antedate Freud's theories but in some respects predict developments after Freud. Second, such an
inquiry illuminates one phase of the historical background of the
problem of anxiety in our society.[1] Thus our investigation in

---

[1] Since an individual's anxiety is conditioned by the fact that he stands at a
particular point in the historical development of his culture, an understanding of

this chapter should cast light on the genesis of certain cultural issues and attitudes which are crucial for much contemporaneous anxiety. One such issue, for example, is the dichotomy between mind and body, which was enunciated in its dominant modern form by Descartes and other thinkers of the seventeenth century and which not only produced psychological disunity and anxiety for large numbers of people in the late nineteenth and twentieth centuries, but in some respects specifically set the problem of anxiety for Freud.[2]

Another such issue is the tendency of our culture to be preoccupied with "rational," mechanical phenomena and to suppress so-called "irrational" experience. We may approach this issue by means of two questions: Why did anxiety not emerge as a specific problem until the middle of the nineteenth century? And why was anxiety not dealt with as a problem in the various schools of psychology (excepting psychoanalysis) until the latter 1930's, despite the fact that during the last half-century the study of fears has been prominent in psychology? Among the varied legitimate answers to these questions, one important factor is our widespread tendency since the Renaissance to avoid and look askance at "irrational" phenomena, and to admit in our own experience as well as to accept as a legitimate area for investigation only those aspects of experience which can be made to appear "rational"—that is, aspects of experience for which intellectual "reasons" can be presented. Since fears are experienced as specific and definite, we can present "logical" reasons for them, and we can study them by mathematical means; but anxiety is generally experienced by an individual as a profoundly irrational phenomenon. The tendency to suppress anxiety because it seems irrational or to rationalize it in terms of "fears," is by no means limited to sophisticated intellectuals in our culture—it continually crops up in clinical or psychoanalytic work as a major hurdle in therapy with anxiety problems.[3] For understanding the

the development of his culture is indispensable to understanding the individual's anxiety. This assumption, which is implicit in the present chapter, is dealt with in some detail in Chapter 5.

    [2] Cf. Rollo May, Historical roots of modern anxiety theories, paper delivered at Symposium on Anxiety of Amer. psychopath. Ass., June 3, 1949 (to be published).

    [3] For example, this tendency appeared in several of the cases in the study of

genesis of such cultural tendencies, an inquiry into the background of the accepted attitudes and normative ideas of our society is necessary.[4]

We begin with the seventeenth century because in that century the systems of thought which have been dominant for the major part of the modern period were formulated.[5]

The philosophies of the seventeenth century had one theme in common with respect to the understanding of human nature: they presented the "rationalistic solution to the problem of man." [6] The common denominator was the confidence that each man was a rational individual who could arrive at autonomy in his intellectual, social, religious, and emotional life. Mathematics was conceived as the chief tool of reason. This belief in "autonomous reason," as Tillich calls it, or "mathematical reason," in Cassirer's phrase, was the guiding intellectual principle of the cultural revolution which, beginning in the Renaissance, resulted in the overthrow of feudalism and absolutism and ultimately led to the supremacy of the bourgeoisie. It was believed that autonomous reason would make possible the control of the individual's emotions (e.g., Spinoza). Autonomous reason would also make possible the mastery of physical nature

---

anxiety in unmarried mothers presented in Chapter 7. See especially the case of Helen (Case 4), who had strong anxiety arising from her extramarital pregnancy but who sought to repress this anxiety beneath a continual concern for the quasi-scientific "facts" of pregnancy. Helen's need to exclude from conscious awareness all ideas and feelings which were not intellectually "acceptable" and explicable is, it probably would be generally admitted, typical of many persons in our society.

4 In the discussion which follows, we do not treat philosophical formulations as either cause or effect, but rather as one expression of the total cultural development of the period. The particular philosophers whose formulations have become important for their own and subsequent centuries (such as those we shall refer to in this chapter) are those who were successful in penetrating and expressing the dominant meaning and direction of development of their culture. It is in this sense that the formulations made by the intellectual leaders of one century become the common currency, in the form of unconscious assumptions, of large numbers of people in succeeding centuries.

Other aspects of the development of modern culture as it affects the problem of anxiety (e.g., the economic and sociological aspects) are referred to in Chapter 5. A summary of the cultural backgrounds of contemporaneous anxiety is given in Chapter 6 and may serve as a supplement to the discussion in this chapter.

5 Many of the formative principles which guided the scientists and philosophers of that century had emerged in the Renaissance, but it was in the seventeenth century—that remarkable classical period of Descartes, Spinoza, Pascal, Leibnitz, Locke, Hobbes, Galileo, Newton—that they received their systematic formulation.

6 Ernst Cassirer, *An essay on man* (New Haven, Conn., 1944), p. 16.

—a confidence which was later to be thoroughly substantiated by far-reaching progress in the physical sciences. Descartes gave impetus to this development by his sharp distinction between mind and the processes of thought on one hand and physical nature (extension) on the other. The crucial point was in a corollary to Descartes' dichotomy, namely that *physical nature, including the body, could be understood and controlled by means of mechanical, mathematical laws.*[7] The way was thus paved for the preoccupation in modern times with phenomena which were susceptible to mechanical and mathematical treatment, a preoccupation which was to be accompanied both by an endeavor to extend the application of the methods of mechanics and mathematics to as many areas of experience as possible and by a tendency to omit from consideration those aspects of experience which were not susceptible to such methods of treatment.[8]

The confidence that physical nature and the human body were mathematically and mechanically controllable had vast anxiety-dispelling effects. This was not only true in the respect of meeting man's material needs and overcoming the actual threats of physical nature but also in the respect of freeing man from "irrational" fears and anxiety. A way was opened for dissolving the multitude of fears of devils, sorcerers, and forms of magic which had been the foci of pervasive anxiety in the last two centuries of the Middle Ages as well as in the Renaissance.[9] Tillich points out that the Cartesians, by means of their assumption that the soul could not influence the body, were able to "disenchant the world." For one example, the persecution of witches, which had occurred through the Renaissance to the early eighteenth century, was overcome through Cartesian formulations.

---

[7] Descartes' endeavor was to "explain all of the world except God and the soul by mechanical and mathematical laws. . . ." Will Durant, *The story of philosophy* (New York, 1926), p. 167.

[8] The suppression of the nonmechanical and "irrational" aspects of experience went hand in hand, both as cause and effect, with the needs of the new industrialism following the Renaissance. What could be calculated and measured had practical utility in the industrial, workaday world, and what was "irrational" did not (Tillich).

[9] Cf. Johan Huizinga and Karl Mannheim in Chapter 5 below.

The confidence in the power of the autonomous, rational individual, which had emerged at the Renaissance and was more explicitly formulated in the seventeenth century, thus had on one side its anxiety-dispelling effects.[10] But on the other side, since the confidence in reason was inseparably connected with the individualism of the Renaissance, it brought in its train new sources of anxiety in feelings of psychological isolation on the part of the individual.[11] This problem was confronted in the thought of the seventeenth century, and the solution presented had far-reaching effects in allaying anxiety. This solution consisted of the belief that the liberation of reason in every person would lead to a realization of a universal humanity and to a system of harmony between individuals and society. That is to say, the individual need not feel isolated, for if he courageously pursued his own reason, his conclusions and his interests would ultimately be in accord with those of his fellow-men and a harmonious community would be achieved. Moreover, a metaphysical basis for overcoming isolation was presented, namely that the pursuit of universal reason would lead the individual into accord with "universal reality."[12] As Cassirer puts it,

---

[10] In some ways, in fact, the doctrine of autonomous reason was in itself an intellectual expression in the seventeenth century of Renaissance individualism. It seems to the present writer that Descartes's classical phrase, "I think, therefore I exist," shows the emphasis on rational processes as a criterion of existence and also implies that one arrives at belief in his own existence *in vacuo* as far as the community is concerned. Compare the present psychological concept that the experience of identity of the self occurs when the child becomes aware of other people as distinct from himself. W. H. Auden phrases this social origin of the self in succinct poetic terms:

> . . . for the ego is a dream
> Till a neighbor's need by
>   name create it.

The age of anxiety (New York, 1947), p. 8.

[11] This point is discussed in Chapter 5.

[12] Both the individualistic character of the thought of this period and the factors compensating for it can be seen in Leibnitz. His basic doctrine of the "monads" is individualistic in the sense that the monads are unitary, separated; but the compensating element is given in his doctrine of "pre-established harmony." Tillich expresses this graphically: "In the system of harmony the metaphysical solitude of every individual is strongly emphasized by the doctrine that there are 'no doors and windows' from one 'monad' to the other one. Every single unit is lonely in itself, without any direct communication. The horror of this idea was overcome by the harmonistic presupposition that in every monad the whole world is potentially present and that the development of each individual is in a natural harmony with the development of all the others. This is the most profound metaphysical symbol for the situation in the early periods of bourgeois civilization. It fitted

"mathematical reason was the bond between man and the universe." [13]

These anxiety-dispelling factors are essential to understanding why the specific problem of anxiety is so rarely confronted by the thinkers of the seventeenth century. We shall demonstrate in the writings of Spinoza that the confidence that fear could be overcome by reason did serve to a considerable extent to obviate the problem of anxiety. We shall also discuss Pascal, a representative of the period who could not accept the prevalent confidence in the power of autonomous reason and for whom, at the same time, anxiety was a central problem.

1. SPINOZA: REASON OVERCOMING FEAR

An eminent example of the method of dealing with fear in terms of mathematical reason is found in the writings of Baruch Spinoza. Spinoza "ventures to make the last and decisive step in this mathematical theory of the world and the human mind," remarks Cassirer; "Spinoza constructs a new ethics . . . a mathematical theory of the moral world." [14] It is well known that Spinoza's writings are replete with acute psychological insights.[15] We can be sure that, if Spinoza does not concern himself with anxiety, it is not because of lack of psychological discernment. At many points he anticipates later psychoanalytic concepts, as, for only one example, when he states that a passion (meaning an emotional complex) "ceases to be a passion when one has formed a clear and distinct idea of it." [16]

this situation because there was still a common world, in spite of the increasing social atomization." *The Protestant era* (Chicago, 1948), p. 246.

[13] Cassirer, *op. cit.*, p. 16.

[14] *Ibid.*, p. 16.

[15] His psychological insights are remarkably close to contemporary scientific psychological theories, such as his statement that mental and physical phenomena are two aspects of the same process. His definition of emotions is a predecessor of the modern James-Lange theory: "By emotion I understand the modifications of the body by which the power of action in the body is increased or diminished, aided or restrained, and at the same time the ideas of these modifications."—Origin and nature of the emotions, *Spinoza's ethics*, Everyman edition (London, 1910), p. 84.

[16] *Spinoza's ethics, The power of the intellect*, p. 203. Spinoza saw the political aspect of "freedom from fear." Indeed, the purpose of the state is "so to free each man from fear that he may live and act with full security and without injury to himself or his neighbor."—Durant, *op. cit.*, p. 211.

Spinoza believed that fear is essentially a subjective problem, that is, a matter of one's state of mind, or attitudes. He defines fear in juxtaposition to hope: they are both characteristic of the person in doubt. Fear is an "uncertain pain" arising from the idea that something we hate may befall us, and hope is an "uncertain pleasure" arising from the idea that a good we wish may come to pass. "It follows from these definitions," he adds, "that fear cannot be without hope, nor hope without fear." [17] Fear *"arises from a weakness of mind and therefore does not appertain to the use of reason."* [18] Hope also is a weakness of mind. "Therefore the more we endeavor to live under the guidance of reason, the less we endeavor to depend on hope, and the more to deliver ourselves and make ourselves free from fear and overcome fortune as much as possible, and finally to direct our actions by the certain advice of reason." [19] Spinoza's guidance on how to overcome fear is consistent with the general rational emphasis of the time, in which emotion is not repressed but rather made amenable to reason. It is true, he holds, that an emotion can be overcome only by a contrary, stronger one. But this can be done by paying attention to the "ordering of our thoughts and images." "We must think of courage in the same manner in order to lay aside fear, that is, we must enumerate and imagine the common perils of life and in what manner they may best be avoided and overcome by courage." [20]

At several points in his analysis Spinoza stands on the threshold of the problem of anxiety, as, for example, when he defines fear in juxtaposition to hope. But he does not cross the threshold into the problem of anxiety itself. The simultaneous presence of fear and hope within the individual, perpetuated over a period of time, is one aspect of the psychic conflict that is seen by later writers as anxiety.[21] But Spinoza, in marked contrast

[17] *Spinoza's ethics, Origin and nature of the emotions,* p. 131.

[18] On the basis of this statement of Spinoza's, one can contemplate with profit how greatly the historical situation in which one lives conditions one's anxiety and fear. One could say that living *without* fear in the twentieth century—the day of atom bombs, totalitarianism, and traumatic social change—shows weakness of mind, or more accurately, insensitivity, atrophy of mind.

[19] *Spinoza's ethics, The strength of the emotions,* p. 175.

[20] *The power of the intellect,* in *Spinoza's ethics* (London, 1910), p. 208.

[21] Cf. Kurt Riezler, The social psychology of fear, *Amer. J. Sociol.,* May, 1944, p. 489. For examples of such psychic conflicts underlying anxiety, see what we

to Kierkegaard in the ninteenth century, does not see conflict between hope and fear as persistent or necessary: fears can be overcome by courageous dedication to reason, and hence the problem of anxiety does not confront him. A similar difference between Spinoza and philosophers of the nineteenth century is evidenced in the treatment of confidence and despair. In Spinoza's terms we are confident when the cause of doubt has been removed from our hope, i.e., we are certain the good event will occur. And we are in despair when the element of doubt is removed from our fear, i.e., when we are certain that the evil event will occur or has occurred. For Kierkegaard, in contrast, confidence is not the removal of doubt (and anxiety) but rather the attitude that we can move ahead *despite* doubt and anxiety. In Spinoza it is that word *certain* which strikes us so boldly. If one believed, as apparently Spinoza in his century could believe, that such intellectual and emotional certainty could be achieved, untold psychological security would result. This belief, of course, underlay Spinoza's constructing a *mathematics* of ethics; one should be as certain about an ethical problem as one is about a proposition in geometry. The essential point is that for Spinoza the removal of doubt and the attainment of certainty is possible if we direct ourselves by the "certain advice of reason."

The central problem of anxiety does not intrude itself into Spinoza's thought. One cannot escape the conclusion that, given the cultural situation in which he lived, his confidence in reason served him satisfactorily.[22]

---

describe as the "rift between expectation and reality" which underlay the neurotic anxiety of the cases in Part II, page 339 ff., below.

[22] It is to be borne in mind not only that Spinoza's seventeenth century cultural situation was different from the situation of the nineteenth and twentieth centuries, but also that his confidence in reason was different from the deteriorated forms of rationalism in the nineteenth century which involved a denial and repression of emotion. Since in the above discussion we are chiefly interested in Spinoza as a spokesman for the confidence in reason in the seventeenth century, it is important to emphasize that he was by no means merely a rationalist in the contemporary connotation of that term. His ethical and mystical interests gave a broad and profound context to his thought which was absent in the later and more limited forms of rationalism. For example, if we should follow out to the ultimate step his analysis of how to overcome fear (and anxiety, so far as anxiety appears as a problem), we should discover that each destructive affect must be overcome by a stronger, constructive one and that he defined the ultimate constructive affect in the curiously mystico-rationalistic phrase, the "intellectual love of God." In other words, fear (and anxiety) can be overcome in the last analysis only by a religious

2. PASCAL: ANXIETY AND THE INSUFFICIENCY OF REASON

Though representative of the eminent intellectuals of the seventeenth century in his mathematical and scientific genius, Blaise Pascal was the exception in that he did not believe human nature, with all its variety, richness, and contradiction, could be comprehended by mathematical rationalism. He believed rational certitude about man was not possible in any sense similar to rational certitude in geometry and physics. The laws that operate in human life are laws of chance and "probabilities." Hence he was impressed by the contingency of human existence.

> When I consider the brief span of my life, swallowed up in the eternity before and behind it, the small space that I fill, or even see, engulfed in the infinite immensity of spaces which I know not, and which know not me, I am afraid, and wonder to see myself here rather than there; for there is no reason why I should be here rather than there, now rather than then.[23]

Pascal was directly concerned with anxiety, not only anxiety which he himself experienced but which he believed he observed underneath the surface of the lives of his contemporaries, evidenced by the "perpetual restlessness in which men pass their lives." [24] He noted the unceasing endeavors of people to divert themselves, to escape ennui, to avoid being alone, until "agitation" becomes an end in itself. The great bulk of diversions, he felt, were actually endeavors of people to avoid "thoughts of

---

attitude toward one's life as a whole. (Cf. Erich Fromm, *Man for himself* [New York, 1947], on this point.) It should also be mentioned, by the way, that one important consequence of the broad base of Spinoza's thinking was that he was able to avoid the dichotomy between mind and body which characterized other philosophies of his day.

[23] *Pascal's pensées,* ed. and trans. G. B. Rawlings (Mt. Vernon, N.Y., 1946), p. 36. Also: "On beholding the blindness and misery of man, on seeing all the universe dumb, and man without light, left to himself, as it were astray in this corner of the universe, knowing not who has set him here, what he is here for, or what will become of him when he dies, incapable of all knowledge, I begin to be afraid, as a man who has been carried while asleep to a fearful desert island, and who will wake not knowing where he is and without any means of quitting the island. And thus I marvel that people are not seized with despair at such a miserable condition."—*Ibid.,* p. 7.

[24] *Pascal's thoughts,* trans. Edward Craig (New York, 1825), p. 110.

themselves," for if they should pause for self-contemplation, they would be miserable and anxious.

In his preoccupation with the contingent and uncertain aspects of human experience, Pascal took cognizance of the fact that reason was offered as a guide to certainty; but he believed that reason is undependable as a practical guide. It is not that he devaluated reason as such. On the contrary, he believed it to be the distinctive quality of man, the source of man's dignity in the midst of unthinking nature, and the source of morality ("to think well . . . is the principle of morality" [25]). But in practical life reason is undependable because it is "pliable to every sense," and sense reports are notoriously deceptive. Moreover the usual confidence in reason is faulty, he held, because it fails to take into account the power of the emotions.[26] Pascal conceived of the emotions in both a positive and a negative sense. He saw values in the emotions that were not comprehended in rationalism: "The heart has reasons which the reason knows not of." On the other hand, the emotions often distort and overrule reason, and reason becomes mere rationalization. Overconfidence in reason often facilitates the abuse of reason to support mere custom, or the power of kings, or injustice. In practice reason is often a matter of "Truth on this side of the Pyrenees, error on that." [27] He was impressed with the frequency with which self-interest and vanity are the actual motivations of men, and are then justified by "reason." Greater trust could be placed in reason, he remarks epigrammatically, if "reason were only reasonable." In all these qualifications of the prevalent confidence in reason, it is clear that Pascal valued very highly what he termed a "genuine love of and respect for wisdom," but he felt that love of and respect for wisdom are rare phenomena in human life. Hence he saw the human situation much less optimistically than his contemporaries: "We are placed in a vast medium, ever floating uncertainly between ignorance and knowledge." [28]

---

25 *Pascal's Pensées* (Rawlings ed. and trans.), *op. cit.,* p. 35.
26 It is interesting to note, in connection with Pascal's lament that the emotions were not reasonable, that it became Freud's endeavor, over three centuries later, to extend the domain of reason to include the emotions.
27 Rawlings (ed. and trans.), *op. cit.,* p. 38.   28 Craig (trans.), *op. cit.,* p. 84.

We have suggested that the confidence in reason, as interpreted by the intellectual leaders of the seventeenth century, served to dispel anxiety. It is some support for this thesis that Pascal, the one who could not accept the rationalistic solution to human problems, was at the same time the one who could not avoid anxiety.

Pascal stands as an exception, however, to the prevalent formulations of his day, and to the central stream of the philosophical developments in the modern period.[29] On the whole, the belief that through reason Nature could be mastered and man's emotions ordered served the intellectual leaders of that day relatively satisfactorily, so that the problem of anxiety rarely is confronted in their thought. We suggest that the cultural position in which Spinoza and the other thinkers of this classical phase of the modern period found themselves did not result in the inner trauma which was to occur to comparable intellectual leaders in the nineteenth century, and to vast numbers of people in the twentieth century. The central belief in the power of autonomous reason gave a psychological unity to the culture which was not to be threatened with serious disintegration until the nineteenth century.

3. Kierkegaard and the Problem of Anxiety in the Nineteenth Century

In the nineteenth century we can observe on a broad scale the occurrence of fissures in the unity of modern culture which underlie much of our contemporary anxiety. The revolutionary belief in autonomous reason which had been central in the inception and structuralization of modern culture was now supplanted by "technical reason." [30] The rapidly increasing mastery over

---

29 The question of why he was an exception, and why he experienced inner trauma and anxiety to a much greater degree than his contemporaries, would take us afield from this discussion. We might, however, mention Cassirer's suggestion that Pascal's view of man is really a carry-over from medievalism, and that despite Pascal's scientific genius, he had not really absorbed the new view of man which had emerged at the Renaissance.

30 The term is Paul Tillich's. It refers to the fact that in the nineteenth century reason, in practice, became increasingly applied to technical problems (cf. Nietszche and Cassirer in next paragraph). The theoretical implications of this

physical nature was accompanied by widespread and profound changes in the structure of human society. The economic and sociological aspects of these changes concern us in a later section, but here it is important to note the changes at that time in man's view of himself.

This was the era of "autonomous sciences." [31] Each science developed in its own direction; but a unifying principle, as Cassirer phrases it, was lacking. It was against the consequences of "science as a factory" that Nietszche warned; he saw technical reason progressing rapidly on one hand and the disintegration of human ideals and values on the other; and he feared the nihilism which would result. The views of man presented in the nineteenth century are not divorced, in most cases, from the empirical data produced by the advancing sciences, but since science itself was without a unifying principle, there was great variance in the interpretations of man. "Each individual thinker," Cassirer remarks, "gives us his own picture of human nature," and whereas each picture is based upon empirical evidence, each "theory becomes a Procrustean bed on which the empirical facts are stretched to fit a preconceived pattern." [32] Cassirer feels that this antagonism of ideas constituted not only "a grave theoretical problem but an imminent threat to the whole extent of our ethical and cultural life." [33]

The nineteenth century was marked by a cultural *compartmentalization*, not only in theories and in the sciences but in other phases of culture as well. In aesthetics, there was the "art for art's sake movement" and an increasing separation of art from the realities of nature—a development attacked toward the end of the century by Cézanne and Van Gogh. In religion there was a separation of theoretical beliefs and Sunday practices

growing emphasis on the technical aspects of reason were not widely appreciated at the time.

[31] Werner Brock, *Contemporary German philosophy* (Cambridge, 1935).

[32] *An essay on man, op. cit.*, p. 21. Cassirer continues: "Owing to this development our modern theory of man lost its intellectual center. We acquired instead a complete anarchy of thought. . . . Theologians, scientists, politicians, sociologists, biologists, psychologists, ethnologists, economists all approached the problem from their own viewpoints. To combine or unify all these particular aspects and perspectives was impossible . . . every author seems in the last count to be led by his own conception and evaluation of human life."

[33] *Ibid.*, p. 22.

from the affairs of weekday life. The compartmentalization in family life is vividly portrayed and attacked by Ibsen in *The Doll's House*. With respect to the psychological life of the individual, the nineteenth century is broadly characterized by a separation of "reason" and "emotions," with voluntaristic effort (will) enthroned as the method of casting the decision between the two—which resulted generally in a denial of the emotions. The seventeenth century *belief in the rational control* of the emotions had now become the *habit of repressing* the emotions. In this light it is easy to understand why the less acceptable emotional impulses, such as sex and hostility, should have undergone particularly widespread repudiation. It is this psychological disunity which set the problem for the work of Sigmund Freud. His discoveries relating to unconscious forces and his techniques designed to assist the individual to find a new basis for psychological unity can be adequately understood only when seen against the background of compartmentalization of personality in the nineteenth century.[34]

In view of this psychological disunity, it is not surprising that anxiety should have emerged as an unavoidable problem in the nineteenth century, and that in the middle of that period we should find Kierkegaard producing the most direct, and in some ways the most profound, study of anxiety to appear up to that point in history. The disunity itself was of course anxiety-creating; and the search for a new basis for unity of personality, as pursued by Kierkegaard and later by Freud, necessitated first of all confronting, and so far as possible solving, the problem of anxiety.

This breakdown in the unity of thought and culture was keenly felt by a number of sensitive and prophetic thinkers of the nineteenth century, many of whom can be grouped under the term Existentialists. The existentialist movement dates

---

[34] Freud often writes of his aim of making unconscious material conscious, and thus increasing the scope of reason. In his more theoretical writings (see *Civilization and its discontents* and *The future of an illusion*), he has a concept of reason and science which is inherited directly from the seventeenth and eighteenth centuries. But in actual practice his concept of reason, involving as it does a union of conscious experience with the vast store of unconscious tendencies within the individual, is a quite different thing from "reason" in traditional rationalism.

from the German philosopher F. W. J. Schelling's Berlin lectures in 1841, delivered before a distinguished audience including Kierkegaard, Engels, and Burckhardt.[35] In addition to Schelling and Kierkegaard, existential thinking is represented on one wing by the "philosophers of life"—Nietzsche, Schopenhauer, and later Bergson—and its sociological wing is seen in Feuerbach and Marx.[36] "What all philosophers of Existence oppose is the 'rational' system of thought and life developed by Western industrial society and its philosophical representatives." [37] Tillich characterizes the endeavors of these existential thinkers as "the desperate struggle to find a new meaning of life in a reality from which men have been estranged, in a cultural situation in which two great traditions, the Christian and the humanistic, have lost their comprehensive character and their convincing power." [38] In their rejection of traditional rationalism, the existential thinkers insisted that reality can be approached and experienced only by *the whole individual, as a feeling and acting as well as a thinking organism.* Kierkegaard felt that Hegel's system, which confuses abstract thought with reality, was nothing short of trickery. Kierkegaard and others in this line believed that passion cannot be divorced from thinking. Feuerbach wrote, "Only that which is the object of passion really is." [39] Said Nietzsche, "We think with our bodies."

---

[35] Paul Tillich, Existential philosophy, *History of Ideas,* 1944, **5:1, 44-70.** Since Tillich's own thinking participates in the Existentialist tradition, his descriptions of the movement have special cogency and will be quoted frequently in this section.

[36] The relationship of this form of thought to American pragmatism, as presented by William James, will be clear. Modern European representatives of existentialism include M. Heidegger and K. Jaspers. We do not wish existentialism in this discussion, to be identified with the present-day popular conception as presented, for example, in the philosophical writings of Sartre. This latter has been termed a "parenthesis" or "deviation" in the history of existentialism.—Guido de Ruggiero, *Existentialism* (New York, 1948).

[37] *Existential philosophy, op. cit.,* p. 66. Tillich continues: "During the last hundred years the implications of this system have become increasingly clear: a logical or naturalistic mechanism which seemed to destroy individual freedom, personal decision and organic community; and analytic rationalism which saps vital forces of life and transforms everything, including man himself, into an object of calculation and control . . ."

[38] *Ibid.,* p. 67.

[39] *Ibid.,* p. 54.

Thus, these thinkers sought to overcome the traditional dichotomy between mind and body and the tendency to suppress the "irrational" aspects of experience. Pure objectivity is an illusion, Kierkegaard held, and even if it weren't it would be undesirable; he emphasizes "the word 'interest' *(inter-est)*, which expresses the fact that we are so intimately involved in the objective world that we cannot be content to regard truth objectively, i.e., disinterestedly." [40] Kierkegaard reacted strongly against rigid definitions of such terms as "self" and "truth"; he felt they could be defined only dynamically, i.e., dialectically. "Away from speculation," he cried, "away from 'the System' and back to reality." [41] He insisted that "truth exists for the particular individual only as he himself produces it in action." [42] This sounds like a radical subjectivity, which on the surface it is; but it must be remembered that Kierkegaard and the others in this movement believed that this was the way to a genuine objectivity as opposed to the *artificial* objectivity of the "rationalistic" systems. As Tillich expresses it, these thinkers "turned toward man's immediate experience, toward 'subjectivity,' not as something opposed to 'objectivity,' but as that living experience in which both objectivity and subjectivity are rooted." [43] It was the aim of these thinkers to overcome the compartmentalization of their culture by a *new emphasis on the individual as a living, experiencing unity*—i.e., the individual as an organism which thinks, feels, and wills at the same time. The existentialists are important in this study, not only because the dichotomy between psychology and philosophy is broken down in their thought, but also because now for the first time in the modern period anxiety comes directly into the foreground as a specific problem.

We turn now to Søren Kierkegaard. He is regarded on the Continent, according to Brock, as "one of the most remarkable psychologists of all time, in depth, if not in breadth,

---

40 Walter Lowrie, *A short life of Kierkegaard* (Princeton, N. J., 1944), p. 172.
41 *Ibid.*, p. 116.
42 *The concept of dread, op. cit.*, p. 123.
43 Tillich, p. 67. Also, "They tried to discover the creative realm of being which is prior to and beyond the distinction between objectivity and subjectivity."

superior to Nietzsche, and in penetration comparable only to Dostoievski." [44]

The keystone idea in Kierkegaard's little book on anxiety,[45] published in 1844, is the relation between anxiety and freedom. Kierkegaard held that anxiety is always to be understood as oriented toward freedom." [46] Freedom is the goal of personality development; psychologically speaking, "the good is freedom." [47] Kierkegaard defines freedom as *possibility*. This he views as the spiritual aspect of man; indeed, it is not inaccurate to read "possibility" whenever Kierkegaard writes "spirit." The distinctive characteristic of man, in contrast to the merely vegetative or the merely animal, lies in the range of man's possibility and in his capacity for self-awareness of his possibility. Kierkegaard sees man as the creature who is continually beckoned by possibility, who conceives of possibility, visualizes it, and by creative activity carries it into actuality. What the specific content of this possibility is, in psychological terms, we shall discuss below in dealing with Kierkegaard's ideas of expansiveness and communicativeness; it suffices here to emphasize that this possibility is man's freedom.

---

[44] Werner Brock, *Contemporary German philosophy* (Cambridge, 1935), p. 75. For an appreciation of Kierkegaard by a contemporary psychologist, see O. H. Mowrer, Anxiety in *Learning theory and personality dynamics* (1950). Mowrer believes that it was necessary for Freud to produce his work before the insights of Kierkegaard could be widely understood.

[45] Translated into English under the title *The concept of dread*, by Walter Lowrie, and published at Princeton, N. J. in 1944. Lowrie states that in English "we have no word which adequately translates *Angst*" (preface to above edition, p. ix). Hence, after much deliberation, Dr. Lowrie and the other translators of Kierkegaard into English unanimously decided to use the term "dread" as a translation of Kierkegaard's *Angst*. It is certainly to be agreed that the term "anxiety" in English often means "eagerness" ("I am anxious to do something") or a mild form of worry or has other connotations which do not at all do justice to the term *Angst*. But the German *Angst* is the word which Freud, Goldstein, and others use for "anxiety"; and it is the common denominator for the term "anxiety" as used in this study. The question is whether the scientific psychological meaning of "anxiety" (in contrast to the literary meaning) is not very close—in fact much closer than the term "dread"—to what Kierkegaard meant by *Angst*. Professor Tillich, who is familiar with both the psychological meaning of *Angst* and Kierkegaard's works, believes this to be true. In any case, Professor Lowrie has generously given the present author permission to render the term "dread" as "anxiety" in the quotations from his translations of Kierkegaard, in order to conform with the usage of terms in this book.

[46] *The concept of dread*, p. 138.

[47] *Ibid.*, p. 99.

Now this capacity for freedom brings with it anxiety. Anxiety is the state of man, says Kierkegaard, when he confronts his freedom. Indeed, he describes anxiety as "the possibility of freedom." Whenever possibility is visualized by an individual, anxiety is potentially present in the same experience. In everyday experiential terms, this may be illustrated by the observation that every person has the opportunity and need to move ahead in his development—the child learns to walk, and moves on into school, and the adult moves into marriage or new jobs. Such possibilities, like roads ahead which cannot be known since one has not yet traversed and experienced them, involve anxiety. (This is "normal anxiety," and is not to be confused with "neurotic anxiety," which will be considered below; Kierkegaard makes it clear that neurotic anxiety is a more constrictive and uncreative form of anxiety which results from the individual's failure to move ahead in situations of normal anxiety.) [48] There is anxiety in any actualizing of possibility. To Kierkegaard, the more possibility (creativity) an individual has, the more potential anxiety he has at the same time. Possibility ("I can") passes over into actuality, but the intermediate determinant is anxiety. [49]

Viewing anxiety developmentally, Kierkegaard begins with the original state of the child. This he terms the state of innocence, in which the child is in immediate unity with his natural condition, his environment. The child has possibility. This entails anxiety, but it is anxiety without specific content. In this original state anxiety is a "seeking after adventure, a

---

[48] For the realization of selfhood, one must always move ahead. "So it is too that in the eyes of the world it is dangerous to venture. And why? Because one may lose. But not to venture is shrewd. And yet, by not venturing, it is so dreadfully easy to lose that which it would be difficult to lose in even the most venturesome venture, and in any case never so easily, so completely as if it were nothing . . . one's self. For if I have ventured amiss—very well, then life helps me by its punishment. But if I have not ventured at all—who then helps me? And, moreover, if by not venturing at all in the highest sense (*and to venture in the highest sense is precisely to become conscious of oneself*) I have gained all earthly advantages . . . and lose my self! What of that?"—Kierkegaard, *Sickness unto death*, trans. Walter Lowrie (Princeton, N. J., 1941), p. 52. (Italics mine.)

[49] *The concept of dread*, p. 44. The full quotation is: "Possibility means *I can*. In a logical system it is convenient enough to say that possibility passes over into actuality. In reality it is not so easy, and an intermediate determinant is necessary. This intermediate determinant is anxiety . . ."

thirst for the prodigious, the mysterious." [50] The child moves ahead, actualizing his possibilities. But in the state of innocence he is not self-consciously aware that the possibility of growth, for example, also involves possibility of crises, of clashes with, and defiance of, parents. In the state of innocence, individuation is a potentiality which has not yet become self-conscious; and the anxiety connected with it is "sheer possibility," i.e., without specific content.

Then in human development comes self-awareness. Kierkegaard cites the story of Adam as a presentation in myth form of this phenomenon. Disposing immediately of the deteriorated view of this myth as a historical event, he insists that "the myth represents as outward that which occurred inwardly." [51] He interprets it as a portrayal of the individual's inner awakening into self-consciousness. At some point in development there occurs the "knowledge of good and evil," as the myth puts it. Then conscious choice enters the picture of possibility. There is a heightened sense both of the portentous nature of possibility and of the responsibility that goes with it. For now the possibility of conflict and crises confronts the individual; possibility is negative as well as positive. Developmentally, the child now moves toward individuation. And the road over which he moves is not one of immediate harmony with environment or specifically with parents, but a road which continually skirts the edges of defiance of this environment; and indeed in many cases the road must move directly through actual experiences of defiance of, and conflict with, parents. Individuation (becoming a self) is gained at the price of confronting the anxiety inherent in taking a stand *against* as well as *with* one's environment. Describing the moment of this heightened awareness of the possibility of freedom, Kierkegaard speaks of "the *alarming* possibility of being able." [52]

---

[50] *Ibid.,* p. 38.
[51] *Ibid.,* p. 92. In this sense the myth of Adam is re-enacted by every human being somewhere between the ages of one and three.
[52] *Ibid.,* p. 40. Cf. Fromm's description in *Escape from freedom* (New York, 1941), p. 29, of the threat of isolation and powerlessness and the consequent potential anxiety which may arise at this point in the child's development (discussed on pages 170 ff. below).

It may be helpful to point out here that Kierkegaard's central problem when he writes psychologically is how a person can will to be himself. *To will to be himself is man's true vocation.* Kierkegaard holds that one cannot define specifically this self one is to be, for the self is freedom; but at considerable length he points out how people try to avoid willing to be themselves: by avoiding consciousness of the self, by willing to be some one else or simply a conventional self, or by willing to be oneself defiantly, which is a form of tragic, stoic despair and therefore doomed to fall short of full selfhood. His word "will" is not to be confused with nineteenth century voluntarism, which consisted chiefly of repression of unacceptable elements within the self. Rather, this willing is a creative decisiveness, based centrally on expanding self-awareness. "Generally speaking, consciousness, i.e. consciousness of self, is the decisive criterion of the self," he writes. "The more consciousness, the more self. . . ." [53] This is not a foreign language to anyone conversant with modern psychotherapy, in which the basic aim is to enlarge self-awareness by means of clarifying inner self-defeating conflicts which have existed because the individual has been forced to block self-awareness at various points.[54] It is clear in psychotherapy that these blockages in self-awareness have occurred because the individual has been unable to move through accumulations of anxiety at various points in his growth. Kierkegaard makes it clear that selfhood depends upon the individual's capacity to confront anxiety and move ahead despite it. Freedom, to Kierkegaard, is not a simple accretion, occurring as spontaneously as the plant grows toward the sun when the rocks that block it are removed (as the problem of freedom is sometimes oversimplified in deteriorated forms of psychotherapy). Freedom, rather, depends on how one relates oneself to oneself at every moment in existence. This means, in present-day

---

[53] *Sickness unto death, op. cit.,* p. 43.

[54] It should be clear that Kierkegaard, like the exponents of modern psychotherapy, is not speaking of what is sometimes called "unhealthy introspection." Such introspection arises not from too much self-awareness (which is a contradiction in terms in Kierkegaard's view) but rather from conditions of blocked self-awareness.

terms, that freedom depends on how responsibly and autonomously one relates to oneself.

When Kierkegaard speaks of the awakening of self-awareness following the state of innocence of the child, one is tempted to compare this with the data of contemporary psychology.[55] It is obviously parallel to what is now meant in some psychological quarters by the "emergence of the ego." This occurs generally somewhere between the ages of one and three; we can observe that in babies this self-awareness does not exist, whereas it is discernible in the child of four or five. So far as Kierkegaard's own view goes, he believed this change is a "qualitative leap," and cannot therefore be adequately described by scientific methods. Kierkegaard's aim is to describe phenomenologically the human situation—of an adult, for example—which he finds as a state of conflict (self-awareness) set against a backdrop of innocence.[56]

As a consequence of this "leap" into self-awareness, anxiety becomes reflective, that is, has more content. Anxiety "in the later individual is more reflective as a consequence of the participation of the individual in the history of the race." [57] Self-awareness makes possible not only self-directed individual development, but also self-conscious historical development. Just as the individual now sees himself as not merely at the mercy of his environment and his natural condition, but as possessing the capacities of choice and independence, so he sees himself likewise as something more than an automaton, swallowed up in a meaningless historical development. Through self-awareness man can mold and to an extent transform his present historical development. This does not annul the determining influences of one's historical environment. "Every individual begins in a historical nexus," Kierkegaard writes, "and the consequences of natural law are still as valid as ever." [58]

---

[55] The difficulty in comparing ideas such as Kierkegaard's to parallel concepts in contemporary psychology is that the equivalence is never entirely complete. For example, his idea of the *self* is only partially contained in the psychological term *ego*, which is its nearest equivalent.

[56] In philosophical terms, this is, of course, the problem of man's "essence" as over against his "existence."

[57] *The concept of dread, op. cit.*, p. 47.

[58] *Ibid.*, p. 65.

But what is of crucial significance is how a man relates himself to his historical nexus.[59]

Anxiety involves inner conflict; this is another consequence of self-awareness. Anxiety "is afraid," says Kierkegaard, "yet it maintains a sly intercourse with its object, cannot look away from it, indeed will not. . . ." [60] And again, anxiety "is a desire for what one dreads, a sympathetic antipathy. Anxiety is an alien power which lays hold of an individual, and yet one cannot tear oneself away, nor has a will to do so; for one fears, but what one fears one desires. Anxiety then makes the individual impotent." [61] This inner conflict which characterizes anxiety is familiar in modern clinical psychology; it has been described specifically by Freud, Stekel, Horney, and others. Ample illustrations of it can be cited from clinical data, especially in its exaggerated form in neurosis: a patient has sexual or aggressive desires, yet he fears these very desires (or the consequences of them), and a persistent inner conflict is engendered. Every person who has been seriously ill physically knows that he has severe anxiety lest he not get well, yet he flirts with the prospect of not getting well; he is sympathetic, in Kierkegaard's words, toward the prospect that he hates and fears most. This seems to be a phenomenon much more profound than the mere desire for the "secondary gain" of illness, be it emotional or physical. Possibly Freud was struggling with this phenomenon when he postulated the much questioned formulation of the "death instinct" as in conflict with the "life instinct." It would seem that Otto Rank comes closer to Kierkegaard (and at the same time avoids the less acceptable elements in Freud's postulation) in his concept of the conflict between the "life will" and the

---

59 Kierkegaard's argument up to this point may be summarized as follows: In the state of innocence there is no separation of the individual from his environment, and anxiety is ambiguous. In the state of self-awareness, there is this possibility of separation as an individual; anxiety is reflective; and the individual can through self-awareness direct his own development as well as participate in the history of the race.

60 *The concept of dread*, p. 92. Kierkegaard adds, for reasons the reader can well understand, "If to one or another this may appear a difficult saying, I can do nothing about it."

61 *Ibid.*, p. xii, quoted from his Journal (III A 233; Dru No. 402).

"death will." [62] In any case, Kierkegaard makes it clear that he would not limit this inner conflict to neurotic phenomena. He believes that in every possibility, in every experience of anxiety beyond infancy, the conflict is present. In every experience the individual wishes to move ahead, actualizing his possibilities, but at the same time wishes not to. Kierkegaard would describe the difference between the "neurotic" and "healthy" state by saying that the healthy individual moves ahead despite the conflict, actualizing his freedom; whereas the unhealthy person retrenches to a "shut-in" condition, sacrificing his freedom.[63] The radical distinction between fear and anxiety appears at this point: in fear one moves in one direction, *away* from the feared object, whereas in anxiety a persistent inner conflict is in operation and one has an ambivalent relation to the object. Kierkegaard always insists that, though anxiety in the reflective stage has more content, it can never be assigned a wholly specific content, for it describes an inner state, a state of conflict.

Another consequence of self-awareness is that responsibility and guilt feeling enter the picture.[64] Guilt feeling is a difficult and perplexing problem, to Kierkegaard as well as in contemporaneous psychology, and in the mind of the present writer the problem is often avoided by oversimplification. We can understand Kierkegaard's ideas on the relation between guilt and anxiety only by emphasizing that he is always speaking of anxiety in its relation to creativity. Because it is possible to create—creating one's self, willing to be one's self, as well as creating in all the innumerable daily activities (and these are two phases of the same process)—one has anxiety. One would

---

62 The present writer does not believe this conflict can be most fruitfully understood as "instinctual" or "biological." Rather, it is psychological; this is why Rank's term *will*, while not entirely satisfactory, is better than *instinct*. The conflict occurs not only *in* anxiety, but is itself the product of anxiety; i.e., one has such conflict to the extent that one already has anxiety in the situation.

63 It is interesting that Otto Rank also holds that the healthy individual is the one who can create despite the inner conflict (between "life will" and "death will," in his terms), whereas the neurotic is the one who cannot manage this conflict except by retrenching and sacrificing his creativity.

64 In contemporary psychopathology it is held that there is always anxiety where there is guilt feeling (fear of punishment) but that the reverse is not necessarily true. It will be seen, however, that Kierkegaard is speaking of a different level, i.e., the relation of guilt feeling to creativity.

have no anxiety if there were no possibility whatever. Now creating, actualizing one's possibilities, always involves negative as well as positive aspects. It always involves destroying the status quo, destroying old patterns within oneself, progressively destroying what one has clung to from childhood on, and creating new and original forms and ways of living. If one does not do this, one is refusing to grow, refusing to avail himself of his possibilities; one is shirking his responsibility to himself. Hence refusal to actualize one's possibilities brings guilt toward one's self. But creating also means destroying the status quo of one's environment, breaking the old forms; it means producing something new and original in human relations as well as in cultural forms (e.g., the creativity of the artist).[65] Thus every experience of creativity has its potentiality of aggression or denial toward other persons in one's environment or established patterns within one's self. To put the matter figuratively, in every experience of creativity something in the past is killed that something new in the present may be born. Hence, for Kierkegaard, guilt feeling is always a concomitant of anxiety : both are aspects of experiencing and actualizing possibility. The more creative the person, he held, the more anxiety and guilt are potentially present.[66]

Although sex and sensuality are often made the content for this guilt, Kierkegaard did not believe that sex and sensuality are in themselves sources of either anxiety or guilt. Sex is significant, rather, because it stands for the problem of individuation and community. In Kierkegaard's culture as well as in ours, sex is often the clearest fulcrum of the problem of being a

---

[65] The process of creativity has not been adequately explored in contemporary psychology. The testimony of the artists would support Kierkegaard at this point: Degas says, "A picture must be painted with the same feeling as that with which a criminal commits his crime," and Thomas Mann speaks of the "precious and guilty secret" which the artist keeps. One can find more insight into this phenomenon in mythology; in the myth of Prometheus, creativity is pictured as a defiance of the gods. One could ask psychologically whether individuation, and the creativity involved, means a progressive breaking from, and defiance of, the mother; or in Freudian terms, whether creativity is a progressive dethroning of the father. Psychologically speaking, we are not yet able to deal with these problems conclusively.

[66] "The greater the genius," writes Kierkegaard, "the more profoundly he discovers guilt."—*The concept of dread, op. cit.,* p. 96.

self—e.g., having individual desires, urges; yet being in expanding relationships with others—e.g., the complete fulfilment of these desires involves other persons. Sex may thus express this individuality-in-community constructively (sex as a form of interpersonal relatedness), or it may be distorted into egocentricity (pseudo-individuality) or into mere symbiotic dependence (pseudo-community).[67]

The belief in fate, says Kierkegaard, is often used as a method of avoiding the anxiety and guilt feeling in creativity. Since "fate is a relation of spirit (possibility) to something external," such as misfortune, necessity, or chance, the full meaning of anxiety and guilt are not felt. But Kierkegaard holds that this taking of refuge in a doctrine of fate sets limits to creativity. Thus he believed that Judaism, in which the problem of guilt was frankly faced, represents a higher level than Hellenism, which rested with a belief in fate. The creative genius in the highest sense does not seek to avoid anxiety and guilt through recourse to belief in fate; he creates by moving *through* anxiety and guilt.

One form of the loss of freedom is the state of "shut-upness."[68] This is the state, points out Kierkegaard, that has been characterized historically as the "demoniacal," and since he cites some biblical cases of hysteria and muteness, we know that he is referring to various clinical forms of neurosis and psychosis. The trouble in such cases he felt to be an "unfree relation to the good." The anxiety takes the form of "dread of the good"; the individual endeavors to shut out freedom and constrict his development. Indeed, "freedom is precisely the expansive," Kierkegaard holds; "freedom is constantly communicating."[69] In the demoniacal state, "unfreedom becomes

---

[67] In what we may take as an analogy, Kierkegaard speaks of anxiety culminating in the woman at the birth of a child, because "at this instant the new individual comes into the world."—(*Ibid.*, p. 65). Anxiety and guilt are potentially present at every instant that individuality is born into community; and this is not only in the figurative sense of the birth of a child, but in the birth of new phases of one's own individuality. According to Kierkegaard, one ought to be continually creating his own selfhood every instant of his life.

[68] "Shut-upness" is a graphic term for the processes of blocked awareness, inhibition, and other common neurotic reactions to anxiety which will be discussed frequently in subsequent chapters. For example, see particularly the cases of Phyllis and Frances in Chapter 7; see also Sections 5 and 6, Chapter 8.

[69] *The concept of dread, op. cit.*, p. 110.

more and more shut-up and wants no communication." [70] Kierkegaard makes it clear that he is not referring, in the phrase "shut-upness," to the reserve of the creative person, but to shut-upness as withdrawal and as a form of continual negation; "the demoniacal does not shut itself up *with* something, but shuts *itself* up." [71] Hence he also holds that the shut-up is the tedious (the impression of being extinct) and the vacuous. The shut-up person has anxiety when confronted with freedom or the "good" (these two terms are used as synonyms at this point). The "good" in Kierkegaard's sense signifies to the shut-up person a challenge to reintegrate himself on the basis of freedom.[72] The "good" furthermore, he describes as expansiveness, ever increasing communicativeness. Shut-up states, in the last analysis, are based upon illusions: "it is easy to see that shut-upness *eo ipso* signifies a lie, or, if you prefer, untruth. But untruth is precisely unfreedom. . . ." [73] He suggests that those who work with shut-up personalities should realize the value of silence, and should

---

[70] *Ibid.* Compare Ibsen's description of inmates of a lunatic asylum: "Each shuts himself in a cask of self, the cask stopped with a bung of self and seasoned in a well of self."—*Peer Gynt.*

[71] *The concept of dread.*

[72] Kierkegaard believed that it is a false compassion to view the shut-up personality as a victim of fate, for this implies that nothing can be done about it. A real compassion involves facing the problem with guilt (i.e., responsibility). This is responsibility on the part of all of us, whether shut-up or not. The courageous man prefers, when ill, to have it said, "this is not fate, this is guilt," for then his possibility of doing something about his condition is not removed from him. For "the ethical individual," Kierkegaard continues, "fears nothing so much as fate and aesthetic folderol which under the cloak of compassion would trick him out of his treasure, *viz,* freedom" (*ibid.,* p. 108 n.). We can illustrate this experientially from a realm of illness which is supposed in our culture to be even more closely referable to fate than psychological disturbances, i.e., infectious illnesses. In observing numbers of tuberculous patients, the writer noted that the sick persons were often reassured by well-meaning friends and medical personnel that the disease was due to an accident of infection by the tubercle bacillus. This explanation on the basis of fate was thought to be a relief to the patient. But actually it threw many of the more psychologically sensitive patients into greater despair; if the disease were an accident, how could they be certain it would not occur again and again? If, on the other hand, the patient feels that his own pattern of life was at fault and that this was one of the causes of his succumbing to the disease, he feels more guilt, to be sure, but at the same time he sees more hopefully what conditions need to be corrected in order to overcome the disease. From this point of view, guilt feeling is not only the more accurate attitude, but it is also the one yielding the more genuine hope. (Needless to say, Kierkegaard and the present author are referring to *rational,* not *irrational* guilt. The latter has unconscious dynamics, is unconstructive, and needs to be weeded out.)

[73] *Ibid.,* p. 114 n.

always keep their "categories very clear." He believed that the shut-up state can be cured by inward revelation, or "transparency," and his references to this on the psychological level are not unlike contemporary ideas of catharsis and clarification.

Freedom may also be lost psychosomatically. To Kierkegaard "the somatic, the psychic, the pneumatic" (possibility) are so interrelated that "a disorganization in one shows itself in the others." [74] He adds a third determinant to the customary psyche and soma, namely the self. It is this "intermediate determinant" which involves possibility and freedom. He did not believe that personality is a mere synthesis of psyche and soma. If it is to be developed to its larger capacities, personality depends upon how the self relates itself to both psyche and soma. (This is another indication that Kierkegaard's concept of the self is not to be identified with merely a portion of the psyche such as the ego.) The self is in operation when an individual is able to view both psyche and soma with freedom and to act on this freedom.

Other forms of the loss of freedom as a result of anxiety are seen in the rigid personalities. These are the personalities, writes Kierkegaard, who lack inward certitude. "A partisan of the most rigid orthodoxy may be demoniacal. He knows it all, he bows before the holy, truth is for him an ensemble of ceremonies, he talks about presenting himself before the throne of God, of how many times one must bow, he knows everything the same way as does the pupil who is able to demonstrate a mathematical proposition with the letters ABC, but not when they are changed to DEF. He is therefore in anxiety whenever he hears something not arranged in the same order. And yet how closely he resembles a modern speculative philosopher who found out a new proof for the immortality of the soul, then came into mortal danger and could not produce his proof because he had not his notebooks with him." [75] The kind of anxiety which is related to lack of inward certitude may show itself on one hand by wilfulness and unbelief—the negating attitude; and on the other hand by superstition. "Superstition and unbelief are both forms

---

[74] *Ibid.*, p. 109.
[75] *Ibid.*, p. 124.

of unfreedom." [76] The bigot and the unbeliever are in the same category with respect to the form of anxiety underlying their frame of mind. Both lack expansiveness; "both lack inwardness and dare not come to themselves." [77]

It is not surprising to Kierkegaard that people should do everything possible to avoid anxiety. He speaks of his "cowardly age" in which "one does everything possible by way of diversions and the Janizary music of loud-voiced enterprises to keep lonely thoughts away, just as in the forests of America they keep away wild beasts by torches, by yells, by the sound of cymbals." [78] For anxiety is an exceedingly painful experience. And again we quote, because of its vividness and aptness, his description of this painfulness: "And no Grand Inquisitor has in readiness such terrible tortures as has anxiety, and no spy knows how to attack more artfully the man he suspects, choosing the instant when he is weakest, nor knows how to lay traps where he will be caught and ensnared, as anxiety knows how, and no sharp-witted judge knows how to interrogate, to examine the accused, as anxiety does, which never lets him escape, neither by diversion nor by noise, neither at work nor at play, neither by day nor by night." [79] But attempts to evade anxiety are not only doomed to failure. In running from anxiety one loses one's most precious opportunity for education as a human being. [80]

Kierkegaard writes in his most engaging vein about anxiety as a "school." Anxiety is an even better teacher than reality, for one can temporarily evade reality by avoiding the distasteful situation; but anxiety is a source of education always present because one carries it within. "Even in relation to the most trifling matters, so soon as the individuality would make an artful turn which is only artful, would steal away from something, and there is every probability that it will succeed, for

---

[76] *Ibid.*
[77] *Ibid.*, p. 129.
[78] *Ibid.*, p. 107.
[79] *Ibid.*, p. 139.
[80] "If a man were a beast or an angel, he would not be able to be in anxiety. Since he is a synthesis he can be in anxiety, and the greater the anxiety the greater the man. This, however, is not affirmed in the sense in which men commonly understand anxiety, as related to something outside a man, but in the sense that man himself produces anxiety."—*Ibid.*, p. 139.

reality is not so sharp an examiner as anxiety—then anxiety is at hand." [81] Accepting anxiety as a teacher may seem a foolish counsel, he admits, especially to those who boast of never having been in anxiety. "To this I would reply that doubtless one should not be in dread of men, or of finite things, but *only that man who has gone through the anxiety of possibility is educated to have no anxiety.*" [82] On one side—which we may term the negative side—this education involves facing and accepting the human situation frankly, facing the fact of death and other aspects of the contingency of existence, and from this *Angst der Kreatur* one learns how to interpret the reality of one's human situation. [83]

On the positive side, going to school of anxiety enables one to move through the finite and petty constrictions and to be freed to actualize the infinite possibilities in personality. The finite to Kierkegaard is that which "shuts up" freedom ; the infinite refers in contrast to "opening up" doors to freedom. The infinite, therefore, is part of his concept of possibility. Finiteness can be defined as one experiences it in the innumerable constrictions and artificial limitations that we observe in the clinic as well as in our own lives. The infinite cannot be so defined, because it represents freedom. In facing anxiety, Kierkegaard extols the attitude of Socrates who "solemnly flourished the poisoned goblet . . . as a patient says to the surgeon when a painful operation is about to begin, 'Now I am ready.' Then anxiety enters into his soul and searches it thoroughly, constraining out of him all the finite and the petty, and leading him hence whither he would go." [84] In such confronting of anxiety the individual is educated to faith, or inward certitude. [85] Then one has the "courage to

---

[81] *Ibid.,* p. 144.

[82] *Ibid,* p. 141. (Italics mine.)

[83] "When such a person, therefore, goes out from the school of possibility, and knows more thoroughly than a child knows the alphabet that he can demand of life absolutely nothing, and that terror, perdition, annihilation, dwell next door to every man, and has learned the profitable lesson that every anxiety which alarms [*Aengste*] may the next instant become a fact, he will interpret reality differently, he will extol reality. . . ."—*Ibid.,* p. 140.

[84] *Ibid.,* p. 142.

[85] Fromm makes a similar definition of faith as *inward firmness* (see *Man for himself* [New York, 1947]). In fact, the thought of Fromm, though it has significant differences from that of Kierkegaard, presents some striking parallels to

renounce anxiety without any anxiety, which only faith is capable of—not that it annihilates anxiety, but remaining ever young, it is continually developing itself out of the death throe of anxiety." [86]

To the scientifically minded reader, it may seem that Kierkegaard in the above quotations is speaking in poetic and paradoxical figures of speech. This is, of course, true; but his meaning may be summarized in clear, experiential terms. On one hand he is anticipating the contention of Horney and others that anxiety indicates the presence of a problem which needs to be solved; and in Kierkegaard's mind, anxiety will dog the steps of the individual (if he does not engage in complete neurotic repression) until the problem is resolved. But on the other hand, Kierkegaard is proclaiming that "self-strength" develops out of the individual's successful confronting of anxiety-creating experiences; this is the way one becomes educated to maturity as a self. What is amazing in Kierkegaard is that despite his lack of the tools for interpreting unconscious material—which tools have been available in their most complete form only since Freud—he so keenly and profoundly anticipated modern psychoanalytic insight into anxiety; and that at the same time he placed these insights in the broad context of a poetic and philosophical understanding of human experience. In Kierkegaard one finds a promise of the dawning of that day for which the French physiologist Claude Bernard yearned, the day when "the physiologist, the philosopher and the poet will talk the same language and understand each other."

---

the psychological work of the nineteenth century Danish thinker. Both Fromm and Kierkegaard are centrally concerned with the individual as an existential unity, and both devote themselves to the problems of individual freedom and the sense of isolation so profoundly experienced by modern man.

[86] *Ibid.*, p. 104.

Chapter 3

ANXIETY INTERPRETED BIOLOGICALLY

> The planning function of the nervous system, in the course of evolution, has culminated in the appearance of ideas, values, and pleasures—the unique manifestations of man's social living. Man, alone, can plan for the distant future and can experience the retrospective pleasures of achievement. Man, alone, can be happy. But man, alone, can be worried and anxious. Sherrington once said that posture accompanies movement as a shadow. I have come to believe that anxiety accompanies intellectual activity as *its* shadow and that the more we know of the nature of anxiety the more we will know of intellect.—Howard Liddell, *The Role of Vigilance in the Development of Animal Neurosis.*

In this chapter we inquire, from the biological viewpoint, what happens to an organism when it is confronted with a danger situation? [1] We begin by noting a protective response which, although not fear or anxiety, is a precursor of these emotions, namely the startle pattern. The study of the startle pattern by Landis and Hunt is of particular interest, since it casts light on the order of emergence in an organism of protective reflex, anxiety, and fear. [2]

1. THE STARTLE PATTERN

On experiencing a violent, sudden stimulus such as a loud noise, a person will bend quickly, jerk his head forward, blink his eyes, and in other ways exhibit the "startle reflex." This reflex is a primary, innate, involuntary reaction which precedes

---

[1] We employ the term "biological" as including not only the immediate neurological reflexive responses to danger, but also in the broader sense of the organism as a biological whole responding to a threat.

[2] C. Landis and W. A. Hunt, *The startle pattern* (New York, 1939).

the emotions of fear and anxiety.[3] Landis and Hunt have performed varied experiments to elicit the startle pattern, using mainly a pistol shot for the stimulus and cinemaphotography to record the instantaneous reactions. The startle pattern has as its most prominent feature a general flexion of the body, "which resembles a protective contraction or 'shrinking' of the individual."[4] The startle pattern always is marked by a blinking of the eyes, and in the normal picture it includes "head movement forward, a characteristic facial expression, raising and drawing forward of the shoulders, abduction of the upper arms, bending of the elbows, pronation of the lower arms, flexion of the fingers, forward movement of the trunk, contraction of the abdomen, and bending of the knees."[5] Neurologically, the startle pattern involves an inhibition of the higher nervous centers, the latter being unable to integrate a stimulus of such suddenness. That is to say, we startle before we know what we are threatened by.

The startle reflex is not fear or anxiety as such. "It seems best to define startle as pre-emotional," Landis and Hunt remark.[6] "It is an immediate reflex response to sudden, intense stimulation which demands some out-of-the-ordinary treatment by the organism. As such it partakes of the nature of an emergency reaction, but it is a rapid, transitory response much more simple in its organization and expression than the so-called 'emotions.' "[7] Emotion proper may follow the startle reflex. The adult subjects in the Landis and Hunt experiments showed such secondary behavior (emotion) as curiosity, annoyance, and fear after the startle. The authors suggest that this secondary behavior is a "bridge from the innate and unlearned response over to the learned, socially conditioned, and often purely volun-

---

[3] We omit from consideration the Moro reflex, which is present in babies but represents an immaturity of neurological development. The Moro reflex disappears after a certain amount of maturation, especially of the higher nervous centers, and is therefore found in adults only in abnormal cases. For adults the startle pattern is the primary protective reflex.

[4] Landis and Hunt, op. cit., p. 23.

[5] Ibid., p. 21. Also: "It is a basic reaction, not amenable to voluntary control, is universal, and is found in Negroes as well as whites, infants as well as adults, in the primates and in certain of the lower animal forms."

[6] Ibid., p. 153.

[7] Ibid.

tary type of response." [8]   Significantly, *the younger the infant in these experiments, the less secondary behavior accompanied the startle*.   During the first month of life the infant showed very little reaction except startle, "while our work shows," continue Landis and Hunt, "that as the infant develops, more and more secondary behavior appears. . . . Crying and escape behavior— either a turning of the head away from the sound source or actual turning of the body and creeping away—became increasingly frequent with age." [9]

This startle pattern, according to Landis and Hunt, belongs to the general type of response which Goldstein calls the "catastrophic reaction."   In the present study we view the startle pattern as a primal, unlearned protective reflex, the precursor of the emotional reactions of the organism which become anxiety and fear.[10]

2. Goldstein: Anxiety as the Catastrophic Reaction

The contribution of Kurt Goldstein is important for our present purposes because it yields a broad biological base for the understanding of anxiety.[11]   Goldstein's concepts arise out of his work as a neurobiologist with diverse mental patients, but especially with patients with brain injuries. These patients, whose capacities for adequate adjustment to the demands of their environment were limited by their brain lesions, responded to a wide variety of stimuli with shock, anxiety, and defense re-

---

8 *Ibid.,* p. 136.

9 *Ibid.,* p. 141.

10 A good deal could be deduced from the startle pattern as a pre-emotional response of anxiety and fear. For example, Kubie finds in this pattern the "ontogeny of anxiety." He holds that the startle pattern is the first indication that a gap exists between the individual and his world. The fetus, Kubie holds, cannot experience startle; in the fetus there is no interval between stimulus and response. But the infant and the startle pattern are born at the same moment. Thereafter there exists a "distance" between the individual and his environment. The infant experiences waiting, postponement, frustration. Anxiety and the thought processes both arise out of this situation of "gap" between the individual and the world, Kubie holds, with anxiety preceding the development of thought. "Anxiety in the life of the individual stands as a bridge between the startle pattern and the dawn of all processes of thought."—L. S. Kubie The ontogeny of anxiety, *Psychoanal. Rev.,* 1941, 28:1, 78-85.

11 Kurt Goldstein, *The organism: a holistic approach to biology* (New York, 1939), and *Human nature in the light of psychopathology* (Cambridge, 1938).

actions. By observing them, as by observing normal individuals in crisis situations, we gain insights into the biological aspects of the dynamics of anxiety in all organisms.[12]

Goldstein's Definition of Anxiety.—Goldstein's central thesis is that anxiety *is the subjective experience of the organism in a catastrophic condition.* An organism is thrown into a catastrophic condition when it cannot cope with the demands of its environment and therefore feels a threat to its existence (or to values it holds essential for its existence). Goldstein's brain-injured patients devised innumerable ways of avoiding catastrophic situations. Some, for example, had developed compulsive patterns of orderliness: they kept their closets in perfect order, and if placed in surroundings in which the objects were in disarray, they were at a loss to react adequately and exhibited profound anxiety. Others, when asked to write their names on a paper, would write in the extreme corner of the paper; any open space (any "emptiness") represented a situation with which they could not cope. Any changes in environment were avoided by these patients, for they were unable to evaluate new stimuli adequately. In all these situations we see the patient unable to cope with the demands of his world and unable to actualize his essential capacities. The normal adult, of course, is able to cope with a much wider range of stimuli, but the problem of *organism-in-catastrophic-condition* remains essentially the same. The objective aspect of being in such a condition is disordered behavior. The subjective aspect is anxiety.

Goldstein denies that an organism is to be understood as a composite of various "drives," the blocking or disturbing of

---

[12] A distinction must be made between "biological," referring to the organism as an acting and reacting totality, and "psychological" referring to one level in that totality. It is true, as some writers have held, that a study of brain-injured patients does not yield data on the specifically psychological aspect of neurotic anxiety, since these patients are neurologically impaired to begin with. For example, Mowrer (1949) holds that the anxiety of Goldstein's patients is more akin to *Urangst* than to neurotic anxiety. Indeed it is doubtful whether the term "neurotic anxiety" has any meaning when applied to these patients. This distinction, however, does not contradict the above statement that Goldstein's findings are of great value in providing a biological base for the understanding of anxiety; and it is the writer's judgment (as will be indicated in detail later) that the understanding of anxiety on the psychological level is not inconsistent with, but complementary to, Goldstein's findings on the biological level.

which results in anxiety.[13]   Rather, there is only one trend in an
organism, namely *to actualize its own nature*.[14]   Each organism's primal need and tendency are to make its environment adequate to itself and vice versa.   Of course the nature of organisms,
animal or human, varies widely.   Each has its own essential
capacities, which determine both what it has to actualize and
how it will endeavor to do so.   A wild animal may actualize its
own nature successfully in its jungle habitat, but placed in cap-
tivity in a cage it is often unable to react adequately and exhibits
frantic behavior.   Sometimes an organism overcomes the hiatus
between its own nature and the environment by sacrificing some
elements in its nature—presumably the wild animal above learns
to avoid the catastrophic condition in the cage by sacrificing its
need to roam freely.   An inadequate organism may seek to
shrink its world to that in which its essential capacities are adequate, thus avoiding the catastrophic situation.   As an example,
Goldstein mentions that Cannon's sympathetomized cats stayed
near a radiator because their capacity to react adequately to cold
(and thus preserve their existence) had been curtailed by the
cutting of the sympathetic nervous chain.

It is not merely or even centrally the threat of pain, according
to Goldstein, that causes the catastrophic condition and consequent anxiety.   Pain can often be borne without anxiety or fear.
Likewise anxiety is not cued off by *any* danger.   It is that particular danger which threatens the existence of the organism—
"existence" here meaning not merely physical life but psychological life as well.   The threat may be to *values the organism
identifies with its existence*.[15]   To one student a particular examination may not be a traumatic experience, whereas to another
student, whose life career depends on passing the examination,

---

13 Though he rejects the concept of "drives," Goldstein holds that one can
speak of the "needs" of the organism in its trend to actualize itself.

14 Note the similarities between this view and Kierkegaard's concept of self-
realization (Chapter 2).

15 We may note, apart from Goldstein's analysis, that in our culture the
so-called "drives"—be they psychophysical like sex or psychocultural like "success"
—are often identified in various ways with the psychological existence of the
individual.   Hence one person may be thrown into anxiety by the frustration of
certain sexual patterns, and another may feel himself to be in a catastrophic situation when his success in terms of money (and prestige) falls below a certain level.

the situation may be catastrophic, reacted to with disordered behavior and anxiety. There are thus two sides to the basic concept of organism-in-catastrophic-situation: one is the objective situation itself, and the other is the nature of the organism involved.

Human beings vary enormously with respect to their capacity for meeting crisis situations. Why some individuals are so ill-prepared for crises because of conflicts within themselves is more strictly the psychological problem and is discussed in the next chapter. Let it suffice to point out here that every human being has his "threshold" beyond which additional stress makes the situation catastrophic. Grinker and Spiegel have illustrated this threshold in their studies of soldiers who have broken down in battle. The function of the various defenses— shown in Goldstein's patients by fanatical orderliness, avoidance of change, and compulsive activity—is to protect the individual from the catastrophic situation.

We now consider Goldstein's interesting discussion of *why anxiety is an emotion without a specific object*. He agrees with Kierkegaard, Freud, and others that anxiety is to be distinguished from fear in that fear has a specific object, whereas anxiety is a vague and unspecific apprehension. The puzzling problem in contemporary psychology is not this definition but the rationale for it. So far as the phenomenon goes, it is readily observable that a person in severe anxiety is unable to say, or to know, what "object" he is afraid of.[16] This is especially clear in patients at the onset of psychoses, says Goldstein, but the same phenomenon can be seen in less extreme cases. When patients are in anxiety states in psychoanalysis, they will report that their inability to know what they are afraid of is precisely what makes the anxiety so painful and disconcerting. Goldstein suggests that "it seems as if, in proportion to the increase of anxiety, objects and contents disappear more and more." And he asks,

---

16 Of course a "pseudo-object" is often found for the anxiety, such as in phobias or superstitions. As is well known, anxiety is often displaced on any acceptable object; there is generally relief from the pain of anxiety if the sufferer can attach it to some object. The presence of pseudo-objects in anxiety ought not to be confused with the real sources of the anxiety.

"Does not anxiety consist intrinsically of that inability to know from whence the danger threatens?" [17] In fear we are aware of ourselves as well as of the object, and we can orient ourselves spatially with reference to the thing feared. But anxiety "attacks us from the rear," to use Goldstein's phrase, or, as the present writer would say, from all sides at once. In fear one's attention is narrowed to the object, tension is mobilized for flight; one can flee from the object because it occupies a particular point spatially. In anxiety, on the other hand, the individual's efforts to flee generally amount to frantic behavior because he does not experience the threat as coming from a particular place, and hence he does not know where to flee. As Goldstein phrases it, "In fear, there is an appropriate defense reaction, a bodily expression of tension and of extreme attention to a certain part of the environment. In anxiety, on the other hand, we find meaningless frenzy, with rigid or distorted expression, accompanied by withdrawal from the world, a shut-off affectivity, in the light of which the world appears irrelevant, and any reference to the world, any useful perception and action is suspended." [18] Goldstein observed that when the brain-injured patients were in anxiety, they were unable to evaluate external stimuli adequately, and hence they were neither able to give an accurate account of their objective environments nor able to see realistically their own positions in relation to these environments. "The fact that the catastrophic condition involves the impossibility of ordered reactions," remarks Goldstein, "precludes a subject 'having' an object in the outer world." [19] Everyone has noticed in his own experience how anxiety tends to confuse not only his awareness of himself but at the same time to confuse his perception of the objective situation. It is understandable that these two phenomena should go together, for, in Goldstein's words, "to be conscious of one's self is only a correlate of being conscious of objects." [20] *The awareness of the relationship between the self*

---

[17] *The organism, op. cit.,* p. 292.
[18] *Ibid.,* p. 293. Also: "Fear sharpens the senses. Whereas anxiety paralyzes the senses and renders them unusable, fear drives them to action."—*Ibid.,* p. 297.
[19] *Ibid.,* p. 295.
[20] *Ibid.*

and objects is precisely what breaks down in anxiety.[21]   Hence
it is not at all illogical that anxiety should appear as an objectless
phenomenon.[22]

In the light of the above discussion, Goldstein holds that
severe anxiety is experienced by a person as a disintegration of
the self, a "dissolution of the existence of his personality." [23]
Thus it is not strictly accurate to speak of "having" anxiety;
rather one "is" anxiety, or "personifies" anxiety.

Relation Between Anxiety and Fear.—What is the developmental relation between anxiety and fears?   In Goldstein's view,
anxiety is the primal and original reaction and fear a later development.   The first reactions of infants to threats are diffuse and
undifferentiated—i.e., anxiety reactions.   Fears are a later differentiation as the individual learns to objectivate and to deal
specifically with those elements in his environment which might
throw him into the catastrophic condition.   In an infant, even an
infant in the first ten days of life, one can observe obvious anxiety
—diffuse, undifferentiated reactions to threats to its security.
Only later as the growing infant becomes neurologically and psychologically mature enough to objectivate—i.e., to distinguish
those items in its environment which might give rise to the
catastrophic condition—do specific fears appear.

Proceeding into his more specific formulation of the relation
between fear and anxiety, Goldstein makes a statement which
may seem confusing to many readers. *"What is it then that
leads to fear?"* he asks, and then asserts, *"Nothing but the experience of the possibility of the onset of anxiety."* [24]   Thus fear,
he holds, is actually an apprehension that one might be thrown
into the catastrophic condition.   This may be illustrated from the

---

[21] Readers who wish a clinical illustration of these points are referred to the
case of Brown in Chapter 7, especially to the discussion on page 249; and also to
Section 6 in Chapter 8.

[22] Of course Goldstein does not intend, in this discussion of the objectless
nature of anxiety, to divorce the organism from its objective environment. The
individual is always faced with an objective environment, and it is only in seeing
the organism-in-environment, that is, the organism reacting to tasks which it
cannot solve, that we are able to understand the onset of anxiety.

[23] *Op. cit.,* p. 295.

[24] *Ibid.,* p. 296.

case to which we have already referred, that of Brown (Chapter 6 of this book). At different times this young man needed to pass certain examinations if he was to be permitted to proceed in his academic plans. On one occasion he felt at the moment of writing the examination that he could not succeed and was seized with panic that he might be dropped from the university and would then again be a "failure." The very pronounced tension and conflict, with all his old symptoms of profound anxiety, were the subjective reactions to his experience of being in a "catastrophic condition." At another time, however, when he approached a similar situation of examinations, he felt apprehension but moved ahead, steadily doing his work, and ultimately succeeded in writing the tests without being thrown into panic. The apprehension on this latter occasion we may define as fear. Now what was he afraid of? Namely, that he would be thrown into the catastrophic condition described in the first instance. Thus, Goldstein holds, fear represents a warning that if the dangerous experience were not coped with adequately, one might be thrown into a situation of danger to the whole organism. Fear boils down to apprehension of specific experiences which might produce the more devastating condition, namely anxiety; fear, in Goldstein's formulation, is fear of the onset of anxiety.

The present writer believes that Goldstein's formulations at this point may seem confusing because of the tendency in much of our past psychological thinking to regard fear as the generic term and anxiety as a derivative from fear.[25] Goldstein's viewpoint is the opposite: fear is a differentiation from anxiety and a later development in the maturation of the organism. He asserts that the customary procedure of understanding anxiety as a form of fear, or the "highest form of fear," is incorrect. "Thus it becomes clear that anxiety cannot be made intelligible from the phenomenon of fear, but that only the opposite procedure is logical."[26] To be sure, fear may pass into anxiety (when the individual finds he cannot cope with the situation) or anxiety

---

[25] See P. M. Symonds, *The dynamics of human adjustment* (New York, 1946), p. 155.

[26] *The organism, op cit.,* p. 297.

may pass into fear (as the individual begins to feel he can cope adequately). But when increasing fear turns eventually into a state of anxiety, for example, Goldstein contends that a qualitative change is occurring—that is, *a change from the perception of the threat as coming from a specific object to an apprehension which engulfs the whole personality so that the person feels his very existence is endangered.*[27]

With regard to the origin of fears and anxiety, Goldstein disagrees with the various theories of hereditary anxiety and inherited fears of certain objects. Stanley Hall went back so far as to assume that children's fears were inherited from the animal ancestors of man. Stern refuted this, but he held, with Groos, that the child has an instinctive fear of the "uncanny." Goldstein feels that this cannot be true, since the child learns by moving ahead into unfamiliar situations. Stern held that certain peculiarities of objects lead to the child's fears of them: sudden appearance, rapid approach, intensity of the stimulus, and so forth. All these have one factor in common, says Goldstein: they make an adequate stimulus evaluation difficult, if not impossible. "For an explanation of anxiety in childhood," Goldstein sums up the question, "it suffices to assume that the organism reacts to inadequate situations with anxiety, and did so in the days of his ancestors, as well as today." [28] This explanation, we might add, saves us from becoming lost in that labyrinth of futile "heredity vs. learning" debates which have heretofore bedevilled much of the discussion of fears and anxiety. Goldstein's view is clarifying in that it becomes no longer necessary to view the individual as a carrier of certain fears, but rather as an organism needing to make itself adequate to its environment and its environment adequate to itself. When this cannot be done, as stated above, anxiety results; and fears, rather than being hereditary, are objectivated forms of this capacity for anxiety.

---

[27] We might remark parenthetically that since anxiety is the much more discomforting state, there is always a tendency to "rationalize" anxiety in terms of fears. This is done unrealistically and unconstructively in the phenomena of phobias and superstitions; but that it can be done constructively is shown in therapeutic sessions in which the individual learns to view his dangers realistically and at the same time develops confidence that he can meet them adequately.

[28] *Ibid.,* p. 300.

The capacity to bear anxiety is important for the individual's self-realization and for his conquest of his environment. Every person experiences continual shocks and threats to his existence; indeed, self-actualization occurs only at the price of moving ahead despite such shocks. This points to the constructive use of anxiety. Goldstein's view is here similar to that of Kierkegaard, who, as indicated in the previous chapter, emphasized that anxiety is from the positive point of view an indication of new possibility for development of the self. Goldstein holds that the freedom of the healthy individual inheres in the fact that he can choose between various alternatives, can avail himself of new possibilities in the overcoming of difficulties in his environment. In moving *through* rather than *away from* anxiety the individual not only achieves self-development but also enlarges the scope of his world of activity. "Not to be afraid of dangers which could lead to anxiety—this represents in itself a successful way of coping with anxiety. . . ." [29] "Courage, in its final analysis, is nothing but an affirmative answer to the shocks of existence, which must be borne for the actualization of one's own nature." [30] The normal child has less power to cope with his world than the adult, but the child has a strong tendency toward action—this inheres in the child's nature, says Goldstein—and hence moves ahead, growing and learning despite shocks and dangers. This is the essential difference between a normal child and a brain-injured patient, though they both represent limited powers of coping with anxiety-creating situations. The capacity to bear anxiety is found least of all in the brain-injured patient, more in the child, and most of all in the creative adult. The creative person, who ventures into many situations which expose him to shock, is more often threatened by anxiety but, assuming the creativity is genuine, he is more able to overcome these threats constructively. Goldstein quotes with approval Kierkegaard's statement, "The more original a human being is, the deeper is his anxiety." [31]

---

[29] *Ibid.,* p. 303.
[30] *Ibid.,* p. 306.
[31] Kurt Goldstein, *Human nature in the light of psychopathology,* p̄. 113.

Culture is the product of man's conquest of anxiety in that culture represents man's progressive making of his environment adequate to himself, and himself adequate to his environment. Goldstein disagrees radically with Freud's negative view of culture—viz., that culture is a result of the sublimation of repressed drives, a result of the desire to avoid anxiety. Creativity and culture are from the positive viewpoint, Goldstein holds, associated with the joy of overcoming tasks and shocks. When creative activities are a direct product of the individual's anxiety, or are substitute phenomena into which the individual is forced by his anxiety, there is evident a stress on partial aspects of action, compulsiveness, and lack of freedom. Hence ". . . as long as these activities are not spontaneous, are not outlets of the free personality, but are merely the sequelae of anxiety, they have only a pseudo-value for the personality." [32]

We conclude with Goldstein's interesting note on the relation of anxiety to the modern cultural phenomenon of fascism. Persistent anxiety on the part of a national group may be an important psychodynamic motive in the social regression represented in fascism, just as the anxiety-ridden individual who can no longer tolerate his anxiety will endeavor to find relief through curtailing his freedom. "Shaken on the one hand by uneasiness about the present situation and by anxiety for their existence, deceived on the other by the mockery of a brilliant future as the political demagogue depicts it, a people may give up freedom and accept virtual slavery. And it may do this in the hope of getting rid of anxiety." [33]

3. NEUROLOGICAL AND PHYSIOLOGICAL ASPECTS OF ANXIETY

In most discussions of the neurophysiological aspects of anxiety, the procedure is to describe the functioning of the sympathetic division of the autonomic nervous system (and the

---

[32] He continues, "This can be illustrated by the difference between the sincere faith of the really religious man, which is based upon willing devotion to the infinite, and superstitious beliefs. Or by the difference between the open-minded scholar who bases his beliefs upon facts and is always ready to change his conceptions when faced with new facts, and the dogmatic scientist. . . ."—*Ibid.*, p. 115.

[33] *Ibid.*, p. 117. See earlier discussion of this "escape from freedom" motif in totalitarianism in Chapter 1, pages 10 ff., and in Chapter 5.

bodily changes for which this division is the medium), and then to assume implicitly or explicitly that this procedure adequately takes care of the problem. While the present writer agrees that an understanding of the function of the sympathetic division is one very important step in the inquiry into the neurophysiology of anxiety, he will later indicate that such a procedure is not in itself adequate. Anxiety is a reaction in the organism so pervasive and fundamental that it cannot be relegated to a "specific" neurophysiological base. As we shall see in the subsequent discussion of psychosomatics, anxiety almost always involves a complex constellation of neurophysiological interrelationships and "balances." In the present section, therefore, we shall proceed from the simpler levels of the question—e.g., the functioning of the sympathetic division when the organism is subjected to threat—to the more complex levels as the organism is seen as a reacting totality in its environment.[34]

When an organism is subjected to threat, certain bodily changes occur which prepare the organism for fighting or fleeing from the danger. These changes are effected by way of the *autonomic* nervous system. Called "autonomic" because it is not subject to direct conscious control,[35] this system leads from the spinal column to the internal organs and the endocrine glands and is the medium by which emotional changes occur in the body.

---

[34] Goldstein offers a challenging corrective to much of the discussion in this field: "There are no 'specific' neurophysiological bases for anxiety or fear," he stated in conversation with the present writer; "if the organism reacts at all, the whole organism reacts." This does not imply, of course, that it is not useful to study sympathetic activity, for example, as one important aspect of the neurophysiology of anxiety and fear, but it does imply that such a study must be subsumed under a more comprehensive view of the organism as a reacting totality. Goldstein's view also does not imply that some reactions of the organism are not more specific than others. For example, fear is a more specific reaction, neurophysiologically as well as psychologically, than anxiety, so the practice of describing the neurophysiology of fear solely in terms of sympathetic activity is less fallacious than the same procedure with anxiety. As we shall later demonstrate, one distinction between fear and anxiety is that anxiety strikes at more fundamental, and hence, more engrossing, "strata" in the organism. Furthermore, the reader should perhaps be warned that while much of great value is known about the neurophysiological reactions of the organism under threat (which knowledge we shall endeavor to review in the remainder of this chapter), there is a great deal about the neurophysiology of anxiety which we do not as yet know.

[35] This is one distinction between the autonomic system and the other two systems in the organism, the central (cerebral-spinal) and skeletal nervous systems, both of which are more directly under conscious control.

It has been called "the bridge between psyche and soma." As will be discussed more fully below, the autonomic system consists of two divisions which work in opposition to each other. The *parasympathetic* division stimulates digestive, vegetative, and other "upbuilding" functions of the organism; the affects connected with these activities are of the comfortable, pleasurable, relaxing sort. The other division, the *sympathetic,* is the medium for accelerating heartbeat, raising blood pressure, releasing adrenalin into the blood, and the other phases of mobilizing the energies of the organism for fighting or fleeing from danger. The affects connected with the "general excitement" of sympathetic stimulation are typically some form of anger, anxiety, or fear.

Perception of the Danger Stimuli.—The impulses moving to the autonomic nervous system go through the lower and middle brain centers (i.e., the thalamus and diencephalon), the last-named being the "coordinating apparatus" for the sympathetic stimuli involved in anxiety and fear. These lower and middle brain centers are, in turn, interrelated with the cerebral cortex, i.e., the higher brain centers which involve the function of "awareness" and "conscious interpretation" of situations.

The stimulus which sets off anxiety and fear may come in two ways, neurologically speaking. In the first place, stimuli may come "directly" to the midbrain, resulting in a reflexive defense reaction. Crude sensory stimuli, such as loud noises or the sudden loss of support, are of this sort; they cause an automatic reflexive reaction relayed through the thalamus to the diencephalon and back to the muscles without intervention of the cerebral cortex. The organism may jump or in other ways show startle, and only afterwards is there a reverberation to the cerebral cortex so that the organism is aware of fear and anxiety. Or, in the second place, the stimuli may come from the cerebral cortex (here roughly equated with the function of conscious awareness). (In this connection it should be noted, as will be discussed later, that the equating of a neurological area with a psychological function can be done only very loosely, not literally.) Such stimuli move "down" through the diencephalon to effect the necessary sympathetic and motor changes. This is the case when the organism interprets some stimuli, external or intrapsychic, as a threat. In the first case the reflexive action "jumps" the cerebral cortex, and in the second the alerting of the organism is from cortex through diencephalon to sympathetic nervous system and motor apparatus.

This function of the cerebral cortex, or psychologically speaking, conscious awareness, is of great importance in clinical dealing with anxiety, since the apprehension depends centrally on how the individual *interprets* potential dangers.[36] For example, a patient with an anxiety neurosis discussed later in this study experienced profound anxiety whenever he engaged in a minor argument or a bridge game, because any suggestion of competition set off associations connected with his early competition with his sisters which had been a great threat to his close dependency on his mother.[37] Thus a relatively harmless situation, objectively speaking, may become the occasion for great anxiety because of the complex ways, involving past experiences, etc., in which the individual interprets the situation.

The stimuli which the individual interprets as dangerous may be *intrapsychic* as well as external. Certain inner promptings of a hostile or sexual nature, for example, may be associated with past experiences in which the carrying out of these promptings produced guilt feelings and fear of punishment or actual punishment. Hence whenever the promptings occur intrapsychically again, guilt feelings and consequent expectation of punishment may arise and the individual may experience intense and undifferentiated anxiety.

Normally the cortex exercises an inhibitory control over the lower centers by which the organism tones down and controls

---

36 Cannon points out that the central difference, neurologically speaking, between animals and man is that in the latter the cerebral cortex is vastly larger. This is the neurological correlate of the fact that the problems of anxiety in the human organism involve intricate and complex interpretations which the person makes of his danger situation. Walter B. Cannon, *The wisdom of the body* (New York, 1932).

37 Case of Brown, Chapter 7. Of course we do not mean that an individual like this patient is consciously aware of all the determinants which go into his interpretations; the influence of unconscious factors is more strictly the psychological problem and falls in the next chapter.

the intensity of the anxiety, fear, or rage responses. This control is proportionate to the maturity of cortical development. Infants, for example, respond to a variety of stimuli with an intensity of undifferentiated rage or anxiety. The closer to the infant state an organism is, the more its reactions take the reflexive or undifferentiated form; "maturing" in this sense means developing increasing cortical differentiation and control. When the cortex is surgically removed from animals, we observe the automatic and excessive "sham rage" reaction (Cannon). Intense fatigue or illness may also weaken the control of the cortex, and hence we find tired or sick persons responding to threats with a greater degree of undifferentiated anxiety.

The matter of cortical direction and control has important bearings on learning theory and maturation which can only be mentioned here. We have noted that on the infant level (and in decorticate animals) the stimuli of threat are responded to in an undifferentiated or reflexive way. "As the cortex becomes better developed with the process of growth and maturing," Grinker and Spiegel hold, "it establishes increasing inhibition over these indiscriminate responses. At first only secondarily aware of the reflex response to stimuli, it attempts on succeeding repetitions of such stimuli to modify the response, segregating those stimuli which are truly dangerous from those which can be dealt with, and learning by trial and error how to deal with the former." [38]

Bodily Changes After Perception of the Threat.—The physiological changes induced in the organism through sympathetic activity are known to everyone in his own experiences of anxiety or fear. The pedestrian feels his heart pounding heavily when he has stepped back on the curb after having been narrowly missed by a speeding taxi. The student feels an urgency to

[38] R. R. Grinker and S. P. Spiegel, *Men under stress* (Philadelphia, 1945), p. 144. When the individual is confronted with a situation beyond his degree of control (e.g., because of the suddenness of the stimuli or their traumatic nature), he may be thrown back into the state of less differentiated response. Grinker and Spiegel hold that this is equivalent to a "regression" to the infant stage when, neurologically speaking, there was no cortical control over the emotional response. While it seems doubtful to the present author whether such undifferentiated reactions can be accurately explained in terms of regression to the infant stage, Grinker and Spiegel's phenomenological description of the behavior seems accurate.

urinate before a crucial examination; or a speaker finds his appetite strangely absent at the dinner after which he must make an important and difficult address. These and many other physical expressions of anxiety-fear can be conveniently linked in the framework of Cannon's "flight-fight" mechanism.[39] The heartbeat is accelerated in order to pump more blood to the muscles which will be needed in the impending struggle. The peripheral blood vessels are contracted (and the blood pressure thereby raised) to maintain arterial pressure for the emergency needs. This peripheral contraction is the physiological aspect of the popular expression "blanching with fear." The "cold sweat" occurs preparatory to the warm sweat of actual muscular activity. The body may shiver and the hairs of the body stand on end to conserve heat and protect the organism from the increased threat of cold caused by the contraction of peripheral blood vessels. Breathing is deeper or more rapid in order to insure a plentiful supply of oxygen; this is the "pant" of strong excitement. The pupils of the eyes dilate, permitting a better view of threatening dangers; hence the expression "eyes wide with fear." The liver releases sugar to provide energy for the struggle. A substance is released into the blood to effect its more rapid clotting, thus protecting the organism from the loss of blood through wounds. As a part of placing the organism on this emergency footing, digestive (parasympathetic) activity is suspended, since all available blood is needed for the skeletal muscles. The mouth may feel dry, because of a decreasing of the flow of saliva parallel to the suspending of the flow of gastric juices in the stomach. The smooth muscles of internal genital organs are contracted, and there is a tendency toward voiding of bladder and bowels—again recognized in vernacular expressions—which has the obvious utilitarian function of freeing the organism for strenuous activity.

It is necessary, now, to expand a point mentioned earlier, namely that the sympathetic and parasympathetic divisions work in opposition to each other. These two branches of the autonomic system are "balanced," as Cannon suggests, somewhat

---

[39] See Walter B. Cannon, *Bodily changes in pain, hunger, fear and rage* (New York, 1915, 1923), and *The wisdom of the body* (New York, 1932).

like extensor and flexor muscles.   The sympathetic is stronger in the sense that it is capable of overruling the parasympathetic. In other words, a moderate amount of fear or anger will inhibit digestion, whereas it requires a considerable degree of parasympathetic stimulation (e.g., eating) to overcome a moderate amount of anger or fear. A slight degree of stimulation of the opposing nervous division, however, may simply serve to "tone up" the activity the organism is engaged in. For example, a low degree of anxiety or fear, amounting to what Cannon calls the feeling of "adventure," may serve to heighten the pleasure in eating or sexual relations. Folklore tells us that "Stolen fruit tastes sweeter," and it is the common experience of many persons that the element of adventure adds some zest to sexual activities. This, of course, may very easily take a neurotic form if carried to any extreme, but it has its normal phase as well. An analogy is seen in the fact that the arm performs better in its extensor movements if there is a slight flexor tension at the same time. This discussion points to one of the constructive uses of moderate amounts of anxiety and fear.

The fact that these two nervous divisions are set in balance against each other is of crucial importance in the understanding of anxiety in psychosomatic phenomena (discussed in the next section). With some persons, for example, anxiety seems to be a cue to begin eating. Clinical literature yields frequent cases of overeating, and consequent obesity, as a result of anxiety states.[40] This may have much to do, of course, with eating as an expression of the need for infantile dependency cued off by anxiety, but it also has its clear neurological corollary in the fact that a considerable amount of parasympathetic stimulation may quiet sympathetic activity.[41]

---

[40] See Leon J. Saul, pages 70-71 below.

[41] A parallel phenomenon can be seen in the area of sex. The early stages of sexual stimulation involve the sacral, or parasympathetic, division; the nervi erigentes, which effect erection, are part of this division. This is the neurological aspect of the feelings of tenderness and comfort experienced in the earlier stages of sexual activity. It is common knowledge that some persons masturbate in order to quiet anxiety. It is said, interestingly enough, that masturbation was prevalent among the Romans while the enemy barbarians were encamped about the city. Socrates remarks in the last pages of the *Phaedo*, on the day he was to drink the hemlock, that it was a customary practice of the condemned to spend their last day in eating and sexual relations. This was no doubt not only for the

Sympathetic stimulation results in a *general* state of excitement of the whole organism. This is effected neurologically by the condition that the sympathetic division has a large number of connecting and bridging fibers, resulting in a "diffuse, widespread discharge of nerve impulses through sympathetic channels, as contrasted with the limited, sharply directed discharge to specific organs in the functioning of the cranial and sacral divisions." [42] The sympatin and adrenin poured into the blood stream also have this generalized effect on the organism. Cannon speaks of adrenin working in "partnership" with direct sympathetic stimulation. "Since secreted adrenin has a general distribution in the blood stream, the sympathetic division, even if it did not have diffuse effects because of the way its fibers are arranged, could have such effects by the action of adrenin." [43] These facts are the neurological and physiological correlates of the experience everyone has observed in himself, that anger, fear, and anxiety are felt as generalized, "over-all" emotions.

Since sympathetic stimulation leads simply to a general state of excitement in the organism, it is impossible to predict on the basis of neurophysiological data alone whether the emotion will take the form of fear, anxiety, anger, or hostility. Except in the reflexive reactions, the form of the emotion will be determined by the interpretation the organism makes of the threatening situation. Speaking in general terms, if the danger is interpreted

---

purpose of getting their last taste of human pleasures, but also for the anxiety-quieting effect such activities afforded. As regards sexual activity as a form of allaying anxiety, it is significant that the sexual ejaculation and orgasm are mediated by the opposite or sympathetic division; this division innervates the seminal vesicles. This is the neurological aspect of the experience of aggression or rage often felt at the height of sexual activity; Havelock Ellis speaks of the "love-bite." From a sheer neurological viewpoint, sexual experience serves to allay anxiety only up to the point of the orgasm. Though the orgasm does release tension, and in normal situations does not produce anxiety, it may leave the individual who engages in masturbation or other sexual activity for anxiety-allaying purposes more anxious than he was to begin with. It is not intended here to leave out of account what may be the most important cause of the anxiety after such sexual activity, namely guilt feeling. Indeed, we do not wish to advance any of these psychoneurological correlations as hard and fast; the neurological functioning is so generally influenced, and so often contravened, by complex psychological factors in the picture that it is necessary to emphasize continually that behavior in a given case can be understood only by viewing that particular organism in the situation to which it is reacting.

[42] Cannon, *Wisdom of the body, op. cit.*, p. 254.
[43] *Ibid.*, p. 253.

to be one which can be mastered by attack, the emotion will be anger.   In such case the activities of the organism become "fight" rather than "flight," and certain physical changes follow from that interpretation.   In anger, for example, the lids of the eyes are often narrowed to restrict the vision to that part of the environment the organism seeks to attack.   If the situation is seen as one which cannot be overcome by assault but can be avoided by flight, the emotion will be fear; or, if the danger is interpreted as putting the organism in a dilemma of helplessness, the emotion will be anxiety.   Certain physical changes likewise occur as a result of these interpretations: in fear and anxiety the eyelids, for example, are generally opened very wide, presumably to give the organism opportunity to see every possible route of escape. Thus the psychological factor in how the organism relates itself to the threat is essential in the defining of an emotion as such. As Landis expresses it, an emotion is "an emotion not because of any particular pattern of bodily reactions or temporal relationships but *because of certain relationships existing between the reacting organism and its environment."* [44]

Since an emotion consists of a certain relation existing between the organism and its environment, and since the sympathetic neurophysiological processes are general rather than specific, it is misleading and erroneous to reason either *from* a so-called specific neurophysiological process *to* a specific psychological experience like fear or anxiety or vice versa.   The intricately balanced neurophysiological apparatus is capable of being employed in an infinite variety of combinations, depending on the needs and patterns of the organism at the time.   Likewise it is erroneous to *identify* a neurophysiological process with an emotion.   An illustration of this latter error is seen in Willoughby.   In describing anxiety he holds that "the initiation of antagonism between strong excitatory and strong inhibitory nervous excitation throws the organism into a condition of generalized activity, as if a general nervous irradiation or overflow were in process. . . ."   The "generalization of excitation," he

---

[44] Summarized by H. Flanders Dunbar, *Emotions and bodily changes* (New York, 1935), p. 128.   (Italics mine.)

suggests, "should be equated with anxiety." [45] We here submit that anxiety cannot be equated with a generalization of neurophysiological excitation. Anxiety, rather, is a term for a certain relation (e.g., one of helplessness, conflict, etc.) existing between the person and the threatening environment, and the neurophysiological processes follow from this relationship. Willoughby's error arises from the fallacy which Dunbar has described as "confounding the physiological mechanism through which psyche operates with the fundamental etiology." [46]

The neurophysiological aspects of anxiety cannot be understood without constant reference to the question: What needs is the organism trying to fulfill in its struggle with its environment? This means that neurophysiological processes are seen as one phase of the "hierarchy of organization" of the organism; it means what Adolph Meyer called "a superordination of physiology by means of the integrating functions and particularly by

---

[45] R. R. Willoughby, Magic and cognate phenomena: an hypothesis, in Carl Murchison (ed.), *Handbook of social psychology,* (Worcester, Mass., 1935), p. 466. That the above quotation is not a mere confusion of words, but that Willoughby really does identify anxiety with neurophysiological processes, is indicated in his description of abnormal anxiety as anxiety which is generated without relief in action until a "considerable 'head' " is attained. It is as though Willoughby were thinking of anxiety as a physiochemical entity like steam. (Cf. note, page 347 below.) Willoughby's paper is based upon Freud's first theory, i.e., that anxiety is the converted form of repressed libido. Now it must be agreed that this theory lends itself to thinking of anxiety as a physiochemical entity. Freud's works, however, reveal an ambivalence with respect to the identification of physiological processes with emotion. On one hand Freud minces no words in insisting that a description of neurophysiological processes was not to be confused with the psychological understanding of the phenomena. In his chapter on anxiety in the *General introduction to psychoanalysis* he writes: "Interest there [in academic medicine] centers upon anatomical processes by which the anxiety condition comes about. We learn that the medulla oblongata is stimulated, and the patient is told that he is suffering from a neurosis of the vagal nerve. The medulla oblongata is a wondrous and beauteous object. I well remember how much time and labor I devoted to the study of it years ago. But today I must say I know of nothing less important for the psychological comprehension of anxiety than a knowledge of the nerve-paths by which the excitations travel" (pp. 341-42). He cautions the psychoanalyst to "resist the temptation to play with endocrinology and the autonomic nervous system, when the important thing is to grasp psychological facts psychologically."—*Emotions and bodily changes, op. cit.,* p. 145. But on the other hand, his libido theory, a physiochemical concept whether one accepts it as referring to actual chemical processes or as an analogy, opens the way for such fallacies as Willoughby's equating of anxiety with a neurophysiological process. The present writer would simply underline Freud's statement that *the important thing is to grasp psychological facts psychologically.*

[46] Dunbar, *op. cit.,* p. 116.

means of the use of symbols as tools." [47]   We believe this organismic approach makes it possible to avoid three common errors : (1) the error, on one side, of identifying an emotion with a neurophysiological process; (2) the error in the middle of "neurologizing tautology" (e.g., merely describing sympathetic activity as the neurophysiological aspect of anxiety) ; and (3) the error on the other side of assuming a dichotomy between neurophysiological processes and psychological processes.[48]   In the following discussion of psychosomatic aspects of anxiety, clinical data will be presented which demonstrate and support the viewpoint here stated.

4. PSYCHOSOMATIC ASPECTS OF ANXIETY

All through history it has been recognized in folklore and by observers of human nature that emotions like anxiety and fear have a profound and pervasive interrelationship with the sickness and health of the organism.   In recent years the studies in psychosomatic relations have begun the scientific exploration of this area and have yielded new illumination on the dynamics and meaning of fear and anxiety.[49]   Though the recently ac-

---

[47] Harry Stack Sullivan, *Conceptions of modern psychiatry* (Washington, D.C., 1947), p. 4. We suggest this rough schema : the organism interprets the reality situation which it confronts in terms of *symbols* and *meanings;* these are productive of *attitudes* toward the reality situation ; and the attitudes, in turn, involve the various emotions (and the neurophysiological components thereof) as *preparations for activity* in meeting the reality situation. We have already emphasized the importance of symbols and meanings by which the human being interprets situations as anxiety-creating ; and we have noted that these interpretations occur chiefly in the cortex, that part of the human being's neurological apparatus which grossly distinguishes him from an animal. Cannon's work on sympathetic activity, which is the basis for most discussions in which the neurophysiological aspects of anxiety are identified with sympathetic activity, was done chiefly with animals. Thus one cannot reason from these studies to human behavior without the clear qualification that the animal reactions represent a parallel to human reactions only when certain aspects of the latter are isolated out of the total context. This observation, of course, is directed only against oversimplified applications of Cannon's findings, not against Cannon's classical work itself.

[48] The reader may recognize that these three errors are parallel to three viewpoints which recur in historical philosophy and science as endeavors to solve the mind-body problem : (1) physiological mechanism (making psychological phenomena merely the epiphenomena of physiological processes), (2) psychophysical parallelism, and (3) dualism.

[49] Psychosomatic symptoms may be viewed as "one of the modes of expression of the emotional life, especially of the unconscious emotional life—one of its

celerated interest and activity in the field of psychosomatics chronologically followed the psychoanalytic work of Freud and his successors and is largely dependent upon psychoanalysis for its conceptual tools, we shall consider the psychosomatic area in this chapter because of its logical relationship with the biological approach to the organism.

In the following brief treatment we shall note one of the extreme forms of psychosomatic interrelations—the relation of anxiety and fear to the possible death of the organism. Then we shall list summarily some of the correlations of anxiety with certain psychosomatic illnesses and proceed to a more detailed consideration of anxiety and fear as exhibited in some very revealing studies of stomach functioning and ulcer formation.

It is hoped that this consideration of anxiety in psychosomatic illnesses will throw light upon three questions. First, how does the organism respond as a pattern (an organized psychophysical hierarchy) to the threatening situation? Second, how may the different affects—anxiety, fear, hostility— be distinguished from each other in the organism's response, and how are these affects related to each other? Third, what is the function of the organic symptom in the organism's adjustment to the threat it confronts?

The condition of traumatic fear and anxiety may be so crucial and devastating for the organism that actual death results. The phrase "scared to death" is not an exaggerated description of what happens in some cases. Cannon has discussed the phenomenon of "voodoo" death in this light.[50] He cites several competently observed cases of death occurring to a primitive who was the victim of some powerful symbolic act held by the tribe to be lethal, such as the magic "bone-pointing" of the witchdoctor, or the eating of tabooed food which the community believed would result in death. One anthropological observer notes, "I have seen a strong young man die the same day he was tapued [tabooed]; the victims die under it as though their

languages, like dreams, slips of the tongue, and neurotic behavior. . . ."—Leon J. Saul, Physiological effects of emotional tension, in J. McV. Hunt [ed.], *Personality and the behavior disorders* (New York, 1944), Vol. I, pp. 269-305.

[50] Walter B. Cannon, "Voodoo" death, *Amer. Anthrop.*, 1942, 44:2, 169-81.

strength ran out like water." [51] It may well be true, says Cannon, that an "ominous and persistent state of fear can end the life of a man." [52]

The physiological aspects of "voodoo" death are not difficult to understand. The reported symptoms of natives dying from voodoo bone-pointing or from having eaten tabooed food are in accord with those of an organism experiencing profound and persistent sympathetic-adrenal stimulation. If this stimulation continues without corresponding outlet in action—and the voodoo victim, paralyzed by anxiety since he himself believes he will die, lacks any effective outlet for action—death may result. Cannon found in his experiments with decorticate cats, which lacked the usual moderating effects of the cortex on emotional excitement, that after several hours of "sham rage" the cat expired.[53] But the psychological questions in "voodoo" death—such as what interpretation the native makes of his environment that leads him to experience such severe threat—are not so easy to answer, chiefly because we lack data on the subjective experiences of the particular natives involved. Cannon suggests one psychological explanation from William James's idea of being "cut dead" when the others in one's group ignore one. The primitive victim of taboo is certainly "cut dead," and he must experience powerful psychological suggestion from the fact that his entire community not only believes he will die but, in fact, behaves toward him as though he were already dead. Dying as the consequence of overwhelming anxiety has likewise been observed in other situations, such as death from shock in war when "neither physical trauma nor any of the known accentuating factors of shock could account for the disastrous condition." [54] Whatever the complex psycho-

---

[51] E. Tregear, in *J. Anthrop. Inst.*, 1890, **19**, 100, quoted by Cannon, in "Voodoo" death, *Amer. Anthrop.*, **44**, 170.

[52] *Ibid.*, p. 176.

[53] "In sham rage, as in wound shock, death can be explained as due to a failure of essential organs to receive a sufficient supply of blood or, specifically, a sufficient supply of oxygen, to maintain their services."—*Ibid.*, p. 178.

[54] *Ibid.*, p. 179. Cannon refers to the work of Mira, a psychiatrist in the Spanish War of 1936-1939, who has reported fatal results in patients afflicted with "malignant anxiety." Mira observed in these patients signs of anguish and perplexity, accompanied by a permanently rapid pulse, rapid respiration, and other symptoms of excessive sympathetic-adrenal stimulation. Mira mentions as pre-

logical determinants of such experiences may be, it is clear *that a threat to an individual's existence can be so powerful that the individual possesses no way of coping with the threat short of giving up his existence, namely dying.*

Of more practical interest is the great variety of psychosomatic disorders in which the organism suffering anxiety maintains its struggle for existence but does so by means of a somatic alteration of function. The general psychosomatic literature has been summarized by Dunbar, Saul, and others, to whom the reader who wishes a detailed survey of the interrelation of emotions and organic symptomatology is referred.[55] We shall here merely list some of the important psychosomatic conditions in which anxiety and fear have been found to play a central role.

There are frequent instances of the overproduction of sugar in the body and ensuing diabetes mellitus in states of anxiety and fear.[56] It is well known that sudden and traumatic fear may be associated with hyperthyroidism and the special form of this called exophthalmic goiter: instances of the appearance of goiter in soldiers after a terrifying experience were frequently known in World War I.[57] It is not surprising that many heart conditions are found accompanying anxiety, since the heart in everyone is directly sensitive to emotional stress. Oswald Bumke holds that most of the "so-called 'cardiac neuroses' are nothing but a somatic manifestation of anxiety." [58] Many cases of excessive appetite (bulimia) and consequent obesity accompanying chronic anxiety have been cited. Saul describes one in which the desires

---

disposing conditions "a previous lability of the sympathetic system" and "a severe mental shock in conditions of physical exhaustion due to lack of food, fatigue, sleeplessness, etc."—*Ibid.*, p. 180.

[55] Saul, *op. cit.*, H. Flanders Dunbar, *Emotions and bodily changes* (New York, 1935); *Psychosomatic diagnosis* (New York, 1943).

[56] Walter B. Cannon, *Bodily changes in pain, hunger, fear, and rage* (New York, 1915), p. 67.

[57] N. D. C. Lewis reviews the literature on exophthalmic goiter, remarking: "All symptoms of hyperthyroidism, chemical, physiological, and psychological, are exact duplicates of those of fear. Exophthalmic goiter is a special type of hyperthyroidism—it is what one might call structuralized fear—the constant flow of the river of emotion has cut its channels definitely in the structure and function of the tissue. Even the eye signs in exophthalmic goiter are those of fear."—Psychological factors in hyperthyroidism, *Med. J. Rec.*, 1925, 122, 121-25. Quoted in Dunbar, *Emotions and bodily changes*, pp. 154-55.

[58] Dunbar, *Emotions and bodily changes*, p. 63.

to eat "were displacements to food of intense frustrated desires for love. . . ." [59] A number of such patients were found to have been children of overprotective mothers—a childhood situation which often predisposed the child to anxiety. The opposite condition, pathological lack of appetite (anorexia nervosa), has been found in subjects in whom there were intense frustrated wishes for love and attention from the mother which led to hostility toward the mother and consequent guilt because of the hostile feelings.[60] The frequent association of diarrhea with anxiety is well known. Saul cites a case from his own analytic practice of a young physician who had been overprotected by his parents as a child. When he graduated from medical school and began to assume his own professional responsibilities, he reacted with anxiety and diarrhea. The diarrhea, remarks Saul, was an expression of his hostility that he should be forced to be independent and responsible: thus the hostility was a reaction to his anxiety.[61]

Though essential hypertension (elevated blood pressure without evidence of other disease) is generally associated in psychosomatic literature with suppressed rage and hostility, a pattern of anxiety is often found underlying the aggressive affects. Saul cites cases of hypertension to illustrate that the rage and hostility are reactions to situations of conflict on the part of persons who were predisposed to anxiety by excessive dependence on a parent and who were, at the same time, submissive to this parent.[62] As regards asthma, Saul remarks on the basis of a number of studies, "It appears that the outstanding personality traits of asthmatics are over-anxiety, lack of self-confidence, and a deep-seated clinging dependence upon the parents which is often a reaction to parental oversolicitude." Asthma attacks "bear a relationship to anxiety and to crying (weeping changing to wheezing)." [63] Frequency of urination has been found accompanying anxiety connected with competi-

---

[59] Saul, *op. cit.*, p. 273.
[60] *Ibid.*, p. 274. This pattern is mentioned to emphasize the interrelation of many anxiety states with dependence on the mother.
[61] For another example, see case of Brown, Chapter 7, below, esp. page 253.
[62] Saul, *op. cit.*, pp. 281-84.
[63] *Ibid.*, p. 286.

tive ambition.[64]   Though epilepsy, to the extent that it can be viewed psychosomatically, is generally conceded to represent a mass discharge of repressed hostility, there is evidence in some cases of epilepsy that anxiety attacks and anxiety-provoking feelings (sometimes specifically related to the mother) underlay the hostility.[65]

We now turn to the highly significant demonstrations of the relation between anxiety and organic changes as found in the experiments with peptic ulcer patients by Mittelmann, Wolff, and Scharf.[66]   A decade and a half ago Franz Alexander had found a recurrent psychological constellation in his psychoanalyses of patients with peptic ulcers. The needs of these patients were of a receptive nature, characterized by cravings to be supported, "fed," cared for in the prototypical form of being given nourishment by the mother. The constellation included, however, a repression of those dependent tendencies in favor of compensatory ambition and the need to appear strong and triumphant in the competitive struggles of life.

Seeking to discover whether the process of ulcer-formation could be related to the emotional changes in the patients, Mittelmann, Wolff, and Scharf carried on interviews with thirteen ulcer subjects, during which physiological changes in the patient were recorded. By inducing the subject to discuss topics such as marriage or vocation which were known from the case history to be anxiety-creating, the experimenters were able to correlate the accompanying changes in gastroduodenal function. It was discovered that when conflicts involving anxiety and related emotions were touched upon, the patients regularly exhibited accelerated gastric activity. Increased stomach acidity, increased peristaltic motility, and hyperaemia were evidenced—conditions which are known to be ulcer-producing. But in interviews in

---

[64] *Ibid.*, p. 294.

[65] *Ibid.*, p. 292.

[66] Bela Mittelmann, H. G. Wolff, and M. P. Scharf, Experimental studies on patients with gastritis, duodenitis and peptic ulcer, *Psychosom. Med.*, 1942, 4: 1, 5-61. We select these studies not because ulcer has any closer relation to anxiety than many other psychosomatic disorders but because we wish to explore one psychosomatic area in some detail and the available investigations in the gastrointestinal area are in some ways the most detailed and illustrative for the study of anxiety.

which reassurance and an allaying of the subject's anxiety occurred, gastric activity was restored toward normal and the symptoms were eliminated. It was clearly demonstrated that the gastric activities which cause or exacerbate the ulcer-formation were *increased by anxiety and were decreased as security supplanted anxiety in the patient's affective condition.*[67] Whether this kind of reaction to anxiety occurs only with persons of a particular psychophysical type, whether it is a general occurrence in our culture or a general human reaction, are still open questions. The thirteen control cases investigated in this study—persons who were healthy and without complaint—exhibited in general similar gastric responses to emotional stress but of lesser magnitude and duration than those of the ulcer patients.

In understanding the function of anxiety in these ulcer patients it is important to consider the psychological patterns they represented. Though they had varied personality features in many respects, they did possess these characteristics in common: "assertive independence and self-sufficiency, covering underlying anxiety and insecurity, and accompanied by feelings of resentment and hostility." [68] They were frequently hard-working, perfectionistic persons, but "even superficial analysis made evident that the drive behind the competitive effort was anxiety and insecurity." [69] In each case the home had failed to provide the subject with a stable childhood background.

---

[67] To quote from the summary given by the experimenters: "In all the patients with peptic lesions it was possible to demonstrate a chronological parallelism between the onset, recrudescence, and course of gastroduodenal symptoms, and the occurrence of untoward emotional reactions. . . . To demonstrate that the above described emotional states [anxiety, etc.] were relevant to the gastroduodenal dysfunction and peptic ulcers in the particular patients studied, situations were experimentally created which induced destructive emotional reactions and precipitated symptoms when the patient was free of symptoms. Moreover, if such affects, symptoms, and tissue defects already existed, all increased in intensity during such experimental procedures. On the other hand, in situations which engendered feelings of emotional security and assurance, gastric function was restored toward normal and symptoms eliminated."—*Op. cit.,* p. 58.

(This and the two excerpts on pages 74 and 78 are quoted from Bela Mittelmann, H. G. Wolff, and M. P. Scharf, Experimental studies on patients with gastritis, duodenitis and peptic ulcer, *Psychosom. Med.,* 4, 5-61, by permission of the authors and of Paul B. Hoeber, Inc., Medical Book Department of Harper & Brothers. Copyright, 1942, by Paul B. Hoeber, Inc.)

[68] *Ibid.,* p. 5.

[69] *Ibid.,* p. 6.

The steps in the development of the original insecurity through anxiety patterns to ultimate ulcer symptoms are noted by Mittelmann, Wolff, and Scharf. These steps are quoted here because they bear significant parallels to the anxiety theory presented later in the present study.[70]

> The insecure and anxious individual gained a degree of assurance by evolving a life pattern of being self-sufficient, independent, or the "lone wolf," or on the other hand by gaining approval through extra effort, conscientiousness, "perfectionism," and meticulousness. Under the usual circumstances of his life, such a system seemed adequate, i.e., the individual was relatively comfortable and effective. Then, because of a change in his situation such as a new position, the assumption of new responsibilities in courtship or marriage, criticism from without was implied or expressed and this again challenged his adequacy. Feelings of insecurity and anxiety were then experienced. One reaction to this challenge was to increase efforts by more work, greater conscientiousness and "perfectionism." Another reaction was seen in the bolstering of self-esteem through additional assertions of independence and the shutting off of much needed affection. There developed frustration, resentment and hostility toward the person or situation which rearoused the feelings of insecurity and inadequacy, causing the fragile system to falter or break down. . . . In short, the patient had evolved an almost adequate pattern for dealing with anxiety and then, through some life incident, was thrown into a disorganized anxious state to which he reacted with hostility. His hostile attitudes toward those whom he wanted to love and the community of which he wished to be a part gave rise in turn to feelings of guilt, remorse and self-condemnation. Coincident with these reactions there occurred epigastric burning, pain, vomiting, and hemorrhage.[71]

Equally significant for our present inquiry is the case of Tom, a subject whose gastric activities during periods of emotional stress could be observed through a fistula in his stomach. Tom was studied intensively by S. G. Wolf and H. G. Wolff over a period of seven months.[72] He was a fifty-seven-year-old man

---

[70] Chapter 6.
[71] Mittelmann, Wolff, and Scharf, *op. cit.,* p. 16.
[72] From *Human gastric function* by Stewart Wolf and H. G. Wolff. Copyright 1943, 1947, by Oxford University Press, Inc.

of Irish stock, who, following an accident to his esophagus as a boy, had had an aperture made surgically through his abdomen and into his stomach. For almost fifty years he had fed himself successfully by means of a funnel through this fistula. Since Tom was an emotionally labile individual who ran through the gamut of fear, anxiety, sadness, anger, and resentment, Wolf and Wolff had abundant opportunity to observe through the aperture the interrelation of these emotions with Tom's gastric functions.

In periods of fear, Tom's gastric activity was sharply *decreased*:

> Sudden fright occurred one morning during a control period of accelerated gastric function, when an irate doctor, a member of the staff, suddenly entered the room, began hastily opening drawers, looking on shelves, and swearing to himself. He was looking for protocols to which he attached great importance. Our subject, who tidies up the laboratory, had mislaid them the previous afternoon, and he was fearful of detection and of losing his precious job. He remained silent and motionless and his face became pallid. The mucous membrane of his stomach also blanched from a level of 90 to 20 and remained so for five minutes until the doctor had located the objects of his search and left the room. Then gastric mucosa gradually resumed its former color.[73]

Other affects associated with such hypofunctioning of the stomach were sadness, discouragement, and self-reproach. Tom and his wife had made tentative arrangements to move into a new apartment, a change they very much desired. But mainly because of their own negligence, the landlord leased the desired apartment to someone else. The morning after this discovery, Tom was downcast, uncommunicative, and sad. He felt defeated and had no desire to fight back; his dominant mood was self-reproach. That morning his gastric activity was markedly decreased.

But in periods of anxiety, Tom, like the ulcer patients in the previous study, showed *accelerated* gastric activity:

---

[73] *Ibid.*, p. 112.

The most marked alterations in gastric functions which were encountered were associated with anxiety provoked by our failure to inform the subject how long he might expect an income from the laboratory. He had been receiving government aid prior to his employment with us, and the rise in his family's standard of living since his new job meant a great deal to him. The subject of how long his job would last had come up in a discussion between his wife and himself the previous evening. He decided to inquire about it the next morning. Both he and his wife were so anxious about the answer, however, that neither of them slept at all. The next morning the values for vascularity and acidity were the highest encountered in any of the studies. . . .[74]

This illustrates a pattern which was regularly found with Tom. "Anxiety and the complex conflicting feelings found associated with it were regularly accompanied by hyperaemia, hypersecretion, and hypermotility of the stomach." [75]

In experiences of hostility and resentment Tom likewise exhibited increased stomach activity. Two different instances are cited when he felt aspersions had been cast upon his ability and conscientiousness by members of the hospital staff; gastric secretions were greatly increased. During one of these periods when Tom was diverted from his hostile feelings by conversation, the overactivity subsided, but it rose afterwards when Tom again lapsed into brooding over his wounds.

Though Tom did not have peptic ulcers, the pattern of his personality was in many ways similar to that of the patients in the prior study. As a child he had been very dependent on his mother, though apparently he did not experience much emotional warmth in his relation with her. "He had a fear and a love for his mother," write Wolf and Wolff, "such as he had for the Lord." [76] He was seized with panic when she died, after which he became dependent on his sister. A like ambivalence was shown in his relation to the doctors: he exhibited considerable dependence, and he frequently reacted with hostility toward

[74] Ibid., p. 120. This, the above quotation in note 73, and the three following excerpts, from Wolf and Wolff, Human gastric function, copyright, 1943, by Oxford University Press, are used by permission of Oxford University Press.
[75] Ibid., pp. 118-19.
[76] Ibid., p. 92.

them when this dependence was frustrated. He placed great emphasis on being the "strong man," the successful provider for his family. "If I couldn't support my family," he remarked, "I'd as soon jump off the end of the dock." [77] He could not release his emotions in crying, since there was the need to keep a firm appearance of strength. This personality pattern, characterized by affective dependence covered over by the need to appear strong, presumably bears a decisive relationship to the fact that Tom reacted to anxiety and hostility with acceleration of gastric function.

That stomach functions and other gastrointestinal activities should be closely related to affective states does not in itself present a problem. Folk language is rich in expressions like "not being able to stomach" or being "fed up" with a situation. The neurophysiological aspects of this interrelationship have been pointed out by Pavlov, Cannon, and others. Psychosomatically the basic consideration is the close association of gastrointestinal functions with desires for care, support, and a dependent form of love, all of which are related genetically to being fed by the mother. Conflict situations, such as in anxiety, hostility, and resentment, accentuate the receptive needs. These needs are bound to be frustrated, partly because of their excessive character and partly because in our culture the dependent needs generally have to be repressed under the façade of the "he-man" who is characterized by ambition and conscientious striving. In the ulcer patients and in Tom, these receptive needs took the somatic expression of increased gastric activity.[78]

The accelerated gastric activity as a response to conflict situations may be viewed in two ways, Mittelmann, Wolff, and Scharf suggest. First, it may be a somatic expression of the

---

[77] This sentence is a vivid revelation of how profound a psychological value was at stake in Tom's façade of the strong, responsible man.

[78] Saul reports from his fusion of evidence that the following causal chain operates as at least one factor in certain cases of peptic ulcer: "Emotional stimulus related to the function of the particular organ (frustrated wishes for love, care, dependence)→stimulation of subcortical centers→disturbance of the autonomic innervation of the organ→dysfunction of the organ→hypersecretion, hypermotility, alterations in blood supply→chronicity and structural damage. Of course it may well be that in other cases the psychogenic element is of no importance and that ulcers are caused by other mechanism."—*Op. cit.*, p. 277.

psychologically repressed needs of the organism to be cared for. The person endeavors to resolve anxiety and hostility and gain security through eating.[79] Second, it may represent a form of aggression and hostility toward those who deny the comfort and solace desired. Eating as a form of aggression is common in animal life, e.g., "eating up" the prey.

These studies demonstrate that it is an oversimplification, and an inaccuracy, to relegate anxiety solely to sympathetic nervous activity. An explanation of the above bodily changes in conflict situations on the basis of the classical antagonism of sympathetic and parasympathetic nervous divisions does not make sense unless Cannon's principle of the *balance* of these divisions is kept clearly in mind. The neurological functions in anxiety cannot be understood except as we see them in the light of the needs and purposes of the organism confronting its threat. "It is not possible with the evidence at hand," remark Wolf and Wolff, "to attribute the pattern of bodily changes observed solely to vagus or sympathetic activity. It seems more profitable to consider gastric changes which accompany emotional disturbances as part of a general bodily reaction pattern." [80] Mittelmann, Wolff, and Scharf state, "The question as to which parts of the nervous system will dominate under stress is of secondary importance; of primary importance is *the interplay or combination which will best serve the needs of the animal in meeting a given life situation.*" [81]

General Comment on Anxiety in Psychosomatic Illnesses. —(1) When a person is faced with a conflict situation which he cannot solve on the level of conscious awareness, somatic symptoms of various types may appear.[82] One type is the hysterical conversion symptom, such as hysterical blindness in situations of terror, or the hysterical paralysis of certain muscles. Hysterical symptoms, having a fairly direct psychological

---

79 Mittelmann, Wolff, and Scharf, *op. cit.,* p. 16.
80 *Op. cit.,* p. 176. Quoted by permission of Oxford University Press.
81 *Op. cit.,* p. 54 (italics mine).
82 What follows is not meant to be an exhaustive listing of all types of symptoms, but merely a summary of some important kinds of symptom formation as a basis for our inquiry into the relation between the organ symptom and anxiety.

etiology, may involve any part of the neuromuscular apparatus. In contrast, the psychosomatic type of symptom, in its limited sense, is a dysfunction mediated by the autonomic nervous system. But in a broader sense, anxiety may be involved in any illness whether it takes specifically hysterical or psychosomatic forms or not. An example of this third type is the infectious diseases. The susceptibility of the organism to infectious diseases may be influenced by anxiety as well as other affects. It is possible that deterioration diseases like tuberculosis may be associated with repressed discouragement following chronic conflict situations which have not been soluble by the person on the level of direct awareness or on the specifically psychosomatic level.[83]

What determines whether a given person will be able to resolve his conflict situation in conscious awareness or will manifest psychosomatic or hysterical symptoms or a different form of disease? This is a complicated question which can be answered only by a thorough study of the person concerned. Certainly the answers would involve constitutional factors, the person's experiences in infancy as well as other past experiences, the nature and intensity of the immediate threat, and the cultural situation. In every case, however, we suggest that the organism is to be viewed as endeavoring to resolve a conflict situation, a conflict characterized in its subjective aspect by anxiety and in its objective aspect by illness; the symptom—when it is present—being one expression of the organism's endeavor at resolution of the conflict.

(2) *Cultural factors are intimately related to the anxiety underlying psychosomatic disorders.* Demonstrations of this could be cited from almost any of the psychosomatic illnesses;

[83] See Jerome Hartz, Tuberculosis and personality conflicts, *Psychosom. Med.,* 1944, 6 : 1, 17-22. We suggest that the progression may be roughly as follows: When the organism is in a catastrophic situation, the endeavor to solve the conflict takes place first on the conscious level; then on the specifically psychosomatic level; and if neither of these is effective, the conflict may involve a disease such as tuberculosis representing a more complete involvement of the organism. Grinker points out that when the conflict cannot be solved on the level of conscious awareness ("cortical," "ego" level), the result may be visceral expressions of the conflict, or organ dysfunctions, which we term organ neuroses, that constitute the first step toward organic disease."—R. R. Grinker, in *Psychosom. Med.,* 1939, 1, 19-47.

we take for illustration again the case of peptic ulcer. The high incidence of ulcer has frequently been related to the excessively competitive aspects of modern Western culture. Ulcer has been called "Wall Street stomach," and is considered by some investigators to be particularly a "disease of the striving and ambitious men of Western civilization." [84] The fact that in modern times ulcer is found more than ten times as frequently in men as in women presents interesting questions. Mittelmann and Wolff suggest that this is because men in our culture are expected to repress their dependent needs under a façade of independence and strength, whereas women are permitted to give vent to their feelings of helplessness, as for example in weeping. In some modern cultural circles expression of dependence on the part of women is even considered a virtue. In the early nineteenth century there was a high incidence of ulcer— so far as statistics can be relied upon—in women in their twenties. Mittelmann and Wolff hold that this is related to the fact that in that culture women experienced considerable need to compete in getting a husband; the prospect of remaining a spinster, dependent on relatives, created marked anxiety. In that period men, on the contrary, occupied the "strong" position vocationally and were able at the same time to express their need for dependence within the family circle. [85]

---

[84] Saul, *op. cit.,* p. 276.

[85] It will be recalled that the control cases (patients without ulcers) studied by Mittelmann, Wolff, and Scharf exhibited the same hyperfunction of gastric activities in periods of emotional conflict, though in lesser degree than the ulcer patients. Tom, also not an ulcer patient, exhibited the same reaction. These data would point to a hypothesis that this psychosomatic reaction pattern is not only a matter of individual type but occurs with some frequency in our culture. Whether there is a specifically American cultural factor present is also an interesting question. In discussing the relation between the repressed needs for dependency and gastrointestinal symptoms frequently found in their work with soldiers in conflict situations, Grinker and Spiegel remark on the accentuated desire to drink milk on the part of their patients. The "particular food so intensely desired is that associated with the earliest signs of maternal affection and care," and they remark that "drinking milk is a cultural trait of most Americans."—*Op. cit.,* p. 140. There would seem to be some presumptive evidence for the hypothesis that the emphasis upon individual competition in Western culture took root with special influence in the American branch of that culture. There has been some suggestion, also, that pronounced dependence on mothers may be more frequently found as a psychological trait in America than in some other countries in the Western world. Whether there exists this specifically American factor in the psychosomatic pattern related to ulcer we suggest here simply in the form of a question.

Since the individual lives and moves and has his being in a given culture, with his own reaction patterns having been formed in terms of that culture and with the conflict situation confronting him likewise given in terms of that culture, it is readily understandable that cultural factors should be interrelated with psychosomatic as well as other behavior disorders. It would seem that the affects, biological needs, and forms of behavior most repressed in a given culture are the ones most likely to give rise to symptoms. In the Victorian period Freud found the repression of sex central in symptom-formation; in our culture it may be true, as Horney suggests, that the repression of hostility is more common than the repression of sex and thus might be expected to be frequently related to psychosomatic symptoms. It would certainly not be gainsaid that our competitive culture generates considerable hostility and, as indicated above, requires widespread repression of the dependent needs of men. As shifts in cultural emphasis occur, corresponding shifts in the incidence of various diseases likewise occur.[86] Another significant point is that in our culture it is considered much more acceptable to have an organic illness than an emotional or mental disorder; this may well be related to the fact that anxiety and other emotional stresses in our culture so often take a somatic form. In short, the culture conditions the way a person tries to resolve his anxiety, and specifically what symptoms he may employ.

(3) The psychosomatic studies throw light upon the *distinction between, and the relative importance of, the various emotions.* We refer, first, to the distinction between *anxiety and fear.* In some treatments of anxiety and fear there has been a reluctance to make a distinction between these two affects, since it was assumed that they had the same neurophysiological base.[87] But when the person is viewed as a functioning unit in a life situation, very important distinctions between anxiety and fear may appear. In the instance of Tom, we recall that his neuropsychological behavior was radically different in fear from what it was in anxiety. His affects indicating a withdrawal

---

[86] E.g., the present rise in incidence of cardiovascular disturbances (Dunbar); the decline of hysterical cases in World War II from World War I.

[87] We have indicated above the questionable nature of this assumption.

without inclination to struggle—such as fear, sadness, self-reproach—were accompanied by a suspension of gastric activity. This is in accord with the classical formulation of sympathetic-parasympathetic antagonism. But in situations in which Tom was engaged in conflict and struggle—when the affect was anxiety, hostility, or resentment—hyperactivity of gastric functions occurred. This is the *opposite* to what would be expected on the basis of the conventional analysis of neurophysiological processes (i.e., anxiety identified with sympathetic activity). [88] We therefore submit that the distinction between fear and anxiety must be made if we are to understand the organism as a behaving unit endeavoring to adjust to a given life situation. How this distinction may be made we propose to summarize in Chapter 6 below. One added observation, however, may be offered at this point: Except in cases of sudden, traumatic fear producing a fairly direct somatic restructuralization via sympathetic overstimulation (e.g., some cases of exophthalmic goiter), *fear does not lead to illness if the organism can flee successfully.* If the individual cannot flee, but is forced to remain in a conflict situation which cannot be resolved, fear may turn into anxiety and psychosomatic changes may then accompany the anxiety.

A distinction is to be drawn between anxiety and the aggressive affects, such as anger and hostility. Though repressed rage and hostility are specific etiological factors in certain psychosomatic disorders, it is significant that these emotions can frequently be discovered on more thorough analysis of the patient to be reactions to an underlying anxiety. (Cf. above discussion of hypertension and epilepsy.) The rationale of this situation can be suggested as follows. Anger does not lead to illness unless it cannot be expressed in fighting or some other direct form. When it must be repressed—because of the dangers to the organ-

---

[88] Dr. P. M. Symonds suggests that the increased gastric function is a defense against anxiety rather than an expression of anxiety. While this distinction can justifiably be made, it does not seem to the present writer that it changes the basic emphasis here made, namely that the organism is in a conflict situation, and that the neurophysiological changes are one aspect of this conflict. It is to be recalled that the thirteen control cases (patients who did not have ulcer) also exhibited the increased gastric activity. The implication would be that these persons, too, were experiencing conflict as part of their anxiety and that the conflict was expressed in such physiological changes.

ism if the aggression were carried out in action—psychosomatic symptoms like hypertension may appear. But if underlying anxiety were not present, the hostility would not have to be repressed. This accords with our emphasis that the basic picture is that of the organism in a conflict situation, the conflict being represented on the psychic side by anxiety. Though we wish to imply no underestimation of the importance of identifying the specific emotions in any given case of psychosomatic illness, we suggest that anxiety is the psychic common denominator. There is ground then for Felix Deutsch's statement that "every disease is an anxiety disease" [89] if we mean by this that anxiety is the psychic component of every disease. In discussing the present focal problems of psychosomatics, Dunbar remarks, "Specific psychic etiology is to be looked for in the anxiety of the organism and in its defenses, the type of defenses developed against inner and outer dangers." [90]

(4) The most intricate problem in the relation of anxiety to somatic changes is *the meaning of the organ symptom.* Somatic symptoms may be approached through two questions, both of which are necessary to an understanding of why the anxiety takes a somatic form. First, how does the organ symptom function in the organism's struggle to cope with the threatening situation, or, to put it somewhat figuratively, what is the organism seeking to do via the symptom? Second, what are the intrapsychic mechanisms by which this interrelationship of anxiety and symptom takes place?

Several pertinent clinical observations throw light upon these questions. *There tends to be an inverse relation between the individual's capacity to tolerate conscious anxiety and the appearance of psychosomatic symptoms.* As Dunbar phrases it, "Whereas conscious anxiety and fears are aggravating factors, there is evidence that the anxiety and fears and conflicts which have been excluded from consciousness are of the greatest significance . . . that is, those most likely to be etiological in illness." [91] She also remarks, "The more overt the anxiety and

---

[89] Quoted in Dunbar, *Emotions and bodily changes,* p. 80.

[90] *Ibid.,* pp. xxix-xxx.

[91] H. Flanders Dunbar, The relationship between anxiety states and organic diseases, *Clinics,* 1942, 1:4, 881.

the greater its manifestation in neurotic behavior, the less severe the organic disease." [92] While the person is endeavoring to master the conflict consciously, he may be experiencing considerable anxiety, but he is still confronting the threat through direct awareness. "In general it may be stated that the existence of anxiety implies lack of serious disintegration. . . . It may be compared with the prognostic significance of fever." [93] But when the conscious struggle can no longer be tolerated, either because of its increasing severity or because of its lack of success, symptomatic changes in the organism take place. These relieve the strain of the conflict and make a quasi- or pseudo-adjustment possible when the conflict cannot actually be solved. Thus it may be said that the symptoms are often ways of containing the anxiety; they are the anxiety in structuralized form.[94] In a case described later in this study, it is observed that the progression taken by anxiety states was roughly as follows: first the patient reported an organ symptom, about which he had no conscious anxiety except the discomfort of the symptom itself. Several days subsequently anxiety dreams began to appear. Later came conscious anxiety, with considerable dependence and many demands upon the therapist. As the anxiety came into consciousness, the patient was more severely discomforted but the organ symptom disappeared.[95] In this same connection Dunbar writes that "the somatic symptomatology of patients . . . becomes exacerbated as the emotional material related to the specific focal conflict and character defenses is brought up, and alleviated as the material is worked through psychotherapeutically." [96] It is significant that the patients with ulcer symptoms discussed above were not aware of conscious anxiety. The symptom is in this sense a protection against the anxiety-creating situation.[97]

---

[92] *Ibid.*, p. 902.

[93] J. C. Yaskins, The psychobiology of anxiety—a clinical study, *Psychoanal. Rev.*, 1936, **23**, 3 & 4, and 1937, **24**, 81-93.

[94] Cf. Freud's remark about psychological symptoms: "The symptom is bound anxiety."

[95] Case of Brown, Chapter 7.

[96] *Emotions and bodily changes, op. cit.*, p. xxx.

[97] It might be mentioned practically that it is often dangerous to remove the symptoms of anxiety patients until the anxiety itself can be clarified. The existence of the symptom indicates roughly that the subject has not been able to handle his anxiety, and it may be a protection against a worse state of deterioration.

It is also of extreme interest that when people become ill in ostensibly organic ways, anxiety tends to disappear. Dunbar reports that patients "with severe organic damage tended to blot out that portion of their experience which really caused them the greatest anxiety." [98] The present author observed a curious phenomenon in patients with tuberculosis. When a patient became aware that he was seriously ill, a considerable amount of anxiety associated with his behavior patterns before the illness seemed to disappear. Conscious anxiety often reappeared as the patient neared the state of physical health when he could return to work and responsibilities. One could remark superficially that the disease served to relieve him from responsibilities, afforded him protection, etc. But the phenomenon seems to be more profound. Assuming that succumbing to the disease in the first place was partly the result of chronic unsolved conflicts, the disease itself may represent one way of shrinking the scope of the conflicts to an area in which they might be solved. Having a disease is one way to resolve a conflict situation. This viewpoint may throw light on the clinically observed phenomenon that when the disease appears, there is a lessened awareness of anxiety, and when the disease is overcome, anxiety may reappear. [99]

The problem of the interchange of symptoms and anxiety is explained by writers using Freud's first anxiety hypothesis in terms of the libido theory. F. Deutsch, for example, holds that the organ symptom results from dammed-up libido. If libido cannot be discharged normally, it takes the form of anxiety, and this anxiety may discharge itself in the form of a somatic symptom. Hence, "psychologically speaking, to remain or to become organically healthy the individual must either invest his libido or get rid of his anxiety." [100] This viewpoint assumes that it is the "dammed-up libido" which causes the anxiety and from

[98] The relationship between anxiety states and organic diseases, 1, *op. cit.*, 879.

[99] Needless to say, we are speaking of the anxiety related to the patient's behavior patterns, not the specific anxiety related to the fact that he has a disease (which may obviously be present during the disease). Many observers have spoken of the "substitution function" of the disease for anxiety. Draper (see Saul, *op. cit.*) mentions also that a neurosis may function as a substitute for organic symptoms.

[100] Quoted by Dunbar, *Emotions and bodily changes,* p. 80.

which the individual seeks relief via his somatic symptom. The present writer believes this is an error resulting from a failure to see the organism in its relation to its environment.[101] The viewpoint taken in the present study is that anxiety occurs not because the individual is a "carrier of libido" but because he is confronted with a threatening situation with which he cannot deal and which therefore throws him into a state of helplessness and inner conflict.[102] *Thus our conclusion is that the purpose of the symptom is not to protect the organism from dammed-up libido, but rather from the anxiety-creating situation.*[103]

---

[101] Freud's partial shift from his first anxiety hypothesis, utilized above by Deutsch, toward the viewpoint taken by the present writer, is discussed in the next chapter, pp. 124-26.

[102] This viewpoint is discussed and demonstrated more fully in later sections on the function of the defense mechanisms (Chapter 8).

[103] This function is obvious in hysterical symptoms. Grinker and Spiegel point out that in cases of psychosomatic disorders among soldiers the symptom often had the same end result as hysterical symptoms, viz., a relief from conflict over going back into battle, which could no longer be tolerated.

Chapter 4

ANXIETY INTERPRETED PSYCHOLOGICALLY

Anxiety is the fundamental phenomenon and the central problem of neurosis.—Sigmund Freud. *The Problem of Anxiety.*

The theory of fear is intrinsically bound up with the theory of anxiety. Since the relation between fears and anxiety should be most clearly discerned by examining those two reactions to threat in the relatively unstructured personalities of children, we shall briefly consider some of the studies of children's fears.[1]

1. THE EXPERIMENTAL STUDY OF CHILDREN'S FEARS

Several decades ago the chief problem of the psychology of fear was to discover the original, unlearned stimuli which give rise to fears, and to account for these fears by instinctive processes. The child was supposed to have instinctive fears of darkness, animals, large bodies of water, slimy things, and so forth —many of these assumed by Stanley Hall to have been inherited from the animal ancestors of man. Then it became the task of many psychologists to disprove these "inherited fears" one after another, until in John B. Watson's behaviorism the field was reduced to two. Says Watson of the infant, "there are just two things which will call out a fear response, namely, a loud sound, and loss of support." [2] All subsequent fears, this hypothesis

---

[1] The order in which we deal with the work of various investigators in this chapter is not based on the importance of their work. If it were, Freud by common consent should come first. We begin with academic psychology and with the studies of fears because that is where the thinking of most of us in this country began. Then we discuss the work of Liddell and Mowrer because their studies form a bridge from the experimental to the psychoanalytic study of anxiety. From then on the chapter proceeds roughly chronologically, with Freud being the pioneer in the line of psychotherapists who have made distinctive contributions to the theory of anxiety.

[2] John B. Watson, *Behaviorism* (New York, 1924).

87

contended, are "built in," i.e., established by conditioning. But later students of children's fears, such as Jersild, have pointed out that Watson's view was a gross oversimplification. Various investigators have been unable to find these two "original fears" with any consistency in infants. As Jersild writes, "the fear stimulus cannot be described as consisting of an isolated stimulus. . . . The circumstances that may give rise to so-called 'unlearned' fears in the infant include not simply noises and loss of support, but any intense, sudden, unexpected, or novel stimulus for which the organism appears to be unprepared." [3] That is to say, situations to which the organism cannot react adequately constitute a threat and are reacted to with anxiety or fear.

The present writer submits that the debate on "original fears," represented by the instinctivists on one hand and the behaviorists on the other, was on a false basis. The endeavor to determine what specific fears the infant is born with causes us to become lost in a labyrinth of misleading questions. The fruitful question, rather, is: What capacities (neurological and psychological) does the organism possess for meeting threatening situations? With respect to inheritance, we need only assume that the organism reacts to situations for which its capacities are inadequate with anxiety or fear and did so in the days of our ancestors as well as today. The problem of the acquisition of anxiety and fears after birth boils down to the two questions of *maturation* and *learning*. We also pose the question of whether these reactions of the infants described by Watson ought accurately to be called "fears" at all. Are they not, rather, *undifferentiated defensive reactions properly to be termed anxiety?* Such a hypothesis would account for the unspecific character of the reactions, i.e., that the "fear" is not found consistently even in the same child in response to a specific stimulus.

Role of Maturation in Anxiety and Fears.—Another defect in the Watsonian approach to children's fears is its neglect of the factor of maturation. As Jersild observes in this connection, "If a child at a certain stage of development exhibits behavior

---

[3] This and following excerpts from *Child psychology* (revised ed., New York, 1940), p. 254, by A. T. Jersild are reprinted by permission of Prentice-Hall, Inc. Copyright, 1933, 1940, by Prentice-Hall, Inc.

that was not shown at an earlier time, it does not follow that the change in behavior is due primarily to learning." [4]

It will be recalled from the discussion of the startle pattern above that in the early weeks of life the infant exhibited the startle reflex and little or nothing which could be called the emotion of fear. But as the infant developed, more and more secondary behavior (anxiety and fear) appeared. Jersild found in his studies that at about five or six months the child showed occasional signs of fear at the approach of a stranger, while before that level of development the child showed no such reaction. Gesell's account of the reaction of the infant at different ages to confinement in a small pen is illuminating. At ten weeks the child was complaisant; at twenty weeks he showed mild apprehension, one sign of which was persistent head-turning.[5] At thirty weeks his response to the same situation "may be so vigorously expressed by crying that we describe his reaction as fear or fright." [6] As Jersild expresses it, "the tendency to respond to an event as actually or potentially dangerous is relative to the child's level of development." [7]

It seems clear that the level of maturation is one determinant in the infant's or child's response to danger situations. The data suggest that the earliest reactions are of the reflexive variety (i.e., startle) and of diffuse, undifferentiated apprehension (anxiety). Though this diffuse apprehension may be elicited in the early weeks of the infant's life in response to certain stimuli (e.g., falling), it is more frequent as the infant develops greater capacity to perceive danger situations. As regards specific fears, we raise the question as to whether these are not the latest to appear in the scale of maturation of the infant. As Goldstein has indicated, responding with a specific fear presupposes the

---

[4] A. T. Jersild and F. B. Holmes, *Children's fears* (Child Development Monograph No. 20, Bureau of Publications, Teachers College, Columbia University, New York, 1935), p. 5. By permission of Teachers College. Copyright, 1935, by Teachers College, Columbia University.

[5] To us, this "persistent head-turning" is a significant picture of mild anxiety; the infant is disquieted, but it cannot spatially locate the object of its apprehension.

[6] See Jersild, *Child psychology, op. cit.,* p. 255. Quotations are from A. L. Gesell, The individual in infancy, in Carl Murchison, ed., *The foundations of experimental psychology* (Worcester, Mass., 1929).

[7] Jersild, *op. cit.,* p. 255.

capacity to objectivate—i.e., to discriminate between specific objects in the environment; and this capacity requires greater neurological and psychological maturation than to respond in a diffuse, undifferentiated way.

As the child develops after the infant period, Jersild points out, new and significant changes occur in the kinds of stimuli which give rise to fears. "With the development of the child's imaginative abilities, his fears become increasingly concerned with imaginary dangers; with the development of understanding of the meaning of competition and of awareness of one's own status as compared with others, there frequently come fears of loss of prestige, ridicule, and failure." [8]

It would seem clear that in the latter of these apprehensions—those related to competition—the child is engaging in a more or less complex interpretation of environmental situations. Such interpretive processes presuppose a certain amount of maturation, but they also patently involve the experience and conditioning which occur as the culture makes impact upon the child. Not only did Jersild find that fears related to competitive status increased as the child matured, but also, interestingly enough, that the adults reporting on their remembered childhood fears gave a much higher percentage of apprehensions related to competitive status than any of the groups of children studied. Jersild rightly explains this as due to the tendency of the adults to "read back" into their childhood the fulcra of fear and anxiety which had become increasingly important to them in adulthood.

It is unnecessary to review in detail the results of Jersild's comprehensive studies of children's fears.[9] But two problems

---

[8] *Ibid.*, p. 256. Whether these reactions which Jersild describes as "fears"— for example, those connected with competition—are actually fears or anxiety is a question which could be answered only on the basis of the actual situation. Also, aside from Jersild's work, clinical studies indicate that intrapsychic conflicts may be projected on the environment and give rise to anxiety; one common example of this is the anxiety underlying phobias. This likewise presupposes not only some level of maturation but also intricate conditioning and experiential processes.

[9] See A. T. Jersild and F. B. Holmes, *Children's fears* (New York, 1935); also Jersild, *Child psychology, op. cit.* The studies reported include experiments designed to elicit possible fear reactions, the reporting of fears observed by a group of mothers in their children, recording fears cited by children in interviews, and the reporting by adults of fears they remembered having had in childhood. Four case studies of children with much fear and four of children with little fear are

arise as one contemplates these results. We cite these problems bcause of the illumination they shed upon the relation of fears to underlying anxiety.

First, Jersild's results show the *"irrational"* qualities of children's fears. There was a sharp discrepancy between the fears the children reported and what they described, later in the interview, as the "worst happenings" in their lives.[10] The worst happenings were cited as illnesses, bodily injuries, misfortunes, and other experiences that had actually befallen the children. Their fears, on the other hand, were "predominantly described in terms of somewhat vague calamities that might occur." [11] Actual terrifying experiences with animals constituted less than 2 per cent of the "worst happenings," whereas fears of animals accounted for 14 per cent. The animals feared were chiefly remote creatures like gorillas, wolves, and lions. Being left alone in the dark and being lost were given as 2 per cent of the actual experiences, while fears of such situations amounted to about 15 per cent. Dangers from mysterious agents like ghosts, witches, and the occult were of course not reported at all as worst happenings, but fears of such things accounted for over 19 per cent (the largest group) of the total fears expressed. As Jersild sums it up, a *"large proportion of fears that were described have little or no direct relation to misfortunes that actually have befallen the children."* [12] If one thinks of fears as responses to a specific threat, the above data are puzzling. One would expect the child to fear what actually has been of danger to him in his past experience. Jersild, noting that the "imaginary fears" of the child increase with age, suggests as one explanation the fact that "imaginative capacities" of the child are developing. Such maturing capacities may explain why the child deals in imaginary

---

also included. Though Jersild recognizes the deficiencies of these various methods, the data yielded are undoubtedly comprehensive and valuable.

[10] Based upon interviews with 398 children aged five to twelve years. See A. T. Jersild, F. V. Markey, and S. L. Jersild.: *Children's fears, dreams, wishes, daydreams, pleasant and unpleasant memories* (Child Development Monograph No. 12; New York: Teachers College, Columbia University, 1933).

[11] Jersild, *Child psychology, op. cit.,* p. 265.

[12] A. T. Jersild and F. B. Holmes, *Children's fears* (Child Development Monograph No. 20, Teachers College, Columbia University [New York, 1935]), p. 328. Italics mine. By permission of Teachers College Bureau of Publications. Copyright, 1935, by Teachers College, Columbia University.

material; but in the present writer's opinion this does not adequately account for the fact that these imaginary things should, in such large measure, be *feared*.

Another problem raised by Jersild's data is the *unpredictability of fears*. Jersild notes that his data emphasize how difficult it is to predict when a child will be afraid: "the same child may face a given situation at a certain time without showing fear but at a later time, with no grossly apparent intervening causal factors, the same situation gives rise to fear." [13] Over half the group of mothers engaged in observing fears of their children reported instances in which the child showed fear of a situation which he had previously encountered without fear. [14] Jersild also notes that a child's fears shift unpredictably. He comments that some process is occurring vastly more complicated than the usual concept of conditioning. But the question of what this process is remains unanswered. [15]

We submit that these two problems—the irrational and unpredictable qualities of children's fears—become intelligible if many of these so-called "fears" are regarded not as specific fright reactions (that is, fears as such) but rather as *appearances in objectivated form of underlying anxiety*. Such an interpretation has logical definition in its support: fear is regularly defined as a specific reaction, and it is apparent that something is occurring in these "fears" which cannot be explained as a specific response inseparably and intrinsically related to a specific stimulus. If the hypothesis is made that these fears are rather expressions of anxiety, the high percentage of "imaginary" fears becomes

---

[13] "Numerous examples of this fact appeared in the data of the present study: a certain noise causes fear and another does not; a child is taken to one strange place and exhibits no fear, while in another strange situation he does show fear; he fears a certain dog on first seeing it, and has no fear of another dog. . . . Undoubtedly there is some feature of the specific situation that is the deciding factor; but just what it is that turns the scale in one specific situation and not in another, is hard to tell. The problem here involved is one that needs a good deal of intensive study. On the basis of present knowledge any general statement as to specific stimuli that are likely to cause fear in the case of a given child is likely to be highly untrustworthy."—*Ibid.*, p. 308.

[14] *Ibid.*

[15] It is significant for our present inquiry that "fear of strange persons" was most often mentioned as a fear that appeared in certain situations and not in other similar situations.

understandable. It is well known that the anxiety of children (as well as of adults) is often displaced upon ghosts, witches, and other objects which do not have a specific relation to the child's objective world but do fulfill significant functions for his subjective needs.[16] In some cases, for example, the process is to be understood as follows: the child feels anxiety about his relation to his parents. He cannot face this directly, in such terms, for example, as "I am afraid my mother does not love me," for such a realization would increase the anxiety. Or he is aided in covering up the direct form of the anxiety by reassurances from the parents (which often have little to do with the real fulcrum of anxiety). The anxiety is then displaced upon "imaginary" objects. We have placed the term "imaginary" in quotation marks frequently in this discussion because it would no doubt be found on more profound analysis of the mysterious fears that the imagined object stands for something real in the child's experience. (Adults, of course, likewise engage in a similar pattern of displacement of anxieties, but adults are much more skilled in rationalizing the anxieties so that the objects become more apparently "logical" or "reasonable"). Our hypothesis would also make clear why the fears of animals were not of animals actually encountered by the child but remote ones like gorillas and lions. Fears of animals are often projections of anxieties the child feels in relations with objects or persons (such as parents) who are by no means remote.[17] Melitta Schmideberg suggests that fears of animals may also be projections of the child's own hostile feelings toward members of his family, feelings which entail anxiety because of the probability of punishment or disapproval if these hostile tendencies were carried into action.[18]

The hypothesis we suggest also throws light upon the unpredictability and shifting quality of children's fears. If these fears are appearances in objectivated form of underlying anxiety, the anxiety could focus now on this object and now on that. What appears as inconsistency on superficial analysis would then

---

16 See P. M. Symonds, *The dynamics of human adjustment* (New York, 1946).
17 See Freud's case of Hans, pages 117-18.
18 Melitta Schmideberg, Anxiety states, *Psychoanal. Rev.*, 1940, 27 : 4, 439-49.

be quite consistent when viewed on a deeper level. Jersild notes this shifting character of fears when the fears are an expression of underlying anxiety:

> As long as there are underlying difficulties that press upon the child from many sides, the elimination of one particular expression of fear may shortly be followed by other fears of a slightly different cast.[19]

Another indication that anxiety rather than fear is occurring in many of these children is in Jersild's observation that his studies indicate the frequent ineffectiveness of verbal reassurance in overcoming children's fears. As Goldstein has held, if the emotion is a specific fear, it can normally be allayed by verbal reassurance. If the child who has a fear that the house is on fire receives adequate demonstration that such is not the case, the fear vanishes. But if this apprehension is actually an objectivated form of anxiety, either the terror will not be allayed (as Jersild reports is often the case), or it will shift to a new object.

There is indirect presumptive support for the hypothesis that anxiety often underlies children's fears in the close relationship between children's "fears" and those of their parents. Hagman's study yields a correlation of .667 between the gross number of children's fears and the gross number of mothers' fears.[20]

---

[19] Jersild continues: "For example, a child's apparent fear of being abandoned, exhibited whenever his mother leaves the house on a brief errand, may be associated with other symptoms of distress that first appeared when a new baby came into the household. This particular expression of fear may abate in response to parental efforts to help the child overcome it, only to be followed by other expressions of fear—such as fear of sleeping alone in a dark room—if the underlying uncertainties still persist."—*Child psychology*, p. 274. As an actual case the present author cites the following: A boy of three was sent to his grandparents' farm for the period during which his mother gave birth to twins. On his mother's arrival with the new babies, the boy began to exhibit a strong "fear" of the tractor on the farm. It was noted by the parents that this "fear" took the form of the boy's running to his parents ostensibly for their protection from the tractor. On the assumption that the underlying cause of the boy's "fear" was feelings of isolation and rejection related to the previous separation from the parents and the advent of the two babies, the parents ignored the item of the tractor as such and devoted their efforts to helping the boy overcome his feelings of isolation. The fear of the tractor shortly vanished. If it had been assumed that the exhibited fear was related specifically to the threat of the tractor, it is not denied that the child could have been conditioned, in the usual meaning of this term, out of the fear of the tractor. But if, as hypothesized by the parents, this fear were really a focus for anxiety which actually had quite different roots, the "fear" would simply have shifted to a new object.

[20] Jersild, *Child psychology, op. cit.*, p. 270.

Jersild found "a good deal of correspondence between the frequency of fears of children of the same family; the correlations ranged from .65 to .74." [21]   It would seem that something more is occurring than the parents' fears having an "influence," as Jersild puts it, upon the fears of the children; i.e., that the child learns to fear certain things because the parents do.   It has been so frequently pointed out as to become a platitude that the development of anxiety in children arises centrally out of their relations with their parents.[22]   "Anxiety in a parent," Symonds writes, "breeds anxiety in children." [23]   We suggest that the close relationship between children's fears and those of their parents, and between fears of children of the same family, can be understood more clearly as a carry-over on the anxiety level. In other words, in families in which the parents have a good deal of anxiety, the interpersonal relations with children will be disrupted by this anxiety, and there will be greater anxiety (i.e., increased tendency to have "fears") on the part of the children.

Summary.—The purpose of this discussion of children's fears, in addition to throwing light upon the specific problem of fear as such, has been to demonstrate that the study of fears leads inexorably to the study of anxiety.   What is necessary is a hypothesis which will include not only the relation between fears and anxiety but also will make intelligible how underlying anxiety comes into expression in the form of specific fears.   We have endeavored to demonstrate the need for such a hypothesis by citing the problems of the "irrational" and unpredictable and shifting qualities of childrens' fears, questions which are puzzling on the level of fears as such, but which can be given con-

---

21 Jersild and Holmes, *op. cit.,* p. 305.   Several studies indicate that a common, if not the chief, fear of school children is that they might fail in school.   Studies also show this fear of failure to be very much out of proportion to the actual experience or reasonable probability of failure on the part of the student (Symonds, *op. cit.,* p. 151).   It is safe to assume that there is operating in these situations not only the child's sensitivity to competitive status and the anxiety connected therewith, so common in our culture, but a carry-over upon the child of the *parents'* anxiety about competitive status.   E.g., the parents will disapprove of the child if he does not rank high in school.

22 See following Sections on Freud, Sullivan, *et al.*

23 Symonds, *op. cit.,* p. 139.

sistent answers on the assumption that anxiety underlies many of the so-called fears.

The particular hypothesis suggested here is that many children's fears are objectivated forms of underlying anxiety.[24] Such a hypothesis emphasizes the difficult problem in experimental work of distinguishing whether a given emotional reaction is properly to be termed a specific fear or is anxiety. Jersild recognizes this problem and suggests that though children's anxiety is outside the scope of his studies, it is an area which merits further investigation.

2. THE PROBLEM OF EXPERIMENTAL STUDY OF ANXIETY

The investigations of anxiety-like reactions in animals have shed peripheral illumination on the problem of anxiety in human beings. We use the term "anxiety-like reactions" because there is considerable difference of opinion as to whether animals experience anxiety or not. Goldstein believes animals do have anxiety, but he is using the term to refer to undifferentiated fright reactions, parallel to the "normal" anxiety which may be seen in the two-weeks-old human infant. Sullivan holds animals do not have anxiety. Mowrer, in his early studies of the "anxiety" of rats (which will be reviewed in the next section), used the terms "fear" and "anxiety" interchangeably. But later on, he concluded that the apprehension his animals were experiencing was fear, and that animals do not have anxiety except as they are placed in a special psychological relationship with human beings, such as the experimenters. In contrast to Goldstein, however, Mowrer is using the term "anxiety" to refer to neurotic anxiety, which by definition presupposes the capacities for self-consciousness, repression, and so forth which are uniquely the possessions of the human mammal.

It is Liddell, in the present writer's judgment, who cuts the Gordian knot of this controversy. In a paper which is remark-

[24] The phenomenon of phobias presents in extreme form a demonstration of the above hypothesis. Phobias appear as specific, but are found on deeper analysis to be concentrations of anxiety at one point in the environment in order to avoid anxiety at other points. See Freud's analysis of Hans, the five-year old boy whose phobia of horses, Freud indicates, was a displacement of anxiety arising out of his relations with his father and mother.

ably pertinent to our study of anxiety, based on his extensive work in experimental neurosis, Liddell holds that animals do not have anxiety in the meaning of that term as applied to human beings, but they do have a primitive, simple counterpart, namely *vigilance*.[25] When an animal is in a situation that involves a possible threat—such as the sheep in the laboratory expecting an electric shock, or the seal sleeping in its natural habitat having to awake every ten seconds to survey the landscape lest Eskimo hunters sneak up on it—the animal exhibits an alertness and a general expectancy of danger. It is as though the animal were asking "What is it?" This vigilance is characterized by generalized suspiciousness (indicating that the animal does not know whence the danger may arise), with tendencies to act but without any clear-cut direction for acting. Such behavior, as will readily be seen, is the parallel on the animal level to the vague and generalized apprehensive behavior of the human being in anxiety.

Liddell holds that Goldstein was describing this vigilance in his concept of the "catastrophic reaction," but he adds that the fact that Goldstein pegged the reactions at a high level of intensity has kept other investigators from identifying the catastrophic reaction. In conditioning experiments, vigilance may be shown not only at a high intensity (as in experimental neurosis, when the animal gives a very clear picture of Goldstein's catastrophic condition), but through all gradations down to such a low intensity as a "small movement of the eyes or a slight acceleration of the heart."

It is this vigilance which supplies the power for the conditioned reflex. While Pavlov was astonishingly accurate in his description of the neurophysiological *mechanics* of conditioning, Liddell believes he was inaccurate when he contended that the motive power for the conditioning came from instinctual sources —e.g., the dog's instinctual desire to get food or to avoid pain and discomfort. Liddell writes that "the conditioning machin-

---

25 Howard Liddell, The role of vigilance in the development of animal neurosis, paper read at the symposium on anxiety of the Amer. psychopath. Ass., New York, June, 1949. (To be published in the transcription of those meetings; page references not available at this writing.)

ery is not powered, as Pavlov believed, by a leakage of energy along a newly formed pathway or channel from a highly energized unconditioned reflex center to a sensory center feebly energized by sensory impulses set up by the conditioned stimulus." Rather, it is powered by the animal's capacity for vigilance or, in other words, by the animal's capacity as a behaving organism to be alert to, and suspicious of, its environment.[26] If the animal is to be conditioned—i.e., if it is to learn to behave in an orderly fashion—it must be able to get some reliable answer to its question, "What is it?" Thus in conditioning experiments consistency is all-important.

Within its limitations (e.g., the sheep can keep track of time, can "plan for the future," only up to about ten minutes, and the dog up to about half an hour), the animal must also be able to get some answer to a second question, "What happens next?" When, as in the laboratory experiments designed to produce the experimental neurosis, the animal cannot get these answers, but continues in tension as though asking "What is it? What is it? What is it?"; when, in other words, the animal is kept in a constant and unrelieved state of vigilance, its behavior soon becomes frantic, disordered, and "neurotic." This, on the animal level, is parallel to what happens when human beings break down under the burden of severe and constant anxiety. Though Liddell cautions that we cannot identify the disturbed behavior of animals with human anxiety, it is possible to state that conditioned reflex behavior in animals bears the same relation to experimental neurosis as intelligent action in human beings bears to anxiety.

This brings Liddell to some exceedingly stimulating and suggestive thoughts about the relation between intelligence and anxiety in human beings. Pavlov had believed that the "What is it?" response was the rudimentary form of human inquisitiveness, which in its flowering became man's capacity for scientific investigation and realistic exploration of his world. Liddell is

---

[26] Liddell's distinction here, which places the problem on a psychobiological rather than a neurophysiological level, is the point we have emphasized in the previous chapter, namely that the neurophysiological *media* by which behavior occurs must not be confused with the *causes* of the behavior.

able to carry this line of thought further, and also to make it more precise, by his distinction between the *sentinel* function of the neurological system, i.e., "What is it?" and the *planner* function, i.e., "What happens next?" The latter function plays a much greater role in human behavior than in animal. Man is the mammal who can foresee, can plan for the future, can retrospectively enjoy past achievements. This capacity to plan has culminated in man's unique capacity for living by means of ideas and values. The capacity to experience anxiety, Liddell states, and the capacity to plan are the two sides of the same coin. He holds "that anxiety accompanies intellectual activity as its shadow, and that the more we know of the nature of anxiety, the more we will know of intellect." Thus Liddell states one aspect of the problem, which was attacked by Kierkegaard and Goldstein, and with which we shall wrestle again and again in the present study, of the relation between man's creative potentialities—his capacity for imaginative reality-testing, for dealing with symbols and meanings, and for changing behavior on the basis of these processes—and man's potentiality for experiencing anxiety.[27]

It remains only to note that Liddell, like so many investigators cited in the present study, as well as the present author, sees the social nature of man as the source of man's uniquely creative intellectual capacities as well as his capacity for anxiety. Liddell asserts "that both intellect and its shadow, anxiety, are products of man's social intercourse." [28]

When we pass on to consider the experimental study of anxiety in human beings, we are confronted by a situation very different from that of the experimental study of animals. At the beginning of a recent paper on anxiety Mowrer remarks, "there is at present no experimental psychology of anxiety, and one may even doubt whether there ever will be." [29] Not only is it true that the problem of human anxiety has been absent from the

---

[27] See Chapter 8, Section 6.

[28] The reasoning which leads Liddell to this conclusion is very similar to that of Sullivan (see Section 9 below), and it also has much in common with the viewpoints of Freud and of Mowrer on the social origins of anxiety.

[29] O. H. Mowrer, Anxiety, chapter in *Learning theory and personality dynamics* (1950).

strictly experimental specialties of psychology, but it has largely been omitted from the other branches of academic and theoretical psychology as well. In searching the psychological books written earlier than the late 1930's (excepting those concerned with psychoanalysis), it is almost impossible to find the topic of anxiety even listed in the indexes. What Kierkegaard wrote a hundred years ago has remained true in our twentieth century until fairly recently, "One almost never sees the concept of anxiety dealt with in psychology." [30] True, there have been a plenitude of studies of fears in the experimental and academic psychology of this century; but on the threshold where the problem of fears moves into the problem of anxiety, the great bulk of investigations has halted. For both practical and theoretical reasons it is important that we inquire into this phenomenon. The practical reasons are partially illustrated in the preceding section, where we observed that even the studies of fears are confused by a lack of clear understanding of the relationship between fears and anxiety and by a lack of differentiation as to when a reaction to threat is fear and when it is anxiety. The theoretical reasons are that, to the extent that fears are investigated and anxiety is not, we tend to base our conceptualizations of anxiety on our knowledge of fears, and the essential nature of anxiety then eludes us.

There is, first, a general cultural reason for the lack of study of anxiety in academic and experimental psychology. Since the Renaissance, science has traditionally been allied with mathematical rationalism (which we have previously seen to be the dominant mode of thought through the four centuries of the modern period).[31] Particularly in its academic manifestations, science has been preoccupied with those aspects of nature which were susceptible to mathematical treatment. In psychology this took the form of preoccupation with those elements in behavior and human nature which could be isolated as discrete entities, tabulated, measured, and in ideal circumstances experimented upon in the laboratory. There has, moreover, been a corollary

---

[30] Søren Kierkegaard, *The concept of dread,* trans. Walter Lowrie (Princeton, N. J., 1944), p. 38.
[31] Chapter 2.

tendency in the scientific tradition of our culture, parallel to tendencies in the culture as a whole, to look askance at phenomena which were not susceptible to mathematical treatment in the above form—such as "irrational" and "unconscious" phenomena. It is no accident (as Mowrer has pointed out) that psychophysics is the most advanced of the psychological specialties, for its methods fit the traditional emphases: the reactions it studies are stable, consistent, and can be measured with some degree of satisfaction. Likewise, there has been no lack of studies of fears by means of enumeration and tabulation, for to the extent that fears could be isolated as specific reactions, their study was amenable to the traditional methods.

There are, secondly, the facts of the dangers and difficulties of studying human anxiety experimentally. The reasons why Mowrer expresses "grave doubt" whether experimental psychology "will ultimately succeed in encompassing this topic" [32] are that the effects of inducing human anxiety in the laboratory are "too damaging" and that the experience itself is so complex. Mowrer himself recommends a flanking approach to the problem through clinical studies, in which it is possible to deal intensively with single individuals in crisis situations, and through inquiries into those aspects of the cultural literature—chiefly philosophy, ethics, and religion—which historically have dealt with anxiety. The present writer agrees heartily with both of these recommendations, and they are employed, implicitly and explicitly, in the present study. [33]

Whatever one's personal predilections about method in psychology may be, several facts stand out clearly when one surveys the whole field of the psychological studies of human anxiety. The first is that experimental studies which have been most fruitful for illuminating this area are those which employed clinical procedures along with experimental techniques—for example, the studies of ulcer patients and the case of Tom, reviewed in the

---

[32] Mowrer, *op. cit.*

[33] The reader will recognize the implicit concern throughout this study with both the cultural and the clinical approaches to the problem of human anxiety. With regard to the explicit use of these approaches, the cultural appears chiefly in Chapters 1, 2, and 5, and the clinical in the case studies in Chapters 7 and 8.

preceding chapter.[34] The second is that the experimental and academic psychologists who have pertinently attacked the problem of anxiety have been those who were led to it via their increasing interest in clinical work and who adopted clinical techniques as their method.[35] The third fact which stands out clearly is that most of the significant data on anxiety comes from the psychotherapists—Freud, Horney, Fromm, Sullivan, and others—whose clinical methods permit an intensive study of the subjective dynamics and whose focus of attention is by definition on the individual as a totality confronting crises in his life situation. We shall discuss in the next section the work of Mowrer, which provides a bridge from the experimental to the clinical approach to anxiety; and then we shall proceed directly to a consideration of the anxiety studies and theories of the various psychotherapists.

3. Mowrer: Anxiety and Learning Theory

Ranging all the way from his original formulations of anxiety in stimulus-response psychology to his latest concept of anxiety and ethics, O. H. Mowrer's indefatigable inquiries and researches present a distinctive contribution to anxiety theory in American experimental and academic psychology. We shall

---

[34] There have been relatively rare endeavors to study individuals in an immediate crisis situation which employ a mixture of experimental and clinical procedures (cf. A. R. Luria, *The nature of human conflicts* [New York, 1932]). In the previous chapter we have discussed the ingenious psychosomatic studies on patients with peptic ulcer which used physiological, psychological, analytical, and case history approaches, combining clinical and experimental procedure. The book-length study of Tom likewise falls in this multimethod category. The writer would add at this point only that these studies have their exceedingly great value for the understanding of anxiety because the investigators were able (1) to inquire into subjective as well as objective factors; (2) to study each individual as a unit in his life situation; and (3) to pursue the study of each over a period of time.

[35] In addition to Mowrer, P. M. Symonds is an example (see the very useful discussion of method in the Preface to *The dynamics of human adjustment* [New York, 1946]). It is by no means irrelevant that both Mowrer and Symonds had established their expertness in the fields of experimental and academic psychology. The former's ingenious experimental work is reviewed in the next section; the latter had pursued with expertness the objective, atomistic measuring methods of psychology for some years. Thus the demand for new methods on the part of such psychologists does not arise out of their lack of appreciation of older methods but rather out of convincing experience that these methods were not ultimately efficacious for the study of anxiety.

trace Mowrer's work developmentally, for the stages of thinking shown in his series of papers represent several significant levels in the changing and broadening approach to anxiety in psychology in this country. Mowrer's analyses of anxiety are based centrally upon his researches in learning theory. In view of the frequently proposed assumption that the ultimate bridge between psychoanalysis on one hand and experimental and academic psychology on the other will probably be learning theory, it is presumable that the learning theory base of Mowrer's work gives his conceptualizations of anxiety added cogency.

In his early stimulus-response formulations, Mowrer explicitly characterized anxiety as a "psychological problem to which the habits known as 'symptoms' provide solutions." [36] Anxiety was defined in his first paper as "the conditioned form of the pain reaction." [37] That is to say, the organism perceives the danger signal (the stimulus), and the conditioned response which then follows in anticipation of the danger—a response characterized by tension, organic discomfort, and pain—is anxiety. Any behavior which reduces this anxiety is rewarding, and hence, by the law of effect, such behavior becomes "stamped in," i.e., learned. This analysis has two important implications. First, anxiety is seen as one of the central motivations of human behavior. And, secondly, as a corollary, the process by which neurotic symptoms are acquired is placed squarely on a basis of learning theory—symptoms are learned because they are anxiety-reducing.

Mowrer's next researches in anxiety were experiments with rats and guinea pigs verifying the above hypothesis that reduction in anxiety serves as a reward and is positively correlated with learning. [38] This hypothesis is now widely accepted in the psychology of learning. [39] It has the practical merits not only of emphasizing how important and pervasive anxiety is as a motiva-

[36] O. H. Mowrer, A stimulus-response analysis of anxiety and its role as a reinforcing agent, *Psychol. Rev.*, 1939, **46**: 6, 553-65.

[37] *Ibid.*, p. 555.

[38] Anxiety-reduction and learning, *J. exp. Psychol.*, 1940, **27**: 5, 497-516.

[39] Cf. N. E. Miller and John Dollard, *Social learning and imitation* (New Haven, Conn., 1941), and P. M. Symonds, *The dynamics of human adjustment* (New York, 1946).

tion in education, but it also sheds light on healthy and constructive methods of management of that anxiety in the classroom.[40]

These early approaches of Mowrer to the problem of anxiety have two elements of definition in common. First, no specific distinction is made between fear and anxiety. In the first paper the terms are used synonymously, and in the second the factor of anxiety is defined as the animals' expectation of the electric shock —a state that could be termed fear as accurately as, if not more accurately than, anxiety.[41] Second, the threat which cues off anxiety is defined as the threat of organic pain and discomfort. During the period when these papers were written, Mowrer was endeavoring to define anxiety in physiological terms.[42]

But radical changes occurred in Mowrer's conception of anxiety following his further researches in learning theory, particularly after his inquiry into the question: Why do people learn nonintegrative ("neurotic," consistently punishing) behavior? Experimenting with animals, he demonstrated that rats exhibited "neurotic" and "criminal" behavior because they were incapable of anticipating future, long-time rewards and punishments and balancing them against the immediate consequences of their behavior.[43] In his stimulating discussion of these findings, Mowrer concludes that the essence of integrative behavior is the capacity to bring the future into the psychological present. Man has the capacity for integrative learning in a form vastly different from animals because he is able to bring the "time determinant" into his learning, to weigh future against immediate consequences. This gives human behavior flexibility and freedom (and, by inference, responsibility).[44]

---

[40] Cf. O. H. Mowrer, *Preparatory set (expectancy)—some methods of measurement* (Psychol. Monogr., 1940), No. 233, pp. 39, 40.

[41] The present writer would call the reactions of Mowrer's animals in this experiment fear, and Mowrer himself, from his present perspective, would likewise term the reactions fear.

[42] Cf. O. H. Mowrer, Freud's theories of anxiety: a reconciliation. Unpublished lecture given at Yale Institute of Human Relations, 1939.

[43] O. H. Mowrer and A. D. Ullman, Time as a determinant in integrative learning, *Psychol. Rev.*, 1945, 52: 2, 61-90.

[44] Mowrer refers to Goldstein's observations that the most characteristic loss of patients with cortical injuries was the capacity to "transcend concrete (immediate) experience," to abstract, to deal with the "possible." Hence these patients were limited to rigid, inflexible behavior. Since the cortex represents the distinctive

Man's capacity for transcending the present in terms of future consequences depends upon several distinctive qualities which set him "well apart" from animals. One is the capacity to *reason,* to use *symbols.* Man communicates by means of symbols, and he thinks by means of setting up "emotionally charged" symbols in his mind and reacting to them. Another quality is man's distinctive *social, historical* development. Weighing the long-time consequences of one's behavior is a social act in that it involves the question of values for the community as well as for one's self (if, indeed, these two can be separated). Mowrer's findings imply a new emphasis on the historical nature of man, on man as the "time-binding" being.[45] As he phrases it, "the capacity, then, to bring the past into the present as a part of the total causal nexus in which living organisms behave (act and react) is the essence of 'mind' and 'personality' alike." [46] To be sure, the importance of the individual's own genetic past—the fact that he carries into the present the experiences from his childhood, for example—has long been generally accepted in clinical psychology. But there is another implication of this emphasis on man as the "time-binding" being which is relatively new in clinical work: namely, since the human being weighs his behavior in terms of symbols which have been developing through many centuries in the history of his culture, he can be understood only in the context of that history in its broader sense. These findings meant for Mowrer a new interest in history in general, and in particular a new interest in ethics and religion, which are the history of man's endeavor to transcend immediate consequences in terms of long-time universal values.[47]

---

neurological difference between man and animals, this capacity which the cortically impaired patients lost may be taken as the distinctively human capacity.

45 Elsewhere the present author (page 67, and Chapter 5) discusses these two qualities of the human being as (1) *man is the mammal who lives by symbols* and (2) *man is the historical mammal* in that he possesses the capacity for self-awareness of his history. He is therefore not just the product of history (as all animals are), but in varying degrees, depending upon his self-awareness of his history, man can exercise selectivity toward his history, can adapt himself to portions of it and correct other portions. Within limits he can mold his history and in other ways use it in his development in self-chosen directions. Cassirer also makes these two qualities distinctive for human beings; cf. *An essay on man* (New Haven, Conn., 1944).

46 O. H. Mowrer, *op. cit.*

47 Through his discussion of integrative learning, Mowrer makes an exceedingly useful distinction between the terms *integrative* and *adjustive.* All learned behavior

The implications of the above considerations for anxiety theory are profound. The problem of neurotic anxiety is placed squarely in its cultural and historical nexus, and is *related specifically to man's distinctive problems of social responsibility and ethics*. (This is in radical contrast to Mowrer's previous definition of anxiety as response to the threat of organic pain or discomfort.) For Mowrer the "social dilemma [as illustrated in the child's ambivalent relation to his parents] is a precondition for anxiety." [48] If animals have neurotic anxiety at all, Mowrer now holds, it is only in artificial environments (e.g., the "experimental neurosis") in which they have become to some extent domesticated, "socialized." That is, by virtue of their relationship with the experimenters, the animals have become something more than "just" animals. We have discussed above Mowrer's present doubts as to whether there ever will be an experimental

is in some sense adjustive; neuroses are adjustive; defense mechanisms are learned because they are means of adjusting to difficult situations. Mowrer's "neurotic" rats gave up taking food, and his "criminal" rats took it despite the future punishment, each group "adjusting" to a difficult situation. But neuroses and defenses, like the behavior of these rats, are not *integrative;* neuroses and defenses do not permit the further constructive development of the individual.

In the light of this distinction, we raise a question in regard to the implications of the concept of *anxiety as a drive.* That anxiety does operate as a drive, a "secondary" drive, as is emphasized by learning theorists (Miller and Dollard, Symonds, etc.) is indisputable. And its reduction, like the reduction of other drives, is rewarding and reinforces learning. But strictly speaking, *behavior which occurs chiefly and directly to lessen the drive of anxiety is adjustive, not integrative.* To this writer it falls in the same category as the learning of neurotic symptoms. This could be illustrated by the many examples given in the above writings (Miller and Dollard, Symonds) concerning children's learning in school in order to avoid punishment and disapproval. Granted that much learning in school is of this variety, we submit that it is a different kind of learning from that which occurs on the motivation of curiosity and the positive satisfactions which the child experiences in the development of his own powers. This is Goldstein's point when he holds that all activity which is a direct product of the individual's anxiety (i.e., when the motivation is the reduction of anxiety as a drive) is marked by a stress on partial aspects of action, compulsiveness, and lack of freedom. And, "as long as these activities are not spontaneous, are not outlets of the free personality, but are merely the sequelae of anxiety, they have only a pseudo-value for the personality." (See Chapter 3 above.) This also is Horney's point when she holds that the concept of "drive" (anxiety or any other motivation as a drive) itself implies compulsive behavior, and in her definition is neurotic, mildly or severely as the case may be. In the present study, therefore, the term *needs* is used in a positive sense and the term *drives* in a negative sense. With regard to anxiety as a drive in learning, a clear distinction must be made between behavior which *allays* anxiety (adjustive, drive-reducing) and behavior which increases the skills and capacities of the organism, thus overcoming the causes of the anxiety and releasing the individual for further development and integrative learning.

[48] Mowrer, *op. cit.*

psychology of anxiety. This does not imply, in Mowrer's writings or in the attitudes of the present writer, any depreciation of the value of animal experiments or laboratory studies of human beings; but it does place such methods of study in perspective. In the study of neurotic anxiety, we find the essence of our problem in precisely those characteristics of man which distinguish him from animals. If we limit ourselves to the areas in human behavior which are identical with the infrahuman or to those elements which can be isolated in the laboratory, or, indeed, if we center our study around the strictly biological and organic impulses and needs of man, the essential significance of anxiety for human beings will elude us.

We now turn to Mowrer's most recent presentation of his concept of anxiety. He notes that the beginning of the "social dilemma" is in the child's early relations with his parents. The child cannot avoid anxiety cued off in the family situation by simple flight (like the animal in nature), for the anxious child is interdependent with his parents at the same time that he fears them.[49] Mowrer agrees with the Freudian theory that repression occurs in the child because of real fears—generally the fear of punishment or deprivation (withdrawal of love). Indeed, Mowrer wholly accepts Freud's description of the *mechanism* by which anxiety occurs: a real fear→repression of this fear→ neurotic anxiety→symptom formation as a solution to the anxiety. But *mechanism* is a different thing from *meaning*. Mowrer contends that Freud "never succeeded in fully comprehending the essential nature of anxiety itself," [50] because of his endeavor to explain anxiety in terms of instincts and his failure to understand the social context of personality. In the maturing of the human individual, social responsibility normally becomes (or should become) a positive, constructive goal. By and large, Mowrer holds, the conflicts which are most likely to cause anxiety are of an ethical nature—a point seen by Kierkegaard but not

---

[49] Cf. Horney's theory that basic (neurotic) anxiety arises out of the conflict in the child between his dependency upon his parents and his hostility toward them (Section 8 below).

[50] Mowrer, *op. cit.*

by Freud.[51]   The sources of the conflicts are social fear and guilt. What the individual fears is social punishment and withdrawal of love and approval on the part of the significant other persons in his constellation of relationships.   It is these fears and the guilt associated with them which become repressed, and in their repressed state they become neurotic anxiety.[52]

Thus Mowrer advances a " 'guilt-theory' of anxiety rather than an 'impulse theory.' " [53]   Anxiety is a product "not of too little self-indulgence and satisfaction . . . but of irresponsibility, guilt, immaturity."   It arises from "repudiated moral urgings, " [54] or in Freudian terminology, anxiety is caused by "repression of the super-ego," not, as Freud would have it, the reverse.   This viewpoint, of course, has radical implications for dealing with anxiety in therapy.   Mowrer points out that the endeavor of many psychoanalysts to dilute and "analyze away" the superego (and concomitantly the individual's sense of responsibility and guilt) only too often results in a " 'deep narcissistic degression' rather than in the growth in personal maturity, social adequacy, and happiness which one has a right to expect from a really competent therapy." [55]

One of the significant implications of Mowrer's viewpoint is that anxiety is seen as playing a constructive, positive role in human development.   He writes:

> There is a common tendency in our day, both on the part of professional psychologists and laymen, to look upon anxiety as a negative, destructive, "abnormal" experience, one which must be

---

[51] The "ethical accomplishment of untold past generations, as imbedded in the conscience of modern men and women, is not a stupid, malevolent, archaic incubus, but a challenge and a guide for the individual in his quest for self-fulfillment and harmonious integration."—*Ibid.*

[52] In summary, Mowrer submits that his data indicate "that it is always *a dissociated fear of some kind* which kindles the fires of anxiety and that such a fear need not be 'instinctual' either in the sense of its being cued off by a frustrated impulse or in the sense of representing a danger that such an impulse is about to 'overwhelm the ego.' Most simply said, any fear which, because of a competing drive or interest, becomes repressed may return from repression as anxiety, and the indications are that the fears which are most likely to suffer such a fate are those originating in connection with social punishments and deprivations."—*Ibid.*, p. 73.

[53] *Op. cit.*

[54] *Ibid.*

[55] *Ibid.*

fought and if possible annihilated. . . . Anxiety, as conceived in these pages, is not the cause of personal disorganization; rather is it the outcome or expression of such a state. The element of disorganization enters with the act of dissociation or repression, and anxiety represents not only an attempted return of the repressed but also a striving on the part of the total personality toward a re-establishment of unity, harmony, oneness, "health." [56]

And, again,

Nothing could be truer in the light of my own clinical, as well as personal, experience than the proposition that psychotherapy must involve acceptance of the essential friendliness and helpfulness of anxiety, which, under such treatment, will eventually again become ordinary guilt and moral fear, to which realistic re-adjustments and new learning can occur.[57]

Comments.—(1) Mowrer's analysis, in the judgment of this reviewer, illuminates aspects of the problem of anxiety in our culture which have been often overlooked in psychology and psychoanalysis. A good demonstration of part of Mowrer's argument is found in the case of Helen (Chapter 7), who would admit none of her extensive guilt feelings about her extra-marital pregnancy because such an admission would conflict with her aim of being a "rationally" emancipated person. As a consequence her strong feelings of anxiety likewise remained repressed and unamenable to therapy. It would seem that Mowrer is accurate in holding that the repression of guilt feelings, with its concomitant generation of neurotic anxiety, is a prevalent characteristic of certain groups in our culture and in some ways is pervasive of our culture as a whole.[58]

Mowrer's concept likewise checks with certain curious anxiety phenomena which have appeared in the writer's own psychoanalytic practice, phenomena which are inexplicable on the basis of

---

[56] *Ibid.*

[57] *Ibid.*

[58] It has been pointed out above (Chapter 2) that our modern culture since the Renaissance has been characterized by rationalistic emphases, with a tendency to repress "irrational" motivations (guilt feelings being one prime example of the latter). We have placed the term *rationally* in quotation marks in the sentence referring to Helen above, since obviously such a standard has only a pseudo-rational character.

the classical psychoanalytic doctrine of anxiety. The writer noticed that some patients did not repress their sexual, aggressive,
or "antisocial" urges (in Freud's sense) in any discernible way,
but instead repressed their needs and desires to have responsible,
friendly, charitable, and constructive relations with other people.
When aggressive, sexual, or other behavior in egocentric form
emerged in the analysis, these patients showed no anxiety. But
when the opposite needs and desires emerged—i.e., to have responsible and constructive social relations—there appeared much
anxiety, accompanied by the typical reactions of patients who
feel a crucial psychological strategy to be threatened. Such repression of constructive social urges occurs particularly, in the
writer's experience, with defiant, aggressive types of patients.[59]
(In Greek terms, this is repression of love in the *agape,* rather
than the *eros,* sense.)[60] While it is true that many persons have
guilt and anxiety because of fear of expressing their own individual capacities and urges, sexual or otherwise, as Freud originally indicated, it is at the same time true that many have guilt
and anxiety because they have become "autonomous" without
becoming "responsible." [61] It is true, also, that many patients

[59] It will no doubt be agreed that there are multitudes of these defiant, aggressive
types in our culture, but they probably do not frequent psychoanalysts' offices
because our competitive culture (in which, to a considerable extent, the individual
who can aggressively exploit others without conscious guilt feeling is "successful")
supports and "cushions" them to a greater extent than the opposite types. It is
generally the culturally "weak" individuals who get to the psychoanalyst; for in
cultural terms they have the "neurosis" and the successfully aggressive person does
not. It is the nonaggressive types who repress their "defiance," along with their
sexual and hostile inclinations. Perhaps these considerations help us understand why
most psychoanalytic theories have emphasized repression of sex and aggression as
causal for anxiety. Possibly if we could analyze more of the aggressive types—
those "successful" people who never get into an analyst's office—we should find
that Mowrer's concept of anxiety is true on a broad scale.

[60] This is repression of what Adler—in superficial ways, perhaps—termed
"social interest." Adler's viewpoint does have the merit of emphasizing a profoundly important point, namely that the needs of the human being to be a responsible social creature are as fundamental as his needs to express his individualistic,
egoistic urgings. It might be argued that urgings for self-gratification are more
primal than those for social interest and generosity, since the latter develop at a
later stage in the child. On the other hand, there is the fact that the human being
is bound by social ties from its fetal, *in utero* stage onward (as Sullivan points out),
regardless of whether awareness of social ties and their meaning emerges into
consciousness sooner or later.

[61] These terms are placed in quotation marks because, in the final analysis,
genuine autonomy is not possible without corresponding responsibility. Elsewhere
in the present study the author indicates that a failure to achieve either the capacity

carry a heavy burden of irrational guilt and anxiety which is not a product of their own irresponsibility (in the writer's experience, borderline psychotics fit this category most dramatically). This irrational guilt certainly needs to be clarified and relieved in any adequate therapy. But there are other patients with whom, when guilt feeling is reduced in therapy by means of the endeavors of the analyst, it eventuates that the genuine, if confused, insights of the patient into himself have been violated and obscured; and that the most valuable and objectively accurate motivation for change is lost. The writer has known of cases in analysis which have been unsuccessful precisely because the analyst joined the patient in diluting and depreciating guilt feelings. Temporary allaying of anxiety was achieved, of course, but the problems which underlay the anxiety were unsolved and only became buried under a more complicated system of repression.

(2) With regard to Mowrer's use of terms the present writer has considerable question. For example, "repression of the superego" seems a confusing phrase. Freud's term "superego" has been so universally identified with the negative and constrictive aspects of authority that we doubt whether it can be salvaged for a theory which does not see all authority in a negative light (to say nothing of the topological difficulties in the terms "ego," "id," and "superego"). This positive use of the term "superego" might give rise to a misinterpretation of Mowrer's view, namely that he is recommending simply an acceding to cultural mores, as though freedom from anxiety and personality health were best exemplified in the conventional person who follows the "rules" and never runs athwart the cultural patterns. Mowrer is certainly not naïve with respect to the shortcomings of our present culture and would not mean to imply an uncritical acceptance of all aspects of the culture. The present writer believes it would be helpful if Mowrer would distinguish more explicitly between the destructive, negative aspects of our cultural tradition on the one hand and the positive, constructive aspects on the other.[62]

---

for expression of individual endowments or the capacity for social responsibility results in the development of conflict and neurotic anxiety (Chapter 6, Section 2).

[62] This is by no means a simple task, and it can be approached with some hope of success only by methods which include the historical perspective. The writer

(3) It is exceedingly clarifying that Mowrer, in his later contributions, makes a clear distinction between anxiety and fear. It is likewise helpful that he energetically tackles the problem of *Urangst* (which he terms *primal,* as over against *derived,* anxiety). But at the same time he endeavors to limit his use of the term "anxiety" to those instances in which it means "neurotic anxiety," and he seeks to identify all objective ("real") anxiety with fear. While this procedure has pedagogical merits (e.g., it is simple, and it makes the distinction between fear and neurotic anxiety even sharper), it results in logical inconsistencies and obstructs the very important inquiry into *Urangst,* or what the present writer would term "normal" anxiety. *Urangst* persists throughout life, for example in the face of death and other aspects of man's contingency, and the present writer submits that it cannot be intelligibly identified with fear or termed "neurotic." Does not *Urangst,* plus the "primal" anxiety of the infant occurring long before the capacity for repression which is prerequisite for neurotic anxiety, require that we retain a category of normal anxiety? [63]

4. Freud's Evolving Theories of Anxiety

Though others, like Kierkegaard, had preceded Freud in recognizing the crucial importance of the problem of anxiety in understanding human behavior, Freud was the first in the scientific tradition to see the fundamental significance of the problem.[64] More specifically, he directed attention to anxiety as the

---

has endeavored in Chapter 5 of this work to make a beginning in this direction by tracing the sources in modern culture of the generally accepted apotheosis of competitive individualistic success. From a historical perspective, it becomes clear that Freud was accepting the common prejudice of our culture since the Renaissance, that the triumphant individual who was able to achieve his own ends of gratification, to a large extent despite society, was the healthy personality. This is the psychological form of what Tawney, speaking from the economic viewpoint, has called the apotheosis of the individual's self-interest and "natural instinct" for aggrandizement which has characterized industrialism in the past several centuries. This is one example of how the ideals accepted in practice by our modern culture run counter to the long-time ethical traditions of the culture.

[63] "Normal" anxiety and *Urangst* are discussed in this study in Chapter 6, Section 1, below.

[64] Freud stands in the line of those explorers of human nature of the nineteenth century—including Kierkegaard, Nietzsche, Schopenhauer—who rediscovered the

basic question for the understanding of emotional and psychological disorders; anxiety, he notes in his later essay devoted to this topic, is the "fundamental phenomenon and the central problem of neurosis." [65]

Students of dynamic psychology would no doubt agree that Freud is the pre-eminent explorer of the psychology of anxiety, that he both showed the way and gave many of the most efficacious techniques for the understanding of the problem, and that therefore his work is of classic importance even though it is now widely believed that many of his conclusions must be qualified and reinterpreted.   To study Freud on anxiety is to become aware that his thinking on the topic was in process of *evolution* throughout his life.   His theories of anxiety underwent many minor changes as well as one revolutionary change.   Since anxiety is so fundamental a question, it cannot be given any simple answers; and Freud significantly confesses in his last writings that he is still presenting hypotheses rather than a "final solution" to the problem.[66]   Therefore we shall endeavor in this survey not only to present Freud's central insights and his innumerable observations into the mechanics of anxiety, but also to plot the *directions* in which his concept of anxiety was evolving.

significance of the irrational, dynamic, "unconscious" elements in personality. (Cf. Thomas Mann, *Freud, Goethe, Wagner* [New York, 1937].)   These aspects of personality had tended to be overlooked—and in many ways suppressed—by the rationalistic preoccupations of most Western thinking since the Renaissance (Cf. Chapter 2).   Though Kierkegaard, Nietzsche, and Freud attacked the rationalism of the nineteenth century for different reasons, they had in common the conviction that the traditional modes of thought omitted elements vital for the understanding of personality.   The so-called irrational springs of human behavior had been left outside the accepted area of scientific investigation or lumped under the so-called instincts.   Freud's reaction against the endeavors of academic medicine of his day to explain anxiety by "describing the nerve-pathways by which the excitations travel" and his conviction that the methods of academic psychology of his day yielded little or no help in the dynamic understanding of human behavior which he sought can be understood, it seems to this writer, in this light.   At the same time, Freud felt himself to be an enthusiastic champion of science in his avowed intention of making the "irrational" elements in behavior explicable in terms of his broader concept of scientific method.   That he carried over into his work some of the presuppositions of the nineteenth century traditional (physical) science is illustrated in his libido theory, which will be commented on below.

[65] *The problem of anxiety*, trans. H. A. Bunker (American ed.; New York, 1936), p. 111.

[66] *New introductory lectures in psychoanalysis* (New York, 1933), p. 113.

To begin with, Freud makes the customary distinction between fear and anxiety which we have already noted in the work of Goldstein and others. Freud holds that in fear the attention is directed to the object, whereas anxiety refers to the condition of the individual and "ignores the object." [67] To him the more significant distinction is between objective (what we would term "normal") and neurotic anxiety. The former, "real" anxiety, is the reaction to an external danger; he conceives it as a natural, rational, and useful function. This objective anxiety is an expression of the "instincts of self-preservation." "The occasions of it, i.e., the objects or situations about which anxiety is felt, will obviously depend to a great extent upon the state of the person's knowledge and feeling of power regarding the outer world." [68] This "anxious readiness," as Freud terms objective anxiety, is an expedient function, since it protects the individual from being surprised by sudden threats (frights) for which he is unprepared. Objective anxiety does not in itself constitute a clinical problem. But any development of anxiety beyond the initial prompting to survey the danger and make the best preparation for flight is inexpedient: it paralyzes action. "The *anxious readiness* therefore seems to me the expedient element, and the *development* of anxiety the inexpedient element, in what we call anxiety or dread." [69] It is, of course, this development of anxiety in amounts out of proportion to the actual dan-

---

[67] *General introduction to psychoanalysis,* p. 343. Beyond this brief distinction, Freud does not—either in the chapter on anxiety in the *General introduction to psychoanalysis* or in his later *Problem of anxiety*—throw much illumination on the problem of fear as such. He treats Stanley Hall's list of allegedly innate fears, such as fear of darkness, fear of bodies of water, of thunder, etc., as phobias, which are by definition expressions of neurotic anxiety. In a summary of Freud's views in W. Healy, A. F. Bronner, and A. M. Bowers, *The structure and meaning of psychoanalysis* (New York, 1930), p. 366, a distinction between real fear and neurotic fear is made which is parallel to Freud's distinction between real and neurotic anxiety. Real fear, it is stated, is the reaction to an objective danger, whereas neurotic fear is the "fear of an impulse claim." Freud is interpreted as holding that "three practically universal childhood fears"—fear of being alone, fear of darkness, and the fear of strangers—arise out of the "unconscious Ego's fear of loss of the protecting object, namely, the mother"—*Ibid.* This is synonymous with his definition of the source of anxiety in similar situations; apparently the terms "fear" and "anxiety" are here used interchangeably, the former being the term for the emergence of anxiety in specific form.

[68] *General introduction to psychoanalysis,* p. 342.

[69] *Ibid.,* p. 343.

ger, or even in situations where no ostensible external danger exists, which constitutes the problem of neurotic anxiety.

Freud's First Theory: Anxiety as Repressed Libido.[70]— How is it possible, Freud asks in his early writing, to bring the phenomenon of neurotic anxiety into logical relationship with objective anxiety?   In the endeavor to answer this question he cites his observations in clinical work.   He had noticed that patients who exhibit inhibitions or symptoms of various sorts are often remarkably free from overt anxiety.   In phobias, for example, the patient exhibits an intense concentration of anxiety on one point in his environment—namely, the object of his phobia—but he is free from anxiety at other points in his environment.   In obsessional acts, likewise, the patient seems to be free of anxiety so long as he is permitted to carry out his act in unmolested fashion, but as soon as he is prevented from performing the obsessional act, intense anxiety appears.   So, Freud reasoned understandably, some substitutive process must be occurring, i.e., the symptom must in some way be taking the place of the anxiety.   He observed at the same time that his patients who experienced continual sexual excitation which was ungratified— he cites cases of coitus interruptus, for one example—also exhibited a good deal of anxiety.   Hence, he concluded, the substitutive process occurring must be the interchange of anxiety, or anxiety-equivalents in the form of symptoms, for unexpressed libido.   He writes, "libidinal excitation disappears and anxiety appears in place of it, both in the form of expectant dread and in that of anxiety attacks and anxiety-equivalents." [71]   Looking back from a later date on the observations which led to this theory, Freud remarks, "I found that certain sexual practices, such as coitus interruptus, frustrated excitement, enforced abstinence, give rise to outbreaks of anxiety and a general predisposition to anxiety—which may be induced whenever, therefore, sexual excitation is inhibited, frustrated, or diverted in the course of its discharge in gratification.   Since sexual excitement

70 The first and second theories have to do with the mechanics, as contrasted with the *origins,* of anxiety.

71 *General introduction to psychoanalysis,* p. 348.

is the expression of libidinal instinctual impulses, it did not seem rash to suppose that through the influence of such disturbances the libido became converted into anxiety." [72]

The first theory, therefore, states that when libido is repressed, it becomes transformed into anxiety, and then reappears as free-floating anxiety or as an anxiety-equivalent (symptom). "Anxiety is thus general current coin for which all the affects are exchanged, or can be exchanged, when the corresponding ideational content is under repression." [73] When an affect is repressed, its fate is "to be converted into anxiety, no matter what quality of affect it would otherwise have been had it run a normal course." [74] The source of the child's anxiety at missing his mother, or at the appearance of strange people (which represents the same danger situation as missing the mother, since the presence of the strange people signifies the mother's absence), lies in the fact that the child cannot then expend his libido towards the mother, and the libido is "discharged through being converted into anxiety." [75]

Recalling that objective anxiety is a flight-reaction to external danger, Freud asks what the individual is afraid of in neurotic anxiety. The latter, he answers, represents a flight from the demands of one's own libido. In neurotic anxiety "the ego is attempting a flight from the demands of its libido, and is treating this internal danger as if it were an external one." "Repression is an attempt at flight on the part of the ego from libido which it feels to be dangerous: the phobia (for example) may be compared to a fortification against the outer danger which now stands for the dreaded libido." [76] To summarize Freud's first theory of neurotic anxiety: the individual experiences libidinal impulses which he interprets as dangerous, the libidinal impulses are repressed, they become automatically converted into anxiety, and they find their expression as free-floating anxiety or as symptoms which are anxiety-equivalents.

---

[72] *The problem of anxiety* (American ed.; New York, 1936), pp. 51-52.
[73] *General introduction to psychoanalysis*, p. 350.
[74] *Ibid.*, p. 355.
[75] *Ibid.*, p. 353.
[76] *Ibid.*, p. 355.

This first endeavor of Freud's to formulate a theory of anxiety is undeniably based initially on observable clinical phenomena: everyone has noticed that when strong and persistent desires are held in check or repressed, the individual will often exhibit chronic restlessness or various forms of anxiety. But this is a phenomenological description, which is a quite different thing from a *causal explanation* of anxiety—as Freud himself was later to acknowledge. Furthermore, the phenomenon of sexual repression resulting in anxiety is by no means consistent; the "frank libertine," as Mowrer puts it, may be a very anxious person, and many well-clarified persons may bear a great deal of sexual abstinence without anxiety. On the positive side, this first theory does have the value of emphasizing the intrapsychic locus of neurotic anxiety. But the suggested mechanism of automatic conversion of libido—an attractive concept, perhaps chiefly because it fits chemical-physiological analogies so handily —is highly dubious, as Freud himself was later to see. Some of the inadequacies of the first theory can best be seen by following the clinical observations and reasoning which led Freud to reject it.

Freud's Second Theory: Anxiety as the Cause of Repressions.—On later analysis of patients with phobias and other anxiety symptoms, Freud found that a quite different process with respect to anxiety was occurring. A new theory was made necessary, too, by his increasing emphasis on the role of the ego, which had played only an auxiliary part in the first theory.[77]

He demonstrates the analysis which led to the new theory with the case of Hans, the five-year-old boy who refused to go out into the street (the inhibition) because of his phobia of horses (the symptom). Hans had considerable ambivalence toward his father, which Freud explains in classical Oedipus fashion. The little boy felt strong desires for the love of his mother and consequent jealousy and hatred of his father. But at the same time he was devoted to his father in so far as his mother did not enter the picture as a cause of dissension. Because of

---

[77] "The division of the mental personality into a super-ego, ego and id . . . has forced us to take up a new position with regard to the problem of anxiety."—*New introductory lectures*, p. 118.

the father's strength, the aggressive impulses in Hans would cue off anxiety. The hostility carries with it frightening possibilities of retaliation, and it also involves the boy in continuous ambivalence toward a father to whom he is at the same time devoted; hence the hostility and related anxiety undergo repression. These affects are then displaced upon horses. Without going into detail about the mechanism of phobia formation, we wish only to make Freud's point that the phobia of horses is a symptomatic representation of Hans's fears of his father. Freud interprets this fear in typical castration terms: the fear of the bite of the horse is fear of having the penis bitten off. "This substitute formation [i.e., the phobia] has two patent advantages: first, that it avoids the conflict due to ambivalence, for the father is an object who is at the same time loved; and secondly, that it allows the ego to prevent any further development of anxiety." [78]

The crucial point in this analysis is that the *ego perceives the danger*. This perception arouses anxiety (Freud speaks of the "ego" arousing anxiety), and as an endeavor to avoid the anxiety the ego effects the repression of the impulses and desires which would lead the person into danger. "It is not the repression that creates the anxiety," Freud now remarks against his first theory, "but the anxiety is there first and creates the repression!" [79] The same process holds true for other symptoms and inhibitions: the ego perceives the danger signal, and the symptoms and inhibitions are then created in the endeavor to avoid the anxiety. We may now, writes Freud, take the new view that the "ego is the real locus of anxiety, and reject the earlier conception that the cathectic energy of the repressed impulse automatically becomes converted into anxiety." [80]

A qualification is now also made by Freud in his earlier statement that the danger feared in neurotic anxiety is that simply of inner instinctual impulses. Speaking of Hans, he writes, "But what sort of anxiety can it be? It can only be fear of a threatening external danger; that is to say, objective anxiety. It is

---

[78] *The problem of anxiety*, p. 80.
[79] *New introductory lectures*, p. 119.
[80] *The problem of anxiety*, p. 22.

true that the boy is afraid of the demands of his libido, in this case of his love for his mother; so that this is really an instance of neurotic anxiety. But this being in love seems to him to be an internal danger, which he must avoid by renouncing his object, only because it involves an external danger-situation [retaliation, castration]." Though this interrelationship of external and internal factors was found by Freud in every case he investigated during this later period, he confesses "that we were not prepared to find that the internal instinctual danger was only a half-way house to an external and real danger-situation." [81]

Many students of anxiety feel that this second theory, with its emphasis on the ego function, makes possible a more adequate description of the mechanics of anxiety. Symonds points out that the second theory is more compatible with other psychological approaches to the problem.[82] In similar vein, Horney holds that whereas the first theory was essentially "physiochemical," the second is "more psychological." In any case, the second hypothesis evidences some clear and significant trends in Freud's understanding of anxiety, which will be discussed below.

Origins of Anxiety.—Freud states that the capacity for anxiety is innate in the organism, that it is part of the self-preservation instinct, and that it is phylogenetically inherited. In his words, "we ascribe to the child a strong tendency to objective anxiety and should regard it as only practical if this apprehensiveness had been transmitted by inheritance." [83] Specific anxi-

---

[81] *New introductory lectures*, p. 120. This interrelationship between internal and external factors, in Freud's viewpoint, can be demonstrated in terms of conditioned-response psychology. If Hans were merely afraid of his father's punishment (as an external danger), Freud would not call his anxiety neurotic. The neurotic element enters because of the ego's perception of the danger inherent in the internal instinctual promptings (Hans's hostility toward his father, for example). Now it is well known that inner promptings in the individual's experience can come easily to stand for external, objective dangers. If hostility toward the parent is met by retaliation, the child will soon be conditioned to experience anxiety whenever the hostile promptings arise intrapsychically.

It is questionable whether one ever encounters purely "internal" or "external" factors in a given organism's behavior and whether, therefore, some falsification is not involved in the use of these terms. This query will be dealt with more fully below.

[82] Symonds, *The dynamics of human adjustment, op. cit.*

[83] *General introduction to psychoanalysis*, p. 353. Whether capacities or traits can logically be said to be "phylogenetically inherited" is, of course, questionable. See Goldstein in Chapter 3 of this book. It is doubtful to the present writer

eties, however, are taught: of genuine "objective anxieties"—
by which Freud means fear of climbing on window sills, fear of
fire, etc.—"the child seems to bring very little into the world."
And "it is entirely due to training that real anxiety does eventually awake in him." [84] We take this to mean that in Freud's
viewpoint the tendency to, or capacity for, anxiety is part of the
individual's innate capacity, whereas the specific forms this
anxiety will take are due to learning.

Beyond the above general statement, Freud finds the origin
of anxiety in the *birth trauma* and *fear of castration*. These two
concepts are interwoven and progressively reinterpreted in his
writings. The *affect* which comes with anxiety, Freud holds in
his early lectures, is a reproduction and repetition of some particular very significant previous experience. This he believed to
be the birth experience—"an experience which involves just
such a concatenation of painful feelings, of discharges and excitation, and of bodily sensations, as to have become a prototype for
all occasions on which life is endangered, ever after to be re-
produced again in us as the dread or 'anxiety' condition." He
adds, foreshadowing his later broadening of the birth concept,
"It is very suggestive too that the first anxiety state arose on the
occasion of the separation from the mother." [85] The child's having anxiety at the appearance of strange people and its fears of
darkness and loneliness (which he terms the first phobias of the
child) have their origin in dread lest the child be separated from
his mother.

It is an important question, in reviewing Freud's later writings, how far he was considering the birth experience as a literal
source of anxiety, to be cued off by later danger situations, and
how far he regarded it as a prototype in a symbolic sense, i.e.,
symbolic for separation from the loved object. Since he places
great emphasis on castration as the specific source of anxiety

---

whether the phylogenetic concept is useful except in terms of transmission via
culture.

[84] *Ibid.* Freud takes maturation into account: "A certain predisposition to
anxiety on the part of the infant is indubitable. It is not at its maximum immediately after birth, to diminish gradually thereafter, but first makes its appearance
later on with the progress of psychic development, and persists over a certain period
of childhood."—*The problem of anxiety*, p. 98.

[85] *General introduction to psychoanalysis*, p. 344.

underlying many neuroses, he is at pains to explain how castration and the birth experience are interrelated. We shall, therefore, now investigate how he progressively reinterprets and interrelates castration and the birth experience page by page in his chief essay on anxiety.[86] Speaking of the danger underlying the development of phobias, conversion hysteria, and compulsion neuroses, he notes, "in all these, we assume castration anxiety as the motive force behind the struggles of the ego." [87] Even fear of death is an analogue of castration, since no one has actually experienced death but everyone has experienced a castration-like experience in the loss of the mother's breast in weaning. He then speaks of the danger of castration "as a reaction to a loss, to a separation," of which the prototype is the birth experience. But he is critical of Rank's too specific deduction of anxiety and consequent neurosis from the severity of the birth trauma. In reaction against Rank, he holds that the danger situation in birth is "the loss of the loved (longed for) person," and the "most basic anxiety of all, the 'primal anxiety' of birth, arises in connection with separation from the mother." [88] Castration he now relates to the loss of the mother by Ferenczi's reasoning: the loss of the genital deprives the individual of the means of later reunion with the mother (or mother substitute). Fear of castration later develops into dread of conscience, i.e., social anxiety; now the ego is afraid of the anger, punishment, loss of love of the superego. The final transformation of this fear of the superego consists of death anxiety.[89]

Thus we are presented with a hierarchy: fear of loss of the mother at birth, loss of the penis in the phallic period, loss of the approval of the superego (social and moral approval) in the latency period, and finally loss of life, all of which go back to the prototype, the separation from the mother. All later anxiety occasions "signify in some sense a separation from the mother," [90] which must mean that castration stands for the loss of a prized object of value, in the same sense as birth stands for

86 *The problem of anxiety.*
87 *Ibid.,* p. 75.
88 *Ibid.,* pp. 99-100.
89 *Ibid.,* p. 105.
90 *Ibid.,* p. 123.

the loss of the mother. Another datum which impelled him to interpret castration in a nonliteral fashion was the fact that the female sex, "certainly more predisposed to neurosis," as he remarks, cannot suffer literal castration because of the absence of a penis to begin with. In the case of women, he states that anxiety arises over fear of the loss of the love of the object (mother, husband) rather than loss of the penis.

Though one cannot be certain as to how far Freud was regarding the birth experience and castration literally and how far symbolically, we submit that the *trend* in Freud's reasoning cited above is toward an increasingly symbolic interpretation. To the present writer this is a positive trend. With respect to castration, there may legitimately be considerable question as to whether literal castration is a source of anxiety on any wide scale. We suggest that castration is a culturally determined symbol around which neurotic anxiety may cluster.[91]

With respect to the birth trauma, we regard Freud's increasingly symbolic interpretation also as a positive trend. It is still an open question in experimental and clinical psychology how far the severity of the birth experience is a literal source of later anxiety.[92] But even if the actual birth experience cannot be accepted as the source of anxiety in literal fashion, it would

---

[91] Since castration and other aspects of the Oedipus situation are so important in Freudian discussions of anxiety, another question may be raised. Does not neurotic anxiety arise around castration or the Oedipus situation only when there are prior disturbances in the relationship between parents and child? To illustrate in the case of Hans, are not the boy's jealousy and consequent hatred of his father themselves the product of anxiety? Apparently Hans had exclusive needs for his mother, needs which her loving the father would threaten. Are not such needs (which may fairly be termed excessive) in themselves an outgrowth of anxiety? It may well be true that the conflict and anxiety leading to the particular phobic construction which Freud analyzes are specifically related to ambivalence and hostility toward the father. But we submit that this hostility and ambivalence would not have developed except as Hans was already in a disturbed relationship with his mother and father which produced anxiety and led to exclusive demands for his mother. One can understandably hold that every child experiences clashes with its parents in its development of individuality and autonomy (*vide* Kierkegaard, Goldstein, etc.), but in the normal child (defined as the child in a relationship to its parents which is not characterized by pronounced anxiety) such clashes do not produce neurotic defenses and symptoms. It is here suggested, *in fine,* that Oedipus situations and castration fears do not emerge as *problems*—i.e., do not become the foci of neurotic anxiety—unless prior anxieties already exist in the family constellation.

[92] For discussion of the possible relation between birth and anxiety, see Symonds, *op. cit.*

certainly be widely agreed that the infant's early relations with its mother, which so intimately condition both its biological and psychological development, are of the greatest significance for later anxiety patterns.   Hence the present writer wishes to emphasize that facet of Freud's thought which holds that *anxiety has its source, as far as a primal source is reactivated in later neurotic anxiety, in the fear of premature loss of or separation from the mother (or mother's love), and thence fear of the loss of subsequent values.*   Indeed, in the development and clinical application of Freudian theory, this interpretation is widely made, often in the form of the primal source of anxiety as being rejection by the mother.[93]

Trends in Freud's Theories of Anxiety.—Since we are concerned with the evolution of Freud's understanding of anxiety, we shall summarize certain directions in which his thinking was moving from his earlier to his later writings on anxiety.[94]   *First, in respect to the role of libido in anxiety.*   There is evidenced in Freud a trend toward removing the libido theory from the primary position in his understanding of anxiety to a secondary position.   Whereas the earlier theory of anxiety was almost wholly a description of what happened to libido (it was an "exclusively economic interpretation," Freud remarks), in his later writing he states that he is now not so much interested in the fate of the libido.   His second theory still presupposes the libido concept, however: the energy which becomes anxiety is still

---

93 Cf. D. M. Levy: "[The] . . . most potent of all influences on social behavior is derived from the primary social experience with the mother."—Maternal overprotection, *Psychiatry*, 1, 561 ff. Grinker and Spiegel, whose viewpoint represents a development of Freudianism, point out in their study of anxiety in combat airmen that fear or anxiety will not develop unless the value or object that is threatened in combat is "something that is loved, highly prized, and held very dear." This may be a person (one's self or a loved one) or a value like an abstract idea.—*Men under stress* (Philadelphia, 1946), p. 120. We here suggest, in line with Freud's discussion above, that the primal form of the prized person is the mother and that the capacity to prize other persons and values is a development from this first prototype.

94 This approach—plotting the trends in Freud's thinking—is fitting in the respect that Freud's thinking was germinal; it was changing and developing through most of his life. This makes dogmatism about his views of very dubious worth; but the changing nature of his views also makes for ambiguity in his writings. For example, at times Freud writes as though he had completely rejected his first theory, but at other times as though he believed it compatible, in a subsumed position, with the second theory.

libido withdrawn from the cathexis of repressed libido, the ego performs its repressive functions by means of "desexualized" libido, and the danger faced (to which anxiety is the reaction) is the "economic disturbance brought about by an increase in stimuli demanding some disposition be made of them." [95] Though Freud retained the libido concept through all his writings, the trend is *from* a description of anxiety as an automatic conversion of libido *to* a description of the individual perceiving a danger and utilizing libido (energy) in coping with this danger. This trend accounts partially for the fact that Freud's second theory presents a more adequate description of the mechanism of anxiety. But the present writer questions whether the secondary emphasis on the libido theory in Freud's later writings on anxiety does not confuse the problem by its emphasis on the individual as a carrier of instinctual or libidinal needs which must be gratified.[96] The view taken in the present study (see Chapter 6 below) involves carrying the above trend in Freud's writing further in the respect that libido or energy factors are seen not as given economic quantities which must be expressed, but as functions of the values or goals the individual seeks to attain as he relates himself to his world.

A second trend is seen in Freud's conception of how anxiety symptoms are formed. This trend is shown most vividly in the reversal of his early view that repression causes anxiety to the later view that anxiety causes repression. What this shift implies is that anxiety and its symptoms are seen not as merely the outcome of a simple intrapsychic process, but *as arising out of the individual's endeavor to avoid danger situations in his world of relationships.*

Another trend, with implications similar to that above, is indicated in Freud's endeavor to overcome the *dichotomy between "internal" and "external"* factors in the occasions of anxi-

---

[95] *The problem of anxiety,* p. 100.

[96] The present writer agrees with those critics of the Freudian libido theory who hold that the theory is a carry-over from nineteenth century physiochemical forms of thought. As an example of this physiochemical form of Freud's thinking, the translator of Freud's latest work makes an analogy between libido and an "electric charge." (*An outline of psychoanalysis,* trans. J. Strachey [New York, 1949], p. 23.)

ety. Whereas in the earlier theory neurotic anxiety was viewed as fear of one's own libidinous impulses, Freud later saw that the libidinous impulses are dangerous because the expression of them would involve an external danger. The external danger was of only minor importance in the first theory when anxiety could be viewed as an automatic intrapsychic transformation of libido, but it became a pressing problem to him in the cases he was analyzing in his later periods when he saw that the internal danger—danger from one's own impulses—arose from the fact that the individual was struggling against an "external and real danger-situation." This same trend toward seeing the anxious individual in a struggle with his environment (past or present) is indicated in the increasing prominence in Freud's later writings of the phrase "danger situation" rather than merely "danger." In his early writings we are informed that the symptom is developed to protect the individual from the demands of his own libido. But in developing his second theory he writes, "One might say, then, that symptoms are created in order to avoid the development of anxiety, but such a formulation does not go below the surface. It is more accurate to say that symptoms are created in order to avoid the *danger situation* of which anxiety sounds the alarm." [97] Later in this same essay he notes, "We have become convinced also that instinctual demands often become an (internal) danger only because of the fact that their gratification would bring about an external danger—because, therefore, this internal danger represents an external one." [98] Therefore the symptom is not merely a protection against inner impulses: "For our point of view the relationships between anxiety and symptom prove to be less close than was supposed, the result of our having interposed between the two the factor of the danger situation." [99] It may seem at first blush that we are laboring a minor point in emphasizing this shift from

---

[97] *The problem of anxiety*, p. 86. This is the point the present writer makes with respect to the function of symptoms (see Chapters 3 and 8).

[98] *Ibid.*, p. 152.

[99] *Ibid.*, p. 112. In some interpretations of Freudian theory the first emphasis of Freud is still made. Cf. Healy, Bronner, and Bowers: "Symptom-formation . . . is now regarded as a defense against or a flight from anxiety" (*The structure and meaning of psychoanalysis*, p. 411). Cf. the view advanced in Chapter 3 above, that the symptom is a protection from the *anxiety-creating situation.*

"danger" to "danger situation," but we believe that it is by no means an unimportant issue or a mere question of terminology. *It involves the whole difference between seeing anxiety as a more or less exclusively intrapsychic process, on the one hand, and the view that anxiety arises out of the individual's endeavor to relate himself to his environment, on the other.* In this second view intrapsychic processes are significant because they are reactions to, and means of coping with, the difficulties in the interpersonal world. The trend in Freud is toward a more organismic view—*organismic* being here defined as connoting a view of the person in his constellation of relationships. But it is well known that Freud never developed this trend to its logical conclusions in terms of a consistent organismic and cultural viewpoint. We believe he was prevented from doing so by both his libido theory and his topological concept of personality.

A final trend in Freud's thinking on anxiety is shown in his increased emphasis on the *topology of the psyche,* arising out of his division of the personality into superego, ego, and id. This makes it possible for him to center more of his attention on anxiety as being a function of the way the individual, via the ego, *perceives and interprets the danger situation.* He remarks that the phrase he employed in his earlier theory, "anxiety of the id," is infelicitous since neither id nor superego can be said to perceive anxiety. While this trend, like the others mentioned above, makes Freud's later concepts of anxiety more adequate and more understandable psychologically, we raise the question as to whether this topology, when employed in any strict sense, does not confuse the problem of anxiety. For example, Freud speaks in his later writing of the ego "creating" repression after it perceives the danger situation. Does not repression involve unconscious ("id," in topological terms) functions as well? Indeed, any symptom formation which is effective must involve elements which are excluded from awareness, as Freud himself, despite his topology, would be the first to admit. We suggest that repressions and symptoms can best be viewed as the organism's means of adjusting to a danger situation. While it is helpful and necessary to see in given cases that certain elements are in awareness and others are excluded from awareness, the strict application of the topology makes not only for inconsistencies in the theory but also shifts the attention away from the real locus of the problem, namely the organism and its danger situation.[100]

Another application of his topology made by Freud which reveals this problem is seen in his discussion of helplessness in anxiety. He holds that in neurotic anxiety the ego is made helpless by its conflict with the id and superego. While the present writer would agree that in all neurotic anxiety the individual is engaged in intrapsychic conflict, a question arises as to whether this conflict, rather than being a lack of accord among ego, superego, and id, is not really a conflict between contradictory values and goals the individual seeks to attain in relating himself to his interpersonal world. It is to be granted that certain poles of these conflicts will be in awareness and others will be repressed, and it is also to be granted that in neurotic anxiety previous conflicts in the individual's life-history are reactivated. But to our mind *both the present and the previous conflicts are to be seen not as between different "parts" of the personality but as between mutually exclusive goals made necessary by the individual's endeavor to adapt to a danger situation.*

It is unnecessary to labor the point of Freud's far-reaching contributions to the understanding of anxiety. For the purposes of the present discussion, these contributions consist chiefly in the many-sided illumination he shed upon symptom formation, in his emergent concern with the primal source of anxiety in the separation of the child from its mother, and in his emphasis on the subjective and intrapsychic aspects of neurotic anxiety.

---

100 The confusing implications of Freud's topology are seen in his tendencies to think of the ego and the id as literally geographical regions in the personality. In his last writing, *Outline of psychoanalysis* (New York, 1949), he refers to his "topographical" viewpoint, speaks of the ego as "developed out of the cortical layer of the id" (p. 110), and uses such phrases as "mental regions" (p. 15) and "the outermost cortex of the ego" (p. 41). The present author believes that the equating of neurological areas with psychological functions can be done only very loosely; the two are never literally equivalent, as we have endeavored to show in Chapter 3. The tendency to locate the "ego function" geographically reminds the present author of the endeavors of Descartes and others of the seventeenth century to locate man's "soul" in the pineal gland at the base of the brain! Again, we can do no better than to quote Freud himself; the essential thing is to grasp psychological facts psychologically.

5. Rank: Anxiety and Individuation

Otto Rank's view of anxiety stems logically from his belief that the central problem in human development is *individuation*. He conceived of the life history of a human being as an endless series of experiences of *separation,* each such experience presenting the possibility of greater autonomy for the individual. Birth is the first and most dramatic event in this continuum of separations, but the same psychological experience occurs, in greater or lesser degree, when the child is weaned, when it goes off to school, when the adult separates from his single state in favor of marriage, and at all steps in personality development until ultimate separation in death. Now, for Rank, *anxiety is the apprehension involved in these separations.* Anxiety is experienced in the breaking of previous situations of relative unity with, and dependence upon, the personal environment: this is anxiety in the face of the need to live as an autonomous individual. But anxiety is also experienced if the individual refuses to separate from his immediate position of security: this is anxiety lest one lose one's individual autonomy.[101]

Rank's understanding of anxiety was influenced by his famous studies of the birth trauma.[102] The symbol of birth has basic significance in Rank's interpretation of psychological events all through the life career of an individual, even though his belief that the infant feels anxiety at the time of parturition is debatable. He held that the "child experiences his first feeling of fear in the act of birth," an apprehension which Rank termed "fear in the face of life." [103] This primal anxiety is anxiety at being separated from the previous situation of wholeness with the mother and being projected into the radically different state of individual existence in the world. Now, we would agree

---

[101] The concept of the "separation of the individual from the whole" has a long history in philosophy, running back to Anaximander in the preclassical period in ancient Greece. It would be agreed that it is a fruitful concept psychologically as well as philosophically, and that Rank has much empirical, experiential data on which to base his psychology.

[102] *The trauma of birth* (English trans.; New York, 1929). (Original publication in German, 1924.)

[103] Otto Rank, *Will therapy; an analysis of the therapeutic process in terms of relationship* (authorized trans. from the German; New York, 1936), p. 168.

that our adult minds can imagine the birth experience to be filled with portentous possibilities, certainly enough to engender profound anxiety. But what the infant being born experiences, or whether it experiences anything which can be called a "feeling," is a different question, and in the judgment of this writer an entirely open question. It seems much more accurate to speak of "potential" anxiety at birth rather than actual, and to treat birth as a symbol. Indeed, it is clear from Rank's later writings (with the exception of such sentences as that quoted above) that he does employ the birth experience symbolically.[104] What Rank insists upon is that anxiety exists in the infant *before* any specific content attaches to it. "The individual comes to the world with fear," he remarks, "and this inner fear exists independently of outside threats, whether of a sexual or other nature." Later in the development of the child the "inner fear" becomes attached to outer experiences of threat, a process which serves to "objectify and make partial the general inner fear." [105] Thus Rank distinguishes between the primal undifferentiated apprehension, which in this study we term "anxiety," and the later specific, objectified forms of apprehension, which we term "fears." [106]

The primal anxiety present in the infant, says Rank, takes two forms throughout the individual's life career, namely *life fear* and *death fear*. These two terms, unspecific as they seem at first glance, refer in Rank's thought to the two aspects of individuation which are shown in an infinite variety of forms in

---

104 For example, Rank held that the patient goes through a birth experience at separation from the analyst in the end phases of psychotherapy. *Ibid.*, p. xii.

105 *Ibid.*, pp. 172-73. This attaching of primal anxiety to specific experiences in the form of fears he describes as "therapeutic," implying that the individual can deal more effectively with specific threats.

106 A confusion is presented by the fact that Rank uses the term *fear* to stand for both fear and anxiety. But it seems clear in the contexts of his writing as well as in the phrases themselves that what he refers to as "fear of life," "inner fear," and the "primal fear" of newborn infants is what other authors such as Freud, Horney, and Goldstein call anxiety. For example, he describes primal fear as the "undifferentiated feeling of insecurity," a phrase which is certainly a sound definition of early anxiety. Indeed, it seems to this writer that such general phrases as "life fear" and "death fear" have no meaning unless they refer to anxiety. One can be afraid one's neighbor will shoot one, but persistent "death fear" is a different matter. The reader will make better sense of Rank's discussion in this connection if he reads "anxiety" in most cases where Rank writes "fear."

every person's experience. The life fear is the anxiety at every new possibility of autonomous activity. It is the "fear of having to live as an isolated individual." [107] Such anxiety occurs, Rank held, when a person apprehends creative capacities within himself; the actualization of these capacities means creating new constellations, not only in works of art (in the cases of artists) but also in new forms of relationship with others and new integration within one's self. Such creative possibilities bring the threat of separation from previous forms of relationship. It is, of course, not coincidental that this concept of anxiety in creative activity is presented by the psychologist who has perhaps done the most penetrating work on the psychology of the artist. It is a concept we have already seen in Kierkegaard and one which is presented in classical form in the Greek myth of Prometheus.[108]

The death fear in Rank's thought is the opposite to the above. Whereas the life fear is anxiety at "going forward," becoming an individual, the death fear is anxiety at "going backward," losing individuality. It is anxiety at being swallowed up in the whole, or in more psychological language, anxiety lest one stagnate in dependent symbiotic relationships.

Rank believed that each person experiences these two forms of anxiety in polarity. "Between these two fear possibilities, these poles of fear, the individual is thrown back and forth all his life, which accounts for the fact that we have not been able to trace fear back to a single root, or to overcome it therapeutically." [109] The neurotic is he who has never been able to manage these two forms of anxiety in balance: his anxiety in the face of individual autonomy keeps him from affirming his own capacities, and his anxiety in the face of dependency on others renders him incapable of giving himself in friendship and love. Hence many neurotics are characterized by a great need to appear inde-

---

[107] Rank, *op. cit.,* p. 175.

[108] Cf. Kierkegaard in Chapter 2 and Fromm in Chapter 5.

[109] *Will therapy,* p. 175. Apparently Rank means it is not possible to overcome *all* anxiety therapeutically; he indicates clearly that neurotic anxiety may be overcome. As regards normal anxiety, he would hold that it may be *surmounted* in the sense that the healthy individual moves ahead despite anxiety. By creativity one surmounts normal anxiety and overcomes neurotic anxiety.

pendent but at the same time an actual excessive dependence. Because of his exaggerated anxiety the neurotic engages in widespread constraint of his impulsive and spontaneous activity; and as a consequence of this constraint, Rank held, the neurotic experiences excessive guilt feelings. The healthy, creative individual, on the other hand, is he who can surmount his anxiety sufficiently to affirm his individual capacities, negotiate the crises of psychological separation necessary for growth, and reunite himself with others in progressively new ways.

Though Rank's chief interest is in individuation, he is well aware that the individual can realize himself only in interaction with his culture, or, as he phrases it, in participation in "collective values." Indeed, the characteristics of the prevalent neurotic type in our culture—characteristics which he describes as "a feeling of inferiority and inadequacy, fear of responsibility and guilt feeling, in addition to a hyper-selfconsciousness"—are to be understood as products of a culture in which "collective values including religion have been overthrown and the individual has been pushed to the fore." [110] The loss of collective values in our culture (or, as we would say, the chaotic condition of social values) is not only a cause of neurotic anxiety but sets for the individual an especially difficult task in overcoming neurotic anxiety.

Many readers will find Rank's terminology and his dualistic mode of thought uncongenial. But, in the present writer's opinion, no one has attacked more insightfully one basic aspect of the problem of anxiety, namely the relation between anxiety and individuation.

6. ADLER: ANXIETY AND INFERIORITY FEELINGS

Alfred Adler does not present a systematic analysis of anxiety, partly because of the unsystematic nature of his thinking as a whole, and partly because the problem of anxiety is swallowed

---

[110] Pearce Bailey, *Theory and therapy: an introduction to the psychology of Dr. Otto Rank* (Paris, 1935). Needless to say, Rank's use of the term "collective values" antedated the appearance in Europe of fascism, a neurotic form of collectivism.

up in his central and inclusive concept of *inferiority feelings*. When Adler refers to "inferiority feelings" as the basic motivation of neuroses, he is using the term as almost every other psychologist would employ the term "anxiety." Hence to discover his understanding of anxiety we must examine his concept of inferiority—a concept which is significant but unfortunately vague and elusive.

Every human being, according to Adler, begins life in a state of biological inferiority and insecurity. Indeed, the whole human race was inferior, tooth for tooth and claw for claw, in the animal world. For Adler, civilization—the development of tools, arts, symbols—is a result of man's endeavor to compensate for his inferiority in nature.[111] Each individual infant begins his existence in a state of helplessness and would not survive except for the social acts of his parents. Normally the child overcomes his helplessness and achieves security through progressively affirming his social relationships—through affirming the "multiplex bonds that bind human being to human being." [112] But normal development is jeopardized by both objective and subjective factors. The objective factors are that the infant's inferiority may be augmented by *organic weaknesses* (of which even in adulthood he may be unaware) ; or by *social discrimination* (e.g., being born into a minority group, or being a woman in a culture which holds masculinity to be superior) ; or by an *adverse position in the family constellation* (for Adler, being an only child was an example of this). Objective inferiority, however, can be adjusted to realistically despite the fact that it sets up hurdles to be surmounted in the individual's development.

---

[111] Adler here slips into a negative view of culture (i.e., civilization is developed because it compensates for weakness), which is not consistent with his general positive valuation of culture. The above view is similar to the Freudian concept that civilization is a product of man's anxiety (or, more accurately, that anxiety leads human beings to sublimate their natural impulses into cultural pursuits). This general viewpoint is a half-truth and has the implication that all constructive activity is a defense against anxiety. It lacks a comprehension of the fact that the human being may act on the basis of positive, spontaneous powers and curiosity or, as Goldstein puts it, on the basis of the "joy of actualizing one's own capacities." Cf. Horney, Fromm, and Goldstein for a corrective to the above view.

[112] W. Beran Wolfe, Introduction to Alfred Adler, *The pattern of life* (New York, 1930).

The crucial factor for the development of the neurotic character is the *subjective attitude toward one's weaknesses*—which brings us to the important distinction Adler makes between inferiority as a fact and inferiority "feelings." It is a characteristic of the human infant, Adler holds, that he apprehends his inferiority long before he can do anything about it. His self-awareness develops in the context of comparison with older siblings and adults who have much more power than he. This may lead to a valuation of the *self* as inferior ("I *am* weak" being a different statement about one's self from "I *have* weaknesses"). Such inferiority feelings about the self, which focus on the objective inferiorities mentioned above, set the stage for the development of neurotic compensatory endeavors to gain security by achieving superiority.[113]

The neurotic inferiority feeling (or, as we would say, anxiety) is the driving force behind neurotic character formation. The neurotic character, writes Adler, "is a product and instrument of a cautious psyche which strengthens its guiding principle [neurotic goal] for the purpose of ridding itself of a feeling of inferiority, an attempt which is destined to be wrecked as a consequence of inner contradictions, on the barriers of civilization or on the rights of others." [114] By "inner contradictions" he refers to the fact that the human being is fundamentally a social creature, biologically and psychologically interdependent

---

[113] This problem of the distinction between inferiority as a fact and inferiority "feelings" is, in different language, the problem of why some persons can accept weaknesses without special anxiety whereas for others weaknesses always become the fulcra for neurotic anxiety. Adler is not clear as to the determinants of these radically different ways of viewing weakness, beyond his helpful point that it depends on whether the valuation of the *self as weak* is made. He would certainly say that the determinants of this kind of self-valuation lie in the relations of the child with its parents, and particularly in the parents' attitudes toward the child. We should go further and suggest that it lies in the nature of the parents' "love" for the child—i.e., is their "love" essentially exploitative (as is the case with parents who regard children as compensations for their own weaknesses or extensions of their own selves, etc.), in which case the child in his own self-valuation will identify himself with power, or its reverse, weakness. Or is the love of the parents based upon an appreciation of the child as a person quite apart from specific strengths or weaknesses the child may have? In such case, the child's valuation of himself will not be identified with power or weakness. In later sections of this study, it is hoped that this distinction will become clearer and more specific (see Chapters 7 and 8).

[114] Alfred Adler, *The neurotic constitution* (New York, 1926), p. xvi.

upon other people, and that therefore inferiority can be constructively overcome only by affirming and increasing social bonds. ⟨The essence of the neurotic endeavor to overcome inferiority is the drive to gain superiority and power *over* other persons, the drive to demote others in prestige and power in order to elevate one's self.⟩ Hence the neurotic endeavors actually undermine the individual's only lasting basis of security. As Horney and others have pointed out more systematically than Adler, striving for power over other persons increases intrasocial hostility and makes the individual's own position in the long run more isolated.

Turning specifically to anxiety, Adler asks: What purpose does it serve? For the anxious individual himself, anxiety serves the purpose of blocking further activity; it is a cue to retreat to previous states of security; and hence it serves as a motivation for evading decisions and responsibility. But even more frequently emphasized by Adler is the function of anxiety as a weapon of aggression, a means of dominating others. "What appears to us as important," he holds, "is that a child will make use of anxiety in order to arrive at its goal of superiority—or *control* over the mother." [115] Adler's writings are replete with illustrations of patients employing anxiety in order to force the household to accept their regimes, of anxious wives controlling their husbands by means of a convenient attack of apprehension, and so forth.

Now no one would dispute the contention that anxiety is often used for these "secondary gains." But to imply that these are the chief motivations of anxiety is to oversimplify and confuse the problem. It is difficult to see how anyone who has experienced or witnessed genuine attacks of anxiety and comprehended the torment they involve would be guilty of the conclusion that such panics are produced chiefly for the benefit of their effects upon others. One has the impression that Adler in these contexts is talking about *pseudo,* rather than genuine, anxiety. This impression is given support by the fact that he treats anxiety often as a "character trait" [116] rather than an emotion. All

---

[115] Alfred Adler, *Problems of neurosis* (New York, 1930), p. 73.
[116] Alfred Adler, *Understanding human nature* (New York, 1927).

of which indicates again that he subsumes the basic, genuine forms of anxiety under his "inferiority feelings"—which he would certainly not hold to have their genesis in the fact that they may be used for controlling others.[117]

With regard to the causes of anxiety, Adler does not yield much illumination beyond his general description of the genesis of inferiority feelings. He remarks that anxiety neurosis is always due to the individual's having been a "pampered" child. This is another example of his tendency toward oversimplification.[118] Again, it is true that anxiety neurotics have learned, generally in early childhood, to depend excessively on others, but this behavior would neither become so firmly intrenched or persist except as the patients are in basic conflict concerning their own capacities.[119]

Concerning methods of overcoming anxiety, Adler is very clear, albeit still general. Anxiety "can be dissolved solely by that bond which binds the individual to humanity. Only that individual can go through life without anxiety who is conscious of belonging to the fellowship of man." [120] The "bond" is affirmed through socially useful work and love. Behind statements like these lies Adler's whole positive evaluation of the social nature of man, an emphasis radically different from Freud's and involving radically different implications for the overcoming of anxiety. Despite his oversimplifications and generalities, Adler has contributed perdurable insights, particularly in the realm of the power struggles between persons and their so-

---

117 In genuine anxiety as contrasted with pseudo anxiety, the control exercised over others is a secondary, not a primary, element; and it occurs as a result of the desperation which the patient experiences in his isolation and powerlessness. The distinction between *pseudo* and *genuine* anxiety is an important problem which has been very little clarified as yet. It is often difficult to distinguish the two because they may be intermixed in the motivations and behavior of the same person. Many anxiety neurotics, having established their neurotic patterns because of genuine anxiety, powerlessness, and helplessness in the family constellation, learn sooner or later that a strategy (façade) of weakness may be an effective means of gaining power. Hence weakness is used as a way of gaining strength. (See discussion of this problem in Chapter 8 of the present study.)

118 But perhaps it is no more of an oversimplification than the early Freudian theory that anxiety neurosis was specifically due to coitus interruptus.

119 See case of Brown, Chapter 7.

120 *Understanding human nature, op. cit.,* p. 238.

cial implications. These insights are especially valuable because they generally occur in the areas of Freud's "blind spots." [121]

7. JUNG: ANXIETY AND THE THREAT OF THE IRRATIONAL

Only a note concerning C. G. Jung is included in this study, chiefly because Jung has never systematized his views of anxiety. So far as the writer can determine, the problem of anxiety is never directly and specifically attacked in Jung's writings, and a comprehensive summary of the implications of his thought for anxiety theory would require a detailed research into all his writings. One distinctive contribution, however, will be cited here, namely, Jung's belief that *anxiety is the individual's reaction to the invasion of his conscious mind by irrational forces and images from the collective unconscious.* Anxiety is "fear of the dominants of the collective unconscious," fear of that residue of the functions of our animal ancestry and the archaic human functions which Jung conceives as still existing on subrational levels in the human personality.[122] This possible upsurging of irrational material constitutes a threat to the orderly, stable existence of the individual.[123] If the barriers within the individual to irrational tendencies and images in the collective unconscious are thin, there is the threat of psychosis, with its concomitant anxiety. But if, on the opposite extreme, the irrational tendencies are blocked off too completely, there is the experience of futility and lack of creativity. Therefore, as Kierkegaard would say, to avoid futility one must have the courage to confront and work through anxiety.

To Jung, the threat of irrational material in the unconscious explains "why people are afraid of becoming conscious of themselves. There might really be something behind the screen—

---

[121] As will be indicated later, the valuable insights of Adler have to a large extent been incorporated in more systematic and profound form as parts of the emphases of such later psychoanalysts as Horney, Fromm, and Sullivan. The influence of Adler on later analysts is no doubt both direct and indirect, with similar emphases arrived at partially independently. The influence on Sullivan may have been indirectly through W. A. White, who was interested in Adler.

[122] Carl G. Jung, *Collected papers on analytical psychology* (London, 1920).

[123] At this point the writer is indebted to Dr. Goodwin Watson's formulation of Jung's concepts.

one never knows—and thus people 'prefer to take into account and to observe carefully' factors external to their consciousness." In most persons "there is a secret fear of the unknown 'perils of the soul.' Of course one is reluctant to admit such a ridiculous fear. But one should realize that this fear is by no means unjustifiable; on the contrary it is only too well founded." [124] Primitive peoples are more readily aware of the "unexpected, dangerous tendencies of the unconscious," Jung holds; and they devise various ceremonies and taboos as protections. Civilized man has likewise devised his defenses against this invasion of irrational forces, which defenses often become systematized and habitual so that the "dominants of the collective unconscious" come into direct control only in such phenomena, for example, as mass panic, or into indirect control in individual psychosis or neurosis. One of Jung's central points is that modern Western man places an excessive emphasis on "rational," intellectual functions, and he holds that in most modern Western individuals this emphasis does not lead to rational integration but rather represents the "misuse of reason and intellect for an egoistical power purpose." [125] He cites the case of a patient of his who was suffering from a cancer phobia. The patient had "forced everything under the inexorable law of reason, but somewhere nature escaped and came back with a vengeance in the form of perfectly unassailable nonsense, the cancer idea." [126]

In the judgment of the present writer, the above-mentioned emphases of Jung have a corrective value, both with respect to characteristics of modern Western culture and with respect to a common aspect of individual neurosis, namely the misuse of rationalistic functions as a defense against, rather than as a means of understanding and clarification of, anxiety. But it appears that these same emphases in Jung lead to a dichotomy between the "rational" and "irrational" (e.g., his concept of the "*autonomy* of the unconscious mind" [127]), and render much of his thought esoteric, and difficult to coordinate with other theories of anxiety.

---

[124] Carl G. Jung, *Psychology and religion* (New Haven, Conn., 1938), pp. 14-15.
[125] *Ibid.,* p. 18.
[126] *Ibid.,* p. 18.
[127] *Psychology and religion,* chap. i. (Italics mine).

8. Horney: Anxiety and Conflicting Personality Trends

Important psychoanalytic developments, based on the work of Freud but presenting new elements, are those in which the problem of anxiety is seen in a sociopsychological setting. These views in essence are that anxiety arises out of disturbed interpersonal relationships, an emphasis made, though in somewhat different ways, by K. Horney, E. Fromm, and H. S. Sullivan.[128]

This approach involves a new emphasis on culture, both in the broader sense of cultural patterns as determinants in the anxiety prevalent in a given historical period,[129] and culture in the more limited sense of the relationship between the child and the significant persons in his environment, in which relationship neurotic anxiety has its source. This approach does not deny, of course, the fact of biological needs in the child or adult; but it holds that the significant psychological question is the role these needs play in interpersonal relations. Fromm, for example, points out that the "particular needs which are *relevant to understanding the personality and its difficulties* are not instinctual in character but are created out of the entirety of conditions under which we live." [130]   Anxiety thus is not specifically the reaction to the anticipation of frustration of instinctual or libidinous needs; considerable frustration of instinctual (such as sexual) need can be borne without anxiety by the normal person. The frustration of instinctual tendencies—again sex is a good example—results in anxiety *only when this frustration threatens some value or mode of interpersonal relationship which the individual holds vital to his security.* Freud conceived of environmental influences chiefly as a factor in molding instinctual drives; the psychoanalytic developments discussed here make the interpersonal context (the environment, viewed psychologically) central, with instinctual factors as important to the extent

---

[128] Since these psychoanalytic developments have large areas of agreement with Freud, we are here concerned with their differences from Freud and with their special contributions to the understanding of anxiety.

[129] See next Chapter.

[130] A viewpoint of Erich Fromm, as phrased by Karen Horney, *New ways in psychoanalysis* (New York, 1939), p. 78.

that they represent vital values in this interpersonal context.[131]

To discuss Horney first, it is significant that her viewpoint places anxiety *prior to the instinctual drives*. What Freud terms instinctual drives, far from being basic, she holds, are themselves a product of anxiety. The concept of "drive" implies some compulsion from within the organism, some stringent and demanding characteristic. (Freud realized that instinctual drives are compulsive in the cases of neurotics; he assumed, however, that the "drive" is biologically determined and that it receives its compulsive strength in neurotics from the fact that they are, for constitutional reasons or because of too much libidinal gratification as infants, unable to tolerate instinctual frustration as much as "normal" persons.) But Horney holds that impulses and desires do not become "drives" except as they are motivated by anxiety. "Compulsive drives are specifically neurotic; they are born of feelings of isolation, helplessness, fear, and hostility, and represent ways of coping with the world despite these feelings; they aim primarily not at satisfaction but at safety; their compulsive character is due to the anxiety lurking behind them." [132] She equates Freud's "instinctual drives" with her "neurotic trends." She believes she thus makes anxiety more basic in personality disturbances than does Freud: "In spite of Freud's recognition of anxiety as 'the central problem

---

[131] Horney's contention is that Freud's instinct theories, and the libido theory which is derivative from them, are based on the assumption that "psychic forces are chemical-physiological in origin." (*Ibid.*, p. 47). The present writer would agree in the respect that psychology for Freud seems to be the science of how an individual uses or misuses libidinal forces. It is not to be denied that the outright frustration of a sheer biological need—such as that for food—would menace life and therefore be a source of anxiety. But beyond such fairly rare cases, it is to be recognized that biological needs assume a wide divergency of forms in different cultures, depending upon the patterns in the culture; and *the point at which a threat to a biological need arouses anxiety depends in the great majority of cases on the psychological patterns of that culture*. This is clearly indicated in a study of what sorts of sexual frustration arouse anxiety in different cultures. Horney believes that Freud's nineteenth-century biological presuppositions prevented him from seeing the psychological context of such problems (she refers to "biological" in the sense of chemical-physical mechanisms, rather than to Goldstein's use of "biological" in the sense of the organism responding as an entirety to its environmental situation).

[132] Karen Horney, *Our inner conflicts* (New York, 1945), pp. 12-13.

of neuroses,' he has nevertheless not seen the all-pervasive role of anxiety as a dynamic factor driving toward certain goals." [133]

Horney agrees with the customary distinction between fears and anxiety. A fear is a reaction to a specific danger, to which the individual can make a specific adjustment. But what characterizes anxiety is the feeling of diffuseness and uncertainty and the experience of helplessness toward the threat. Anxiety is a reaction to a threat to something belonging to the "core or essence" of the personality; she is here in agreement with Goldstein's concept, described earlier, that anxiety, as inhering in the "catastrophic condition," is a reaction to a threat to some value which the individual holds essential to his existence as a personality. The question basic for the understanding of anxiety, therefore, is: *What* is endangered by the threat which provokes anxiety? Her answers to this question can best be understood if we outline first her conception of the origins of anxiety.

Types and Sources of Anxiety.—Horney takes account of the normal anxiety which is implicit in the human situation of contingency in the face of death, powers of Nature, and so forth. This is the anxiety which has been termed *Urangst* or *Angst der Kreatur*.[134] But this is to be differentiated from neurotic anxiety, in that *Urangst* does not connote hostility on the part of Nature or the conditions which make for human contingency; it does not provoke inner conflict or lead to neurotic defense measures.[135] Neurotic anxiety and helplessness are not the result of a realistic view of inadequacy of power but arise out of an inner conflict between dependency and hostility, and what is felt as the source of danger is primarily the anticipated hostility of others.

---

[133] *New ways in psychoanalysis* (New York, 1939), p. 76.

[134] Cf. Goldstein, Kierkegaard, *et al.*

[135] In fact, *Urangst,* in contradistinction to neurotic anxiety, can be used constructively. Cf. Fromm's idea that contingency in the face of death, common to all organisms, may be used as a motivation for increasing the common bonds between human beings. Cf. also Adler's concept that the real weakness of the human being in the face of Nature is related on the positive side to the development of civilization. Neurotic anxiety is unconstructive in the respect that it leads to the development of self-limiting defense measures. Horney indicates that the only way neurotic anxiety can be used constructively is in its being taken as a challenge that some inner problem needs clarification.

Basic anxiety is Horney's term for the anxiety which leads to the formation of neurotic defenses. Such anxiety, itself a neurotic manifestation, is "basic" in two senses: first, it is the basis for neurosis; and secondly, it is basic in the sense that it develops in early life out of disturbed relationships between the child and the significant individuals in his personal environment, normally his parents. "The typical conflict leading to anxiety in a child is that between dependency on the parents—enhanced by the child's feeling of being isolated and intimidated—and hostile impulses against the parents." [136] The hostility involved in this conflict with the parents has to be repressed because of the child's dependency on the parents; and since repressed hostility deprives the individual of the capacity to recognize and fight against real dangers, and also since the act of repression itself creates inner unconscious conflict, such repression contributes to the child's feeling of defenselessness and helplessness.[137] We have here one example of the reciprocal functioning of anxiety and hostility, each affect accentuating the other.[138] Thus helplessness inheres in the very nature of basic anxiety itself. Horney is well aware that every person—the "normal" adult, for example—has to struggle against opposing forces in the culture, many of which are in fact hostile, but this in itself does not provoke neurotic anxiety. The difference she feels is that the normal adult had the bulk of his unfortunate experiences at a period when he could integrate them, whereas the child in a dependent relationship with essentially hostile parents is *in fact* helpless and can do nothing about the conflict except develop neurotic defenses. Basic

---

136 *New ways in psychoanalysis, op. cit.,* p. 82. The reasons why the child may find his dependency upon his parents surrounded by a hostile context are of course multifarious. Horney mentions some having to do with the attitudes and behavior of the parents: "by the parents' lack of respect for him; by unreasonable demands and prohibitions; by injustice; by unreliability; by suppression of criticism; by the parents dominating him and ascribing these tendencies to love; by misusing children for the sake of prestige or ambitious goals. If a child, in addition to being dependent on his parents, is grossly or subtly intimidated by them and hence feels that any expression of hostile impulses against them endangers his security, then the existence of such hostile impulses is bound to create anxiety."— *Ibid.,* p. 83.

137 Basic anxiety is "inseparably interwoven with a basic hostility" *(The neurotic personality of our time* [New York, 1937], p. 89).

138 In other language this would be termed the "vicious circle" of anxiety and hostility.

anxiety is anxiety in the face of a potentially hostile world. The multifarious forms of personality disturbances are neurotic defenses created in the effort to cope with this potentially hostile world despite one's feeling of weakness and helplessness. Neurotic trends, in Horney's viewpoint, are thus essentially security measures arising out of basic anxiety.

It becomes possible, now, to answer the question: What is endangered by the threat which produces an anxiety attack? Anxiety is the reaction to the *threat to any pattern which the individual has developed upon which he feels his safety to depend.* The adult in a period of personality disturbance feels the threatening of a neurotic trend which was his only method of coping with earlier basic anxiety, and hence the prospect is one of renewed helplessness and defenselessness. In contradistinction to Freud, Horney holds that it is not the expression of instinctual drives which is threatened, but rather the neurotic trends which operate as safety devices. Thus neurotic anxiety will be cued off in different persons by different threats; what is important is the particular neurotic trend in the given person upon which he feels his security rests. In a person characterized by masochistic dependence—i.e., a person whose basic anxiety can be allayed only by clinging indiscriminately to another—the threat of desertion by the partner will arouse an anxiety attack. In the case of a narcissistic person—for example, one whose basic anxiety as a child could be allayed only by the unqualified admiration of the parents—anxiety will arise at the prospect of being thrust into a situation in which he is unrecognized and unadmired. If a person's safety depends on being unobtrusive, anxiety will emerge when he is thrust into the limelight.

In the problem of anxiety we must therefore always ask the question of what vital value is being threatened; and specifically in neurotic anxiety, what neurotic trend vital to the preservation of the personality against previous helplessness is being threatened. Thus, "anything may provoke anxiety," Horney writes, "which is likely to jeopardize the individual's specific protective pursuits, his specific neurotic trends." [139] Of course

---

[139] *Ibid.,* p. 199.

the threat may be not only ostensibly external, like desertion by the partner, but it may be any kind of intrapsychic impulse or desire which, if expressed, would threaten the security pattern. Thus certain sexual or hostile inclinations arouse anxiety not because of the anticipation of their frustration per se, but rather because the expression of the inclinations would threaten some pattern of interpersonal relationships which the individual feels vital to his existence as a personality.

A central reason why neurotic anxiety possesses such stringent qualities is that a neurosis involves *contradictory trends within the personality.* The original form of this was indicated above in the discussion of basic anxiety: such anxiety involves excessive feelings of dependency and helplessness, but it also involves excessive feelings of hostility toward those persons upon whom one is dependent. These are mutually exclusive on the conscious level because the hostility would alienate the persons upon whom one is dependent. For example, a common neurotic pattern in our culture takes the form of a man's needing to view his wife as completely dependent upon him, and to see himself as the independent one, the "strong provider," but at the same time he feels compulsively dependent on his wife's admiring everything he does.[140] The presence of both independent and dependent needs at the same time, in the compulsive form these needs take in neurosis, would understandably result in a shaky psychological equilibrium which would be bound to be frequently threatened in the course of everyday life. In fact, such patterns are threatened by the very nature of the contradiction involved. The fact that one or the other of the sides of the contradiction will be either continually or at various times repressed only removes the problem to a deeper level. Again in contradistinction to Freud's concept of neurotic helplessness as the weakness of the "ego" in the face of the power of the "id" and "superego," Horney feels that the helplessness inheres in the fact that the

---

[140] Cf. the contradictory trends in the studies of patients with gastric ulcers, and in the case of Tom (Chapter 3). The fact that one trend may have been developed as a compensation for an opposite trend does not change the fact that the trends exist in contradiction in the same personality.

person is in conflict between contradictory drives, each of which possesses a compulsive nature.[141]

It will already have been noted that Horney places a great deal of emphasis on the *reciprocal relation of hostility and anxiety*. She believes that by far the most common intrapsychic factor provoking anxiety is hostility. In fact, "hostile impulses of various kinds form the main source from which neurotic anxiety springs." [142] Anxiety generates hostility, and hostile impulses, in the anxious person, generate new anxiety. One is understandably hostile against those experiences and persons which threaten him and which give him the painful experience of helplessness and anxiety. But since anxiety is characterized by weakness and dependence on other powerful persons, any hostile impulses toward these persons would threaten this dependency, which must be maintained at all costs. Likewise, intrapsychic impulses to attack those persons cue off fears of retaliation and counterattack, the prospects of which increase anxiety. It is understandable that anxious persons would have a good deal of hostility, which is a commonplace discovery in clinical experience. And it is understandable also that the hostility would be largely repressed for fear of counterattack. Now when repression of hostility occurs, it is often accompanied by projection of hostile impulses on others, normally upon those toward whom one feels hostile. This can be illustrated clearly in the case of the child, who frequently projects his own hostile feelings on his parents and other powerful persons and thereby experiences an increase of the feeling that he lives in a hostile

---

141 One is reminded of W. Stekel's central idea that all anxiety is psychic conflict.—*Conditions of neurotic anxiety and their treatment*. However, in his epigrammatic statements, some of which show penetrating insight, Stekel did not work out systematically the nature of the psychic conflict as Horney has done.

142 *The neurotic personality of our time, op. cit.*, p. 62. Horney feels it is entirely understandable that Freud in his Victorian culture considered that the expression of various sexual inclinations on the part, let us say, of the upper middle-class girl would incur real dangers in terms of social ostracism. But she warns against taking Freud's culturally conditioned data as the basis for a generalization about personality. Except in unusual cases, her experience has been that anxiety which on superficial observation is related to sexual impulses often turns out to have its source in hostile or counter-hostile feelings about the sexual partner. This is plausible in the light of the consideration that sex is a very ready focus for dependent and symbiotic tendencies and that such tendencies are generally found in exaggerated form in anxious persons.

world. The repression of hostility results in the individual's being less able to distinguish and take a stand against real dangers and hence contributes again to his state of helplessness.[143]

Noting all these reciprocal interactions of hostility and anxiety, Horney concludes that there is a "specific cause" of anxiety in "repressed hostile impulses." [144] Whether such a statement can be made as a generalization without constant reference to our culture we leave an open question. But it probably would be generally agreed that in our culture, which, as Horney herself has most persistently emphasized, "generates a good deal of hostility," the interrelation of hostility and anxiety is a demonstrated clinical fact.

The exceedingly valuable contribution of Horney to anxiety theory lies in her elucidation of the conflicting trends in personality as the sources of neurotic anxiety, and in her placing of the problem of anxiety squarely on the psychological level, with its necessary social aspects, in contrast to Freud's tendencies toward quasi-physiochemical forms of thinking. A criticism frequently made against Horney is that her emphasis on how the patient's conflicts are manifested in his present relationships (an emphasis developed partly in reaction against what she felt to be Freud's too exclusive emphasis on past origins) has led her and members of her school to neglect the origins of psychological conflict in early childhood. In the judgment of the present writer, this criticism is justified. True, Horney makes clear reference in her writings to the childhood origins of neurotic conflict, and so do her associates who elucidate her viewpoint.[145] But the over-all

---

143 Often persons who repress considerable amounts of hostility develop a passive or compliant attitude toward persons who exploit them, and this increases the likelihood that they will be exploited by the environment.

144 It is not to be implied that all hostility leads to anxiety; conscious hostility does not necessarily produce anxiety, but may be a constructive function, resulting in actions which decrease the threat. Horney is speaking of repressed hostility. Apart from the hostile content of repressions, one could remark that *any* repression sets the intrapsychic stage for anxiety in that the nature of repression itself involves some surrender of the autonomous power of the individual (some curtailment of the "ego," as it would be stated in Freudian topology). The repression, of course, does not result in itself in conscious anxiety—indeed, its immediate purpose is precisely the opposite—but it represents a retrenchment of autonomy on the part of the individual and thereby accentuates his situation of weakness.

145 See Muriel Ivimey, *The genesis of basic anxiety,* unpublished paper delivered before the Association for the Advancement of Psychoanalysis, 1946.

weight she places on present manifestations of conflict, an emphasis shown particularly in the clinical practice of members of the Horney group as this writer has observed it, does result in a tendency to by-pass the very dynamic sources of conflict (and hence neurotic anxiety) in the patient's early relationships with his parents. We would grant that Freud dealt too exclusively with childhood and infantile origins (as Rank pointed out in the 1920's). We would also grant that the conflicts the child had (and has) with his parents carry over into all his present relationships as an adult. Nevertheless, the roots of the neurotic patient's problems lie in his relations with his parents—a point which is one aspect of Freud's perdurable contribution. Therapy with respect to neurotic anxiety must certainly aim to clarify present relationships as the immediate manifestations of underlying conflict, as Horney insists. But at the same time the early conflicts with parents, carrying over into the present in the patient's emotional life, must be clarified as well.

9. Sullivan: Anxiety as Apprehension of Disapproval in Interpersonal Relations

The concept of anxiety as arising in the locus of interpersonal relations has been most cogently stated by Harry Stack Sullivan. Though his theory of anxiety was never completely formulated, the salient points presented by him are of considerable importance for any comprehensive understanding of anxiety.

Basic for his theory of anxiety is Sullivan's concept of personality as essentially an interpersonal phenomenon, developing out of the relations of the infant with the significant persons in his environment. Even in the sheer biological beginnings of life—the fertilized ovum *in utero*—the cell and environment are unitary, are indissolubly bound. After birth the infant is in intimate relationship with the mother (or mother substitutes), which is both the prototype and the real beginning of those relationships with significant other persons out of which matrix his personality will be formed.

Sullivan divides the activities of the human organism into two classes. First, there are those activities the aim of which is to gain *satisfactions,* such as eating, drinking, and sleeping. These satisfactions pertain rather closely to the bodily organization of man. The second class is those activities which are in pursuit of *security,* and these pertain "more closely to man's cultural equipment than to his bodily organization." [146] A central factor in this pursuit of security is, of course, the organism's feeling of ability and power. The "power motive"—by which Sullivan means the need and tendency of the organism to expand in ability and achievement—is to some extent inborn.[147] It is a "given" in the human organism *qua* organism. This second class of activities—directed toward the pursuit of security—is "ordinarily much more important in the human being than the impulses resulting from a feeling of hunger, or thirst," or as he goes on to say, of sex as it later emerges in the maturing organism.[148] These needs of the organism which are biological, in the more limited sense of that term, are really to be seen as "manifestations of the organism's efforts not merely to maintain itself in stable balance with and in its environment, but to expand, to 'reach out' to, and interact with, widening circles of the environment." [149] The growth and characteristics of personality depend largely on how this power motive, and the pursuit of security it entails, are fulfilled in interpersonal relations. The infant is first in a state of relative powerlessness. His cry becomes an early tool in his interpersonal relations, and later there develop

---

146 From Harry Stack Sullivan, *Conceptions of modern psychiatry,* copyright 1947 by William Alanson White Psychiatric Foundation (Washington, D. C.: The Foundation, 1947).

147 "Power motive" is to be sharply distinguished from "power drive," the latter being a neurotic phenomenon which may be motivated by the accumulated frustration of normal needs for achievement. Sullivan's concept of the expansion of the organism in terms of ability and achievement is parallel to Goldstein's concept of self-actualization. Goldstein's interest is more biological, whereas Sullivan's persistent emphasis is that this expansion occurs and has its meaning almost wholly in interpersonal relationships.

148 *Op. cit.,* p. 6. One thinks at this point of the anxiety experiments which are based on a sheer physiological frustration or threat—such as the threat of pain. It ought to be borne in mind that such experiments, useful as they may be in throwing light upon some aspects of anxiety, involve a laboratory isolation of the personality from its cultural setting. This qualification ought to be especially borne in mind in interpreting the results of animal experiments. In laboratory experiments with human beings, of course, the manner in which the person reacts to the threat of pain will be affected by his previous cultural conditioning.

149 Patrick Mullahy, A theory of interpersonal relations and the evolution of personality, in Sullivan, *op. cit.,* p. 121 (a review of Sullivan's theories).

language and the use of symbols, both of which are powerful
cultural instrumentalities in man's pursuit of security in relations
with his fellow-men. But long before language or specific emotional expression or comprehension is possible for the infant, the
acculturalization is proceeding apace through *empathy*, the
"emotional contagion and communion" that occurs between the
infant and the early significant persons, again chiefly the mother.
In this interpersonal matrix, governed chiefly by the needs of the
organism for security and self-expression, anxiety is born.

Anxiety, to Sullivan, *arises out of the infant's apprehension
of the disapproval of the significant persons in his interpersonal
world.* Anxiety is felt empathically, in a sensing of the mother's
disapprobation, long before conscious awareness is possible for
the infant. It is self-evident that the mother's disapproval will
be very portentous for the infant. Disapproval in the present
sense refers to a threatening of the relationship between the infant and its human world—a relationship which is all-important
to the infant in the respect that he depends upon it not only for
the satisfaction of his physical needs but for his more inclusive
sense of security as well.[150] Hence anxiety is felt as an all-over,
a "cosmic," experience.

With the mother's approbation come rewards, and with her
disapproval come punishment and the peculiar discomfort of
anxiety. This system of approbation and rewards versus disapprobation and discomfort (anxiety) becomes the most powerful
fulcrum on which the acculturalization and education of the individual proceeds throughout life.[151]

Anxiety serves to restrain the infant, to restrict his development to those activities of which the significant other persons
approve. Sullivan presents the highly significant idea that the

---

[150] The term "disapproval" may not have a strong enough connotation to suggest the degree of threat involved or the degree of discomfort the infant experiences
when this threat cues off anxiety. Certainly "disapproval" does not refer to reproof,
a great deal of which, it is known, can be assimilated by the infant if the mother-
child relationship is fundamentally secure.

[151] Sullivan's summary of the importance of the mother in this system is as
follows: "I have spoken of the functional interaction, in infancy and childhood,
of the significant other person, the mother, as a source of satisfaction, as an agency
of acculturation, and finally as a source of anxiety and insecurity in the development of social habits which is the basis of development of the self system." *Op. cit.*,
p. 16.

self is *formed* out of the growing infant's necessity to deal with anxiety-creating experiences. The self is formed out of the need to distinguish between activities which produce approval and those which result in disapprobation. "The self-dynamism is built up out of this experience of approbation and disapproval, reward and punishment." [152] The self "comes into being as a dynamism to preserve the feeling of security." [153] The self is a dynamic process by which the organism incorporates those experiences which produce approbation and reward, and learns to exclude those activities which have resulted in disapproval and anxiety. The limitations thus set by early experience tend to be maintained year after year "by our experiencing anxiety whenever we tend to overstep the margin." [154]

We now need to make explicit what is implied above, namely, that the limitations set by anxiety-creating experiences are not merely prohibitions of action, but are *limitations of awareness* as well. Whatever tendencies would arouse anxiety tend to be excluded from awareness, or, in Sullivan's term, *dissociated*. Sullivan summarizes as follows: "The self comes to control awareness, to restrict one's consciousness of what is going on in one's situation very largely by the instrumentality of anxiety with, as a result, a dissociation from personal awareness of those tendencies of the personality which are not included or incorporated in the approved structure of the self." [155]

These concepts throw new light upon some of the common phenomena in anxiety. The restriction of awareness in anxiety states—an occurrence discernible in everyone's experience as well as a daily observation in clinical work—is Sullivan's reinterpretation of the classical psychoanalytic idea that anxiety leads to repression. Sullivan sheds new light on why and how this restriction of awareness takes place in his elucidation of the dynamics of interpersonal relations, especially between infant and mother, and the centrally important need of the organism to preserve security. With respect to anxiety and the formation of

---

152 *Ibid.*, p. 9.
153 *Ibid.*, p. 21.
154 *Ibid.*, p. 10.
155 *Ibid.*, pp. 21-22.

symptoms, it can readily be seen that, when the dissociation of strong anxiety-creating experience or impulses becomes difficult for the organism to accomplish (as in neurotic states), substitutive and compulsive symptoms develop as a more rigid means of demarcating awareness.[156] In Sullivan's contribution there are also stimulating formulations of the relation between emotional health and anxiety which might be phrased as follows: Anxiety restricts growth and awareness, shrinking the area of effective living; emotional health is equal to the degree of personal awareness; hence clarification of anxiety makes possible expanded awareness and an expansion of the self, which means the achieving of emotional health.

[156] Hence it follows that the dissociated tendencies and experiences will remain dissociated so long as the anxiety connected with them is felt by the person to be too great to be borne.

Chapter 5

ANXIETY INTERPRETED CULTURALLY

Man's nature, his passions, and anxieties are a cultural product; as a matter of fact, man himself is the most important creation and achievement of the continuous human effort, the record of which we call history.—Erich Fromm, *Escape from Freedom.*

People whose course of life has reached a crisis must confront their collective past as fully as a neurotic patient must unbury his personal life: long-forgotten traumas in history may have a disastrous effect upon millions who remain unaware of them.— Lewis Mumford, *The Condition of Man.*

We have observed in the previous chapters that cultural factors emerge at almost every point in a discussion of anxiety. Whether one is investigating children's fears or anxiety in psychosomatic disorders or anxiety in the various forms of individual neurosis, it is clear that one cannot avoid the realization that the cultural milieu is always part of the warp and woof of the anxiety experience. In the last chapter we have also noted the rationale for this significance of cultural factors as presented by various investigators, such as Sullivan in his description of the indissoluble interrelation of the individual with his environment at every point in development from the cell *in utero* to the adult interrelated in love and work with the other members of his society. The general importance of cultural factors in an individual's anxiety is now widely admitted and does not in itself require laboring in present-day psychology and psychoanalysis. Our purposes in this chapter are therefore more specific, namely to show how the *occasions* of an individual's anxiety are conditioned by the standards and values of his culture and also to show

how the quantities of his anxiety are conditioned by the relative unity and stability—or lack of them—in his culture.

By "occasions" we mean that the *kinds* of threats which cue off anxiety are largely defined by the culture in which the individual lives. On the level of primitive societies, Hallowell has shown that the occasions of threat vary from culture to culture and that anxiety is a function of the beliefs accepted in the culture superimposed on the actual danger situation.[1] This may be illustrated in our own culture by the crucial weight accorded the goal of individual competitive ambition. We have seen in the survey of anxiety in the psychosomatic studies of patients with peptic ulcer (the "disease of the striving and ambitious men of Western civilization") that the anxiety is a function of the needs of men in our society to appear strong, independent, and triumphant in the competitive struggle and to repress dependent needs. We have seen also in the studies of children's fears that as children grow older, and absorb more of the accepted attitudes of the culture, fears and anxiety related to competitive status increase. Apparently the weight given the goal of competitive success increases as the individual moves into adulthood: we noted that adults reporting their childhood fears gave a much larger incidence of fears related to competitive success and failure than did the children, which Jersild interpreted as a "reading back" into childhood of the fulcra of fear and anxiety which had become important to them as adults. Indeed, studies of the worries of school children regularly show the most pronounced anxiety to lie in the area of competitive success, whether in school itself or in work.[2] In the study of anxiety in unmarried mothers reported later in the present discussion,[3] one might reasonably have expected that the girls' chief occasions of anxiety would be social disapproval or guilt; but this turned out not to be the case. The predominant occasion of anxiety reported by the girls was competitive ambition—i.e., whether they would measure up to cultural standards of "success." The weight placed upon the

---

[1] A. I. Hallowell, The social function of anxiety in a primitive society, *Amer. Sociol. Rev.*, 1941, 6: 6, 869-81.

[2] P. M. Symonds, *The dynamics of human adjustment* (New York, 1946), p. 149.

[3] Chapter 7.

value of competitive success is so great in our culture and the anxiety occasioned by the possibility of failure to achieve this goal is so frequent that there is reason for assuming that *individual competitive success is both the dominant goal in our culture and the most pervasive occasion for anxiety*.

The question of why this particular threat, i.e., the threat of failure to achieve competitive success, should be so prevalent as an occasion for anxiety in our culture obviously cannot be answered by definitions of "normality." It may be assumed that every individual has normal needs to gain security and acceptance, but this does not explain why in our culture such security is conceived chiefly in *competitive* terms. And although it may be assumed that every individual has normal needs to expand in his achievement and to increase his capacities and power, why is it that in our society this "normal" ambition takes an individualistic form, i.e., is defined chiefly in inverse relation to the community, so that the failure of others has the same relative effect as the success of one's self? [4] And why does competition in our culture carry such stringent penalties and rewards, so that (as will be indicated presently) the individual's feeling of value as a person so regularly depends upon his competitive triumph? These questions indicate that a goal like competitive individual success is not an "immutable attribute" of human nature, but a cultural product. The goal is the expression of a cultural pattern in which there exists a particular confluence of individualism with competitive ambition. This pattern is discernible in our culture from the time of the Renaissance, but it was almost entirely absent in the Middle Ages.[5] Therefore the value of individual competitive success, as a prevailing occasion for anxiety, has its particular historical genesis and development.

---

[4] Discussing the culture of the Comanche Indians, Abram Kardiner points out that there is a great deal of competition, "but it does not interfere with security or with the common goal of the society." *The psychological frontiers of society* (New York, 1945), p. 99.

[5] Cf. "It is the very task of social psychology to understand this process of man's creation in history. . . . Why is the spirit of the Renaissance different from that in the nineteenth century? . . . Thus we find, for instance, that from the Renaissance up until our day men have been filled with a burning ambition for fame, while this striving which today seems so natural was little present in man of the medieval society." Erich Fromm, *Escape from freedom* (New York, 1941), p. 13.

1. The Historical Dimension of Anxiety-Creating Cultural Patterns

The generally accepted statement that the culture conditions anxiety must, therefore, be expanded to read: *An individual's anxiety is conditioned by the fact that he lives in a given culture at a particular point in the historical development of that culture.* This brings in the genetic, long-term, developmental background of the patterns which are the occasions of contemporaneous anxiety.[6]   In his discussion of "man as the time-binding creature," Dilthey emphasized the importance of this historical dimension: "man is a historical being as well as a mammal," he held, and what is needed is "to relate the total personality to the various manifestations of an historically conditioned personality." [7] While there has been broad acceptance in contemporary psychology and psychoanalysis of the importance of cultural factors in the contemporaneous scene, the historical dimension has been largely neglected to date (the prominent exceptions to this generalization being the work of Fromm [8] and the beginnings of historical analysis by Kardiner).[9]   But there is an increasing realization on the part of students of anxiety that an investigation of anxiety, as of other aspects of personality in its cultural setting, raises questions which can only be answered in terms of seeing the individual in his historical position.[10]   Mannheim describes the problem in terms of the need for a psychology which would be historically relevant as well as socially relevant, a type of psychology "which could explain how particular historical types were derived from the general faculties of man."   He asks, for exam-

---

[6] While we are referring at the moment to the *occasions* of anxiety, it is obvious that the *quantities* of anxiety experienced by a given individual are likewise conditioned by the particular stage of the historical development of his culture. This will be discussed later.

[7] Quoted in Gardner Murphy, *Historical introduction to modern psychology* (New York, 1932), p. 446.

[8] Fromm, *op. cit.*

[9] Kardiner, *op. cit.*

[10] Lawrence K. Frank, writing of the "growing realization among thoughtful people that our culture is sick," remarks, "the individual striving ushered in at the Renaissance now leads us into error." Society as the patient, *Amer. J. Sociol.,* 1936, 42, 335.

ple, "Why did the Middle Ages and the Renaissance produce entirely different types of men?" [11] In general terms, the historical is to the man-in-society what the genetic dimension is to man-as-adult. That is to say, the understanding of the historical development of modern man's character structure is as necessary to an understanding of contemporaneous anxiety as an analysis of childhood factors is to the understanding of the anxiety of a particular adult.[12]

The historical approach which is recommended here—and which will guide the discussion throughout this chapter—does not consist of a mere garnering of historical facts. It involves the more difficult procedure of *historical consciousness*—a consciousness of history as it is embodied in one's own attitudes and psychological patterns as well as in the patterns of the culture as a whole. Since every member of a society is to a greater or lesser extent the product of the patterns and attitudes which have been developing in the history of his culture, an awareness of the cultural past is to an extent self-awareness. The capacity for awareness of history as embodied within one's self has been described by Kierkegaard, Cassirer, and others as one of the distinctive capacities of the human being as differentiated from infrahuman beings.[13] The capacity for historical consciousness is a development of the capacity for self-consciousness, i.e., the ability of man to see himself as subject and object at the same time. This approach involves seeing one's own presuppositions (and the presuppositions of one's culture) as historically relative, whether those presuppositions are religious or scientific or whether they refer to a general psychological attitude like the high valuation of competitive individualism in our own culture.[14]

---

11 Karl Mannheim, *Man and society in an age of reconstruction* (New York, 1941).

12 Cf. Lewis Mumford: ". . . the truth is that all history is important *because* it is contemporary and nothing is perhaps more so than those hidden parts of the past that still survive without our being aware of their daily impact." *The condition of man* (New York, 1944), p. 12.

13 We have previously discussed Mowrer's conclusion that the capacity to bring the past into the present as part of the total causal nexus is the essence of "mind" and "personality" alike.

14 Some cultural analysts take certain presuppositions from modern science as an absolute base from which to study other historical periods (Kardiner, *op. cit.*, does this). But it is manifestly impossible to understand such periods as those of

By means of an historical study of the patterns which under-lie contemporaneous anxiety, a way is opened for a *dynamic* approach by which it is possible to take a corrective attitude toward cultural patterns. Thus we may avoid being merely the objects of historical determinism. The cultural past is rig-idly deterministic to the extent that the individual is unaware of it.[15] Through his capacity for historical consciousness man is able to achieve a measure of freedom with respect to his historical past, to modify the historical influences which come to bear upon him, to reform his history as well as to be formed by it. "But man is not only made by history," Fromm points out, "history is made by man. The solution of this seeming contradiction constitutes the field of social psychology. Its task is to show not only how passions, desires, anxieties change and develop as a result of the social process, but also how man's energies thus shaped into specific forms in their turn become productive forces, molding the social process." [16]

The following discussion will endeavor to show that both the occasions and the quantities of an individual's anxiety are condi-tioned by his character structure as it has developed in his culture and by the unity or disunity in the culture at its particular stage of development. Since the total historical development of the character structure of modern man is too broad a topic for treat-ment in this study, we shall limit ourselves to one central aspect of that character structure, namely competitive individual ambi-tion. And since it is manifestly impossible to treat this problem throughout all ages of Western history, we shall begin with the Renaissance, the *formative* period of the modern age.[17] In the Renaissance, the aim will be to show the emergence and extent

---

ancient Greece or the Middle Ages without realizing that our own presuppositions are as relative to a point in history, and as much products of history, as were the presuppositions in those periods.

[15] An analogy, of course, is found in any psychoanalytic treatment: the patient is rigidly determined by past experiences and previously developed patterns to the extent that he is unaware of these experiences and patterns.

[16] Fromm, *op. cit.*, p. 14.

[17] Our concern with the Renaissance, the beginning of the modern period and thus the time when many of the cultural patterns which underlie contemporaneous anxiety received their formative influences, corresponds roughly to the emphasis in individual psychotherapy upon the period of early childhood, when the patterns which underlie the individual adult's anxiety were formed.

of individualism, how the individualism became competitive in nature, and the consequences of this competitive individualism for interpersonal isolation and anxiety.

2. COMPETITIVE INDIVIDUALISM EMERGING IN THE RENAISSANCE

The individualistic nature of Western man's character structure can be seen as a reaction to, and a contrast with, medieval collectivism. The citizen of the Middle Ages "was conscious of himself only as a member of a race, people, party, family or corporation—only through some general category," in Burckhardt's words.[18] Each person theoretically knew his place in the economic structure of the guilds, in the psychological structure of the family and the hierarchy of feudal loyalties, and in the moral and spiritual structure of the church. Emotional expression was channeled communally, the conjunctive emotions in festivals and the aggressive emotions in such movements as the crusades. "All emotions required a rigid system of conventional forms," Huizinga remarks, "for without them passion and ferocity would have made havoc of life." [19]

But by the fourteenth and fifteenth centuries, Huizinga points out, the hierarchal forms of church and society, previously serving as ways of channeling emotions and experience, had become methods of suppressing individual vitality. The use of symbols was rampant in this period at the end of the Middle Ages, the symbols now having become ends in themselves, forms emptied of vital content and divorced from reality. The last two centuries of the Middle Ages were pervaded by feelings of depression, melancholy, skepticism, and much anxiety. The anxiety took the form of excessive dread of death and pervasive fears of devils and sorcerers.[20] Renaissance individualism is partially to

---

18 Jakob Burckhardt, *Civilization of the Renaissance in Italy*, trans. S. G. C. Middlemore (New York, 1935).

19 Johan Huizinga, *The waning of the Middle Ages* (New York, 1924), p. 40.

20 *Ibid.* Cf. also Karl Mannheim, "One has only to look at pictures like those of Bosch and Grunewald in order to see that the disorganization of the medieval order expressed itself in a general fear and anxiety, the symbolic expression of which was the widespread fear of the devil."—*Man and society in an age of reconstruction* (New York, 1941), p. 117.

be understood as a reaction against this deteriorated collectivism of the closing period of medievalism.

The new valuation of the individual and the new conception of the individual's relation to nature, which were to become the central motifs of the Renaissance, can be seen graphically in the paintings of Giotto.[21] In contrast to the symbolic, stiff, frontal figures in medieval painting, Giotto's figures are presented in three-quarter perspective and are given *independent movement*. In contrast to the generalized, otherworldly, typed, and therefore often rigid sentiments in preceding painting, Giotto begins to portray *individual emotions*. He presents the individual sorrow, joy, passion, and surprise of simple people in everyday, concrete situations—a father kissing his daughter, a friend mourning at the grave of the deceased. The delight in natural sentiment carries over into his sympathetic portrayal of animals; and the relish with which he paints trees and rocks foreshadows the new enjoyment of natural forms for their own sakes. Retaining some of the symbolic character of medieval art, Giotto presents at the same time the emerging attitudes which are to characterize the Renaissance, namely the *new humanism* and the *new naturalism*.[22]

In contradistinction to the medieval concept of man as a unit in the social organism, the Renaissance viewed the individual as a discrete entity and the social setting as a background against which the individual achieved eminence. The chief difference between Giotto and the Renaissance in bloom is that for the former the simple individual was valued,[23] but in the full development of the Renaissance it became the *powerful* individual who was valued. This phenomenon, which is basic for anxiety-creating patterns in modern culture, we now wish to trace developmentally.

---

[21] It is between Giotto and his master, Cimabue, that many authorities hold the new age to have begun. Giotto actually lived in the "first Italian Renaissance," which preceded the main Renaissance.

[22] In this chapter we refer to the work of artists on the presupposition that the artist expresses the underlying assumptions and meaning of his culture and that artistic symbols are often not only less distorted than the expressions in word symbols but also can communicate the meaning of the cultural period more directly.

[23] The influence of St. Francis upon Giotto is important in this valuation of simple persons.

The revolutionary cultural changes and expansion which characterized the Renaissance in almost every area—economic, intellectual, geographic, and political—are too well known to require description. All these cultural changes had a relationship of both cause and effect with the new confidence in the power of the free, autonomous individual.[24] On one hand, the revolutionary changes were based upon the new view of the individual, and on the other the sociological changes placed a premium on the exercise of individual power, initiative, courage, knowledge, and shrewdness. Social motility released the individual from medieval family caste; by courageous action he could now achieve eminence regardless of the level of his birth. The riches available from expanding trade and growing capitalism gave new opportunities for enterprise and reward to the individual who was bold enough to take the risks. The new appreciation of education and learning was both an expression of intellectual freedom and released curiosity (the itinerant student, making the known world his university, is symbolic of the relation of the new learning to freedom of movement) ; but at the same time knowledge was valued as a means of gaining power. "Only he who has learned everything," remarked Lorenzo Ghiberti, a Renaissance writer who spoke for his times, "can fearlessly despise the changes of fortune." [25]

The political ferment of the Renaissance, when the rule of cities rapidly passed from the hands of one despot to another, likewise placed a premium on the free exercise of power. It was often a case of each man for himself, and the individual of courage and ability could gain and hold a position of eminence. "The impulse to the free play of ambitious individuality which this state of things communicated was enormous. Capacity might raise the meanest monk to the chair of St. Peter's, the meanest soldier to the duchy of Milan. Audacity, vigour, unscrupulous crime were the chief requisites for success." [26] Speaking of the violence connected with the expression of individuality in this period, Burckhardt remarks, "The fundamental vice of the char-

---

[24] Cf. Chapter 2.
[25] Quoted in Burckhardt, op. cit., p. 146.
[26] John Addington Symonds, The Italian Renaissance (New York, 1935), p. 60.

acter was at the same time a condition of its greatness, namely, excessive individualism. . . . The sight of victorious egoism in others drives him [the individual] to defend his own right by his own arm." [27]

The high valuation of the individual in the Renaissance was not a valuation of persons as such. Rather, as mentioned above, it referred to the *strong* individual. It was presupposed that the weak could be exploited and manipulated by the strong without remorse or regret.[28] *Virtu* in the Renaissance was conceived largely in terms of courage and other characteristics which made for success. "Success was the standard by which acts were judged; and the man who could help his friends, intimidate his enemies, and carve a way to fortune for himself by any means he chose, was regarded as a hero. Machiavelli's use of the term 'virtu' . . . retains only so much of the Roman 'virtus' as is applicable to the courage, intellectual ability, and personal prowess of one who has achieved his purpose, be that what it may." [29] We note here the confluence of individualism and *competitiveness*. Granted the apotheosis of the strong individual, who regarded the community chiefly as the arena in which he battled for eminence, the concept of success was bound to be competitive. The whole cultural constellation placed a premium on self-realization by means of excelling and triumphing *over* other persons.

The confidence in the power of the free individual was an entirely conscious attitude on the part of the men of the Renaissance.[30] There were no boundaries to human creativity if, as

---

[27] Burckhardt, *op. cit.*

[28] In this connection it is important to emphasize that, though in many respects the Renaissance set the principles which were to be unconsciously assimilated by large segments of modern society in succeeding centuries, it was a movement not of masses of people but of a handful of strong, creative individuals.

[29] Symonds, *op. cit.*, p. 87.

[30] Leon Alberti, one of those towering personalities who excelled at everything from gymnastics to mathematics, formulated what may be considered the motto of these strong individuals, "Men can do all things if they will."—Burckhardt, *op. cit.*, p. 150. But nowhere is the attitude of the Renaissance better articulated than in Pico della Mirandola, who wrote twelve books to prove that man is master of his own fate. In his notable *Oration on the dignity of man*, he pictures the Creator saying to Adam, "Neither a fixed abode, nor a form in thine own likeness . . . have we given thee. . . . Thou, restrained by no narrow bounds, according to thine own free will, in whose power I have placed thee, shalt define thy nature for

Michelangelo put it, the individual could but "trust himself." The conscious ideal was *l'uomo universale,* the fully developed, many-sided individual.

But on a less conscious level, beneath this optimism and confidence there was an *undercurrent of despair with nascent feelings of anxiety.* This undercurrent, coming to the surface only toward the end of the Renaissance, can be vividly seen in Michelangelo. Consciously Michelangelo gloried in the individualistic struggle, defiantly accepting the isolation it involved. "I have no friend of any kind, and I do not want any," he wrote. "Whoever follows others will never go forward, and whoever does not know how to create by his own abilities can gain no profit from the works of other men." [31] But in his paintings can be seen the tension and conflict which were the underlying psychological counterpart of the excessive individualism of the period. His figures on the Sistine ceiling exhibit a continuous restlessness and perturbation. The human form in Michelangelo, Symonds points out, "is turbid with a strange and awful sense of inbreathed agitation." [32] Almost all of Michelangelo's human beings, powerful and triumphant as they appear at first glance, present on closer inspection the *dilated eyes which are a tell-tale sign of anxiety.* One would expect an expression of intense apprehension on the faces of the figures in his painting "The Damned Frightened by Their Fall," but the remarkable point is that the same frightened expression in less intense form is present in the other figures in the Sistine Chapel as well. As if to demonstrate that he is expressing the inner tensions not only of his age but

thyself. I have set thee midmost in the world, that thence thou mightest the more conveniently survey whatsoever is in the world. Nor have we made thee either heavenly or earthly, mortal or immortal, to the end that thou, being, as it were, thy own free maker and moulder, shouldst fashion thyself in what form may like thee best. Thou shalt have power to decline into the lower or brute creatures. Thou shalt have power to be born into the higher, or divine, according to the sentence of thy intellect."—Quoted in Symonds, *op. cit.,* p. 352. This sweeping conception of man's power and his vast freedom to move into any realm he chooses— which is to be accomplished by the power of his intellect—is described by Symonds as the "epiphany of the modern spirit."

[31] Romain Rolland, *Michelangelo,* trans. F. Street (New York, 1915), p. 161.

[32] Symonds, *op. cit.,* p. 775. The men of the Renaissance felt they were renewing the spirit of classical Greece, but the essential difference, Symonds indicates, can be seen in the "sedate serenity" of Phidias contrasted with this agitation in Michelangelo.

of himself as a member of his age, Michelangelo in his self-portrait paints eyes which are again pronouncedly distended in the way typical of apprehension. The figures of Michelangelo may be taken as symbols both of the conscious ideal and the psychological undercurrent of the Renaissance—triumphant, strong, fully developed human beings, who are at the same moment tense, agitated, and anxious.[33]

It is significant that the undercurrent of tension and despair is to be found in those persons who, like Michelangelo, actually were *successful* in the individualistic struggle. Thus the nascent anxiety is not due to any frustration of the goal of individual success. Rather, we submit, it is due to the state of psychological isolation and the lack of the positive value of community which result from excessive individualism.

These two characteristics of the strong individuals of the Renaissance are described by Fromm: "It seems that the new freedom brought two things to them: an increased feeling of strength and at the same time an increased isolation, doubt, scepticism, and—resulting from all these—anxiety." [34] An outstanding symptom of the psychological undercurrent was the "morbid craving for fame," as Burckhardt phrases it. Sometimes the driving desire for fame was so great that the individual committed assassination or other flagrantly antisocial acts in the hope that he might thereby be remembered by posterity.[35] This bespeaks considerable isolation and frustration in the individual's relatedness to others and a powerful need to gain some recognition from one's fellows even by way of aggression against them. Whether one was remembered for villainous or constructive deeds seems not to have been the point. This suggests an aspect of individualism which is present in competitive economic

---

[33] By and large the conscious ideal covered over the nascent anxiety in the bulk of the Renaissance artists (*vide* the harmonious human beings in Raphael). But Michelangelo, both because his long life carried him beyond the youthful confidence of the Renaissance at its height and because by his genius and profundity he carried the goals of his period into actuality to a greater extent than the earlier representatives, brings the undercurrents of the period into more overt expression.

[34] Fromm, *op. cit.*, p. 48.

[35] Fromm points out that "if one's relations to others and to one's self do not offer full security, then fame is one means to silence one's doubts."—*Op. cit.*, p. 49.

striving of the present day, namely that aggression against one's fellows is accepted as the way to gain recognition from them.[36]

The competitive individualistic ambition had important psychological repercussions on *the individual's relation to himself.* By an understandable psychological process, a person's attitudes toward others become his attitudes toward himself; alienation from others leads sooner or later to self-alienation. Fromm points out that as a result of the manipulation of others for purposes of increasing his wealth and power (as exemplified in the nobles and burghers), the "successful individual's relation to his own self, his sense of security and confidence were poisoned too. His own self became as much an object of manipulation to him as other persons had become." [37] Moreover the individual's own *self-valuation* depended upon his achieving competitive success. In the unconditioned weight then given success—"unconditioned" in the sense that both one's social esteem and one's self-esteem depended upon it—we see the beginnings of the stringent drive for competitive success which characterizes contemporaneous individuals. Kardiner describes the problem this sets for modern man:

> The anxieties of Western man are therefore concerned with success as a form of self-realization in the same way that salvation was in the Middle Ages. But in comparison with the individual who merely sought salvation, the psychological task for modern man is much more arduous. It is a responsibility, and failure brings with it less social censure and contempt than it does self-contempt, a feeling of inferiority and hopelessness. Success is a goal without a satiation point, and the desire for it, instead of abating, increases with achievement. The use made of success is largely power over others.[38]

As an explanation for the emergence of the new concern for individual success, Kardiner emphasizes the shift from the "otherworldly," post-mortem rewards and punishments of the Middle Ages to the concern in the Renaissance with rewards and punish-

---

[36] This reminds one of the fact that an isolated child will commit delinquencies in order to gain at least an inverted form of concern and recognition.

[37] *Op. cit.,* p. 48.

[38] Kardiner, *op. cit.,* p. 445.

ments here and now. The present writer agrees that the Renaissance was marked by a new appreciation of the values and possibilities for satisfactions in the present world; this is evidenced as far back as Boccaccio and has been indicated in the humanism and naturalism appearing in Giotto. But what impresses the present writer is that whereas rewards in the Middle Ages were gained by virtue of one's participation in a corporate body—family, feudal group, or church—the rewards in the Renaissance always were gained by virtue of the striving of the separated individual in competition with his group. The above-mentioned driving desire for fame in the Renaissance is a seeking of post-mortem reward in the present world. What is significant is the highly individualistic character of this reward: one gains fame, or remembrance by posterity, by excelling, standing *out from* one's fellows.[39]

The positive aspects of the individualism emerging at the Renaissance, especially in respect to the new possibilities for individual self-realization, do not require laboring since they have become an integral part of the conscious and unconscious assumptions of modern culture. But the negative aspects, which

---

[39] Kardiner's viewpoint is that the post-mortem rewards and punishments of medieval ecclesiasticism kept aggressions under control and gave validation to the self. As the power of post-mortem rewards and punishments diminished, there developed an increasing emphasis on rewards here and now and an increased concern for social well-being (prestige, success). The self, no longer validated by post-mortem rewards, then found validation in present success. In the judgment of the present writer, Kardiner's point is partially accurate—specifically in the new concern for present rewards in the Renaissance and the modern development since. But the distinction between *when* rewards and punishments are received—post-mortem in the Middle Ages or here and now in the modern period—easily lends itself to oversimplification, and covers only one aspect of a complex picture. For one example, Boccaccio lauds the pursuit of present satisfactions, in the spirit of the Renaissance; but he also holds that a suprapersonal force, *fortuna*, seeks to block man in his pursuit of pleasure. The important point, however, is that Boccaccio holds that the bold individual has the power to outwit fortuna. *It is this confidence that rewards are gained through individual power which strikes the present writer as the essential characteristic of the Renaissance.* To approach the same problems from a different angle: the tendency to make the distinction between post-mortem and present rewards central as an explanation of the modern concern with success is an oversimplification in the respect that post-mortem religious rewards were presupposed throughout most of the modern period. Immortality was not widely questioned until the nineteenth century (Tillich). But again, the significant aspect of the modern period is not *when* the rewards are received, but *the relation between rewards and the individual's own striving*: the good deeds for which one was rewarded in immortality were the same deeds as made for individual economic success, namely industrious work and conforming to bourgeois morality.

have not been so widely recognized, are pertinent to the present study: namely, (1) the essentially competitive nature of this individualism, (2) the emphasis placed on individual power as against communal values, (3) the beginnings of the unconditional weight placed in modern culture on the goal of individual competitive success, and (4) the psychological concomitants of these developments, present in the Renaissance but to re-emerge in the nineteenth and twentieth centuries in more serious form, namely interpersonal isolation and anxiety. We have used the term "nascent" anxiety in the Renaissance because the consequences of the individualistic pattern in overt, conscious anxiety were largely avoided at the time. Anxiety is discernible in the Renaissance chiefly in symptomatic form. We have seen in the case of Michelangelo that, although isolation was defiantly admitted, there was no conscious admission of anxiety. In this respect there is a sharp difference between the isolated individuals of the fifteenth and sixteenth centuries and those of the nineteenth and twentieth centuries, who, like Kierkegaard, were consciously aware of the anxiety resulting from individual isolation. The central reason that the full implications of interpersonal isolation were evaded in the Renaissance and consequently the full impact of conscious anxiety was avoided, was the great expansiveness of the period. New areas were always available into which the individual could direct his striving if he were frustrated at any one point. This is one way of emphasizing that it was the *beginning* phase of a historical period.

The problem for modern Western culture, with respect to anxiety, was set in the Renaissance: *How is interpersonal community (psychological, economic, ethical, etc.) to be developed and integrated with the values of individual self-realization, thus freeing the members of the society from the sense of isolation and concomitant anxiety inhering in excessive individualism?*

3. Tawney: Competitive Individualism in Economic Developments

The competitive tendencies of the individual in our society have been greatly abetted and reinforced by economic developments since the Renaissance. The breakdown of the medieval guild (in which competition was impossible) opened the door for intensive individual economic competition. Hence it is particularly important to inquire how individual competitive ambition in modern man's character structure is intertwined with the development of industrialism and capitalism. We here follow Tawney's discussion of economic developments in the centuries since the Renaissance, with particular reference to the psychological implications of these developments. In this section we are concerned with the application and working out of the principles which we have described in their emergent form in the Renaissance.

Modern industrialism and capitalism were conditioned by many factors, but on the psychological side the new view of the power of the free individual was of central importance. The rationale for modern industrialism and capitalism was given by the emphasis on the "right" of the individual to amass wealth and employ it as power. Tawney points out that the individual's self-interest and "natural instinct" for aggrandizement were apotheosized as the accepted economic motivations. Industrialism, especially in the last two centuries, is based upon "the repudiation of any authority [such as social value and function] superior to individual reason." [40] This "left men free to follow their own interests or ambitions or appetites, untrammeled by subordination to any common center of allegiance." [41] In this respect modern "industrialism is the perversion of individualism." [42]

This "economic egotism," as Tawney calls it, was based on the assumption that the free pursuit of individual self-interest would automatically lead to economic harmony in society at large.[43] This assumption served to allay anxieties arising from the intrasocial isolation and hostility in economic competition. The competitive individual could believe that the community was

---

[40] R. H. Tawney, *The acquisitive society* (New York, 1920), p. 47.

[41] *Ibid.*, p. 47.

[42] *Ibid.*, p. 49.

[43] This is one form of the assumption in the autonomous rationalism of the seventeenth and eighteenth centuries that the free pursuit of individual reason would lead automatically to a harmony of the individual with society and with "universal reason" (see Chapter 2).

enhanced by his strivings for aggrandizement. During the major part of the modern period this assumption was pragmatically true. It was dramatically substantiated in the respect that the growth of industrialism did greatly increase the means of satisfying everyone's material needs. But in other respects, especially in the later development of monopoly capitalism, the individualistic economic developments here discussed were to have a very harmful effect upon the individual's relation to himself, as well as to his fellow men.

The full psychological implications and results of economic individualism were not to emerge until the middle of the nineteenth century. One of the psychological results of industrialism, especially in its recent phases, is that for the majority of people work has lost its intrinsic meaning. Work has become a "job," in which the criterion of value is not the productive activity itself but the relatively fortuitous results of labor—wages or salary. This shifts the basis of both social esteem and self-esteem from the creative activity itself (the satisfactions from which genuinely increase the individual's feeling of self-strength and thereby realistically decrease anxiety) to the acquisition of wealth. The value placed highest in the industrial system is the aggrandizement of wealth. Thus another of the psychological results of industrialism is that wealth becomes the accepted criterion of prestige and success, "the foundation of public esteem," in Tawney's phrase. The aggrandizement of wealth is by its very nature competitive; success consists of having more wealth than one's neighbors; others going down the scale is the same as one's self going up. Tawney sees from the economic point of view what will later be pointed out from a psychological viewpoint, namely that success defined as the acquisition of wealth involves a vicious circle. One can never be certain one's neighbors and competitors will not gain more wealth; one can never be sure one has attained a position of unassailable security, and hence one is driven by the need always to increase his wealth.[44]

---

[44] In their chapter Why do they work so hard? the Lynds, in their first study of Middletown, note that "both business men and working men seem to be running for dear life in this business of making the money they earn keep pace with the

It is important to note that the acquisition of wealth, as the accepted standard of success, does not refer to increasing material goods for sustenance purposes, or even for the purpose of increasing enjoyment. It refers rather to wealth as a sign of individual power, a proof of achievement and self-worth.

Modern economic individualism, though based on belief in the power of the free individual, has resulted in the phenomenon that increasingly larger numbers of people have to work on the property (capital) of a few powerful owners. It is not surprising that such a situation should lead to widespread insecurity, for not only is the individual faced with a criterion of success over which he has only partial control but also his opportunities for a job are in considerable measure out of his control.[45] *Thus the actual economic developments, particularly in the monopolistic phase of capitalism, work directly against the assumption of freedom for individual endeavor upon which industrialism and capitalism are based.* But, as Tawney points out, the individualistic assumptions are implanted so firmly in our culture that great numbers of people cling to these assumptions despite their contradiction with the reality situation. When anxiety is experienced by members of the middle and lower middle classes, they redouble their efforts to gain security on the basis of the same cultural assumption of individual (property) rights, e.g., saving, investing in property, annuities, etc. Anxiety in members of these classes often becomes an added motivation for their endeavor to defend the individualistic assumptions which are part of the cause of their insecurity. The "hunger for security is so imperious that those who suffer most from the abuses of property [and the assumptions of individual rights upon which property rights are based] . . . will tolerate and even defend them, for fear lest the knife which trims dead matter should cut into the quick." [46]

---

even more rapid growth of their subjective wants."—R. S. Lynd and H. M. Lynd, *Middletown* (New York, 1929), p. 87. It is fair to infer that these "subjective wants" are largely competitive in motivation, i.e., "keeping up with the Joneses."

[45] Tawney writes that the "need for security is fundamental, and almost the gravest indictment of our civilization is that the mass of mankind are without it."— *Op. cit.,* p. 72. In very recent decades the insecurity arising from lack of control of opportunities for a job has been considerably mitigated by the labor union movement.

[46] Tawney, *op. cit.,* pp. 72 ff.

Tawney also makes the highly significant point that the revolutions which served to better the conditions of the middle and
lower classes (as in the eighteenth century) were based upon
the same assumptions as the ruling classes held, namely the
sovereignty of individual rights and the derivative assumption of
property rights.   These revolutions did have valuable results in
extending the base of individual rights.   But for Tawney they
rested on the same fallacious assumption, that individual freedom for aggrandizement is sovereign over social function.   This
point is of fundamental importance for our later question of
whether there is an essential difference between the revolutions
and social changes which have occurred in the previous centuries
of the modern period and the revolutions and upheavals which
confront our contemporaneous culture.

What is lacking in the individualism which has characterized
economic developments since the Renaissance is, in Tawney's
view, a sense of the social function of work and property.   The
individualistic assumption "cannot unite men, for what unites
them is the bond of service to a common purpose, and that bond it
repudiates, since its very essence is the maintenance of rights
irrespective of service." [47]   This is in accord with the hypothesis
of the present study, that competitive individualism militates
against the experience of community, and that lack of community
is a centrally important factor in contemporaneous anxiety.[48]

4. Fromm: Individual Isolation in Modern Culture

In the previous sections of this chapter we have been surveying the historical situation out of which competitive individualism developed, as presented by historians of the Renaissance and

---

[47] *Ibid.,* pp. 81-82.

[48] Tawney gives several explanations for the fact that the contradictions in
modern industrial development were largely held in check in the modern period
until the nineteenth and twentieth centuries. One reason was that industrialism
seemed capable of infinite expansion. Another reason was that the motivations of
hunger and fear on the part of the workers kept the system working with some
efficiency. But when it became manifest that capitalism in its monopolistic phases
contradicted the very assumptions of individual freedom on which it was based;
and when in the nineteenth and twentieth centuries the threats of fear and hunger
had been mitigated by the growth of the labor unions, the contradictions inherent in
individualistic economic development became more overt.

by the economic historian Tawney. We now turn to two writers who interpret the psychological and cultural meaning of these facts, Erich Fromm and Abram Kardiner.

Fromm's central concern is with the psychological isolation of modern man which has accompanied the individual freedom emerging at the Renaissance.[49] His discussion is particularly cogent in respect to the interrelationship of this isolation with economic developments; he shows that "certain factors in the modern industrial system in general and in its monopolistic phase in particular make for the development of a personality which feels powerless and alone, anxious and insecure."[50] It is self-evident that the experience of isolation is first cousin to anxiety; more specifically, psychological isolation beyond a certain point always results in anxiety. The human being develops as an individual in a social matrix; hence the problem Fromm attacks is how the individual, with his freedom, is able or unable to relate himself to his interpersonal world. It is significant that Fromm is like Kierkegaard in the nineteenth century in the respect that both see the problem of anxiety in terms of individuality, freedom, and isolation.[51]

Anxiety and Freedom.—It is necessary first to note Fromm's concept of the *dialectical* nature of freedom. Freedom always has two aspects: in its negative aspect it is freedom *from* restraints and authority, but in its positive aspect it always involves the question of whether this freedom will be used *for* new relatedness. Mere negative freedom results in the isolation of the individual.

This dialectical nature of freedom can be seen in the genesis of the individual child as well as in the phylogenesis of character structure in a culture like that of Western man since the Renaissance. The child begins life bound to parents by "primary ties."

---

[49] Erich Fromm, *Escape from freedom* (New York, 1941). Fromm's contribution is also particularly significant because of its method. The psychological and sociological approaches are interfused; he endeavors to understand modern man's character structure as a progressive cultural product, with the individual seen as a psychological entity having its meaning and taking its form in its interpersonal relations.

[50] *Op. cit.,* p. 240.

[51] See footnote 85, pages 44-45.

His growth involves an increasing freedom from dependence on parents—the process called individuation. But individuation brings with it threats, potential or actual; it involves a progressive breaking of the original unity of the primary ties; the child becomes aware of being a separate entity, of being alone. "This separation from a world which in comparison with one's own individual existence is overwhelmingly strong and powerful, and often threatening and dangerous, creates a feeling of powerlessness and anxiety. As long as one was an integral part of that world, unaware of the possibilities and responsibilities of individual action, one did not need to be afraid of it." [52] This sense of isolation and concomitant anxiety cannot be tolerated indefinitely. Ideally, one expects the child to develop new and positive relatedness on the basis of his growing strength as an individual, a relatedness which is expressed as he becomes an adult by means of love and productive work. But actually the problem is never solved ideally or simply; individual freedom involves a persistent dialectic at every point of growth. How the issue is met—whether by new positive relatedness on one hand, or by surrendering freedom in order to avoid isolation and anxiety, by developing new dependencies, or by the formation of the innumerable compromise solutions which allay anxiety (the "neurotic patterns")—will be decisive for the development of the personality.

The same dialectic of freedom can be observed on the cultural level. The emergence of individuality at the Renaissance brought freedom *from* medieval authority and regulation—freedom from ecclesiastical, economic, social, and political restraints. But simultaneously the freedom meant a severing of those ties which had afforded security and the sense of belonging. This severance, in Fromm's terms, was "bound to create a deep feeling of insecurity, powerlessness, doubt, aloneness and anxiety." [53]

The freedom from medieval restraints in the economic area—the freeing of the markets from guild regulation, the lifting of the proscriptions on usury and the accumulation of wealth—was both an expression of the new individualism and a powerful in-

---

[52] Fromm, *op. cit.*, p. 29.
[53] *Op. cit.*, p. 63.

centive for it. One could now devote one's self to economic aggrandizement to the extent of one's abilities (and luck). But this economic freedom involved increasing tendencies toward individual isolation and subjection to new powers. The individual is now "threatened by powerful suprapersonal forces, capital and the market. His relationship to his fellow-men, with everyone a potential competitor, has become hostile and estranged; he is free—that is, alone, isolated, threatened from all sides." [54]

It is particularly important to observe the effect of these developments on the middle class, not only because this class was to become increasingly dominant in the modern period, but also because there is some reason for hypothesizing that neurotic anxiety in modern culture is especially a middle-class problem.[55] At first chiefly the concern of a few powerful capitalists of the Renaissance, the accumulation of wealth became an increasingly dominant concern of the urban middle classes. In the sixteenth century the middle class was caught between the very rich, who made considerable exhibition of their luxury and power, and the very poor. Though threatened by the rising capitalists, the members of the middle class were concerned with preserving law and order, Fromm points out. It might be added that they accepted the assumptions underlying the new capitalism. Hence the hostility which members of the middle class experienced in their threatened situation was not expressed in open rebellion as was the case with the peasants in Central Europe. Middle-class hostility was largely repressed and took the form of indignation and resentment. It is a known phenomenon that repressed hostility generates more anxiety,[56] and hence an intra-psychic dynamic served to increase middle-class anxiety.

One means of allaying anxiety is frantic activity. The anxiety arising out of the dilemma of powerlessness in the face of suprapersonal economic forces on one hand, but theoretical belief in the efficacy of individual effort on the other, was symptomized partly by excessive activism. Fromm points out

---

[54] *Ibid.*, p. 62.
[55] See discussion of fascism and the middle classes below; see also Chapter 8.
[56] See Horney, Chapter 4.

that the great emphasis in the sixteenth and subsequent centuries on work had as one of its psychodynamics the allaying of anxiety. Work became a virtue in itself, quite apart from the creative and social values emerging from work. (In Calvinism, successful work, though not a means of gaining salvation, is a visible sign that one is among the chosen.) A high valuation on the importance of time and regularity accompanied this emphasis on work.[57] "The drive for relentless work," Fromm writes of the sixteenth century, "was one of the fundamental productive forces, no less important for the development of our industrial system than steam and electricity." [58]

Anxiety and the Ideals of the Market Place.—The consequences of these developments for the character structure of Western man are, of course, profound. Since the values of the market were the highest criteria, persons also became valued as commodities which could be bought and sold. A person's worth, Fromm remarks, is then his salable market value, whether it is skill or "personality" that is up for sale. This commercial valuing (or, more accurately, devaluing) of persons and its consequences in our culture has been vividly and penetratingly described by Auden in his poem, *The Age of Anxiety*. When a young man in that poem wonders whether he can find a useful vocation, another character answers:

> . . . Well, you will soon
> Not bother but acknowledge yourself
> As market-made, a commodity
> Whose value varies, a vendor who has
> To obey his buyer. . . .[59]

The market value, then, becomes the individual's valuation of himself, so that self-confidence and "self-feeling" (one's experi-

---

[57] See also Lewis Mumford, *op. cit.*

[58] Fromm, *op. cit.*, p. 94.

[59] W. H. Auden, *The age of anxiety* (New York, 1947), p. 42. Just as there are many significant parallels between the thought of Fromm and that of Kierkegaard, there is also a remarkable similarity between the picture of our culture presented in Auden's poetry and that given in Fromm's psychological interpretations. Auden and Fromm are impressed by the same characteristics of our society : the automaton conformity, the alienation of man from himself and his fellows, and the destruction of individuality and originality resulting from the apotheosis of commercial values. See discussion of Auden in Chapter 1, pages 5-6.

ence of identity with one's self) are largely reflections of what others think of one, in this case the "others" being those who represent the market. Thus contemporary economic processes have contributed not only to an alienation of man from man, but likewise to "self-alienation"—an alienation of the individual from himself. Feelings of isolation and anxiety consequently occur not only because the individual is set in competition with his fellows, but also because he is thrown into conflict about his inner valuation of himself. As Fromm very well summarizes the point:

> Since modern man experiences himself both as the seller and as the commodity to be sold on the market, his self-esteem depends on conditions beyond his control. If he is "successful," he is valuable; if he is not, he is worthless. The degree of insecurity which results from this orientation can hardly be overestimated. If one feels that one's own value is not constituted primarily by the human qualities one possesses, but by one's success on a competitive market with ever-changing conditions, one's self-esteem is bound to be shaky and in constant need of confirmation by others.[60]

In such a situation one is driven to strive relentlessly for "success"; this is the chief way to validate one's self and to allay anxiety. And any failure in the competitive struggle is a threat to the quasi-esteem for one's self—which, quasi though it be, is all one has in such a situation—and releases powerful feelings of helplessness and inferiority.[61]

Mechanisms of Escape from Anxiety.—It is to be expected that certain "mechanisms of escape" from the situation of isola-

---

[60] Erich Fromm, *Man for himself: an inquiry into the psychology of ethics* (New York, 1947), p. 72.

[61] Fromm points out that in the more recent developments of monopoly capitalism, the tendencies toward devaluation of persons have been accelerated. Not only workers, but middle-sized businessmen, white-collar workers, and even consumers as well, play an increasingly impersonal role. The function of each is, by and large, to be a cog in a technical machine too vast for the ordinary individual to understand, let alone to influence. There exists the theoretical freedom to change one's job or buy a different kind of product, but this generally is a negative freedom in that one changes from being one cog to being another; the "market" continues to operate on the basis of suprapersonal forces over which the ordinary individual has little if any control. To be sure, such movements as labor unions and consumer co-operatives have made headway against these developments, but it would

tion and anxiety should have developed. The mechanism most frequently employed in our culture, Fromm submits, is that of *automaton conformity*. An individual "adopts entirely the kind of personality offered to him by cultural patterns; and he therefore becomes exactly as all others are and as they expect him to be." [62] This conformity proceeds on the assumption that the "person who gives up his individual self and becomes an automaton, identical with millions of other automatons around him, need not feel alone and anxious any more." [63] Such conformity can be understood again in terms of Fromm's idea of the dialectical nature of freedom: there has been much progress in our culture in regard to the negative aspect of freedom, e.g., freedom from outward authority over individual belief, faith, opinion, but this has resulted to a great extent in a psychological and spiritual vacuum. Since the isolation involved in mere freedom from authority cannot long be maintained, there develop new inner substitutes for the rejected authority, which Fromm terms the "anonymous authorities" like public opinion and common sense.[64] For example, one phase of modern freedom has been the right of each individual to worship as he chooses, but, adds Fromm, "we do not sufficiently recognize that while it is a victory against those powers of Church and State which did not allow man to worship according to his own conscience, the modern individual has lost to a great extent the inner capacity to have faith in anything which is not provable by the methods of the natural sciences." [65] The "inner restraints, compulsions, fears" which fill the vacuum left by mere negative freedom provide strong motivations for automaton conformity. Though this conformity is acquired by the individual as a means of avoiding isolation and anxiety, it actually works the other way: the individual conforms at the price of renouncing his autonomous strength, and hence he becomes more helpless, powerless, and insecure.

---

probably be generally agreed that their influence has been so far to mitigate the impersonality of economic life rather than to overcome it.

[62] *Escape from freedom,* p. 185.
[63] *Ibid.,* p. 186.
[64] *Ibid.,* p. 105.
[65] *Ibid.,* p. 105.

Other mechanisms of escape from individual isolation which Fromm describes are sado-masochism and destructiveness. Though sadism and masochism may have as one of their expressions the desire to inflict pain or have pain inflicted on one's self, they are more basically forms of symbiosis in which an individual endeavors to overcome isolation by becoming absorbed in the existence of another person or persons. "The different forms which the masochistic strivings assume have one aim: *to get rid of the individual self, to lose one's self;* in other words, *to get rid of the burden of freedom.*" [66] In masochism we also find the individual endeavoring to compensate for helplessness by becoming part of the "bigger" power. Destructiveness—a phenomenon much evidenced in recent sociopolitical developments like fascism—is likewise related to the need to escape from unbearable feelings of powerlessness and isolation. The rationale for this can be seen in the relation of anxiety (in this context, anxiety arising from isolation) to hostility. Anxiety creates hostility (see earlier discussions in this study), and destructiveness is one of the overt forms this hostility assumes.

Fascism is a complex socioeconomic phenomenon, but certainly on its psychological side it cannot be understood without reference to anxiety, and particularly to the phases of anxiety which Fromm discusses, namely the feeling of isolation, insignificance, and powerlessness of the individual.[67] It is accepted that fascism begins chiefly as a lower-middle-class phenomenon. In analyzing the origins of the German form of fascism, Fromm describes the powerlessness experienced by the middle class after World War I and especially after the depression of 1929.[68] This class was not only economically, but also psychologically, insecure; it had lost its previous centers of authority, the monarchy and the family. The fascist authoritarianism, characterized by sado-masochism and destructiveness, had a function which is

---

[66] *Ibid.,* p. 152.

[67] Many of the same things may be observed in communism in its sociopolitical authoritarian form.

[68] It is not meant to exclude the increased feelings of powerlessness on the part of the workers and peasants also. "The vast majority of the population was seized with the feeling of individual insignificance and powerlessness which we have described as typical for monopolistic capitalism in general."—*Escape from freedom,* p. 217.

comparable psychologically to a neurotic symptom; namely, fascism compensated for powerlessness and individual isolation and protected the individual from the anxiety-creating situation.[69] If one compares fascism to a neurotic symptom, it seems to the present writer that fascism is a neurotic form of "community." [70]

5. KARDINER: ANXIETY AND WESTERN MAN'S PSYCHOLOGICAL GROWTH PATTERN

Kardiner's psychodynamic analysis of Plainville, a Midwestern rural village, and his outline of the psychological growth pattern of Western man furnish an approach to the problem of the cultural sources of modern anxiety somewhat different from Fromm's. Kardiner's focus is on the *basic personality structure* of Western man, which he feels has changed very little in the last 2,000 years, whereas Fromm's concern is with the *particular character structure* of Western man in the modern period. Using Plainville as his base, Kardiner outlines the personality growth pattern out of which anxiety arises, and he briefly suggests how this growth pattern and its anxieties are manifested in the historical development of Western man.[71]

In Plainville Kardiner finds a great deal of anxiety and much intrasocial hostility. Social-prestige goals are dominant, and in the competition for these goals the individual person finds his self-validation on the one hand or his loss of self-esteem and feelings of inferiority and failure on the other. How the social-prestige goals become dominant, why the striving for them is characterized by such compulsive competitiveness, and how anxiety and hostility are thereby aroused are questions the understanding of which requires noting briefly the psychological growth pattern of the individual in Plainville.

The growth pattern in Plainville and in Western man is characterized, first, by a strong affective relation with the

---

69 Cf. Kurt Goldstein, Chapter 3 above. Also cf. Kurt Riezler, The social psychology of fear, *Amer. J. Sociol.*, 1944, 49, 489.

70 This point is discussed further in Section 3 of the next chapter.

71 Abram Kardiner, *The psychological frontiers of society* (New York, 1945).

mother. Compared to primitive cultures, the maternal care, affective satisfaction, and protection given the baby in Plainville are very good. This lays the groundwork in the child for a high valuation of himself. Such good early affective development makes for the building of both a strong ego and a strong superego (idealization of parents). Though this close affective relationship with the mother may open the way for passivity and excessive affective dependence on the part of the individual as he confronts later crises, its effect is normally very constructive in that it lays a solid base for personality development.

But the second characteristic of the growth pattern is the *introduction of taboos,* via parental discipline. Kardiner sees these taboos as relating chiefly to sex and toilet training. This considerably distorts the psychological growth which has begun so constructively. Doubt arises in the child's mind concerning the continuation of parental care and the satisfaction of his affective needs which have been cultivated by this care. The relaxor (pleasure) patterns of the child become blocked. The ensuing conflict may have several results. Hostility may develop as a result of the blocked pleasure patterns. This hostility may be directed toward parents—in which case, in proportion to the severity of the hostility, it tends to be repressed. Or the hostility may be directed toward siblings, who are rivals in the striving for affective support the child has learned to expect but now sees threatened. Since the satisfaction of affective needs was originally associated with parents (especially the mother), the anxiety arising from blocked pleasure patterns may lead to increased dependence on the mother or (with lesser probability) on the father. Parents may thus occupy an inflated position as relievers of anxiety. Finally, and of considerable significance in this growth pattern, the concept of *obedience* is greatly inflated. Special force attaches to allaying anxiety by obedience, and conversely special force is given to guilt feeling and concomitant anxiety cued off by disobedience.

The personality growing up with the above pattern will be characterized by considerable "emotional potential," as Kardiner phrases it, but also by an incapacity for direct expression of this emotional potential because of the blocked action patterns. This conflict has its positive aspect in the high degree of productivity of which Western man is capable, but its negative aspect lies in the fact that it makes Western man vulnerable to considerable anxiety.

How do the particular occasions of anxiety in Plainville and in Western man, such as anxiety related to success, competition for social prestige, and so forth, arise out of this growth pattern? Kardiner holds that the "socially approved goal of success is made the vehicle of compensation for all other shortcomings in pleasure and relaxor functions. As long as the individual can pretend to some goal of success or security, he can claim some self-esteem." [72] The extensive capacities for self-expression which the personality in such a culture has developed are channeled in the direction of achieving social prestige, or wealth as a symbol of prestige. "The struggle for success becomes such a powerful force because it is the equivalent of self-preservation and self-esteem." [73] The personality produced by the above growth pattern has strong needs for validation of his self-esteem and at the same time experiences considerable frustration of that self-esteem. Hence it is understandable that, whenever anxiety arises, the individual's tendency would be to endeavor to allay the anxiety and re-establish his self-esteem by striving for new success.

The intrasocial hostility is an added motivation for competitive striving. Kardiner describes this intrasocial hostility as arising chiefly from blocked pleasure drives. The hostility tends to be self-increasing in the society, since when one is prohibited from pleasures himself, he joins with the group in prohibiting others (e.g., gossip). The intrasocial hostility can then be expressed in socially approved aggressive competition, generally in competitive work. But such hostility and aggression prevent the individual from establishing friendly relations with his fellows, and hence his feeling of isolation tends to increase. The personality in Plainville and in Western society generally has a firm base set for community, and strong needs for community, by virtue of the good early affective relationships. But com-

[72] *Op. cit.*, pp. 411-12.
[73] *Op. cit.*, p. 376.

munity tends to be blocked by these other factors in the constellation, e.g., the intrasocial hostility leading to aggression and competition.

The values in Kardiner's analysis of the psychological growth
pattern will be self-evident. A question is raised here, in line
with the viewpoint expressed previously in the present study:
Is it the blocking of pleasure patterns through taboos which accounts for the conflict, anxiety, and hostility arising in this
growth pattern, or are these taboos, rather, the *locus* in which
the control and domination of the child by parents and consequent limitation of the normal requirements for expansion of the
child's personality take place? The emphasis in the present
study is that the fact of control and suppression of development
of the child and the arbitrary uses made of parental discipline are
the important elements in the growth pattern, and that sexual
and toilet taboos are one form (in some phases of our culture,
such as Plainville, the most prominent form) in which the par-
ent-child struggle occurs. To the present writer what seems
most crucial as the psychological source of later anxiety is the
inconsistencies in the child-training in Western culture as
Kardiner describes it. This is borne out by Kardiner's analysis
of the Alorese society, in which the parental behavior toward
children is marked by irregularity, deceit, and undependability
and the child typically grows up to be isolated, mistrustful, and
anxious.

How did competitive social prestige emerge as the dominant
goal in the historical trajectory of Western man? Kardiner
holds that there has been very little change in the basic personality structure of Western man from the time of Job and Sophocles
to the modern citizen of New York.[74] The good early parental

---

[74] There would be considerable question about this statement. (See Robert K.
Merton, *New York Times,* Book Review Section, July 1, 1945.) It may be true
that the citizens of Greece in the fifth century B.C. and those of modern New York
exhibit great similarities in basic personality structure when both are compared to
the Eskimo. But the crucial practical problem historically is how differences occurred between different periods in our own culture; in the words of Mannheim,
to which we have referred above, "Why did the Middle Ages and the Renaissance
produce entirely different types of men?" It may be that "basic personality structure" is a concept which does not lend itself to an illumination of the changes of
character structure which produce different types in different periods. In any case,
the present writer feels in the summary of the historical viewpoint which Kardiner

care, the subsequent extensive taboos and systems of impulse control, and the hostility and aggression arising from these taboos and control have been fairly constant throughout Western history, according to Kardiner. There has normally been a strong system of parental obedience, with rewards and punishments to keep the system of taboos and concomitant aggressions under control. Kardiner's view is that this control was maintained in the Middle Ages by the immobile family constellation, by the protection and power of the lord in feudalism, and by the religious system of post-mortem rewards and punishments. Obedience could be obtained and anxiety allayed by family, feudal lord, and church. When the power of these sources of control radically diminished at the Renaissance, the concern with social well-being (success, prestige) was substituted. This concern with social well-being was greatly facilitated by the development of science and capitalism. The self now found its validation in social prestige; tensions and anxiety were allayed by success in terms of social well-being; and intrasocial hostility and aggression, no longer held in check by ecclesiastical, family, and feudal controls, now became motivations for self-validation *via* competitive striving.

6. SUMMARY AND CONCLUSIONS

We have discussed the genetic background of a pattern which is the *occasion* for much anxiety in contemporaneous culture, namely, individual competitive ambition. It remains to summarize the status of the personality in our society with respect to this pattern and then to consider particularly the *quantity* of contemporaneous anxiety in relation to the historical stage of development of modern culture.

Social prestige goals are dominant in our culture, social prestige being defined as success and this success in turn being de-

---

has so far published the lack of a historical-genetic approach, an approach which sees the progressive changes in personality as both cause and effect of the changing historical situation. It is also the present writer's judgment that Kardiner fails to see the historical relativity of all presuppositions, including the presuppositions upon which our contemporaneous psychological science is based. We have indicated above that this sense of historical relativity is necessary for historical consciousness.

fined chiefly in economic terms. Individual economic success —i.e., the acquisition of wealth—is accepted as proof and symbol of individual power. Since success is measured against the status of others, the striving for success is essentially competitive: one is successful if one excels and triumphs over others. The goal of competitive success not only arose by virtue of an emphasis on individual power set over against the community in the Renaissance, but as this goal persists it tends always to increase the juxtaposition of the individual and the community. Being the dominant cultural value, competitive success is likewise the dominant criterion of self-valuation; it is accepted as the means of validating the self in one's own eyes as well as in the eyes of others. *Whatever threatens this goal is therefore the occasion for profound anxiety for the individual in our culture because the threat is to values held essential to his existence as a personality, i.e., essential to his worth and prestige as a personality.*

The dominant goal of competitive success, though defined chiefly in economic terms, carries over to become the individual's goal in his personal relationships as well. Horney has excellently described this phenomenon in our culture:

> It must be emphasized that competitiveness, and the potential hostility that accompanies it, pervades all human relationships. Competitiveness is one of the predominant factors in social relationships. It pervades the relationships between men and men, between women and women, and whether the point of competition be popularity, competence, attractiveness, or any other social value, it greatly impairs the possibilities of reliable friendship. It also as already indicated disturbs the relations between men and women, not only in the choice of the partner but in the entire struggle with him for superiority. It pervades school life. And perhaps most important of all, it pervades the family situation, so that as a rule the child is inoculated with this germ from the very beginning.[75]

Thus love, for example, instead of being a constructive means of overcoming individual isolation, is often a means of self-

---

[75] Karen Horney, *The neurotic personality of our time* (New York, 1937), p. 284.

aggrandizement.[76] In our culture love is frequently sought as a means of allaying anxiety, but when it occurs in a competitive, depersonalized framework, it increases feelings of isolation and hostility and thereby increases anxiety.

Anxiety arises as a result of the individualistic competitive pattern here discussed not simply when the individual finds his possibilities for success threatened but in many more subtle ways. Anxiety arises out of the interpersonal isolation and alienation from others that inheres in a pattern in which self-validation depends upon triumphing over others, which was already discernible in many of the powerful and successful individuals of the Renaissance. Anxiety likewise arises out of the intrasocial hostility produced by competitive individualism. Finally, anxiety arises out of the self-alienation resulting from viewing one's self as an object of the market, or making one's feeling of self-strength dependent upon extrinsic wealth rather than intrinsic capacity and productivity. These attitudes not only distort one's relation to one's self, but to the extent that they make one's criterion of self-worth contingent upon a kind of success which can be threatened every day by one's neighbors' counter-successes, they augment one's feelings of vulnerability, helplessness, and powerlessness.

Moreover, "vicious circle" mechanisms operate in the individualistic competitive pattern which tend to make anxiety self-increasing. The culturally accepted method of allaying anxiety is redoubling one's efforts to achieve success. Since intrasocial hostility and aggression can be expressed in the socially approved method of competition, the anxious individual increases his competitive striving. But the more competitive, aggressive striving, the more isolation, hostility, and anxiety. This vicious circle may be graphed as follows: competitive individual striving→ intrasocial hostility→ isolation→ anxiety→ increased competitive striving. Thus the methods most generally used to

---

[76] Two examples of this use of "love" for competitive purposes are (1) the winning of a socially desirable ("beautiful") mate as a proof of one's social competence, and the consequent viewing of this mate as an acquisition in much the same way as one would view winning profits on the stock market; or (2) the valuing of one's children because they win prizes in college or in other ways add to the competitive status of the family name.

allay anxiety in such a constellation actually increase anxiety in the long run.

We now turn to the problem of the relation between the quantity of anxiety experienced by contemporaneous individuals and the present state of our culture. The conviction that Western civilization in the twentieth century is permeated by considerable quantities of anxiety (or anxiety-like states) has been expressed in different ways by Tawney, Tillich, Fromm, Horney, Mannheim, Cassirer, Riezler, and others. Each presents the evidence and the explanation for the situation from the particular viewpoint of his investigation. The common agreement is that underlying this anxiety are profound cultural changes, which are described in varying terms of "the crisis in man's view of himself," the "disintegration" of traditional cultural forms, and so forth. We have discussed earlier in this study the combinations of attitudes and circumstances which dispelled and allayed [77] anxiety in the earlier centuries of the modern period. The attitudes—consisting chiefly of the confidence that the pursuit of individual reason and individual economic striving would enhance community weal and lead automatically to social harmony —served to dispel the feelings of isolation inherent in individualism. Certain circumstances (taking our example from the economic sphere, the expanding state of capitalism and industrialism) made these attitudes efficacious during a major part of the modern period. But in the late ninteenth and twentieth centuries it has become progressively manifest that individual competitive ambition does not result automatically in the advance of social weal but rather produces increasing feelings of powerlessness and isolation and increasing "dehumanization" of persons (Karl Marx), estrangement of people from each other (Tillich), and self-estrangement (Fromm).

---

[77] The term "dispel" is used in connection with an attitude which realistically obviates anxiety, and "allay" for an attitude which permits the avoidance of anxiety without solving the problem underlying the anxiety. The same attitude may dispel anxiety at one period but become a means of allaying (avoiding) anxiety at another. For example, the assumption that individualistic economic striving furthers community weal was realistically true, and did dispel anxiety during the expanding stages of capitalism; in recent economic developments the assumption is considerably less efficacious, but it persists as a means of allaying anxiety.

Hence almost every investigator describes the present period as one of cultural disunity. This disunity is derived from a number of different kinds of analysis: Mannheim, from the sociological viewpoint, speaks of the "phase of disintegration" through which Western society is passing; Cassirer, from the philosophical viewpoint, derives the disunity from the "loss of conceptual unity"; and Riezler, from the viewpoint of social psychology, derives the disunity from the "lack of a universe of discourse" in our culture.

Psychological disunity is shown by inconsistencies of attitudes and contradictions in standards in a culture. That our contemporaneous society is replete with psychological contradictions and inconsistencies has been attested by too many investigators to be cited here.[78] We shall here describe two contradictions related to the special problem of competitive individualism. First there is the contradiction between the accepted theoretical ideal that each individual is free to gain economic success by his own efforts and merit and the actuality that he is to a great extent dependent upon suprapersonal technical forces (e.g., the market) over which he has little or no control. Kardiner notes that the people in Plainville "subscribe in the main to the American credo of vertical mobility and believe that a man can become anything he wants to. Actually, opportunities are very limited for them . . . even if they go away." [79] Horney phrases this contradiction as between "the alleged freedom of the individual and all his factual limitations. The individual is told by society that he is free, independent, can decide his life according to his own free will; 'the great game of life' is open to him, and he can get what he wants if he is efficient and energetic. In actual fact, for the majority of people all these possibilities are limited. . . . The result for the individual is a wavering between a feeling of boundless power in determining his own fate and a feeling of entire helplessness." [80]

---

78 Cf. Karen Horney, *Our inner conflicts* (New York, 1945), p. 24; Kardiner, *op. cit.,* p. 377, pp. 447-48; H. Flanders Dunbar, *Psychosomatic diagnosis* (New York, 1943), p. 678; etc.

79 Kardiner, *op. cit.,* p. 264.

80 *Neurotic personality of our time,* p. 289.

Another contradiction is between the accepted individualistic rationalism ("each individual can decide on the basis of the facts") and the actuality that most decisions of the individual are based on motivations quite beyond conscious rational appraisal of the situation. The psychological helplessness arising out of this contradiction often leads the individual to cling to the illusion of rational power under what Fromm terms the "anonymous authorities of public opinion," "science," etc.[81] This illusion of rationality temporarily allays anxiety by suppressing the contradiction.[82]

Contradictions and inconsistencies in a culture make the member of the society more vulnerable to anxiety because they increase the number of situations in which he is unable to decide on an approved course of action.[83] But such contradictions also increase anxiety in that, when the individual's values and goals are threatened, he cannot orient himself by reference to consistent systems of value within his culture. The threat the individual experiences is therefore not just to his possibility of attaining his goal, but almost any threat may likewise raise doubts as to whether the goal is worth attaining; i.e., the threat becomes a threat to the goal itself. Thus what might objectively appear to be only a minor threat to an individual's values may in our culture throw the individual into panic and profound disorientation.

---

[81] "To the rational man of the industrial age everything has a 'natural cause'; no demons interfere. Yet in times of crisis, he too can be gripped by indefinite fear. . . . Rational man is the heir of a long period of relative security in which he accumulated a great many matters of course to be taken for granted. This dubious training may be partly responsible for his vulnerability. His scheme of order is rational only in theory."—Kurt Riezler, Social psychology of fear, *Amer. J. Socio.,* 1944, **44,** 496.

[82] Beyond the fact that any unclarified contradiction increases insecurity and anxiety, the contradiction between individualistic rationalism and anonymous authority has special point for the problem of anxiety in that the facing of anxiety is often avoided because of its "irrational" nature. The tendency in our culture in this regard is to "rationalize" anxiety into specific fears, which the individual may then believe he confronts in a rational way. But this involves a suppression of the real source of the anxiety. See Horney, *The neurotic personality of our time,* p. 49.

[83] Cf. the reference in Chapter 1 to the Lynds's statement that the individual in Middletown is frequently "caught in a chaos of conflicting patterns, none of them wholly condemned, but no one of them clearly approved and free from confusion."

We now go further and raise the question of *what* values and goals are threatened in our culture? Mannheim holds that "it is important to remember that our society is faced, not with brief unrest, but with a radical change of structure." [84] In periods of unemployment, for example, anxiety arises not simply because of the temporary threat to subsistence:

> For man, however, the catastrophe [of unemployment] lies not merely in the disappearance of external opportunities for work but also in the fact that his elaborate emotional system, intricately connected as it is with the smooth working of social institutions, now loses its object-fixation. The petty aims towards which almost all his strivings are directed suddenly disappear, and, not merely does he now lack a place to work, a daily task, and an opportunity for using the integrated labor attitudes formed through long training, but his habitual desires and impulses remain ungratified. Even if the immediate needs of life are satisfied, by means of unemployment relief, the whole life-organization and the family hopes and expectations are annihilated.[85]

Then Mannheim proceeds to the point which seems to this writer of crucial significance:

> The panic reaches its height when the individual comes to realize that his insecurity is not simply a personal one, but is common to masses of his fellows, and it becomes clear to him that there is no longer any social authority to set unquestioned standards and determine his behavior. *Herein lies the difference between individual unemployment and general insecurity.* If in normal times an individual loses his job, he may indeed despair,

---

[84] Karl Mannheim, *Man and society in an age of reconstruction* (New York, 1941), p. 6. Mannheim sees the "phase of disintegration" through which Western society is now passing as consisting of a conflict between traditional principles of "laissez-faire" and "planless regulation" (totalitarianism). Laissez faire, as an economic and social principle, was serviceable during the major part of the modern period. When, due to various developments in the late industrial age, the principles of laissez-faire were no longer serviceable, some form of regulation was bound to appear. The "morbid" forms of regulation which did appear are, in his terms, "dictatorship, conformity and barbarism." Mannheim is convinced that the endeavor to return to laissez-faire principles is neither a possible nor a constructive solution, nor obviously is acquiescence to planless regulation. His recommendation is democracy based upon economic planning. In many respects the analysis in the present study parallels Mannheim's analysis, his term "laissez-faire" being parallel to the term "competitive individualism" as used here.

[85] *Ibid.,* p. 128.

but his reactions are more or less prescribed and he follows a general pattern in his distress.[86]

In other words, in individual unemployment the person can still believe in the validity of the cultural values and goals, despite the fact that his achieving the goals himself is at the time threatened. But in mass unemployment and insecurity (such as preceded the fascist developments in Europe) the individual cannot even believe in the values and goals basic to his culture.

We here submit that the *quantity of anxiety prevalent in the present period arises from the fact that the assumptions underlying modern culture are themselves threatened.*[87] The distinction is between a peripheral threat—i.e., a threat which members of the society can meet on the basis of the assumptions of their culture—and a threat on a deeper level, namely a threat to the underlying assumptions, the "charter" [88] of the culture itself. The reader will recall Tawney's argument that the previous revolutions in the modern period occurred on the accepted cultural assumption of the sovereignty of individual rights; the revolutions sought and obtained a broadening of the base of individual rights, but this underlying assumption of the culture was itself unquestioned and unthreatened. It is here submitted that the threats involved in the present social changes are different in the respect that they are not threats which can be met on the basis of the assumptions of the culture but rather are threats to those assumptions themselves. It seems to the writer that only thus can we understand the profound anxiety which occurs in many an individual in our society at the prospect of some minor economic change, an anxiety entirely out of proportion to the actual threat. The threat is experienced not as a threat to subsistence, nor even chiefly to the prestige of the individual concerned, but is rather *a threat to basic assumptions which have been identified with the existence of the culture, and which the*

---

[86] *Ibid.,* p. 130 (italics mine).

[87] See Rollo May, Historical roots of modern anxiety theories, paper delivered at symposium on "Anxiety" of the Amer. Psychopath. Ass., June 3, 1949 (to be published).

[88] The term is B. Malinowski's, used in a lecture.

individual, as a participant in the culture, has identified with his own existence.[89]

It is implicit in this analysis that the basic assumptions threatened in our present culture are those connected with the pattern of competitive individualistic ambition which has been central in our society since the Renaissance. The individualistic assumptions are threatened because in the present phases of social development they destroy the individual's experience of community. Totalitarianism in this discussion has been viewed as a cultural neurotic symptom of the need for community—a symptom in the respect that it is grasped as a means of allaying anxiety resulting from the feelings of powerlessness and helplessness of the isolated, alienated individuals produced in a society in which competitive individualism has been the dominant goal. In this sense totalitarianism is the substitution of collectivism for community, as Tillich has pointed out. It is submitted in this analysis that one of the central requirements for the constructive overcoming of anxiety in our society is the development of adequate forms of community.[90]

---

[89] In this respect what is threatened is the individual's "faith"—a faith which has been described in this analysis as confidence in the efficacy of competitive individualistic ambition.

[90] The term "community," as used here, implies a positive quality of relatedness of the individual to the other persons in his social environment. In this sense it is to be differentiated from the neutral term "society." Everyone belongs to a society whether he wishes it or not, whether he contributes constructively to its development or does the reverse. Community implies one's relating one's self to others affirmatively and responsibly. For example, community in the economic sense implies (following Tawney) an emphasis on the social values and functions of work. Community in the psychological sense involves the individual's relating himself to others in love as well as creative work (Fromm).

Chapter 6

SUMMARY AND SYNTHESIS OF THEORIES
OF ANXIETY

I speak purposely of "hypotheses." This [the formulating of hypotheses on anxiety] is the most difficult task that has been set us, but the difficulty does not lie in the incompleteness of our observations, for it is actually the commonest and most familiar phenomena that present us with such riddles; nor does it lie in the remoteness of the speculations to which these phenomena give rise, for speculation hardly comes into the picture in this connection. No, it is genuinely a question of hypotheses; that is to say, of the introduction of the right abstract ideas, and of their application to the raw material of observation so as to bring order and lucidity into it.—Sigmund Freud, in opening paragraph in chapter on "Anxiety" in *New Introductory Lectures*.

In this chapter our purpose is to synthesize the theories and data on anxiety presented in the preceding chapters. Our aim is to construct a comprehensive theory of anxiety so far as this is possible and, where integration is impossible, to point out the crucial areas of difference among the various theories. The author's own viewpoint will be discernible both implicitly and explicitly in this synthesis.

1. THE NATURE OF ANXIETY AND ITS RELATION TO FEAR

It is agreed by students of anxiety—Freud, Goldstein, Horney, to mention only three—that anxiety is a *diffuse* apprehension, and that the central difference between fear and anxiety is that fear is a reaction to a specific danger while anxiety is unspecific, "vague," "objectless." The special characteristics of anxiety are the feelings of *uncertainty* and *helplessness* in the face of the danger. The nature of anxiety can be understood when we ask *what* is threatened in the experience which produces anxiety. The threat is to something in the "core or essence" of the personality. *Anxiety is the apprehension cued off by a threat to some value which the individual holds essential to his existence as a personality.* The threat may be to physical or psychological life (death, or loss of freedom), or it may be to some other value which the individual identifies with his existence (patriotism, the love of another person, "success," etc.). This identification of a value with one's existence as a personality is vividly illustrated in the remark of Tom [1] in his period of anxiety over whether he would be retained in his job or be forced to resort again to government relief: "If I couldn't support my family, I'd as soon jump off the end of the dock." This, put simply, is his way of saying that if he could not preserve the self-respecting position of being the responsible wage-earner, his whole life would have no meaning and he might as well not exist. The occasions of anxiety will vary with different people as widely as the values on which they depend vary, but what will always be true in anxiety is that the threat is to a value held by that particular individual to be essential to his existence and consequently to his security as a personality.

The terms "diffuse" and "vague" do not mean that anxiety is less intense in its painfulness than other affects. Indeed, other things being equal, anxiety is regularly more painful than fear. Nor do these terms refer merely to the generalized, "over-all" psychophysical quality of anxiety. Other emotions, like fear, anger, hostility, also permeate the whole organism. Rather, the diffuse and undifferentiated quality of anxiety refers to the *level* in the personality on which the threat is experienced. An individual experiences various fears on the basis of a security pattern he has developed; *but in anxiety it is this security pattern itself which is threatened.* However uncomfortable a fear may be, it is experienced as a threat which can be located spatially and to

---

[1] See Chapter 3, page 77. For another clear example, see the case of Nancy, Chapter 7. The value upon which she depended for security as a self was the assurance of other people's "love" and acceptance of her; she remarked, when speaking about her fiancé, "If anything went wrong with his love for me, I'd break down completely."

which an adjustment can, at least in theory, be made. The relation of the organism to a given object is what is important, and if that object can be removed, either by reassurance or appropriate flight, the apprehension disappears. But since anxiety attacks the foundation (core, essence) of the personality, the individual cannot "stand outside" the threat, cannot objectify it, and thereby is powerless to take steps to meet it. In common parlance, he feels caught, or if the anxiety is severe, overwhelmed; he is afraid but uncertain of what he fears. The fact that anxiety is a threat to the essential, rather than to the peripheral, security of the person has led some authors to describe it as a "cosmic" experience (Sullivan).

These considerations aid in understanding why anxiety appears as a subjective, objectless experience. When Kierkegaard emphasizes that anxiety refers to an inner state and Freud holds that in anxiety the object is "ignored," it is not meant (or *ought* not to be meant) that the danger situation which cues off the anxiety is unimportant. Nor does the term "objectless" refer simply to the fact that the danger causing the anxiety, in the case of neurotic anxiety, has been repressed into unconsciousness. Rather anxiety is objectless because it strikes at that basis of the psychological structure on which the perception of one's self as distinct from the world of objects occurs. Sullivan has remarked that the self-dynamism is developed in order to protect the individual from anxiety; the converse is as true, that mounting anxiety reduces self-awareness. In proportion to the increase in anxiety, the awareness of one's self as a subject related to objects in the external world is confused. Awareness of one's self is simply a correlate of awareness of objects in the external world. It is precisely this differentiation between subjectivity and objectivity which breaks down in proportion to the severity of the anxiety experienced. Hence the expression that anxiety "attacks from the rear," or from all sides at once. In anxiety the individual is proportionately less able to see himself in relation to stimuli and hence less able to make adequate evaluation of the stimuli. In various languages the usual expressions, accurately enough, are "One *has* a fear" but "One *is* anxious." Thus in severe clinical cases anxiety is often experienced as a "dissolution of the self." [2] *In fine*, the objectless nature of anxiety arises from the fact that *the security base itself of the individual is threatened, and since it is in terms of this security base that the individual has been able to experience himself as a self, in relation to objects, the distinction between subject and object also breaks down.*

Since anxiety threatens the basis of selfhood, it is described on the philosophical level as the realization that one may cease to exist as a self. This is phrased by Tillich as the threat of "nonbeing." One is a being, a self, but there is at any moment the possibility of "not being." The normal anxiety associated in the minds of most people with death is one common form of this anxiety. But the dissolution of the self may consist not simply of physical death; it may consist also of the loss of psychological or spiritual meaning which is identified with one's existence as a self—i.e., *the threat of meaninglessness*. Hence Kierkegaard's statement that anxiety is the "fear of nothingness" means in this context the fear of becoming nothing. [3]

Distinction Between Normal and Neurotic Anxiety.—The phenomenological description of anxiety given in the above several pages is applicable to different kinds of anxiety, not only to neurotic anxiety. It can be applied, for example, to the reaction to the catastrophic condition seen in Goldstein's brain-injured patients; it is also applicable, making allowance for differences in the intensity of the reaction, to normal anxiety experienced by all kinds of people in a variety of situations. As an example of normal anxiety, let us consider an illustration which is pieced together from what persons who have existed under totalitarian governments have reported to the present writer.

A prominent Socialist was living in Germany when Hitler came into power. Over a period of some months he knew that some of his colleagues were being imprisoned in concentration camps or taken off to other unknown fates. During this period

---

[2] See case of Brown, Chapter 7.

[3] As will be seen later, the courageous and constructive confronting and working through of this anxiety connected with the threat of dissolution of the self actually results in the strengthening of the experience of being a self as distinct from objects and distinct from nonbeing.

he existed in the continual awareness that he himself was in danger, but he never could be certain *if* he would be apprehended, or, if he were, *when* the Gestapo would come, or, finally, *what* would happen to him if he were arrested. Throughout this period he experienced the diffuse, painful, and persistent feelings of uncertainty and helplessness which we have described above as characteristic of anxiety. And the threat confronting him was not merely that of possible death or the inconvenience and discomfort of the concentration camp; it was a threat to the meaning of his existence as a person, since the freedom to work for his beliefs was a value which he identified with his existence. This individual's reactions to threat had all the essential characteristics of anxiety, yet it was proportionate to the actual threat and could not be termed neurotic.

Normal anxiety is, like any anxiety, a reaction to threats to values the individual holds essential to his existence as a personality; but normal anxiety is that reaction which (1) is not disproportionate to the objective threat, (2) does not involve repression or other mechanisms of intrapsychic conflict, and, as a corollary to the second point, (3) does not require neurotic defense mechanisms for its management, but can be confronted constructively on the level of conscious awareness *or* can be relieved if the objective situation is altered. The undifferentiated and diffuse reactions of the very young infant to threats— such as falling or not being fed—fall in the category of normal anxiety, since they occur before the infant is mature enough for the intrapsychic processes of repression and conflict involved in neurotic anxiety and since, so far as we know, the threats may be experienced by the infant in its state of relative helplessness as objectively real dangers to its existence.

Normal anxiety continues throughout life in the form of what Freud termed "objective anxiety." The existence of normal anxiety in adults is frequently overlooked because the intensity of the experience is often so much less than that of neurotic anxiety; and, since one characteristic of normal anxiety is that it can be managed constructively, it does not show itself in "panic" or in other dramatic forms. But the *quantity* of reaction should not be confused with its *quality*. The intensity of the reaction is important as a distinction between neurotic and normal anxiety only when we are considering the question of whether the reaction is proportionate to the objective threat. Every individual experiences greater or lesser threats to his existence and to values he identifies with his existence in the course of his normal development as a human being. But he normally confronts these experiences constructively, uses them as "learning experiences" (in the broad and profound meaning of that term), and moves on in his development.

One common form of normal anxiety is that inhering in man's contingency—i.e., man's vulnerability to the powers of Nature, to sickness, and to eventual death. This form, termed *Urangst* [4] or *Angst der Kreatur* in German philosophical thought, is referred to by contemporary students of anxiety such as Horney and Mowrer. This kind of anxiety is distinguished from neurotic anxiety in that *Urangst* does not imply the hostility of Nature. Furthermore, *Urangst* does not lead to neurotic anxiety defense mechanisms, except as human contingency becomes the *symbol or focus for other conflicts and problems* within the individual.

Practically speaking, it is often very difficult to distinguish the normal from the neurotic elements in anxiety connected with death, for example, or with other aspects of the contingency of the human situation. In most persons the two kinds of anxiety are intermingled. It is certainly true that much anxiety about death falls in the neurotic category—e.g., the excessive concern with death in periods of adolescent melancholy. It may well be true that, in our culture, whatever neurotic conflicts the individual has in adolescence, old age, or any other period of development may cluster around the symbols of man's helplessness and powerlessness in the face of eventual death.[5] Hence the present

---

4 The literal translation of *Urangst* into English is "original anxiety."

5 The writer wishes to suggest that the reason death, whenever it is discussed in our culture, may be a symbol for neurotic anxiety is that the normal recognition of death as an objective fact is so widely repressed. In our culture one is supposed to ignore the fact that he will sometime die, as though the less said about it the better and as though the experience of living is somehow enhanced if one can remain oblivious to the fact of death. Actually, as Fromm has pointed out (*Escape*

writer does not wish to leave the way open for the rationalization of neurotic anxiety under the façade of normal anxiety about man's contingency.   As a practical measure in clinical work, it may be that, whenever concern about death arises, it is best to work first on the assumption that neurotic elements may be present and to endeavor to ferret them out.   But scientific concern with neurotic elements in such anxiety should not be permitted to obscure the fact that death can be admitted and confronted as an objective fact.[6]   The normal anxiety associated with death does not at all imply depression or melancholy.   Like any normal anxiety it can be used constructively.   The realization that we shall be eventually separated from our fellows can be, as Fromm has indicated, a motivation for achieving closer bonds to other human beings now.   And the normal anxiety inherent in the realization that our activity and creativity will eventually be cut off can be motivations for the more responsible, zestful, and purposeful use of the period in which we do live.

Another common form of normal anxiety is that related to the fact that each human being develops as an individual in a social matrix, a world of other individuals.   As seen most clearly in the development of the child, this growth as an individual in a context of social relationships involves a progressive breaking

---

from freedom) [New York, 1941], the exact opposite occurs: the experience of living tends to become vacuous and to lose some of its zest and savor if the fact of death is ignored.

[6] At points like this, the work of the poets and writers who, as Sophocles put it, seek to "see life steadily and see it whole," may be a useful corrective to any constrictive tendencies in our scientific preoccupation with the neurotic forms of behavior.   Death is a concern in poetry of all sorts, and one certainly would not presume to lump all the poets under the category of neurotics.   A person of poetic imagination, for example, may contemplate the ocean from a rocky promontory and "consider the brief span of my life, swallowed up in the eternity before and behind it, the small space that I fill, or even see, engulfed in the infinite immensity of spaces which I know not, and which know not me," and he may "wonder to see myself here rather than there . . . now rather than then."   Such feelings are radically different from those of the person who looks at the ocean, is seized with terror that he may drown, and retreats from the visual experience and the contemplation.   On the contrary, the poetic feelings of the immensity of time and space and the brevity of one individual's existence (together, of course, with the realization that man is the mammal who can transcend this brevity in the respect that he *knows* it, as other animals do not, and that man is the mammal who can *wonder*)—these feelings can high-light the value and significance of the individual's present experience and his creative possibilities, whether these be in the aesthetic, scientific, or any other realm.

of dependent ties with parents, which in turn involves greater or lesser crises and clashes with parents. This source of anxiety has been discussed by Kierkegaard and Fromm.[7] Otto Rank, likewise, has emphasized that normal anxiety inheres in all experiences of "separation" throughout the individual's life career. If these potentially anxiety-creating experiences are negotiated successfully, they lead not only to greater independence on the part of the child but to re-establishment of relations with parents and other persons on new levels. The anxiety in such cases should then be described as "normal" rather than "neurotic."

In the above examples of normal anxiety, it will be seen that in each case the anxiety is proportionate to an objective threat, does not involve repression or intrapsychic conflict, and can be met by constructive development and increasing employment of the person's own courage and powers rather than retrenchment into neurotic defense mechanisms.[8]

Neurotic anxiety, on the other hand, is a reaction to threat which is (1) disproportionate to the objective danger, (2) involves repression (dissociation) and other forms of intrapsychic conflict, and, as a corollary, (3) is managed by means of various forms of retrenchment of activity and awareness, such as inhibitions, the development of symptoms, and the varied neurotic defense mechanisms.[9] It will be noted that these characteristics are related to each other; the reaction is disproportionate to the objective danger *because* some intrapsychic conflict is involved.

---

[7] Cf. Kierkegaard in Chapter 2 and Fromm in Chapter 5. Fromm calls this individual-social nature of man one of the "existential dichotomies" of human life (*Man for himself* [New York, 1948], p. 40).

[8] Some persons might wish to call these situations of normal anxiety *"potentially anxiety-creating situations."* They would feel that, when the individual is not overwhelmed or does not exhibit the anxiety in any pronounced ways, the term "potential" is more accurate. In one sense it is pedagogically useful to refer to normal anxiety as potential. But strictly speaking, the present writer does not believe that the distinction has meaning beyond its useful connotation; potential anxiety is still anxiety. If a person is aware that a situation confronting him *may* involve anxiety, he is already experiencing anxiety; and he will presumably take steps to meet the situation in such a way that he will not be overwhelmed or defeated by it.

[9] Generally when the term "anxiety" is used in scientific literature, "neurotic anxiety" is meant; this ambiguity is one of the reasons it is important to make a clear distinction between the two kinds of anxiety.

Thus the reaction is never disproportionate to the subjective threat. It will likewise be noted that each one of the above characteristics involves a subjective reference. The definition of neurotic anxiety can be made only when the subjective approach to the problem—i.e., the approach based on the question of what is going on intrapsychically in the individual—is included.

It may be useful to note in greater detail why the subjective aspect is essential to the understanding of neurotic anxiety. If one were merely to phrase the problem of anxiety objectively, i.e., in terms of the relative capacity of the individual to cope adequately with threatening situations, it certainly could justifiably be argued that there is no logical need to distinguish between neurotic and normal anxiety. All one could say is that anxious individuals are less able than other individuals to cope with threats. In the cases, for example, of feeble-minded persons, or of Goldstein's brain-injured patients, one cannot term the frequent vulnerability to threats neurotic. So far as we know, the threats which cue off their frequent and severe anxiety are for them objectively real threats. To one of Goldstein's "compulsively orderly" brain-injured patients, finding the objects in his closet in disarray might be an objective threat and plenty of cause for the profound anxiety which ensues, since because of his curtailed capacities he could not then orient himself to the objects. As we have indicated above, the same would be true for young infants and might very well be true in many cases for children or others who are in fact relatively weak and powerless.

But, as is obvious to any observer, many people are thrown into anxiety by situations which are not objectively threatening either in kind or degree.[10] The person may very often state himself that the occasion of his anxiety is a relatively minor event, that his apprehension is "silly"; but he still feels it. Sometimes persons who respond to relatively minor threats as though they were catastrophic situations are described as persons who

---

[10] It is perhaps unnecessary to add that it is the neurotic element in anxiety experiences, rather than the anxiety arising from curtailment of capacity by brain-injury or actual inferiority, which accounts for the fact that anxiety is such a widespread problem, both clinically and culturally, and also for the fact that the problem is so difficult of understanding and solution.

"carry" an "inordinate quantity" of anxiety within themselves. This, however, is a misleading description. Actually these are persons who are inordinately vulnerable to threats, and the problem is why they are so vulnerable.

It was largely through Freud's genius that scientific attention was focused on the inner psychological patterns and conflicts which render the individual unable to cope with a relatively minor objective threat. Thus the problem of understanding neurotic anxiety boils down to the question of understanding the inner psychological patterns which underlie the individual's excessive vulnerability to threats. The distinction made in Freud's early writing—a viewpoint carried through his work with only slight modification—is that objective anxiety refers to "real," external threats and neurotic anxiety is a fear of one's own instinctual "impulse claims." This distinction has the merit of underlining the subjective locale of neurotic anxiety. But it is not strictly accurate in the respect that an impulse arising within the individual constitutes a threat only if its expression would result in a "real" danger, such as punishment or disapproval by other persons. Though Freud modified his earlier view to some extent in this direction (Chapter 4 above), he did not fully carry through the implications of this insight to ask the question: What is involved in the relationship between the individual and other persons to bring it about that a given impulse, if expressed, should constitute a threat? [11]

Thus neurotic anxiety is that which occurs when the incapacity for coping adequately with threats is not objective but subjective, i.e., is due not to objective weakness but to inner psychological patterns and conflicts which prevent the individual from using his powers.[12] These patterns generally have their genesis (as will be discussed more fully in succeeding sections) in the situation in early childhood, when the child was not able objectively to

---

[11] Cf. next Section.

[12] In dealing with persons in situations with which their age and objective capacities fit them to cope adequately, a handy distinction between normal and neurotic anxiety is *ex post facto*, i.e., how the anxiety is used; normal anxiety being that which is used for a constructive solution to the problem which causes the anxiety, and neurotic anxiety being that which results in defense from and avoidance of the problem.

meet the problems of a threatening interpersonal situation and when at the same time he could not admit consciously the source of the threat (as, for example, in parental rejection). Hence repression of the object of the anxiety is a central feature of neurotic anxiety.[13] Though the repression generally begins in the child's relations with its parents, it continues in the form of repression of similar threats as they occur throughout life.[14] Repression of fear of the threat results in the individual's being unaware of the source of his apprehension; thus in neurotic anxiety there is a specific reason why the affect is "objectless," in addition to the general source mentioned earlier of the objectless nature of all anxiety. The repression (dissociation, blocking off of awareness) which occurs in neurotic anxiety in itself renders the individual more vulnerable to threats and thus increases neurotic anxiety. First, repression sets up inner contradictions within the personality, thus making for a shaky psychological equilibrium bound to be easily threatened in the course of everyday life. Secondly, because of the repression the individual is less able to distinguish and fight against real dangers as they occur. For example, the person who represses a good deal of aggression and hostility may at the same time assume a compliant and passive attitude toward others, which in turn increases the likelihood that he will be exploited by others.[15] Finally, repression increases the individual's feeling of helplessness in that it involves a curtailing of his own autonomy, an inner retrenchment and shelving of his own power.

We have presented this brief discussion of neurotic anxiety at this point as an aid to defining what we mean by the term; more complete discussion of the dynamics and sources of such anxiety appears in succeeding sections.

Maturation of the Organism's Capacity for Anxiety and Fear Responses.—In preceding chapters we have considered three types of response to danger which are exhibited by the de-

---

[13] In this sense, Mowrer is correct in saying that anxiety is the result of a repressed fear (see page 108 note above).

[14] This could be illustrated in practically any clinical case: see especially the cases of Brown, Nancy, and Frances in Chapter 7, and the discussion on page 340.

[15] How repression of aggression and a compliant attitude would go together in a child's endeavor to adjust to dominating parents is obvious.

veloping human organism:[16] (1) the *startle pattern,* a pre-emotional, innate reflexive reaction; (2) *anxiety,* the undifferentiated emotional response; (3) *fear,* a differentiated emotional reaction. The startle reflex can be elicited very early in the infant's career; Landis and Hunt found it in babies in the first month of life. They found very little anxiety or fear during this month, but as the infant grew older more and more secondary behavior of the anxiety-fear variety appeared in the child's responses. Similarly, the studies of children by Jersild and by Gesell show anxiety and fear emerging after some maturation on the part of the child. Gesell's infant confined to a pen showed no discomfort at all in the early weeks, but at five months he exhibited mild apprehension, one sign of which was persistent head-turning. (Head-turning is a significant picture of anxiety; the individual does not know where the threat comes from, or how to relate himself to it spatially.) Several months later, the same infant in response to the same stimulus exhibited reactions marked by crying, which Gesell terms "fear."

The neurological data indicate that maturation is a development from the less differentiated toward the more differentiated type of response. At birth the infant's perceptive and discriminative capacities are not sufficiently developed to permit him adequately to identify and localize dangers. Maturing neurologically means not only an increasing capacity to locate possible threats visually, for example, but it also means increasing capacity for cortical interpretation of stimuli. The behavior correlates of this maturing process are a decreasing reliance on simple reflexive behavior and an increasing amount of emotional behavior, which in turn involves an increasing degree of discrimination of stimuli and voluntary control of response. In other words, some neurological maturation is presupposed before the infant can respond to threatening stimuli with undifferentiated emotion (anxiety), and greater maturation is necessary before the infant can differentiate between various stimuli, objectivate the danger, and respond to it as a fear.[17]

---

[16] The Moro reflex, present in the new-born infant but normally disappearing by the second year, is omitted from this discussion.

[17] A converse demonstration of this order is seen in the behavior of the soldiers studied by Grinker and Spiegel: under severe stress the tendency of the men in

It is clear that the factor of maturation must be taken into account in understanding the child's protective reactions. Freud noted this when he remarked that the capacity for anxiety is not at its maximum at birth, but emerges and develops in the maturing infant to a high point which he believed occurred in early childhood. Goldstein holds that anxiety may be observable in the new-born infant in some situations, but that the capacity to respond with specific fears is a later development. Agreeing, therefore, that maturation must be taken into account, we proceed to the more controversial problem—and the problem which has very important implications for anxiety theory—of whether anxiety or fear appears first. It is widely agreed that the infant may exhibit anxiety responses in its very early days; Lauretta Bender remarks that clear anxiety responses can be observed as early as the eighth or ninth day of the infant's life. But whereas responses which can be called fear are described in infants in later months, the present writer has never come across descriptions of behavior in these first weeks of the infant's life which could be termed fear. Or when very early responses are called fear—as by Watson in his theory of the "two original fears"—it seems clear to the present writer that what is being described is the diffuse, undifferentiated apprehension properly to be termed anxiety.[18]

---

combat was to respond to the threat by means of diffuse, undifferentiated behavior, and Grinker and Spiegel remark that this is equivalent to behavior on a level of lessened cortical differentiation and control, i.e., a level closer to that of the infant.

[18] To the present writer it seems a curious phenomenon that many writers in the field of anxiety and fear speak of the "early fears" of the infant but no one, as indicated above, identifies these so-called early fears. For example, Symonds speaks of anxiety as growing out of "primitive fear states" and as a corollary he employs fear as the more inclusive, generic term and anxiety as the derived emotion (P. M. Symonds, *Dynamics of human adjustment* [New York, 1946]). But the apprehensive behavior Symonds so well describes in the very young infant seems certainly to be anxiety—as he, in fact, terms it. He actually describes no reactions which he calls fears in these earliest experiences of the infant. It seems to the present writer that there is a general uncriticized assumption in much psychological thinking that somehow fears must be the first to emerge and anxiety must be a later development. Perhaps that assumption is due partially to the fact that the study of anxiety has chiefly dealt with *neurotic* anxiety—which is certainly a complex affect and does not appear before the development of the capacity for self-awareness and other complicated psychological processes in the child. Perhaps, also, the uncriticized tendency to employ fear as the generic term is partially a product of the tendency in our culture (discussed in Chapters 2 and 4) to be preoccupied with the specific items of behavior which traditionally have fitted the

In fine, after the first reflexive protective reactions, there emerge *the diffuse, undifferentiated emotional responses to threat, namely anxiety; and last to emerge in maturation are the differentiated emotional responses to specific, localized dangers, namely fears.*[19]

Relation Between Anxiety and Fear.—Until recent years the distinction between fears and anxiety has been frequently overlooked in psychological studies, or the two affects have been lumped together on the assumption that they have the same neurophysiological base. But this failure to make a differentiation confuses the understanding of both fears and anxiety. The reactions of an organism in times of fear and of anxiety may be radically different, due to the fact that these reactions occur on different psychological levels of the personality. This difference may be clearly seen in the psychosomatic studies of gastrointestinal activities in states of fear and anxiety. When Tom, the subject with the gastric fistula, was confronted with a specific danger, e.g., that the irate doctor would discover the mistake he had made, Tom's gastric activity was suspended and his psychological and physiological state was that of the familiar pattern of mobilization for flight.[20] But when Tom was in a state of anxiety, as was the case after he had lain awake at night distressed about how long his employment at the hospital would last, his neurophysiological reactions were the exact opposite: gastric activity was accelerated and sympathetic ("flight") activity was at a minimum. The difference in these two reactions may be described as follows: in the fear Tom knew what he was afraid of, and a specific adaptation in one direction was possible, namely flight. In the anxiety, though the tension was occasioned by an apparently specific danger, the threat cued off in Tom an internal conflict on whether he could be a self-supporting man or would

---

methods of the dominant form of thought in our period, namely mathematical rationalism.

[19] This order is also discernible in an adult's reaction to a danger stimulus, let us say to the sudden hearing of a gunshot. First, the adult responds with startle. Secondly, as he becomes aware of the threat but is unable to localize the source of the shooting or to tell whether it is aimed at him, he is in the state of anxiety. Third, as he is able to spot the source of the gunshot and to take steps to get out of the way, he is in the state of fear.

[20] See Chapter 3.

have to return to government relief. Detection by the doctor in the instance of fear would have been uncomfortable but not catastrophic, but *the threat in the second instance was to values Tom held essential to his existence as a self-respecting personality.* The point emphasized here is not only that the reactions in fear and in anxiety may be quite different, but that fear and anxiety represent threats to different levels in the personality.

In some psychological studies purporting to be of fear, the affect involved frequently turns out on further examination to be anxiety. As has been pointed out, John B. Watson, in his theory of the "two fears" of the new-born infant, seems really to be talking of the diffuse, undifferentiated apprehensions we would term "anxiety." In studies of children's fears (Jersild) it is highly significant that a large proportion of the fears are "irrational," i.e., have no direct relation to the misfortunes which had actually befallen the children. The "shifting," "unpredictable" quality of children's fears in these studies is also a datum of considerable significance. Both of these data suggest that some affect is present underlying the so-called fears. Indeed, the phrase "irrational fear" is strictly speaking a contradiction in terms; if a fear cannot be understood as a flight from a danger that one has learned in experience is painful or harmful, then something else is involved in the reactions of the person toward the threat. It may be countered that "irrational fear" is not a contradiction in terms, since Freud and others speak of "neurotic fears," i.e., fears which are irrational in the respect that they are out of proportion to the reality situation. But Freud cites various phobias as examples of neurotic fears, and phobias are by definition forms of anxiety localized on one object. *It is the anxiety underlying the neurotic fear which lends it its unrealistic, "irrational" quality.* The study of fears points toward a process of reaction more basic than the specific fears themselves.

It is now possible to answer the question, what is the relation between anxiety and fears? The capacity of the organism to react to threats to its existence and to its values is, in its general and original form, anxiety. Later, as the organism becomes mature enough neurologically and psychologically to differentiate specific objects of danger, the protective reactions can likewise become specific; such differentiated reactions to specific dangers are fears. *Thus anxiety is the basic, underlying reaction—the generic term; and fear is the expression of the same capacity in its specific, objectivated form.*[21] In Mowrer's phrase, anxiety is "primal" rather than "derived." [22] If one is to speak of either emotion as derived, it is fear that is derived rather than anxiety. In any case, the customary procedure of subsuming the study of anxiety under the study of fear, or trying to make anxiety intelligible through a study of fear, is, the present writer believes, illogical. The understanding of fears hinges upon the understanding of the prior problem, anxiety. The present writer believes this conceptualization fits the biological data (cf. Goldstein), the neurological data of maturation, and the psychoanalytic data (cf. Freud, page 114, Horney, *et al.*).

We speak of anxiety as "basic" not only in the sense that it is the general, original response to threat, but also because it is a response to threat on the basic level of the personality; i.e., it is a response to a threat to the "core" or "essence" of the personality rather than to a peripheral danger. Fears are the responses to threats before they get to this basic level. By reacting adequately to the various specific dangers which threaten him (i.e., by reacting adequately on the level of fears), the individual avoids having his essential values threatened, avoids being threatened at the "inner citadel" of his security system. If however he cannot cope with dangers in their specific forms, he will be threatened on the deeper level which we have called the "core" or "essence" of personality. Using a military analogy supplied by the Battle of France in the last war, battles on various segments of the front lines represent specific threats; so long as the battle can be fought out on the periphery, so long as the dangers can be warded off in the area of the outer fortifications, the vital areas are not threatened. But when the enemy breaks through into the capital of the country, when the inner lines of communication are broken and the battle is no longer localized; when, that

---

[21] This relation between anxiety and fear holds for the neurotic as well as for the normal forms of these affects. A neurotic fear is a specific, differentiated, objectivated expression of underlying neurotic anxiety. In other words, neurotic fears bear the same relation to neurotic anxiety as normal fears do to normal anxiety.

[22] O. H. Mowrer, *op. cit.*

is, the enemy attacks from all directions and the defending soldiers do not know which way to march or where to take a stand, we have the threat of being overwhelmed, with its corollaries, panic and frantic behavior. This latter is analogous to the threat to the basic values, the "inner citadel" of the personality; and *in individual psychological terms it is the threat responded to as anxiety*. Thus, figuratively speaking, we may describe fear as the armor against anxiety. The phrase "fear of fear," employed by President Franklin D. Roosevelt as well as by several other previous figures in history, refers to the apprehension that one will not be able to cope with dangers as they arise and will thereby be thrown into a catastrophic situation. "Fear of fear," thus, really means anxiety.[23]

General Origins of Anxiety.—The origins of normal anxiety do not require extensive hypotheses. Normal anxiety is an expression of the capacity of the organism to react to threats; this capacity is innate and has its inherited neurophysiological modus. Freud remarks that the "tendency toward objective anxiety" is inherent in the child, his belief being that it is an expression of the self-preservation instinct and has an obvious biological utility. The particular forms this capacity to react to threats will assume in a given individual are conditioned by the nature of the threats (environment) and by how the individual has learned to deal with them (past and present experience).

The problem of the origin of normal anxiety raises the question of *whether and to what extent anxiety and fears are learned*. In past decades this question has been approached through debates on which fears are inherited and which are not. The present writer believes that these debates were based on a confused statement of the problem, and therefore have largely been beside

---

[23] Several references to "fear of fear" preceding Roosevelt's are cited by J. Donald Adams (*New York Times Book Review*, p. 2, Jan. 11, 1948): Emerson, quoting from Thoreau's *Journals*, "Nothing is terrible except fear itself." Carlyle, "We must get rid of fear; we cannot act at all till then." Sir Francis Bacon, "Nothing is terrible except fear itself." Such statements do not make sense on the level of fear. Strictly speaking, a fear does not prevent action; it prepares the organism *for* action. It is doubtful whether the phrase "fear itself" has logical meaning—one is afraid *of* something. "Fear itself" is more logically to be termed anxiety. Indeed, if the term "anxiety" is substituted, all the above quotations make sense.

the point. The accepting of a list of "inherited" fears (Stanley Hall) had both practical and theoretical weaknesses—the former in the respect that assuming certain fears and foci of anxiety to be instinctual implied that little or nothing could be done to correct or alleviate them, and the latter in the respect that these so-called instinctual fears could be disproved (Watson). But Watson's theory proposed in rebuttal—namely, that there are only two instinctual fear stimuli, loud noises and loss of support—is likewise based upon the same false statement of the problem. Watsonian behaviorism had the practical weakness of oversimplifying the problem of anxiety and fear in its implication that no fears or anxiety were "necessary" except the "two original fears," and thus it played into the hands of the general cultural tendency to repress anxiety. Watsonian behaviorism also had the theoretical weaknesses that it neglected the factor of maturation and that even the "two fears" themselves could not be found with any consistency by later investigators.[24] With respect to the problem of the "inheritance" of anxiety or fear, we submit that the only assumption necessary is that the human organism has the capacity to react to threats, a capacity which its ancestors possessed likewise.

But the question of *which* particular events will have threat value for an individual depends upon learning. These events are the "conditioned stimuli." This is especially clear in the matter of fears: they are conditioned responses to particular events which the individual has learned are a threat to him. The same is true for particular foci of anxiety.[25]

---

[24] Given the fact that very few protective responses are present in the new-born infant, it does not follow that all later responses are due solely to learning. (Cf. Jersild in Chapter 4 above.)

[25] The above paragraphs are presented merely as some reactions to the problem of learning; the writer does not propose, nor is he competent, to discuss comprehensively or in detail the complex question of the relation of learning theory to anxiety and fear. The reader is referred to the writings and the investigations which are now being pursued on this question by learning psychologists such as Mowrer, Miller and Dollard, Symonds, etc. In a personal communication to the present writer, Mowrer has the following to say on the problem: "I would put it this way: we are so constructed that traumatic (painful) experiences produce the emergency reaction of Cannon. Objects and events associated with trauma take on threat value, i.e., become capable of producing the emergency reaction. When this reaction thus occurs, as a conditioned response, it is fear. The capacity to react to threats then means (a) the capacity to *learn* to do so, or (b) the actual end-results of learning." (Quoted by permission.)

One general comment may be added. At the present time the different approaches to the problem of whether anxiety is learned not only involve the question of definition (i.e., is the author talking about normal or neurotic anxiety or fears), but also the approaches involve divergent emphases. The tendency is for learning psychologists, observing that each particular fear or focus of anxiety is demonstrably closely related to the given individual's experience, to state simply that anxiety is learned. On the other hand, the neurophysiologists, centering their attention on the given capacities of the organism, have tended to assume that anxiety is not learned (Cannon). The present writer believes that there does not need to be a conflict between these two emphases. It is here suggested that the capacity for anxiety is not learned, but the quantities and forms of anxiety in a given individual are learned. This means that normal anxiety is a function of the organism *qua* organism; every human being would experience anxiety in situations of threat to its vital values. But *what* the individual regards as a situation of threat to vital values *is* largely due to learning. Particular fears and foci of anxiety are the expression of patterns which develop out of the interrelation of the individual's capacities for reacting to threat with his environment and conditioning. The matrix in which these patterns develop, i.e., in which the conditioning occurs, is the family situation in particular, which in turn is part of the larger general culture in which the individual lives.

Specific Origins of Neurotic Anxiety.—With regard to the specific sources of neurotic anxiety, Freud centers his attention chiefly on the *birth trauma* and on the fear of *castration*. In his early writings he treats the birth trauma as a literal source of anxiety, later anxiety being a "repetition" of affect which originally occurred with the birth trauma. It has been pointed out (Mowrer) that the "repetition of affect" is a dubious concept; a threat must continue to be present or the affect would not be present. Later Freud tended to employ the birth experience more symbolically; it stood for "separation from the mother." This is more understandable, for although there is no way of knowing on the basis of present data whether literal severity of birth predisposes to later anxiety, the symbol of early anxiety as dread of separation from the mother does have meaning. Symonds speaks of birth as breaking one set of ties and moving into a new and strange situation, a symbol which is similar to Kierke-gaard's concept of anxiety as arising at every new possibility in one's experience.[26] In any case, if separation from the mother is seen as the origin of anxiety, the crucial question for understanding the development of patterns which underlie later anxiety is the meaning of this separation, i.e., what particular values are involved in the relation of the child to its mother which are threatened by the separation? With regard to castration, again Freud's position is ambiguous: at times he treats castration as a literal source of anxiety (Hans is afraid the horse will bite his penis off), and at times he uses the term symbolically, castration standing for the loss of a prized object or value. There would not be radical disagreement with the contention that castration is often a symbol in our culture for the child's being deprived of individual power at the hands of stronger adults, power here referring not only to sexual activity but to work or any sort of individual creative activity. If fear of the loss of the penis is seen as the origin of anxiety, the crucial question again is the meaning of this loss, i.e., what is the nature of the relation between the child and its parents that the child should feel threatened, and what particular *values* significant for the child are threatened? [27]

Since anxiety is a reaction to a threat to values held essential to the existence of the personality, and since the human organism owes its existence to its relation to certain significant persons in its infancy, *the essential values are originally the security patterns existing between the infant and these significant persons.* Hence there is considerable agreement that the relation between the child and its parents is crucial for the origins of anxiety (Sullivan, Horney, etc.). In Sullivan's concept of anxiety, the mother occupies the significant position. The mother is not only the source of the satisfaction of the infant's physical needs; she is

---

26 Cf. also Rank in Chapter 4 above.

27 The term "castration" is often used by present Freudian analysts as equivalent to punishment. This generalized meaning of the term has the merit of placing the emphasis on the relationship between the child and his parents, but it still leaves open the question of what values are threatened by the punishment.

the source of its over-all emotional security as well; and whatever would endanger that relationship would be a threat to the infant's total status in his interpersonal world. Hence Sullivan holds that anxiety has its origin in the infant's apprehension of disapproval by its mother. This apprehension occurs via empathy between infant and mother long before the infant is sufficiently mature to be consciously aware of approval or disapproval. For Horney, basic anxiety—which in an individual's later life becomes neurotic anxiety—has its origin in the child's conflict between his dependency on his parents and his hostility toward them. Several writers hold that anxiety has its origin in the conflicts in the developing individuality of the child and the need to relate to other persons in its community (Fromm, Kierkegaard).

It will be noted that the term "conflict" emerges in the above two statements. Further understanding of the origins of neurotic anxiety requires an examination of the nature and sources of the conflicts which underlie neurotic anxiety.

2. ANXIETY AND CONFLICT

Neurotic anxiety always involves inner conflict. There is often a reciprocal relation between the two: a state of persistent unresolved conflict may lead eventually to the person's repressing one side of the conflict, which then produces neurotic anxiety; and anxiety, in turn, brings in its train feelings of helplessness, impotence, and a paralysis of action which tend to cause or increase psychological conflict. The descriptions of this state of conflict range from Stekel's summary statement, "anxiety *is* psychic conflict," to the systematic endeavors of Freud, Kierkegaard, Horney, and Fromm to discover the nature of this conflict.

The view that the conflict underlying anxiety is between instinctual needs within the individual and social prohibitions stems from Freud. His topological description is that the ego is caught between id (instinctual urges chiefly of libidinous character) on one hand and superego (cultural requirements) on the other. Though Freud modified his first theory that anxiety was simply converted repressed libido to the theory that the ego perceives the danger situation and then represses the libido, the content of the conflict is still the same, namely whether libidinal needs can or cannot be gratified. The threat which cues off anxiety is seen in Freud as the threat of frustration of libido or, what amounts to the same thing, the threat of punishment if the libido is gratified. This question of whether frustration of libido per se causes conflict and concomitant anxiety has been examined by numerous students of anxiety after Freud (Horney, Sullivan, Mowrer, etc.). The consensus of these investigators is that frustration itself does not cause conflict; the basic question is, rather: What essential value is threatened by the frustration? This may be illustrated in the area of sex. Some persons have a great deal of sexual expression (i.e., suffer no frustration) and still have much anxiety. Other persons bear considerable sexual privation and are not prey to excessive anxiety. Still others, significantly, *are thrown into conflict and anxiety when their sexual desires are frustrated by one possible partner but not when the same desires are frustrated by another person.* Thus something more than the need for mere sexual gratification is occurring. (The problem is not the frustration in itself, but whether the frustration threatens some mode of interpersonal relationship which the individual holds vital to his security and self-esteem (Horney).)In our culture sexual activity is often identified by the individual with his sense of power, esteem, and prestige; in such an individual the threat of sexual frustration is very likely to cause conflict and anxiety. Our disagreement is not with Freud's phenomenological description of the frequent relation between sexual repression and anxiety in his Victorian culture (as well as in our own culture to a considerable extent). This relation is due to the fact that sexual prohibitions are very frequently the modus in our culture of authoritative constraint of the child by his parents and later by society. These constraints result in a suppression of the child's development and expansion. Sexual impulses will then involve a conflict with these authorities (usually parents) and will arouse the prospect of punishment by and alienation from the authorities; and this conflict will certainly in many cases produce anxiety. But that does not mean that the libidinal frustration itself causes the conflict and anxiety. The threat of frustration of a biological urge does not cause conflict and anxiety unless that urge is identified with some value essential to the existence of the personality. When Sullivan states that the activities directed toward the pursuit of security are ordinarily of much more importance to the human being than those directed toward physical satisfactions like hunger and sex, he does not mean to discount the biological (in its limited sense) aspect of behavior but to indicate that the physical needs are subsumed under the more comprehensive need of the organism to maintain and extend its total security and power.

Kardiner sees the conflict underlying anxiety in Western man as caused by the introduction of taboos early in the child's development which block relaxor pleasure patterns. While similar to Freud in his emphasis on the biological content of this conflict, Kardiner goes on to state that the severity of the conflict is due to the fact that in the psychological growth pattern of Western culture the introduction of taboos occurs after the parents have cultivated strong affective needs and expectations in the infant. Thus the anxiety is due not merely to frustration of pleasure patterns as such but to the child's experience of the undependability and inconsistency of his parents in their failure to fulfill the expectations which they have engendered in him.

To Horney the early conflict in the child between his dependency on his parents and his hostility toward them sets the basis for the contradictory trends in the adult personality which underlie later anxiety. Neurotic strategies are devices for preserving security despite the presence of underlying conflicts. Whenever these neurotic strategies are threatened, the conflicts are reactivated and anxiety is the result.

Is there any common denominator of these conflicts which underlie anxiety? The present writer believes that such a common denominator can be found in the dialectical relationship of the individual and his community.[28] On one hand the human being develops as an individual; the fact of individuality is a

---

[28] The term "community" is used rather than "society" because it implies a positive quality of relatedness, achieved by the individual by means of his own self-awareness. See footnote, page 189.

given datum in the respect that each person is unique and to an extent discrete from other individuals. Actions, no matter how much conditioned by social factors, are still actions by an individual. At the point in development at which self-awareness emerges, there also emerges a measure of freedom and responsibility in each individual action. But on the other hand this individual develops at every moment as a member of a social nexus, upon which he is dependent not only for the early meeting of his biological needs but also for his emotional security. It is only in interaction with other individuals in a social nexus that the development of a "self" and the development of personality are understandable. The infant's and child's existence consists of a progressive differentiation of himself from his parents. When he is viewed from the individual aspect of the dialectical relationship, his growth consists of decreasing dependence on parents and increasing reliance upon and use of his own powers. When he is viewed from the social aspect, the child's growth consists of his progressive relating to the parents on new levels. *Blockage of development at either pole in this dialectic engenders psychological conflict, the end result of which is anxiety.* Where there is "freedom from" without corresponding interrelationship, there is the anxiety of the defiant and isolated individual. Where there is dependence without freedom (symbiosis), there will be a lack of capacity to act on the basis of one's own powers and therefore a readiness to be threatened by every new situation which requires autonomous action.

To the extent that development is blocked at either pole in this dialectical relationship, inner mechanisms will be set in operation within the individual which increase the conflict and anxiety. In the individual who is characterized by independence without corresponding relatedness, there will develop hostility toward those whom he believes to be the occasion of his isolation. In the individual who is symbiotically dependent, there will develop hostility toward those whom he regards as instrumental in the suppression of his capacities and freedom. In each case, the hostility increases the conflict and anxiety. Another mechanism will also be present, namely repression. The unutilized capacities and the unfulfilled needs are not lost but repressed. The phenomenon is often observed clinically that the defiantly independent, isolated individual is repressing considerable need and desire to make affirmative relationships with other people, and the symbiotically dependent person is repressing need and desire to act independently. It is well known, as has already been pointed out, that the mechanism of repression itself decreases autonomy and increases helplessness and conflict.

In this discussion it is not meant to imply that the conflict is *between* the individual and society, either in the Freudian negative usage of the term "society" or in the opposite Adlerian positive sense. The point, rather, is that a failure of development at either pole in the dialectical relationship of individual-in-community results in a conflict which affects both poles. For example, if a person avoids autonomous individual decisions, he retrenches to a shut-in condition (Kierkegaard) and his possibilities of communicating with others is sacrificed along with his autonomy as an individual. In Kierkegaard's terms, the shut-in condition is a result of the endeavor to avoid conflict, but it actually results later in greater conflict, i.e., neurotic conflict and neurotic anxiety.

This description of the basic conflict underlying anxiety in terms of individual-in-community has the demerit of generality, but it has the merit of emphasizing both sides of the development that is necessary for the overcoming of conflict and anxiety. It also has the merit of providing a frame of reference for the divergent theories of conflict presented in the literature of anxiety. The various emphases on the origin of conflict in early childhood (Freud, Horney, etc.) are understandable, since this is the first arena in which the conflicts relating to individual-in-community are fought out. The theories of conflict which hold that persistent restraint of individual impulses will sooner or later result in conflict and anxiety (Freud) are true but incomplete.[29] The theories which emphasize the community pole in the dialectic (Sullivan, Adler) present another phase of the pic-

---

[29] Sexual desire and relationships are a very significant form of the dialectical relationship here discussed, since sex may express individual-in-community or may be distorted into egocentricity (pseudo-individuality) or into symbiotic dependence (pseudo-community).

ture as well as provide a corrective to overemphasis on the expression of individual impulses per se.[30]   It seems safe to conclude, on the basis of the various analyses of the conflict underlying anxiety, that the constructive solution of the conflict involves the individual's progressive actualization of his capacities in expanding community.

3. ANXIETY AND CULTURE

The anxiety of a given individual is conditioned by the fact that he lives in a given culture at a particular point in the historical development of that culture.   Though the majority of writers on anxiety would agree with this statement in some measure, there are wide divergencies in the literature with respect to the relative emphasis placed on culture and how culture is treated.   In general, those who have viewed the problem of anxiety in terms of the expression of indigenous individual drives have tended to omit cultural factors (like the early Freud) or to treat culture negatively (like the later Freud).   On the other hand, those who see personality development as occurring at every moment within a social matrix have emphasized that the problem of anxiety must always be viewed in the context of the interrelation of the individual with his culture (Horney, Sullivan, Fromm, etc.). It is fair to say that there has been in recent years a considerable trend in the latter direction, with an emergence only lately of an endeavor to trace the historical backgrounds of cultural patterns which underlie contemporaneous anxiety (Fromm, Kardiner).

The problem of anxiety and culture may be broken down into two phases.   First, the *kinds* (forms, occasions) of anxiety experienced by a given individual are culturally conditioned in the respect that *the values or goals held by an individual to be essential to his existence as a personality are largely cultural products.* Second, the *quantities* of anxiety experienced by a given individual are conditioned by the degree of unity and stability in his culture.   If the culture is relatively unified and stable, the indi-

---

[30] Also see Mowrer in Chapter 5.   To him anxiety and conflict are often caused by guilt feeling which arises from the failure of the individual to relate himself maturely and responsibly to his social group.

vidual will be able to orient himself (whether he is in accord with cultural mores or not) and his experiences of anxiety will be relatively less frequent and less intense. If, as in the case of the contemporaneous period, the culture is in a state of disunity and traumatic change, the individual will not only reflect this disunity in his own psychological life, but also his orientation to his changing culture will be proportionately more difficult. Hence his anxiety will be more frequent and more intense.[31]

Competitive Individual Success as an Example of a Cultural Value.—There are many demonstrations of the fact that social prestige goals are dominant in our culture, and that these social prestige goals take the chief form of a high valuation of individual competitive success. If that value is threatened, conflict and anxiety ensue. It is generally agreed, for one example, that the high incidence of gastric ulcer among men in our times is related to the highly competitive nature of our culture, which takes the form of the stringent need of many men to appear independent and triumphant and to repress dependent needs. For another example, in the studies of children's fears it was found that as the child grew older fears related to competitive status increased. Jersild interprets this as a sign of the increasing impact of the culture upon the child. The adults reporting their childhood fears, moreover, gave a much larger incidence of fears related to competitive success and failure than the children, which Jersild interprets as a "reading back" into childhood of fears which have become important to them as adults. The literature indicates that the goal of individual competitive success is not only *a* dominant goal but probably *the* dominant goal in our culture from Wall Street at one extreme to Plainville at the other, and in varying forms from the Renaissance to the present day. This goal is by no means limited to economic activity, though in that realm it receives its clearest definition; it carries over into school and family, sex and love as well.

---

[31] O. H. Mowrer makes the interesting formulation that society is formed to solve problems, and that only when the society breaks down do the underlying problems confront the individual in conscious awareness. In this sense society protects the individual from anxiety; and when this protection is withdrawn, as in periods of traumatic social change, the anxiety which confronts the individual is proportionately more severe.

The goal of individual competitive success is accorded such crucial weight because it is identified with self-esteem and self-worth. It is to the modern man what salvation was to the citizen of the Middle Ages (Kardiner). Competitive success in our culture is not essentially a matter of achieving material security, nor is it in the realms of sex and love a matter of achieving an abundance of libidinal satisfactions. Rather, it is a means of gaining security, because it is accepted as a proof of one's power in one's own eyes and in the eyes of others. In this sense the economic valuation becomes the valuation of persons. Since success is competitive, it involves a striving to triumph over others, augmenting intrasocial hostility and interpersonal isolation. Since it is a value which is always relative to the success of others, it is insatiable. Failure in the struggle to achieve competitive success involves not only social contempt but, more important, self-contempt and feelings of worthlessness. The above observations indicate why, when this value is threatened, the individual in our culture generally experiences profound anxiety. Since success is the chief form of self-validation, feelings of anxiety generally lead to redoubled efforts to attain success. Hence, as was pointed out above (page 183), a vicious circle results: competitive striving→ intrasocial hostility→ interpersonal isolation→ anxiety→ increased competitive striving.

A goal like competitive individual success, in the stringent form it takes in modern society, is not an "immutable attribute" of human nature but *a cultural product which has its historical genesis and development*.[32] This historical background must be understood if the anxiety-creating conflicts involved in the high valuation of competitive individual success are to be resolved. The formative outlines of this goal are to be found in the great emphasis on the power of the free individual which characterized the beginnings of the modern period, the Renaissance. In almost every phase of culture—economic, religious,

---

[32] Such a goal uses in its service legitimate and healthy needs of the individual for self-realization, but it is important not to identify such normal needs with *competitive* individualism. In this sense, the problem is how such normal needs for self-fulfilment became distorted in our culture into a competitive pattern which requires triumphing over others (i.e., anticommunal striving) if the goal is to be achieved.

intellectual, political—the Renaissance emphasized individual capacity and power as over against the corporate cultural patterns of medievalism. The unifying concept of the revolutionary culture changes in and following the Renaissance was the confidence in the power of autonomous reason.

Great room for the exercise of the capacities and initiative of the bold individual was afforded by the unparalleled expansion as well as by the social motility and political ferment of the Renaissance. The cultural situation placed a premium not only on the exercise of individual power as such, but on the use of this power to triumph over and exploit others if necessary for one's own achievement. It was not personality as such which was so highly valued in the Renaissance, but *strong* personality; the accepted ideal was the powerful, free, creative individual, whose power was implemented by his knowledge and reason (as well as cunning). On the positive side this pattern made possible many gains for individual self-realization and freedom; on the negative side it laid the groundwork for interpersonal isolation and compulsive competition. This "excessive" individualism (Burckhardt) consisted chiefly of "freedom from" ties which had bound the citizen of the corporate Middle Ages (Fromm); it lacked the dimension of responsible relatedness to others. Evidences of interpersonal isolation and concomitant anxiety can be discerned already in the Renaissance, especially in the late Renaissance. The "morbid craving for fame" which characterized that age testifies to the sense of frustration of the individual in his relation to others and also demonstrates again the assumption that the chief means of gaining esteem was competitive (fame). The Renaissance set the problem for the modern period, namely: *How can interpersonal community (ethical, psychological, economic, etc.) be attained which, integrated with the values of individual freedom, will liberate the individual from the sense of isolation and concomitant anxiety inhering in excessive individualism?*

After the Renaissance the isolation and anxiety inhering in competitive individualism were held in check and a partial experience of community was obtained on the basis of several generally accepted attitudes. We shall mention two: first, the attitude that *individual economic striving (laissez faire) would redound to the benefit of the social group.*[33] It is true that the social weal *was* furthered by individual economic striving; the great technological progress in the expanding stages of capitalism vastly increased the possibilities of satisfying everyone's material needs. But the individualistic economic developments had further implications for the psychological pattern here discussed. (1) The competitive aspect of individualism was greatly reinforced by the competitive processes of industrialism. It was observable to everyone during the expanding stages of capitalism that certain individuals could gain wealth and power by the exercise of economic initiative and shrewdness. The Renaissance concern with well-being in "this world" became increasingly allied with the assumption that wealth equals well-being. Moreover, the Renaissance concern with individual self-realization in all phases of creative activity became superceded by the emphasis on self-realization chiefly in economic terms, i.e., success in terms of economic wealth. (2) Individual economic competition set the stage for a considerable increase of intrasocial aggression and hostility. This aggression and hostility could be expressed in the socially accepted form of augmented competitive striving, and the anxiety inhering in the intrasocial hostility could be allayed by increased striving for success.

The second attitude which came into clear formulation in the century after the Renaissance and served to allay anxiety was the confidence that *the free pursuit of individual reason would lead automatically to a harmony of the individual with society and a harmony of the individual with "universal reality."* The individual of free intellect need not feel isolated because his conclusions would eventually be in accord with those of his fellow-thinkers, and the combined process would lead not only to the control of nature but to a harmonious society and to the reasonable direction of the individual's emotions as well. Given the cultural situation of the seventeenth century, it seems necessary to conclude that this confidence in individual reason did protect

---

33 Modern industrialism is an outworking of Renaissance individualism in the respect that it is based on the concept of the right of each individual to pursue his own economic self-interest (Tawney).

the intellectuals of the period from the basic, persistent conflicts which lead to anxiety. Threats could be dealt with as fears and overcome by a courageous following of the "certain advice of reason" (Spinoza). The outstanding figure in that period who did confront anxiety, Pascal, was the one who could not accept the prevailing confidence in the rationalistic solutions to individual and social problems. On the positive side the confidence in the power of individual reason not only served to dispel anxiety, but it also aided in the spread of knowledge and the liberation of science. On the negative side, it contributed to the later rationalistic tendency to suppress emotions and "irrational" experience, which was to create profound psychological disunity within the individual in the nineteenth century.

In the nineteenth century an increasing disunity in modern culture became evident. The autonomous sciences were characterized by far-reaching progress in garnering empirical data, but there was a lack of conceptual unity (Cassirer). The tendencies toward compartmentalization in nineteenth-century culture took the psychological form of suppression of vitality and emotions, a disunity attacked in different ways by Kierkegaard and Freud.[34] The attitudes which previously had allayed anxiety were seen by advanced members of the nineteenth century to be no longer efficacious (Kierkegaard, Nietsche, etc.). For example, individual economic striving in the monopolistic stages of capitalism was seen not as leading automatically to the advance of social weal but as increasingly resulting in the dehumanization and alienation of persons (Marx, Tawney, Tillich, etc.).

There is wide agreement that in Western culture the present century is characterized by disunity and traumatic change. Hence the culture is marked by many inconsistencies and contradictions, which are reflected as contradictions in the psychological patterns of the individuals in the culture. For one example, in our culture the individual is taught that he can attain competitive success by hard work and initiative, whereas in actual fact his success is to a great extent determined by such suprapersonal

---

[34] Indeed, the emergence of psychoanalysis in all its branches may be regarded as evidence of the increasing disunity of the culture. It is this disunity which provided the need to which psychoanalysis was one answer.

forces as capital and the market. Since our culture is itself in contradiction, the values the individual members of the culture identify with their existence are bound to be frequently threatened, and widespread anxiety is the result.

It is the present writer's belief, based on his understanding of the evidence, that the trauma of our culture is not peripheral but involves *a threatening of the basic patterns on which the culture itself has depended for security*. On this assumption it can be understood why a relatively minor trauma—like a stock-market fluctuation [35]—is experienced by many individuals as a catastrophic situation. It is not a peripheral threat, to be responded to as a fear, but a threat to values which the individuals in the culture hold essential to their existence as personalities.[36]

The trauma of modern Western culture may be understood as directly connected with the high valuation of competitive individual success which has characterized modern culture since the Renaissance. One demonstration of this connection is presented in Fromm's discussion of the psychological isolation of modern man, an isolation which arises from individualism coupled with failure to create new forms of relatedness. The prevalent attempts to overcome this isolation and concomitant anxiety which Fromm describes—sado-masochistic symbiosis, automaton conformity, submission to external and internalized authority, etc.—may all be viewed as endeavors to compensate for a lack of community and to obtain some form of community albeit in neurotic or unconstructive terms. Totalitarianism (a social form of neurosis) is also an endeavor to overcome isolation and anxiety by means of pseudo-community (Fromm, Goldstein). In Tillich's phrase, totalitarianism is a substitution of collectivism for community. The overcoming of the cultural origins of anxiety in our day involves particularly the development of adequate forms of community.

---

[35] Cf. Karl Mannheim's similar discussion of anxiety in periods of unemployment.

[36] The realization that contemporary social upheavals represent a threat to the basic patterns of modern Western culture occurred in Europe before it occurred in America. Hence W. H. Auden's observation, "In America there are many fears, in Europe much anxiety." It is fair, no doubt, to say that this realization has been increasing in America.

4. Anxiety and Hostility

Anxiety and hostility are interrelated; one affect usually generates the other. *First, anxiety gives rise to hostility.* This can be understood in its simplest form in the fact that anxiety, with its concomitant feelings of helplessness, isolation, and conflict, is an exceedingly painful experience; and one tends to be angry and resentful toward those responsible for placing one in such a situation of pain. Clinical experience yields many examples like the following: A dependent person, finding himself in a situation of responsibility with which he feels he cannot cope, reacts with hostility both toward those who have placed him in the situation and toward those (usually parents) who caused him to be unable to cope with it.

Second, hostility in anxious persons gives rise to increased anxiety. In Freud's example, Hans was hostile toward his father because he stood in the way of the gratification of Hans's excessive libidinal needs for his mother. But if Hans were to express this hostility, the result would be retaliation by the stronger father, the prospect of which would increase Hans's anxiety. Another example is presented by Kardiner in his study of Plainville: the intrasocial hostility in the village, arising chiefly out of reciprocal blocking of pleasure patterns (e.g., gossip), served to increase the individual's feeling of isolation and hence to increase his anxiety.

The most comprehensive analysis of the reciprocal relation of anxiety and hostility is given by Horney. In the child, she holds, basic anxiety is always related to basic hostility. The anxious child is excessively dependent upon his parents but at the same time hostile toward them in proportion to his dependence. In adult patterns this interrelationship between anxiety and hostility often takes the form of the anxious individual's being very closely attached to some other person, e.g., wife or husband, but simultaneously feeling hostile toward this other person because the attachment not only symbolizes the individual's own helplessness but also increases his feelings of weakness. In both child and adult the hostility will be repressed in proportion to the dependence, for fear of arousing counter-hostility or alienating the very persons on whom one is dependent. Repressed hostility generates more anxiety in several ways, among them being: (1) the repressed hostility is often projected on other persons, and thus the feeling that one lives in a hostile and threatening world is increased; (2) the individual who is struggling against repressed hostility is less able to distinguish and protect himself against real threats and exploitation, and hence he is rendered more helpless. Repressed hostility is a specific source of anxiety (Horney).

Granted the interrelation between hostility and anxiety, which affect is generally basic? There is ground for believing that, even though hostility may be the specific affect present in many situations, anxiety is often present below the hostility. This is especially observable in cases of repressed hostility. For one example, in some of the psychosomatic studies of patients with hypertension (a somatic symptom generally associated with repressed hostility) it has been found that the reason the patients repressed their hostility was that they were anxious and dependent. The rationale of such patterns can be broadened to cover many situations in which repressed hostility and anxiety are interrelated: *The hostility would not have to be repressed in the first place except that the individual is anxious and fears counter-hostility or alienation.*[37] It may be hypothesized that in neurotic patterns, including the special group of these patterns termed psychosomatic illnesses, anxiety is the primary etiological phenomenon. In this sense anxiety is the *psychic* common denominator of all disease as well as of all behavior disturbances.

5. METHODS OF DEALING WITH ANXIETY

Negative Methods.—The negative methods of dealing with anxiety range all the way from simple behavior traits like shyness, through the gamut of neuroses and psychosomatic illnesses, to the extreme of psychosis and, in very severe conflict

---

[37] It is not meant to subsume all hostility under the problem of anxiety; it is certainly true that normal hostility may arise whenever an individual's activity is constrained. We are speaking here specifically of *repressed* hostility.

situations, death. The negative methods consist of allaying or avoiding the anxiety without solving the conflict which causes the anxiety; or, in other terms, evading the danger situation rather than resolving it.

The avoidance of anxiety is the purpose of many behavior traits which could be called relatively "normal" and are "neurotic" only in their compulsive forms. For example rigidity of thinking, which may be observed in religious or scientific dogmatism, is a way of armoring one's values so that they are protected from threat. Avoidance of anxiety is temporarily achieved, but at the price of the possibilities of discovering new truth, the exclusion of new learning, and the stunting of capacities to adapt to new situations. Kierkegaard adds that the belief in fate or necessity, like the belief in superstition, is a method of avoiding full responsibility for one's conflicts, thus circumventing anxiety but at the price of loss of creativity. When the values the individual needs to protect are especially vulnerable to threat (often because of their own inner contradictions) and the individual is relatively less able to adapt to new situations, rigidity of thinking and behavior may take the form of compulsion neurosis.

The many methods of relieving tension involved in conflict and anxiety vary from the normal function of laughter to alcoholism or compulsive sexual activity. Frantic activity of any sort—e.g., compulsive work—may serve to relieve the tension mobilized in the organism by anxiety. But frantic activity is generally neither productive nor directed toward solving the problem which causes the tension. The significant question is whether the activity pursued permits the release of tension without resolving the underlying conflict, in which case the activity tends to become compulsive, since the conflict remains.

When persistent anxiety becomes too great to be tolerated in conscious awareness, the neurotic methods of avoiding anxiety occur. It is agreed in the literature that neurotic patterns have their origin in the individual's need to protect himself from anxiety or, more accurately, from the anxiety-creating situation. A neurosis is an intrapsychic compensatory pattern by which security can be preserved despite conflict. It involves some form of *repression* of tendencies which are associated with the conflict situation (Freud), or, in Sullivan's term, dissociation, a demarcation of awareness. It also involves *inhibition* of those activities which would place the individual in a situation of danger. The psychological symptoms in neurosis are various forms of compromise which facilitate the avoidance of the danger situation: e.g., the anxiety generated by Hans's conflict with his father was displaced in the form of a phobia of horses, and so long as Hans could avoid horses by not going out on the street, he need not feel threatened. Likewise the symptoms in hysterical and psychosomatic forms of illness may be viewed as endeavors to adapt to a conflict situation when the problem causing the conflict cannot be solved. The inverse relation between conscious anxiety and the existence of somatic symptoms is one demonstration of the above statement: in proportion to the degree anxiety can be tolerated consciously, somatic symptoms do not appear; but when the anxiety related to the conflict becomes too great to be dealt with, symptoms may appear and the anxiety disappear from consciousness. The symptom is thus a method of coping with the conflict situation by means of alleviating the anxiety without resolving the problem. Indeed, it may be stated that all forms of disease are in one way or another endeavors to cope with a conflict situation, generally by means of shrinking the scope of the conflict to an area in which there is a greater chance of coping with it. In situations of severest conflict the individual may be powerless to cope with the threat by means of the above-mentioned compromises, and may be forced to renounce a large area of activity or reality (e.g., psychosis) or even to renounce existence itself (e.g., "voodoo" death).

It will be seen that the common denominator of the negative methods of avoiding anxiety is a *shrinking of the area of awareness and activity,* thus obviating the conflict which causes the anxiety. Goldstein's brain-injured patients, whose capacities for coping with threats were greatly curtailed, sought to limit their environments (e.g., writing in the extreme corner of the paper) or to avoid change in behavior (e.g., fanatical orderliness in their rooms). The demarcation of awareness and limitation of activity as methods of avoiding anxiety-creating situations amounts

to a curtailing of the freedom of the individual. Thus Kierkegaard holds that the renouncing of possibility, both in the individual's own self-realization and in his communication with
others, is the essential element in the endeavor to avoid anxiety;
his suggestive term for the neurotic forms of avoiding anxiety is
"shut-upness." [38] The negative methods of avoiding anxiety
always involve some sacrifice of possibility both for self-development and for interrelation with one's community.[39]

Constructive Methods.—With respect to neurotic anxiety,
it is agreed that the anxiety indicates the presence of a problem
which needs to be solved. Neurotic anxiety can be treated constructively as a warning that something is amiss within the personality (and at the same time amiss in one's interpersonal relations). And the anxiety can be accepted as a challenge to clarify
and resolve the underlying problem (Horney). Anxiety indicates that a conflict is ensuing, and so long as there is conflict a
positive solution is within the realm of possibility. In this respect anxiety has been likened to the prognostic value of fever:
it is a sign of struggle within the personality and an indication,
speaking in psychopathological terms, that serious disintegration
has not yet occurred (Yaskin). In regard to the method of solving the problem causing the anxiety, two processes are held in
common by the various schools of psychotherapy: (1) *an expansion of awareness*—the individual sees what value (goal) is
threatened, together with becoming aware of the conflicts between his goals and how this conflict developed; (2) *re-education*
—the individual restructures his goals, makes a conscious choice
of values, and proceeds toward the attainment of these values
responsibly and realistically.

But whereas the use of neurotic anxiety as a challenge for
problem-solving has been agreed upon, it has often been overlooked that *normal* anxiety also indicates possibility and may be
used constructively. The tendency in our culture to regard fears

---

[38] Anent the element of distortion of reality (repression, demarcation of awareness) involved in the surrender of freedom and possibility as methods of avoiding
anxiety, Kierkegaard remarks in poetic fashion. "Shut-upness is *ipso facto* an
untruth."

[39] Cf. Sullivan's concept that anxiety is the "great disjunctive force."

and anxiety chiefly in a negative light, as results of unfortunate learning, is not only an oversimplification but tends by implication to remove the possibility of the constructive acceptance and use of the day-to-day anxiety experiences which cannot be called specifically neurotic. To be sure, neurotic anxiety *is* the result of unfortunate learning in the respect that the individual was forced to deal with threatening situations at a period—usually in early childhood—when he was incapable of coping directly or constructively with such experiences. In this respect, *neurotic anxiety is the result of the failure to cope with the previous anxiety situations in one's experiences.* But normal anxiety is not the result of unfortunate learning; it arises rather from a realistic appraisal of one's situation of danger. To the extent that a person can succeed in constructively meeting the normal day-to-day anxiety experiences as they arise, he avoids the repression and retrenchment which make for later neurotic anxiety.

In fine, the goal with regard to neurotic anxiety is the solving of the underlying problem and thus the overcoming of the anxiety. When we are thinking of neurotic anxiety, the oft-expressed criterion of mental health, "the ability to live without anxiety," is sound.[40] But with regard to normal anxiety—the anxiety which arises from real threats, and which, as we have earlier pointed out, inheres in such aspects of human contingency as death, in the threat of isolation which accompanies the development of individuality, and so forth—the desideratum cannot be the complete absence of anxiety.

Our problem, therefore, is *how may normal anxiety-creating situations be used constructively?* Though this question has not generally been attacked in scientific writings, it was confronted

---

[40] The phrase, "living without anxiety", has its valuable ideal meaning, but when it is oversimplified, as it often is in general usage, to mean that the goal is a total absence of anxiety rather than the capacity for confronting and working through anxiety, the phrase becomes delusive and even dangerous. Needless to say, living totally without anxiety in a historical period like the present would imply an unrealistic and insensitive view of one's cultural situation and would betoken an irresponsible attitude toward one's duties as a citizen. One could cite many demonstrations from the rise of fascism in Spain and Germany that the citizens who were unaware of the social danger became putty in the hands of the rising dictatorships. For another illustration, an officer who had no anxiety whatever for his men in time of battle would be irresponsible, and it would be dangerous to serve under him.

directly by Kierkegaard [41] a century ago, and in our times has been attacked by Goldstein and, to a lesser extent, by Mowrer. The reader will recall Goldstein's emphasis (reviewed in Chapter 3 of the present study) that every human being encounters frequent anxiety shocks in the course of his normal development, and that his capacities can be actualized only through an affirmative response to these threats to his existence. Goldstein's simple illustration is the healthy child's learning to walk despite the fact that he falls and gets hurt many times in the process. When we try to understand the constructive use of normal anxiety from the *objective* side, we note that it is characterized by the individual's confronting the anxiety-creating situation directly, admitting his apprehensions but moving ahead despite the anxiety. In other words, it consists of moving *through* anxiety-creating experiences rather than moving *around* them or *retrenching* in the face of them. These ways of meeting anxiety were described countless times in studies of anxiety and fear among soldiers in combat during World War II. The most constructive attitude consisted of the soldier's frankly admitting his fear or anxiety about going into battle, but being subjectively prepared to act *despite* his apprehension. As a corollary it has been frequently pointed out in these studies of soldiers that courage consisted not of the absence of fear and anxiety but of the capacity to move ahead even though one is afraid. This constructive confronting of normal anxiety in daily life and in crises which require moral rather than physical courage (such as the crises in self-development, often attended with profound anxiety, which occur during psychoanalysis), is sometimes accompanied by the affect of "adventure." At other times, however, when the anxiety-creating experience is more severe, confronting it may entail no pleasurable affect

---

[41] The constructive use of anxiety has been described at length by Kierkegaard. To him anxiety is a better "teacher" than reality, for while reality situations may be temporarily evaded, anxiety is an inner function which cannot be escaped short of constriction of the personality. Kierkegaard writes that only he who has been educated in the "school of anxiety"—i.e., has confronted and worked through previous anxiety experiences—is able to meet present and future anxiety experiences without being overwhelmed. In this connection, there is some evidence that soldiers in the last war who had experienced a fair degree of anxiety in their past lives and were in some cases relatively "high-strung" were better able to face anxiety experiences of combat than soldiers who had experienced relatively little anxiety before combat (Grinker and Spiegel).

whatever but be accomplished only by the sheerest kind of dogged determination.

When we view this process *subjectively*—that is, when we ask what is going on within one individual which enables him to confront the danger directly whereas others in the same situation may flee—we discover some very significant data. To draw an illustration again from the studies of soldiers, it has been pointed out that often the subjective motivation which enabled soldiers to confront dangers was their conviction that the threat connected with backing out was greater than the threat faced in battle. Put positively, this is to say that there were values to be achieved in confronting the danger greater than the values in flight. For many a soldier the common value was probably the expectation of his fellow soldiers; he must not let the group down. In simple terms this would be verbalized as the desire not to appear "yellow" to one's buddies; in the more sophisticated soldiers it might be articulated as community responsibility. Thus, the sometimes platitudinous statement that one confronts and overcomes dangers by having a "cause" which more than counter-balances the threat is profoundly true. The one trouble with the platitude is that only in more sophisticated soldiers, to continue our example, does the value one fights for become verbalized in the broader terms of a "cause" such as patriotism, freedom, or human welfare.

We hope that the above illustrative paragraph has prepared the ground for the following generalized statement: *A person is subjectively prepared to confront unavoidable anxiety constructively when he is convinced (consciously or unconsciously) that the values to be gained in moving ahead are greater than those to be gained by escape.* We have pointed out in earlier parts of this study that anxiety arises when the values the individual identifies with his existence are threatened. The converse of this statement may now be made: the individual confronts anxiety-creating experiences and moves ahead without succumbing to them because the values he identifies with his existence (e.g., freedom, prestige, etc.) are stronger than the threat. If one pictures anxiety as resulting from a war between the threat and the values the person identifies with his existence, one can say that neurosis and emotional morbidity mean that the struggle is won by the former (the threat), whereas the constructive approach to anxiety means that the struggle is won by the latter (the individual's values).

The term "values" may seem to many readers to be a vague concept. It is used here purposely because it is a neutral term and gives the maximum amount of psychological leeway for the right of each person to have his own goals. It is thus obvious that the values on the basis of which one confronts anxiety-creating experiences will vary—as indeed we have already seen to be the case with soldiers. Most people are motivated by elemental values which they may never articulate—the need to preserve life itself or some elemental trend toward "health," which, as Sullivan has remarked, we always assume (and with pragmatic justification) when doing psychotherapy. On other levels social prestige is certainly a very important value on the basis of which the individual confronts dangers. Another is the satisfaction to be achieved by the expansion and wider use of one's own powers (as Sullivan, Goldstein, and others have emphasized)—which presumably is operative in the child's learning to walk and many other phases of development through crises. More highly differentiated forms of value occur, for example, in artists and scientists who, in creating new art forms or radically new hypotheses, experience many shocks to their existence; but to the healthy artist or scientist, the discovery of new truth and the adventure of moving into unexplored fields are sufficiently rewarding that he moves ahead despite the threat of isolation and anxiety. In the long run, the confronting of normal anxiety depends on what one regards as of value in himself and his existence. The system of value on the basis of which one confronts normal anxiety is termed by Fromm one's "frame of orientation and devotion." [42] Broadly speaking, this is the person's religious attitude toward life, with the term "religious" defined as the person's basic presupposition of what is and is not of worth. Such an assumption of value is illustrated in Freud's passionate devotion to science in general and to the discovery of psychologi-

---

[42] Erich Fromm, *Man for himself* (New York, 1947), p. 48. Paul Tillich uses the term "ultimate concern" for this religious valuing.

cal truth in particular. Though, as is well known, Freud attacked the orthodox religious formulations severely, there is no doubt that his own passionate affirmation of value—his "religion of science"—enabled him with remarkable courage to persevere in his solitary and individual investigations for the first ten years, and then to continue in his explorations for several decades despite vilification and attack.[43] Our point may likewise be illustrated by Kierkegaard's devotion to "infinite possibility," i.e., devotion to his conviction that unless a man pursues with inner integrity and individually sustained courage the intellectual and moral insights which arise as part of his new experience of every day, he is forfeiting the possibilities for expansion and meaning in his existence as a human being. Thus Kierkegaard, in ways not dissimilar to Freud, was able to produce astonishingly creative works despite social misunderstanding and conflict, and despite very great isolation and anxiety. We can now arrive at a more complete understanding of Spinoza's statement, referred to above (page 24 n), that negative affects like fear and anxiety can be overcome in the long run only by more powerful, constructive affects and that the ultimate constructive affect consists of the individual's "intellectual love of God." In the terms of the present discussion, his term God may be taken as a symbol standing for what the individual conceives to be of ultimate worth.

As already pointed out, the values on the basis of which people meet anxiety-creating experiences may vary from simple preservation of physical life to the classical hedonistic, stoic, and humanistic values, to the "frames of orientation and devotion" given in the classical religions. It is not the purpose of the writer in this study either to imply that all these assumptions of value are of equal efficacy, or to make a judgment among them. Our interest here is only in indicating that the experiences of normal anxiety are confronted constructively because there is more at stake, more to be achieved in moving ahead than in retrenching.

---

[43] Both Freud's critical attitude toward religious formulations and his own passionate devotion to science as the means of attaining human happiness are given in his two books: *The future of an illusion* (London, 1928) and *Civilization and its discontents* (London, 1929).

In this discussion we wish to remain on the psychological level by simply holding to the point that these values will vary greatly from person to person and from culture to culture. The only implicit psychological criterion is that those formulations of value which release the individual's capacities and permit greater expansion in the development of his own powers as well as expansion of his communication with others will serve most constructively as a basis for confronting anxiety.

6. Anxiety and the Development of the Self

The term "self" is used in two senses by writers on anxiety. In its broader meaning, self refers to the sum total of the individual's capacities (Goldstein). In its more limited sense, "self" refers to the capacity of the human organism to have conscious awareness of its activities and through this awareness to exercise a measure of freedom in directing these activities (Kierkegaard, Sullivan, Fromm). Anxiety is involved in the development of the self in both of these meanings of the term.

Goldstein holds that self-actualization—i.e., expression and creative use of the individual's capacities—can occur only as the individual confronts and moves through anxiety-creating experiences. The freedom of the healthy individual inheres in his capacity to avail himself of new possibilities in the meeting and overcoming of potential threats to his existence. By moving through anxiety-creating experiences one achieves self-realization, i.e., one enlarges the scope of his activity and at the same time increases his freedom. The capacity to bear anxiety is one measure of selfhood.[44] This capacity is found least of all in the brain-injured patient, more in the child, and most of all in the creative adult.

Using the term "self" in its more limited sense, namely the function of awareness of one's activities, Sullivan has made a significant contribution. He holds that it is in anxiety experiences in the young child that the self comes into being. The infant in its early relations with its mother learns which activities

---

[44] The capacity to bear anxiety is in this sense a prerequisite to working through the anxiety.

will receive approbation and reward and which will receive disapproval and possible punishment. The latter activities arouse anxiety. The self-dynamism, as Sullivan terms it, develops as a process by which the anxiety-creating experiences are excluded from activity and awareness and the approved activities are incorporated into the child's awareness and behavior. In this sense, the self comes into being to preserve the individual's security, to protect him from anxiety. This view emphasizes the negative function of anxiety in the development of the self and illuminates the very common phenomenon that anxiety experiences which are dealt with unconstructively lead to a constriction of the self. Sullivan also indicates—pointing toward the constructive use of anxiety—that the areas in the personality marked by anxiety often become the areas of significant growth when, as in psychotherapy or favorable human relationships, the individual can deal with his anxiety constructively.

We turn now to the positive aspects of selfhood—freedom, enlarged self-awareness, responsibility. The emergence of individual freedom is very closely connected with anxiety; indeed, the possibility of freedom always arouses anxiety, and how the anxiety is met will determine whether the freedom is utilized or sacrificed by the individual (Kierkegaard, Fromm). The child's need progressively to break the primary ties of dependence on its parents always involves some anxiety (Fromm). In the healthy child this anxiety is overcome by new relatedness on the basis of a larger degree of self-direction and autonomy. But if independence from parents brings with it an insupportable degree of anxiety (as in the case of the child of hostile or excessively anxious parents), if the price in increased feelings of helplessness and isolation is too great, the child retreats into new forms of dependency and that particular possibility of enlarged selfhood is sacrificed. An enlarging of self-awareness occurs whenever one moves through new possibilities (Kierkegaard). Whereas the first anxiety of the infant is without content, a change occurs after the emergence of self-awareness. (Kierkegaard terms this emergence of self-awareness a "qualitative leap"; it is described in a different context in dynamic psychology as the emergence of the ego.) Now the child becomes aware that freedom involves responsibility—responsibility to "be one's self" as well as responsibility to others. The converse side of this responsibility is guilt feeling. To the extent that an individual seeks to avoid anxiety, responsibility, and guilt feeling by refusing to avail himself of his new possibilities, by refusing to move from the familiar to the unfamiliar, he sacrifices his freedom and constricts his autonomy and his self-awareness.[45] Availing oneself of possibilities, confronting the anxiety, and accepting the responsibility and guilt feeling involved result in increased self-awareness and freedom and enlarged spheres of creativity. The more creative the individual, the more possibilities he has, the more he is confronted with anxiety and its concomitant responsibility and guilt feeling (Kierkegaard, Goldstein). Increased self-awareness means increased selfhood (Sullivan); or, as Kierkegaard phrases it, "The more consciousness, the more self." *In fine, the positive aspects of selfhood develop as the individual confronts, moves through, and overcomes anxiety-creating experiences.*

---

[45] "To venture causes anxiety, but not to venture is to lose oneself."— Kierkegaard.

PART II
CLINICAL ANALYSIS
OF ANXIETY

Chapter 7

CASE STUDIES DEMONSTRATING ANXIETY

Anxiety is the dynamic center of neuroses and thus we shall have to deal with it all the time.—Karen Horney, *The Neurotic Personality of Our Time.*

1. INTRODUCTION

What We Seek to Discover.—The following case studies are presented in the light of the summary and synthesis of anxiety theory given in the preceding chapter. While no clinical case can be placed on the Procrustean bed of our expectation that it answer certain questions and no others; while, that is, each case must be taken on its own merit so far as the yielding of data goes, and should be approached in the open-minded mood typified by the inquiry, "what has this particular case to teach us about anxiety"?—nonetheless, our keeping certain more specific questions in mind as we investigate each case makes for greater clarity and concreteness. We shall, therefore, here list some crucial questions for the theory of anxiety to which special attention will be paid in the subsequent case studies. The reader will note that the areas in which these questions occur are parallel to the headings in Chapter 6, "Summary and Synthesis of Theories of Anxiety."

(1) THE NATURE OF ANXIETY AND ITS RELATION TO FEARS. The description of the subject's behavior and feelings in anxiety, which throws phenomenological light on the nature of anxiety, will of course occur as a matter of course in the discussion of each case. More specifically, we shall ask the question: *Can we ascertain whether specific fears are the foci of underlying anxiety?* There is a corollary to the above question

which is also worthy of inquiry. If neurotic fears are the expression in specific form of neurotic anxiety and if, as we have indicated, the latter arises from basic conflicts within the individual, it should be true that the neurotic fears will focus now on this object and now on that, but that the underlying pattern of anxiety will remain fairly constant. Hence, *can we ascertain whether neurotic fears shift as the issues and problems the individual confronts shift, while the underlying neurotic anxiety remains relatively constant?*

(2) ANXIETY AND CONFLICT. In the preceding chapter it was held that neurotic anxiety always has some psychological conflict at its source and that the conflict originally occurs in the child's relation to its parents. Two questions emerge from this aspect of anxiety theory: (a) *Can it be shown in the following cases that subjective, inner conflict is always present as the dynamic source of neurotic anxiety?* (b) *Can it be shown that individuals who have experienced rejection by their parents (especially by the mother) have a greater predisposition for neurotic anxiety?* [1]

(3) ANXIETY AND CULTURE. The interrelation of the subject's anxiety to cultural factors should be illustrated at almost every turn in the following cases. Out of this complex area, we select one question: *Does the individual's socioeconomic status in the society (e.g., middle-class, proletarian) appear to have significant bearing on the kinds and quantities of his anxiety?*

(4) ANXIETY AND HOSTILITY. *Can it be shown that anxiety is related to hostile feelings,* i.e., that the more anxious a person is, the greater is his tendency to have feelings of hostility; and when the anxiety subsides, do the hostile feelings abate likewise?

(5) METHODS OF DEALING WITH ANXIETY. *Can we discover whether, when an individual is confronted with an anxiety-creating situation, characteristic behavioral mechanisms are*

---

[1] This is one way of stating the classical hypothesis, propounded in various ways by Freud, Horney, Sullivan, Fromm, *et al.*, and widely accepted in the field of clinical psychology and psychoanalysis, that the origin of psychological patterns which predispose to neurotic anxiety are in the child's early relations with its parents, especially with its mother.

*called into play (defenses, symptoms, etc.), and that these serve
to protect the individual from the anxiety-creating situation?*

(6) ANXIETY AND THE DEVELOPMENT OF THE SELF. We
shall approach this problem from its reverse side in the first two
of the following three questions, seeking to determine whether
the presence of anxiety tends to retard the development of the
self.[2] (a) *Can it be shown that the presence of severe neurotic
anxiety impoverishes the personality?* (b) *Does the acceptance
of impoverishment on the part of the individual serve as a defense
against the anxiety-creating situation?* (c) *Can we discover
whether the more creative and productive the individual, the
more he is confronted with anxiety-creating situations?*

The reader will note that the headings in the next chapter,
which contains conclusions from the case studies, refer roughly
to the six areas listed above.

The Problem of Method.—How are we to study anxiety in
human beings? In a previous section we have referred to the
lack of investigations of anxiety in experimental and academic
psychology, and we have likewise discussed the realization of
some psychologists that the traditional experimental and mathematical methods were inefficacious for inquiries into human
anxiety.[3] We have noted the reasons that Mowrer, for one
example, has "grave doubts" whether experimental psychology
or experimental methods "will ultimately succeed in encompassing this topic." The reasons for his doubts are not only that the
effects of inducing human anxiety experimentally are too damaging, but that the experience itself is so complex. "Anxiety is
the 'fever' of the 'total personality,'" he continues, "with its
occurrence and nonoccurrence dependent upon a multitude of
factors."[4] In most cases, indeed, we need to know a good deal
both objectively and subjectively about the individual we are
studying before we can even tell *whether* his reaction is anxiety,
let alone understand it.

---

2 The phrase we employ for this retardation of development is "impoverishment
of the personality." While the terms "self" and "personality" are not identical,
they are closely interrelated, as will be seen in the discussion of the actual cases.

3 Chapter 4, Section 2, pages 99-102.

4 O. H. Mowrer, *Learning theory and personality dynamics* (1950).

A chief reason the experience of anxiety in human beings is so complex is that its determinants are often unconscious. As illustrated in such cases as those of Brown and Helen in the following pages, the person in severe anxiety may actually be driven to *deny* the existence of the apprehension—not by caprice or by any uncooperativeness, but simply as a function of the severity of the anxiety itself. The subject can protect himself from the overwhelming effects of anxiety only by trying to persuade himself that he is not afraid![5] Small wonder, then, that check-lists on which the subject reports conscious data about his "anxieties" are of such indifferent value (as the present writer was himself to discover in the study reported later in this chapter).

Symonds, discussing this problem, holds that we must have some methods—often of the "indirect" variety—which will enable us to get at the subjective content of the individual's experience. He reviews the direct methods advanced in academic psychology in recent years for dealing with fears and observes that all these methods fail "to recognize the underlying meaning of anxiety."[6] In Symonds' view it is in understanding *fantasy* that we come to the "heart of the anxiety problem."[7] That is to say, a method is needed which will make accessible the subjective and unconscious forms of motivation as well as motivation in its conscious manifestations. To comprehend an individual's anxiety we need to know how he subjectively interprets his crisis situation; anxiety has an "inner locus," as Kierkegaard and Freud insisted, and to the extent that we cannot get at that, the essential meaning of anxiety in human beings will elude us. Symonds bases his dynamic psychology not only on the assumption that the individual-in-a-life-situation is to be taken as the unit for study, but also on the conviction that psychoanalytic methods are the most fruitful for such inquiries. He recognizes that the scientific character of the clinical and psychoanalytic approaches may be questioned because of the irreproducibility

---

[5] This is a very common phenomenon in human experience, as everyone knows, and not at all limited to the consulting room, *vide* the war experiences of many soldiers; also the "whistling in the dark" phenomenon in daily life.

[6] P. M. Symonds, *The dynamics of human adjustment* (New York, 1946), p. 165.

[7] *Ibid.*, p. 145.

of the data (each individual being in some ways unique, and each requiring a special relationship with counselor or psychotherapist before the meaningful data are accessible). But he holds that the conclusions gain credence because the relationships between behavior and dynamic processes are verified by scores of different investigators.

There are two phases of this problem of method as presented by Symonds, Mowrer, and others. The first is whether the individual-in-a-life-situation is to be taken as the unit of study. The present writer would answer this emphatically in the affirmative. It is his judgment that there is a growing awareness in contemporary academic psychology, to say nothing of the clinical branches of psychology, that if the essential nature of human anxiety is to be fruitfully investigated, dynamic methods are required. The second phase is the more specific one of determining what particular methods within the dynamic field are to be employed. In the present writer's judgment, psychoanalysis has given us a method of great importance. Until the advent of psychoanalysis there was no technique of ascertaining the subjective meanings of an experience like anxiety except the insightful self-observation and intuitive understanding of others by gifted individuals like Pascal and Kierkegaard. But if the term "psychoanalytic" is used to refer to method, it must be employed broadly to stand for all those methods which illuminate unconscious motivations.[8] For example, the projective method of the Rorschach, giving what the subject "will not or cannot tell," in Murray's phrase,[9] was invaluable in the following studies for yielding keys to the dynamics and underlying patterns in the individual's behavior, which were later corroborated by a multitude of other data.

---

[8] The present writer would make a distinction between psychoanalytic *method* and the doctrines which form the *content* of any given psychoanalytic approach. With regard to our use of the term "psychoanalytic" broadly to refer to those methods which uncover unconscious motivation, there may be question by dynamic psychologists who feel they have sound methods which are not psychoanalytical. But we believe there is historical justification for the assumption that practically all methods which get at unconscious motivations, such as the Rorschach, owe much to the original methods worked out by Freud and succeeding psychoanalysts of various schools.

[9] Henry A. Murray, *Explorations in personality* (New York, 1938).

The first case presented in this chapter, that of Brown, is one studied by means of intensive psychoanalysis. This case, selected from the writer's clinical experience, is included on the assumption that certain aspects of the problem of anxiety (such as unconscious conflicts) could best be illustrated by the comprehensive subjective data yielded by this intensive method.

The other thirteen cases comprise a study, made by the writer, of anxiety as found in unmarried mothers at Walnut House, a shelter in New York City.[10] It is important to make clear the assumptions governing the selection of this group. The writer wished to study a group of persons who were in a *crisis situation.* The presupposition was that, when an individual is in a crisis situation, the dynamics of individual behavior are more accessible to study than in so-called "normal" situations.[11] Since one cannot with impunity induce crisis situations in the experimental laboratory, we take what may be called "nature's experiments" for study. The condition of extramarital pregnancy is presumably an anxiety-creating situation in our society. Furthermore, it was believed that it would be useful to study a group of which all the members were in the same anxiety-creating situation. The possibility, which the writer considered, of presenting a number of cases from his own analytical experience, like that of Brown, was therefore rejected in favor of investigating a group of persons presumably in the same crisis situation.

It should be emphasized that we are *not* concerned chiefly in this study with investigating the relation between extramarital pregnancy and anxiety. In theory, another anxiety-creating situation might have served our purpose just as well.[12] The important point is that it be sufficiently a crisis situation to bring the subject's underlying patterns to the fore. Furthermore, we are accepting the presupposition that when an individual is in an anxiety-creating situation, the anxiety reactions he exhibits are not only specifically related to that particular situation but also

---

[10] Walnut House is a fictitious name employed for the customary purposes of anonymity.

[11] Cf. J. A. Plant, *Personality and the cultural pattern* (New York, 1937) and Karl Mannheim, *Man and society in an age of reconstruction* (New York, 1941).

[12] It will be recalled that Luria selected criminals in jail and students at the time of crucial examinations for his study of psychological conflict.

reveal a pattern which is characteristic of that particular individual and would be revealed by him in other anxiety-creating situations. As will be seen in the actual case studies, the data that emerge in the study of these girls have to do with anxiety and competitive ambition, anxiety in phobial patterns, anxiety related to hostility and aggression, anxiety connected with various inner conflicts, and other forms of anxiety which have very little, if anything, to do specifically with the condition of extramarital pregnancy as such. The reader will note that many of the patterns related to anxiety in these cases could be as applicable to students, businessmen, university professors, housewives, and other groups in our society. It is, of course, all to the good that sooner or later studies be made of anxiety in persons in all kinds of groups; in this respect, the more cross-sectional studies we have, the better. But this writer would like to caution against the easily oversimplified critical criterion applied to intensive studies—that they deal with "specialized groups"—in the same way that it is applied to groups selected for investigation of a particular factor. The critical criteria used for "horizontal" (extensive) studies cannot be employed in the same way as yardsticks for "vertical" (intensive) studies, to use Allport's terms.[13] The more intensively we study a given individual, the more we tend to uncover patterns which this individual holds in common with other persons in other groups in the society. That is to say, the more intensively we study one man, the more we arrive at data which lie below individual differences and the more, therefore, we arrive at data which are applicable to "man in general." If this seems a controversial assumption as presented here, the writer can only refer to the previous intensive studies which have yielded data that have been helpful far beyond the confines of the particular individual studied [14] and permit the reader to draw his own conclusions after he has studied the cases which follow.

---

[13] See G. Allport, *The use of personal documents in psychological science* (New York, 1942). The present writer does not mean, of course, to imply that there are not critical criteria which must be applied very conscientiously to intensive case studies; he means simply that these are different in important respects from ways of judging horizontal studies. See next pages for a discussion of critical criteria useful for case studies.

[14] To cite some examples: Exceedingly useful data on anxiety and other aspects of psychosomatics were afforded by the book-length study of one person, Tom,

Methods Used in the Following Cases.—A variety of techniques of collecting data were employed in the case studies of unmarried mothers. The methods of gaining information directly from the girl consisted of personal interviews, Rorschachs,[15] and anxiety check-lists. The writer had from four to eight personal interviews, each generally of an hour's length, with each girl. The social workers had from a score to twoscore of personal interviews with each girl, and while these interviews were not geared specifically to the purposes of this study, they yielded a wealth of pertinent data concerning the girl's attitudes, behavior, and background.[16] Three check-lists—checked by the girl—were employed. The first was designed to elicit the foci of anxiety which the girl remembered from her childhood, the second to elicit foci of anxiety in her present state of pregnancy, and the third (administered after parturition) to elicit foci of anxiety as she faced her problems after the birth of the baby.[17] Observations of the girls' behavior in Walnut House were contributed by the nurses and other personnel of the house as well as by the social workers. A great amount of collateral data was also available, such as the report of the medical examinations of

---

reviewed in Chapter 3. These data are certainly not applicable solely to men of Irish extraction in their fifties, such as Tom was as an individual. Much valuable information about phobias was yielded by Freud's study of Hans, information which is by no means limited to the area of phobias in five-year-old boys. For even more extreme examples; the work of Kierkegaard yields pertinent and profound insights which are applicable to many kinds of people in many situations. Yet Kierkegaard gained his insights chiefly by the intensive study of one person, namely himself. The same is true of Freud's early theories on dreams, which have been very widely accepted and have proven applicable to many different kinds of persons; Freud arrived at these theories chiefly through a study of his own dreams.

[15] One Rorschach was given to every girl before parturition, and second Rorschachs were administered to five girls after parturition.

[16] Every girl was interviewed on entering Walnut House by the head social worker, and the girl then became the case of one of the other social workers, who held conferences with her regularly during her stay (lasting on the average between three and four months) at the house.

[17] Copies of these check-lists are given in the Appendix. One purpose in the use of the second Rorschach and the third check-list was to discover, if possible, the changes in foci of anxiety after parturition. To this end, the items in the third check-list are almost identical, except for rewording, with the items in the second check-list. Due to temporal difficulties—e.g., some girls did not return to Walnut House after parturition—it was not possible to administer the second Rorschach and the third check-list to a majority of the girls. Hence we have only limited data on the changes in foci of anxiety after the birth. In the cases where the tests were given after parturition, the chief use of the results has been to show the shifts in that particular girl's attitudes and anxiety.

each girl, psychometric examinations where deemed necessary, reports from the girl's school or college, and in most of the cases objective data on the girl's home background gained through connecting social agencies. In more than half the cases, the parents and relatives of the girl were interviewed by the social workers at Walnut House.

The scoring of each Rorschach, done originally by the author, was checked independently by a Rorschach specialist. The author's interpretation of each Rorschach was checked by Dr. Bruno Klopfer, who also rated each Rorschach according to *depth* and *width* of anxiety, as well as to the effectiveness of the subject's *handling* of the anxiety.[18] One purpose of the check-lists was to gain additional data on the amount of the girl's anxiety (i.e., number of items checked); in the purely quantitative ranking, a check in the "often" column (indicating the girl believed she "often" had that item of anxiety) was given double the weight of a check in the "sometimes" column. But a second purpose (and, as it turned out, the more useful purpose) of the check-lists was to gain information on the *kinds* (or *areas*) of anxiety the girl experienced. For this purpose the items of the check-lists were classified in five categories: (1) apprehensions of a phobial nature; (2) the girl's anxiety about what her family thought of her; (3) anxiety about what her peers thought of her; (4) anxiety in the area of ambition—e.g., success or failure in work or school; (5) miscellaneous.[19]

An almost unlimited number of data are available in each case study of this sort, data which are neither quantitatively nor qualitatively parallel.[20] In the light of all the data in each case, the author endeavored to see each girl in three dimensions: *structurally* (chiefly by means of the Rorschach), *behaviorally*

---

18 The rating is from 1 to 5, 1 equaling the optimum, or lowest, degree of anxiety. "Depth" refers to how penetrating and profound the anxiety is; this is intensity in its qualitative sense. "Width" refers to whether the anxiety is generalized or limited to special areas; this is intensity in the sense of the quantity of symptoms. "Handling" refers to the degree of efficient effort of the subject in managing her anxiety.

19 The items in these check-lists were classified independently by three persons: Dr. P. M. Symonds, a social worker at Walnut House, and the author.

20 Instead of one factor in 500 cases, as in horizontal studies, we have in studies of this sort 500 factors (roughly speaking) in each case. See G. Allport, *The use of personal documents in psychological science* (New York, 1942).

(the girl's present behavior), and *genetically* (the developmental dimension, an important aspect of which is the childhood background). Using these three dimensions, he sought to arrive at a conceptualization of each case, or a picture of the constellation of each personality. The quantities and qualities of anxiety in each case are integral parts of this constellation. It was necessary, then, to relate the anxiety in each case to other elements in the constellation, such as the rejection each girl experienced in her relation with her parents. To expedite this interrelating process, each subject was ranked by the investigator as to the degree of anxiety and the degree of rejection in one of four categories: high, moderately high, moderately low, and low. These rankings are based on all the data available and also upon the judgments, independently arrived at, of the investigator and the social workers.[21]

The central criterion of validity as to whether we have arrived at a sound conceptualization of each case, as well as a sound estimate and understanding of the anxiety in each case, is *internal consistency*.[22] The author has continually asked, for example: Do the data arrived at by the various methods (interviews, Rorschachs, check-lists) exhibit *inner consistency within the framework of the conceptualization of the case?* And is inner consistency shown in the conceptualization from the structural, behavioral, and genetic aspects of each case? Likewise, if the anxiety has been correctly assessed, it should show inner consistency with the other elements in the constellation of each case.[23]

---

[21] The ratings for anxiety in the Rorschach are given separately in the discussion of the Rorschach in each case, and also a summary rating of the girl against the other girls according to anxiety in the Rorschach is given. In this latter, the rating for *depth* and *width* of anxiety are combined; the *handling* is omitted, since it refers to something different from quantity or kind of anxiety. Though the Rorschach ranking often agrees, or almost agrees, with the investigator's over-all anxiety ranking for the girl, the two are not to be confused.

[22] Cf. Allport, *op. cit.*

[23] Whether a sound conceptualization has been arrived at in each case is a question which is, of course, left to the reader's judgment. The writer may say that in his judgment the data from the different sources did make a consistent picture, with the one exception of the quantities of anxiety on the check-lists. The reasons why this item was at times at odds with an otherwise consistent picture are noted in the case discussions.

Presentation of the Cases.—The cases which illustrate several aspects of the problem of anxiety are presented at some length; other cases, through which it was desired to illustrate or demonstrate only one or two points, are presented briefly. As frequently as practicable, the subject's own words are given. In the face of the great mass of data in each case, some selection in presentation was obviously necessary. It is hoped that enough of each case is presented to make evident the conceptualization of the case and to clarify the points it is desired to illustrate or demonstrate. The Rorschach numerical scoring data in each case are given, with the full understanding, however, that the configuration in each Rorschach is more crucial for its interpretation than the numerical scoring. Unless otherwise stated, the parents in each case will be understood to be white, American, and Protestant. The writer is referred to as the "analyst" in the first case and the "psychologist" in the other thirteen, terms which correspond to his roles in the two methods of study.

2. BROWN: CONFLICT UNDERLYING SEVERE ANXIETY

This man, thirty-two years of age, had been suffering for the preceding nine years from a very severe, recurring anxiety condition. On graduation from college (where he had received high academic honors), he had entered medical school. After two months he had felt increasingly inadequate and helpless in the face of his assignments; the first anxiety state then developed, the symptoms of which were inability to sleep or work, difficulty in making the simplest decisions, and fear that he was "losing his mind." The anxiety state was relieved by his discontinuing school. During the next years he tried several different vocations, only to have to discontinue each on the recurrence of anxiety attacks. The anxiety states, generally lasting several months (or until he dropped the particular work he was doing), were accompanied by profound depression and suicidal thoughts. In two of the more severe anxiety spells he had committed himself to mental hospitals for periods of one and eleven months. He had finally enrolled in another graduate school, and when, in his third and final year, another developing anxiety state incapacitated him for work, he applied for psychoanalytic treatment.[24]

The chief features of the Rorschach which was administered at the beginning of his analysis, when he was in a relatively severe anxiety state, were the great predominance of vague, unelaborated whole responses, the low degree of responsiveness and productivity of both the extratensive and intratensive kinds, and the absence of any originality.[25] When this Rorschach was compared with the one taken a year later, when he was not in an anxiety state, it was plausible to conclude that the anxiety was the significant etiological factor in producing the features described above.[26] In other words, we have in the first Rorschach the picture of an individual whose anxiety blocks his capacity to relate to specific, concrete details, renders his relation to reality "blurred" and vague, and likewise impoverishes both his feeling and thinking capacities.

During the early part of his analysis his mood oscillated between lethargy and inertia on one hand and intense anxiety on the other. In the former passive states he characterized himself

[24] This report is based upon the more than 300 hours of analytical work of the author with this patient. The author wishes especially to acknowledge the penetrating help given by Dr. Erich Fromm on the interpretations during the early part of the psychoanalysis and the collaborative aid given by Dr. Edwin Weinstein on the medical aspects of the case. Only certain phases of the psychoanalysis which are illustrative for the present study—chiefly the early portions—are presented here.

This case might be diagnosed as severe anxiety neurosis or as schizophrenia. If the latter term is used, it should be made clear that it refers not to a distorting of reality, but to the fact that the patient is so radically incapacitated by his anxiety that he cannot take care of himself in the real world. In such conditions, the diagnosis of severe anxiety neurosis may merge into a diagnosis of schizophrenia. In any case, we are concerned here primarily with the behavior dynamics rather than the diagnostic label.

[25] Total responses, 18 : 1 M, 2 FM, 1 k, 6 F, 3 Fc, 3 FC (of which 2 were F/C, 2 CF; 13 responses (76%) were W, 5 responses (28%) D.

[26] The second Rorschach taken after ten months of analysis, when he was relatively free from anxiety, showed a radically different picture. There were 50 responses; W percentage was reduced to 44 (almost normal); D was 40 per cent, and d, Dd, and S together were 16 per cent. This indicates a much greater capacity to relate himself to concrete, specific realities. The number of M had risen to 6 and FC to 4, which indicates much more use of intratensive productivity and also more effective extratensive productivity. There were 3 original responses on the second record, compared to no originality at all and much banality of response on the first. No matter to what one attributes the change—to the year of psychoanalysis, to a transference situation, or what not—the fact remains that at the time of the first record he was in an anxiety state and at the time of the second he was not. It seems to the present writer a tenable conclusion that we have in

as "like a dog lying in the sun hoping somebody will feed it" and produced many "blissful" memories of the care he had received as a child. In the latter anxiety states he exhibited considerable tension and talked very rapidly, as though driven to get the material out. He described his feelings in anxiety as a general emotional vagueness, which corresponds to the "blurred" quality of the Rorschach reactions noted above. When in anxiety it was *difficult or impossible for him to have any clear and distinct feelings,* whether of a sexual nature or otherwise. This state of emotional "vacuum" was excruciatingly uncomfortable for him. He would often go to movies or try to become engrossed in a novel, for, as he phrased it, if he could gain "empathy" with other persons, if he could feel something which other people were feeling, he would to that extent find relief from his anxiety. He is apparently here describing the state of diminished awareness of one's self which characterizes severe anxiety, and his very significant insight is that if he could become aware on a feeling level of the reality of other persons, he would to that extent become aware of himself as a subject differentiated from objects and thus avoid being overwhelmed by his anxiety.

He had been born in India, the son of American missionaries. While his mother was pregnant with him, the only two other children in the family died in a plague. In his childhood he felt he had been "coddled," not only by his mother but by the native women servants, who insisted on dressing him until he was seven. Three girl siblings were born later, with one of whom he engaged in very severe and violent competition for the favor of his parents. "I wanted to be the baby," he phrased it; and when his parents would adjudicate a dispute in the sister's favor, he would feel deeply incensed and threatened. When the patient was in his teens, his father broke down in what was diagnosed as manic-depressive psychosis and the family returned to this country, where the father was hospitalized. Several years later the father committed suicide.

The crucial factor in this patient's anxiety pattern was his very dependent, symbiotic relationship with his mother. Two

these two records the contrasted pictures of the same individual's behavior and personality when in a state of anxiety and when relatively free from anxiety.

significant memories illuminate the early relationship: when he was five, his mother, while nursing one of the babies, had offered him her breast with the remark, "Do you want a drink too?" The intense humiliation he had felt at this implication of his being a baby came up repeatedly in the analysis in many different contexts of his relations with his mother. When he had engaged in a prank at the age of eight, his mother had punished him by making him whip her, which clearly suggests that the symbiosis was nurtured by the mother's sado-masochistic needs concentrated upon him. The traumatic experience of his being forced to whip her became the focus for his later feeling that he could never hold any opinion or exercise any judgment independently of his mother, for she would then assume a martyr role and "my hands would be tied." He was dominated by the mother under the formula, "If you go against my authority, you do not love me." At the time of the analysis he was being supported by his mother, as he had been during his previous periods of incapacitation; both he and his mother were worried about how he would be supported when she died. Even at his present age his mother's letters addressed him as "my darling boy," after receiving which he often had anxiety dreams of "some one trying to kill me," or, in one illuminating example, of "Russia trying to converge on a small country." In one of the letters he received from his mother during the analysis, his mother stated that if *she* had sufficient faith in God, he would be cured of his illnesses through *her* faith. He was understandably resentful at her implication that he could do nothing whatever, religiously or psychologically, to help himself apart from her. We have pictured this relationship with his mother in some detail, for the origins of the patient's anxiety pattern can be understood only in the context of his having to deal from the time of birth onward with a dominating, sado-masochistic mother, who exercised her tyranny at one moment by an assumption of strength but at other times by the more effective—and, for the patient, more confusing—means of cloaking the tyranny under a pretense of her weakness.

The conflict underlying his anxiety was shown in two dreams during the first months of analysis:

I was in bed enjoying a close physical embrace with a woman. It became apparent that it was my mother. My penis was erect, and I was embarrassed. As I tried to pull away, she said, "You've got to grant me some satisfaction." So I fondled her breasts. Then an emission of semen came from her breasts, as from a male genital.

The significant points in the dream are that the mother *commands* him to devote himself to her satisfactions, and that he imputes to her the sexual functions of the male. Several weeks later he received word that his mother had hurt her arm, which news so perturbed him that he had phoned her in a distant city. That night the following dream occurred:

A rotting, putrid arm had reached out from a hole in a rock and grabbed my penis, pulling it away from me. I was mad, and I reached in the hole to grab the hand, pull it out, and make it let go of my penis. Then I felt some one punch me in the back with a knife or pistol, to force me to let go. It seemed to be another person, an accomplice of the hand, who was going to kill me if I didn't let go. I awoke in great fright.

His associations with penis—"strength," "power," "my own penis is small"—indicated that the word for him, as for many people in our culture, stood for his own individual power. Since the arm obviously is his mother's, the dream says that his mother has taken his individual power away from him, and if he tries to regain it he will be killed. In both dreams he sees his mother as possessing great power, even including masculine power, and himself as the victim of her demands.

His conflict, therefore, may be stated: *If he tries to use his own power, to produce and achieve independently of his mother, he will be killed; but the opposite path, namely remaining dependent upon her, can be pursued only at the price of continued feelings of inadequacy and helplessness.* The latter way out of the conflict requires a renunciation of his individual autonomy and strength, but, in symbolic language, it is better to be castrated than to be dead.[27]

---

27 These dreams might be interpreted in the classical mode of Oedipus, incest and castration. But in the judgment of the present writer, the meaning of the symbols is significant rather than the sexual content per se. From this viewpoint

The above dreams indicate how severe the conflict underlying neurotic anxiety may be. It is not surprising that such a conflict has thoroughly paralyzing and incapacitating effects upon the patient. Much of the superficial material in this case could be interpreted in Adlerian fashion, e.g., as anxiety used as a strategy for remaining under the care of the mother and mother substitutes. But such an interpretation overlooks the crippling conflict which underlies the anxiety. It is comprehensible why this patient should describe his feelings during anxiety as "like fighting something in the dark, when you don't know what it is." When he received letters of moralistic advice from his friends, he reacted with an insightful and illuminating analogy, "They [the friends] are like people calling to a drowning man to swim, when they don't know that under the water his hands and feet are tied." [28]

From the dreams and other material so far related it is evident that the patient had much repressed hostility against his mother. (Indeed, from the standpoint of almost any form of

---

the essential point about the first dream is not simply that the subject has sexual contact with the mother, but that the mother commands it. In the second dream it is the mother who castrates the patient, not the father. There are, of course, many incest references in a case of this sort. The significant point in the incest aspect of this patient's pattern is illustrated in the following dream: "I was secretly married to an older woman. *I didn't want to be, so I had myself committed to an institution.*" This is an eloquent statement of his struggle to get away from his mother—even to the point of having himself committed to an institution (which suggests, also, that his psychological illness has some function of protection against the mother). One might hypothesize that his not wanting to be married to her and his having himself incarcerated are the result of guilt feelings arising from the incest desires; but it does not seem necessary to make that interpretation. To the present writer the dream says more simply and directly that he knows what marriage to his mother really means, i.e., to be enslaved by a tyrant, and being incarcerated is preferable if that is the only way one can avoid such a relationship. In the present study incest phenomena are treated as indicative of very dependent relations of the person with the parent, beyond which the person has been unable to "grow up."

[28] We have not said much about the patient's relation to his father, since we must select and the mother relation seems to us crucial in the case. We do not mean to imply, however, that the father's problems, his psychosis and eventual suicide were not exceedingly important influences on the young man. His relation to his father, from childhood on, was characterized by (1) identification with his father, (2) belief that his father was excessively strong, (3) subsequent feelings of being pushed down by the father, and finally (4) being convinced by his father's suicide that "my father, whom I thought was so strong, turned out to be so weak—so how can there be any hope for me?" Thus his relation to his father exacerbated his own profound dilemma of weakness.

psychology it would be impossible to conceive of a human being existing in such a dilemma without his experiencing great hostility). During the analysis the hostility of this patient was manifested in two opposite forms. First, he exhibited hostility whenever he felt he was not being allowed to remain in a dependent state: this is hostility as a reaction to anxiety at having to assume independent responsibility for which he felt inadequate. When he felt that being analyzed required too much effort and responsibility on his part, he would demand that the analyst give him specific advice and authoritative directions for his behavior, as he felt a minister would give him "specific moral and religious instruction" or a physician would tell him exactly what was wrong and exactly what he should do without his having to assume any self-direction whatever. The psychosomatic symptom often accompanying this hostility at having to assume independent responsibility was diarrhea.[29] The other form of hostility emerged whenever he was placed in a dependent, helpless position. Most of the repressed hostility toward the mother falls in this category. We have noted the evidence for this hostility as early as the fifth year, when he was humiliated by his mother's implication that he was still a baby in proffering him milk from her breast.

It will be noted that these occasions of hostility are really contradictory and that they correspond to the two aspects of the patient's fundamental conflict. In other words, hostility was a reaction to the exacerbation of either side of his conflict. There was a roughly direct relation between the exacerbation of the conflict and hostility in the respect that the more anxiety he felt, the more hostility (covert or overt) was present, and when his anxiety abated his hostility did likewise. It was almost impossible for him to admit overt hostility toward his mother, despite the presence of this hostility in dreams and its evidence as a general undercurrent of resentment toward her and specific annoyance at her letters. The hostility had to be in large measure repressed, lest the great dependence upon the mother be threat-

---

29 This association is shown in a remark, "I feel all plugged up; if I could just have a big bowel movement—if I could just get mad!"

ened.[30] His associations suggested that two secondary gains of
his recurring psychological illness were that since his mother
was then required to support him, he could both remain dependent upon her and at the same time get even with her.

We turn now to the problem of the *occasions* which cued off
anxiety in this patient. In spells of acute anxiety, which generally lasted from three days to a week, it was almost impossible
to discover at the time what situation in his present experience
had cued off the panic. When the analyst would suggest inquiring into the occasion of the present anxiety spell, or "what" he
was then afraid of, he would insist that the occasion had nothing
whatever to do with the anxiety, and assert, "I'm afraid of
everything, I'm afraid of life." He was aware only of intense,
paralyzing conflict. Despite the fact that the event or experience
which cued off that particular anxiety spell could often be re-
covered in retrospect after the panic was over, there is logic
in his feeling that the occasion was of secondary importance.
We do not refer simply to the fact that his severe anxiety rendered him incapable of surveying his reality situation objectively.
We refer, rather, to the fact that the *occasion* was not the *cause*
of his anxiety. As he felt, whatever had cued the conflict off, it
was none the less the conflict which caused his anxiety, i.e.,
produced his paralysis and helplessness. If we are to interpret
his "logic," it would be that the particular event or experience
which activated the conflict might be objectively a relatively
minor event, had its subjective significance in the fact that it
served to cue off the conflict, and receded in objective importance
as the conflict became activated.

In less severe anxiety attacks, it was possible to discover the
occasions of his anxiety with fair accuracy. These occasions,
together with the occasions reconstructed in retrospect after severe panics, fall into three main categories. First, anxiety was
occasioned by *situations in which he had to assume individual
responsibility*. For one example, in a period just before the

---

[30] This difficulty in admitting overt hostility was present in his relation with
the analyst as well as with almost all other persons and was particularly in evidence
when he was anxious. Generally his hostility took the forms of general resentment, occasional hostile dreams, or displacement on other persons; during his
anxious periods, a radically demarcated displacement usually occurred.

analytical work had to be suspended for the summer, he experienced a great deal of tension and talked at length about his dread that he might have cancer. This cancer fear was associated with an anxiety panic in childhood when he feared that he might have leprosy and would have to be separated from his family.[31] The fear of cancer vanished on this occasion when the anxiety at separation from the analyst was clarified. Another example of anxiety at having to assume responsibility is seen when, after a year of analysis, he re-enrolled for his final year of study for his graduate degree. Several severe anxiety attacks ensued, during which he was overwhelmed with feelings of helplessness and inadequacy at the prospect of having to produce papers and write examinations. He felt that he "would not measure up," would "lose out in the race," would "lose face," etc. Since he subsequently did accomplish these dreaded academic requirements successfully, with no intervening factor except a reduction in anxiety, it is clear that the anxiety arose not from a realistic appraisal of inadequacy in the face of tasks (i.e., the occasion) but rather from the neurotic conflict which facing these tasks activated.

The second category of occasions of his anxiety was *situations of competition*. These occasions were not only major events such as academic examinations, but also relatively minor events like bridge games or discussions with his colleagues.[32]

But most significant of all is the third group of occasions of anxiety, namely *anxiety after achieving success*. During his final year of graduate study he was invited to preside at a meeting of an important professional society, an event which represented considerable achievement to him. Some undercurrent of tension

---

31 It goes without saying that a person with such pronounced feelings of inadequacy would profoundly dread separation and isolation from those upon whom he depended.

32 This anxiety in competition was generally associated with his severe rivalry with his sister during childhood. The prototype for this anxiety, therefore, seems to be the threat to his excessive needs to be in an approved and favored position with his mother. In such matters as academic examinations, this approval could be gained by his being successful in competition. But on a level quite below his feeling of lack of personal power to achieve, he is faced with the dilemma that if he does achieve, i.e., does use his own power, he will be threatened with death at the hands of his mother. It is understandable, therefore, that the most minor competitive situation would thus activate a major subjective conflict.

which he experienced before this event was clarified, and he discharged his responsibility successfully, receiving compliments from persons who were important in his eyes. The next day began one of his most severe attacks of anxiety and depression. This is understandable on the basis of the conflict outlined above, since using his own powers raises the threat of being killed. His general practice was to refuse to admit any achievement, such as wearing his Phi Beta Kappa key, for, as he phrased it, "When I'm succeeding, I'm afraid it will be a barrier between me and others." If he awoke in the morning feeling rested and strong, he reported apprehension lest he be "separated from other people." He felt he could overcome anxiety spells by crying in the analytic sessions, by "showing my weakness." This use of weakness alleviated his conflict in at least two respects: (1) by being weak he would be accepted, "loved"—prototypically by his mother—while being strong would mean isolation and separation from his mother; and (2) being weak and unsuccessful obviated the threat of being killed.

The *regular pattern of progression assumed by most of his anxiety spells* is revealing. First, he would report a fear that he had cancer, or that he had recently experienced a momentary spell of dizziness as "though some one had struck me in the back of the neck." This latter symptom, associated with some electric shock treatments he had received several years earlier, was felt by him to indicate that he had some organic brain injury.[33] Both the fear of cancer and the dizziness were presented by the patient as entirely rational, with supporting evidence from the daily papers, for example, about the contemporary high incidence of deaths from cancer.[34] When it was suggested that the psychological meaning of the fears be explored, he would show offense and insist he felt no conscious anxiety whatever.

---

[33] Physical examinations of this patient had always been negative. A special medical conference was held concerning this symptom of dizziness, the conclusion of which was that it was in all probability a psychogenic symptom of anxiety. The dizziness almost always occurred in the context of an anxiety situation, such as on his assumption of some responsibility he dreaded. The similarity of the phrase "being struck in the back of the neck" with the anxiety dream of being killed (in which his assailant also struck him in the back) is obvious.

[34] The fear that he had cancer was associated with a dream of being a patient in a hospital with nurses taking care of him. This suggests one of the functions, or purposes, of the symptom.

The second stage would follow a day or so later; the fears associated with cancer and the dizziness would be forgotten, but anxiety dreams would appear, generally about his mother. Still there would be no conscious admission of anxiety.

In the third stage he would exhibit increased dependence on the analyst, insisting that authoritative guidance be given, with increasing covert or overt hostility if these demands were unmet.

The final, fourth step in the progression, again appearing a day or two later, would be the emergence of a conscious anxiety attack, with concomitant severe tension, discouragement, and eventually depression. It seems to the writer that we have in these steps the progressive emergence of anxiety into conscious awareness, the anxiety assumedly occasioned by some experience or event just prior to the reporting of the dizzy spell or the fear of cancer.

Conclusions.—This case illustrates a number of significant aspects of the dynamics of anxiety, several of which we shall here summarize.

(1) RELATION BETWEEN FEARS AND ANXIETY. How anxiety relates to fear is illustrated in the phenomenon of the cancer dread, which appeared as a specific, "realistic" fear but was later demonstrated to be an objectivated manifestation of underlying neurotic anxiety.

(2) CONFLICT UNDERLYING NEUROTIC ANXIETY. We have seen that his anxiety arose out of his symbiotic relation with his mother and that this relationship was characterized by a conflict between his own needs to achieve some autonomy and use of his powers and the conviction that if he did appropriate his own power he would be subject to dire threat (being killed) at the hands of his mother. Consequently his behavior was characterized by passivity, a subordination of himself to others (prototypically the mother), a need to have others take care of him; and at the same time he experienced overwhelming feelings of inadequacy and helplessness. Severe anxiety ensued whenever this conflict was activated.[35]

---

[35] In theory one might assume that there would be no conflict if he simply subordinated himself to his mother's power; but such a prospect only increased

(3) RELATION BETWEEN HOSTILITY AND ANXIETY. This relation is illustrated in that the above conflict (and concomitant anxiety) was greatly abetted by his repressed hostility toward his mother. And speaking more specifically, we noted the relation between hostility and anxiety in the fact that when the patient was in relatively greater anxiety, he exhibited increased hostility (covert or overt); and when his anxiety abated, his hostile feelings did likewise.

(4) RELATION BETWEEN SYMPTOMS AND ANXIETY. The symptom of dizziness (a psychosomatic symptom) and the fear of cancer (a psychological symptom) appeared as the first step in the progression of unconscious anxiety into awareness. These symptoms disappeared as the anxiety became conscious. This is in accord with the contention advanced earlier in this study that the presence of symptoms bears an inverse relation to conscious anxiety. The function of these symptoms was *to protect the patient from the anxiety-creating situation, i.e., any situation which would cue off his conflict.* This can be seen when we consider that if the patient could really believe he had cancer or organic injury, his conflict would be obviated in several respects: (a) he could remain in a dependent role (such as being hospitalized) without guilt feeling, (b) he could avoid having to undertake tasks for which he felt inadequate, and (c) he could get even with his mother by her having to support him in the illness.

(5) RELATION BETWEEN SEVERE ANXIETY AND IMPOVERISHMENT OF PERSONALITY. This relation is seen in a comparison of the two Rorschachs. The one taken when the patient was in anxiety is characterized by meager productivity, vague-

---

his feelings of worthlessness and inadequacy. Whether any human being could permanently surrender his own autonomy to some one else, in this case the mother-figure, and thus avoid conflict is very much open to doubt. It might be added that the progress of this patient toward overcoming his anxiety neurosis was characterized by development on three flanks: (1) a gradual clarification of the previously unconscious mother relation; (2) a renunciation of the excessive aspects of his ambition (which had previously shown themselves in perfectionistic academic striving); and (3) a gradual growth in, and experiencing of, his capacity to use his own strength without thereafter feeling threatened. This account of the direction of his development is grossly oversimplified, but at least it may illustrate how the two sides of his conflict were relieved.

ness, no originality, and a blockage both of "inner" activity and the capacity to respond to emotional stimuli from the outside. The Rorschach taken when the patient was relatively free from anxiety shows much greater productivity, radically increased capacity to deal with concrete realities, a fair degree of originality, and greatly increased "inner" activity as well as increased extratensive emotional responsiveness. The "blurred" relation to reality which characterized the first Rorschach corresponds to his testimony that in severe anxiety he could not experience "distinct feelings"; it is as though the inner, subjective vagueness involved in the anxiety carried over into a general vagueness in his manner of evaluating outside, objective stimuli as well. This is an illustration of the thesis advanced earlier that severe anxiety breaks down the capacity to experience the self in relation to objects and is, correspondingly, an experience of "dissolution" of the self. His endeavor to overcome his anxiety by becoming aware of other people's feelings is insightful in the respect that he could then become aware of himself in relation to other people and to this extent overcome the state which we have termed the "dissolution" of the self.

(6) OCCASIONS DISTINGUISHED FROM CAUSE OF ANXIETY. We have referred to the cause of the anxiety as the neurotic conflict and the occasions of it as the experiences or events which activated that conflict. It was noted that the more severe his anxiety, the more the conflict predominated and the more the occasion receded in importance in his experience. In this respect the significance of the occasion lay in its subjective function of cuing off the conflict. We have also noted that the occasions always bore a logical and consistent relationship to the particular nature of his conflict; e.g., it was not fortuitous that occasions of responsibility, competition, and achieving success cued off this particular patient's conflict. The occasion always involved some anticipated threat (defeat in competition, "loss of face," etc.). But what the present writer wishes to emphasize is that when the conflict was activated, the patient was faced with threat whichever way he turned. *The anxiety was therefore due not just to the anticipation of threat inhering in the occasion* (e.g., he might

fail in an examination), *but rather was due to the experience of being in a dilemma in which he was threatened from both sides at once.* If he achieved some success, he was threatened with death by his mother; if he failed to achieve the success and remained dependent, he was threatened with continued feelings of helplessness and inadequacy.

3. NANCY: ANXIETY AND CONFLICTING ATTITUDES TOWARD THE MOTHER

The mother of Nancy (age nineteen) had divorced her father, a chauffeur, when Nancy was two, and two years later had married a musician whom Nancy described as "very intelligent like my mother." Until the age of twelve Nancy had lived with her mother and stepfather in an upper-middle-class suburb, the cultural level of which, as well as the "good home we had and the good upbringing I received during that period" were greatly prized by Nancy. When she was sixteen, her mother separated from the stepfather, which unstable behavior Nancy described as "too much for me," and she then left her mother and school (having completed the ninth grade) and went to work as a clerk, then as a cashier, and later as a milliner. Nancy's friends, work, and that part of her background with which she identifies place her in the middle class.

Because of her loneliness in living in New York rather than "love" or sexual interest, she explained, she had accepted the relationship with the young man who was the baby's father. Through him she had met another young man with whom she had fallen in love and to whom she was now engaged. The college education and good family standing of her fiancé (his father being a member of a university faculty) were very important points to Nancy. The fiancé knew of her pregnancy and apparently accepted it with understanding, expressing his willingness that they keep the baby as their own after their marriage. Nancy, however, had decided to give the baby up for adoption.

Nancy impressed almost everyone at Walnut House as a well-adjusted, very responsible, conscientious, and considerate person, with a marked capacity for avoiding conflict in her personal relations. She was described by a social worker as "one of the nicest girls we have ever had at Walnut House." Physically and socially attractive, she had cultivated an educated bearing; and in the first interviews she seemed poised and uninhibited, with no apparent indications of the pervasive anxiety we were later to discover.

Nancy's Rorschach showed an intelligent, original person with a marked anxiety neurosis of the type in which the "anxious attitude" toward life was accepted and so well systematized that it gave her the outward appearance of "success" in her personal relations.[36] The outstanding feature of the Rorschach was the very high proportion of responses using the tiny details; indeed, her regular procedure was to go around the circumference of the blot, responding to each small detail as she went, but being careful to cling to the edge and avoiding any threat of losing her bearings by going into the larger areas of the blot itself. Figuratively, this is the picture of an individual who believes herself to be perpetually walking on the edge of a precipice and therefore must step very cautiously from stone to stone lest she fall.[37] The content of these responses was chiefly faces, which suggested that Nancy's anxiety was connected with a great concern with other people looking at her and what they thought of her. The record indicated an isolated personality, with an almost complete absence of outgoing, affective response to other people. Though much "inner" activity was present, the instinctual aspects of inner promptings were subordinated. (The Rorschach thus corroborated her statement that the motives for her sexual relations leading to the pregnancy were something other than "love" or sexual interest.) In the few responses in the Rorschach in which she did become emotionally involved, the pattern of clinging to tiny details was broken and considerable anxiety ensued. This indicated that one of the functions of the emotional con-

---

[36] Total responses, 41: 6 *M*, 3 *FM*, 1 *K*, 22 *F*, 7 *Fc*, 1 *C'*, 1 *CF*; popular responses, 5; originals, 8; *W*% 10, *D*% 41, *d*% 24½, *Dd*% 24½; (*H* plus *A*): (*Hd* plus *Ad*) is 12:13.; percentage of responses in wholly colored cards, 29; intelligence estimate from Rorschach: efficiency 115, potentiality 125.

[37] Nancy's behavior in the Rorschach corresponds to the behavior of Goldstein's patients who, in a much more pathological degree than Nancy, would write their names only in the very corner of the paper, any venture away from clear boundaries being too severe a threat (cf. Chapter 3).

striction was to protect her from the anxiety-creating situation of emotional involvement with other persons.[38]   Much ambition was shown in the record, taking the form of compulsions to produce in quantity, to get everything in (as though she must cover all of experience by including every tiny detail), to produce perfectly, and to show originality.   The perfectionism was partly a way of gaining security by sticking to details in which she could be meticulously accurate, but it was also an endeavor to gain acceptance and reassurance from the tester.   Her ambition was not to gain power over others (like Helen's) but rather served as a way of getting acceptance; e.g., "If I do well, if I am 'interesting,' I will not be rejected."   Her rating for anxiety on the Rorschach was: depth 3, width 5, handling 1, which placed her highest among all the girls.

Nancy filled out the anxiety check-lists with the same meticulous care for accuracy, pondering each item ("I don't like to check them unless I'm sure"), and returning to reconsider items and revise her checking.   In quantity, she ranked in the high category on the childhood list, moderately high on the present list, and low on the future list.[39]   All three lists showed the chief areas of anxiety to be success and failure in work and what her peers thought of her.

It became clear in Nancy's behavior and in the interviews that her security, and consequently her ability to keep anxiety at bay, depended almost entirely on whether she could convince herself that other people accepted her.   She was intensely worried about

---

[38] With the appearance of bright color in Card II, she gives one of her few whole responses, but it is a severely disturbed response, and she drops the card immediately for the next. A similar reaction, though not quite so pronounced, occurs with the appearance of the totally colored cards (VIII).

[39] A curious phenomenon was evidenced in her behavior in checking the lists, which may partially explain why the "future" anxiety list shows less quantity of anxiety than the other two. Every item of anxiety suggested on the lists threw Nancy into a dilemma, which she verbalized by saying she had thought a lot about the item in point. *It was very difficult for her to separate herself enough from her anxiety to know whether she was anxious about a given item or not.* Her criterion seemed to be: if she had been able to manage the suggested item of anxiety, she checked it as not a source of anxiety, despite the fact that her way of managing it generally involved obvious anxiety. The "future" anxieties had not yet proved unmanageable, and hence they would be less frequently checked. Another partial explanation for her checking fewer items of anxiety on this list is that she tended to idealize the future (as will be seen below).

whether her fiancé's parents would continue to like her, and tried constantly to reassure herself by the fact that they seemed to like her now. Her continual reference to them, as to most people she admired, was, "They are such nice people, and they like me." She searched the letters from her fiancé for assurances that he still loved her. It was only by the security she found in him, she emphasized, that she could go through her present difficulties: "If anything went wrong with his love for me, I'd break down completely." The criterion of whether the fiancé, or anyone else for that matter, loved her was whether he could be *depended upon,* as her mother and her first boy friend could not be, but as she believed her fiancé could be. Though Nancy had amicable relations with everyone, she stated that she was very cautious in choosing real girl friends, for "most girls can't be depended upon to help you." She never brought up any references to her own feelings which would indicate affective, outgoing response to these other people who were so important to her. Her own emotional response, even to her fiancé, seemed not to enter the picture, her only reference being the general statement that she loved him. The important point was whether the other person "loved" *her*—by which she meant a condition in which the other would not reject her. Thus "love" for Nancy was essentially *a security device* by which she could keep anxiety at bay.

Her behavior was a revelation of expertly devised means of placating others and keeping them in a benevolent attitude toward her. She apologized effusively when she was late for an interview and showed excessive gratitude when anyone helped her. In one interview with the social worker, Nancy, in trying to avoid discussing her childhood, made a remark that was only in the most minor way aggressive: but she made a special visit to the social worker's office the next day in considerable anxiety to ask whether the social worker had been offended. She never permitted herself outbursts toward other people, even toward her stepfather, who apparently had often given her just cause; "you have to live with people" was Nancy's formula, "so you might as well get along with them." Her repeated statements that loneliness was her motivation for having sexual relations with the first boy friend now make sense in the respect that sexual activity was apparently a way of placating him and thereby holding him. She was upset by the need to deceive anyone; she stated several times that she hoped she could some day tell her prospective mother-in-law about the pregnancy—though this was certainly not an objective problem at the moment—because she hated to have that deceit between them. As an adolescent she had often been given money by her stepfather for her personal needs; she could never keep this fact from her mother despite the fact that she knew her mother would then take the money from her to spend on liquor. All of the above indications give us a picture of Nancy as a person to whom any rejection is a profound threat, and who must therefore placate other people at all costs. Her interpersonal security was so tenuous that the slightest ill-will, aggression, discord, or deceit (however justified) would destroy it, and unmanageable anxiety would ensue.

Her conscientiousness in her work, as on her Rorschach, was a method of buying acceptance. Though objectively Nancy had never had any problems in getting and retaining jobs, she had always been anxious about her work, feeling she would be discharged if she did not keep constantly alert. "There's always some one to take your place if you don't keep on your toes." (This repeated phrase "keeping on your toes" is a very apt expression for this type of anxiety, in which the individual feels that disaster can be avoided only by remaining perpetually in a state of tense balance.)

We now inquire into the sources of this anxiety pattern in Nancy's childhood. The following memories piece together a picture of a child who was clung to by the mother but at the same time severely rejected. Nancy reported (on the basis of information she had received from an aunt) that it had been the mother's practice frequently to leave her alone in the house before the divorce (when Nancy was two), as well as after the separation from the father. Once when she had been left alone (this was one of Nancy's earliest memories, dating from about the age of three), her father had kidnapped her from the mother's house. In the ensuing taxi ride to the father's house, Nancy had cried violently for her mother. Later the mother came with a policeman to get her back. Nancy related a variety of other early memories all of which had these elements: (a) the mother had left Nancy alone; (b) not having proper supervision, Nancy would get hurt (e.g., fall down the cellar steps); and (c) the mother would come home but be "unconcerned." Nancy's explanation was, "My mother cared more about going out to bars than having children." Apparently this rejection of the child continued, though on a somewhat diminished scale, after the mother remarried. The subsequent period, when "we had a good home in the suburbs," is emphasized by Nancy as a kind of Garden of Eden period of happy childhood. In her interpretation of her background, she dates her real misfortunes from the time of their losing this house, when she was twelve. "After that my mother became unsteady, and she and my stepfather began to go out to bars all the time. They'd take me sometimes, but I didn't like that. Sometimes they wouldn't come home all night. They'd leave a girl with me, of course, but I'd wake up in the morning and not find them there. That's not right. . . . I'd worry for fear something had happened to them. Then, when I got to be sixteen, my mother really did go bad." Nancy was not condemnatory toward her mother in a moral sense, but only in the sense that the mother could not then be depended upon. What the "going bad" consisted of Nancy would not tell. At that point in the interview she reverted to reminiscence, "But she was such a *good* mother in the suburbs."

Nancy intensely disliked talking about her childhood, a discomfort which was shown in inordinate smoking and in her stating that such conversation made her "nervous." She remarked that she could remember the events but not the feelings and added, "That's strange—the way I seemed to want my mother as a child, you'd think I would remember the feelings about her." She exhibited a need not only to block off the affect connected with these childhood rejections themselves but also to block off the immediate affect in telling about the events. The fact that she had shown emotional involvement, "nervousness," in telling of these childhood rejections very much upset her; during the subsequent two interviews she remained carefully poised and exhibited an unspoken determination not to display any emotional involvement again.

It will already be evident to the reader that there was a patent contradiction in Nancy's description of her childhood. This contradiction, consisting of conflicting attitudes toward her mother, was of fundamental importance. On one hand there was the actual fact that Nancy felt (with considerable basis in reality) that she was rejected as a child, and that this rejection was exceedingly painful to her. But on the other hand there was her tendency to idealize her mother and parts of her background.[40] In Nancy's discussion of her childhood there emerged time and again the refrain about the "good home in the suburbs, with a little brown road leading up to it," and the accompanying assertion, "My mother was *such* a good mother then." When Nancy would approach some aspect of her childhood which was repugnant to her, she would interpolate as a vague but intense hope, "But my mother *could* have been such a good mother." The facts would seem clearly to contradict this emphasis on the mother being "good" even part of the time; so far as could be determined, the mother left Nancy alone a good deal even during the period in the suburbs, though perhaps not as much as during the later and earlier periods. In any case, the supposition that the mother was "good" (in the sense of "stable") part of the time and "bad" the rest of the time does not make objective sense; even the outward appearance of change suggests profound inconsistency in the behavior of the mother. The conclusion seems justified that this motif of the "good" mother and the "happy" childhood period was brought in by Nancy because she could not bear to face the reality of her rejection by her mother and her feelings toward her mother. The fact that the recurrent refrain that the mother *could* have been good came up in the interviews whenever Nancy found the discussion of her early rejection too painful to continue supports the conclusion that the idealization of the mother was used to cover up the reality of her relationship with her mother.

Conclusions.—(1) As an over-all rating, we found in Nancy a *high* degree of anxiety. She illustrated one type of anxiety neurosis, characterized by the adoption of the "anxious atti-

---

[40] We take the romanticized references to the "good home in the suburbs" as one symbol of her idealization of her relationship with her mother.

tude" toward life as her own, so that practically everything she thought or did was motivated by anxiety. The goal of her behavior was not to *avoid* anxiety; rather, it was to keep anxiety at bay.[41] She was characterized by continual foreboding and a constant endeavor to keep herself precariously balanced in her relations with people lest catastrophe (in Nancy's sense, rejection) should occur. It may be said that this is not a case of the person having anxiety, but of "anxiety having the person."

(2) Her well-systematized *methods of keeping anxiety at bay* were, on the objective level, placating others, avoiding all discord, and doing conscientious work. The goals of these methods were to be accepted and to be "loved," in which state she was temporarily secure. In the case of Nancy these methods were eminently successful in the sense that she did get herself universally liked; but the security she achieved was very tentative, and she exhibited the persistent expectation that tomorrow she might be rejected. On the subjective level, Nancy's methods of keeping anxiety at bay were to avoid emotional entanglements, to suppress the affect connected with her childhood rejection and anxiety, and to idealize anxiety-creating situations.[42] The method of avoiding emotional entanglements was not successful for Nancy, however, since she depended almost entirely for her security on what other people thought of her.[43] When all is said, it is notable that Nancy had no effective subjective protections against anxiety-creating situations. It may be said that her only protection against anxiety was to be anxious—i.e.,

---

41 It may seem confusing to make this distinction between *avoiding* anxiety and *holding anxiety at bay*. But a real distinction is referred to, namely, the fact that in this type of anxiety neurosis the anxious attitude is so intimately a part of the individual's method of evaluating stimuli, of orienting himself to every experience, that he cannot separate himself enough from anxiety to comprehend the goal of avoidance of, or freedom from, anxiety. To pursue our earlier figure of speech, what Nancy sought was to be able to step cautiously from rock to rock without falling; the idea or possibility of not being on a precipice did not occur to her.

42 This was not only evidenced in her attitudes toward her mother, but also in her present situation: she stated that whenever she now felt worried, she put the worry out of her mind by thinking about her fiancé and "what a nice future we will have."

43 Compare in this respect with the case of Phyllis, who, at the price of impoverishment of personality, was able to avoid anxiety by avoiding emotional involvement with other persons.

to live continually "on her toes," and in a state of constant preparedness.

(3) *A high degree of rejection by the mother* was simultaneously present in Nancy with her high degree of anxiety. This rejection by the mother was not accepted as an objective reality, but was continually held in juxtaposition with idealized expectation about her mother. Hence the rejection led to subjective conflict. The feelings of rejection and the idealization of the mother reinforced each other. Feeling rejected, she yearned more strongly for an idealized acceptance by the mother; and having the idealized picture of what her mother "could" have been, the rejection was experienced as especially painful, and the feelings connected with her rejection tended to be repressed (and therefore increased).[44] The conflict underlying her neurotic anxiety may be described as arising from a *hiatus between expectations and reality* in her relation with her mother. The conflict was perpetuated in the form of an excessive need on one hand to depend on others (specifically, on their accepting, liking her) as her security device; but an underlying conviction on the other hand that other people were not dependable and would reject her. We have observed this conflict in its original form in her attitudes toward her mother, and in its present form in her attitudes toward her fiancé as well as toward her other contemporaries.[45]

---

[44] Nancy's case is an illustration of the fact that what is significant about rejection, as a source of neurotic anxiety, is how it is interpreted by the child. In impact upon the child, there is a radical difference between rejection as an *objective* experience (which does not necessarily result in subjective conflict for the child), and rejection as a subjective experience. The important question psychologically is whether the child *felt himself* rejected. That Nancy felt herself greatly rejected is clear, though in actual fact she was objectively less rejected than some of the other girls discussed below (Louise, Bessie) who did not subjectively weight their rejection nearly so much. Our contention above is that Nancy's idealization of her mother is the essential element in understanding why she gave such a pronounced subjective weight to her rejection.

[45] A more specific formulation of Nancy's conflict would require psychoanalytic knowledge of her unconscious patterns—data which the above methods do not yield. It is certainly a justified hypothesis that a great deal of hostility would be present in a pattern in which the individual is so dependent on other people but believes these others to be undependable; and it is entirely understandable that such hostility, in a person as anxious as Nancy, would be radically repressed.

4. Helen: Intellectualizing as a Defense Against the Anxiety-Creating Situation

The impression Helen created in her first interview presented a snapshot of aspects of her behavior which were later to prove to be of considerable significance. On arrival at Walnut House she walked into the office smoking a cigarette, appearing poised and nonchalant. On her own initiative she stated immediately that she had no guilt feeling whatever about her pregnancy. She volunteered the information that she had lived with two different men since arriving in New York, asserting in the same breath that "only priggish people have any feelings about such matters." But there were indications of anxiety and tension beneath her ostensibly friendly and free manner of talking; this tension was particularly suggested in the fact that during her frequent breezy laughter, her eyes remained dilated, giving the appearance of some fright even while she laughed. It was the immediate impression both of the social workers and the psychologist that Helen was employing an evasive, laugh-it-off technique in order to cover over some anxiety, the nature of which was not yet apparent.

She was the twenty-two-year-old daughter of middle-class, Catholic parents, the father being of Italian extraction. During her childhood the family had alternated between very good and straitened financial conditions because of the father's erratic work habits. Helen had attended parochial schools and a Catholic college for two years, but at the time of this study she felt she had emancipated herself from the religious aspects of her background. There were two siblings, a brother a year older and a sister two years younger, with whom Helen had close and affectionate relationships; she stated that the three children had learned to stick together because their parents quarreled so much. Her parents had been divorced when she was eleven and had both remarried. She had lived intermittently with one and the other, having to leave the father at one time because her stepmother was "jealous of my being more attractive," and having to leave the mother because the stepfather, and later the mother's lovers, made advances to her. Her two years at college had been on a scholarship, and she had done brilliant but erratic academic work. Since leaving college she had held routine jobs, such as operating mimeograph machines. Because of boredom she would quit her job every two or three months, "and then is when I would get into difficulty," i.e., would live with a man. Her hope was to write radio scripts.[46] Two years before she had come to New York with an unmarried aunt two years her senior, with whom her relationship was very affectionate. The aunt was also now pregnant and had gone to another city; Helen commented, "She has made a mess of her life too." The father of Helen's baby was a member of the merchant marine, the second man with whom she had shared an apartment since coming to New York. Though she described him as an intelligent person whom she had liked, she had experienced a profound revulsion toward him after she discovered she was pregnant and had broken off all contact with him.[47]

Helen's Rorschach indicated superior intellectual capacity but uneven performance; much originality and variety of interest; much emotional responsiveness but of an impulsive variety, unintegrated with her intellectual functions.[48] Her emotional responsiveness was regularly experienced as disturbing and upsetting to her rational control. Her response to several of the colored cards, "muddy, turbid waters," was an apt description of how she viewed her emotional responsiveness when she could not control it intellectually. Anxiety signs were: slight shading shock (connected in part with sexual problems), a large number of diffusion responses, and intermittent vagueness and evasiveness. The Whole compulsion (66 per cent) in this record is not only indicative of evasiveness as a symptom of anxiety, but also

---

[46] The scripts she showed the writer seemed to be very good technically but artificial in content and lacking in feeling.

[47] Helen's medical examination was negative; she was described as "nervous and high-strung" and was placed by the psychiatrist on a daily dose of phenolbarbital.

[48] Total responses, 46: 10 M, 7 FM, 1 m, 2 k, 1 K (with three additionals), 4 FK (with four additionals), 8 F, 4 Fc, 4 FC, 5 CF; popular responses 7, originals 15; $W\%$ 66, $D\%$ 34; intelligence estimate on basis of Rorschach: potentiality 130 (or higher), efficiency 120. (This intelligence estimate accords with the reports received of two intelligence tests she had taken in school and college.)

of intellectual ambition. With regard to content, the anxiety in the record was connected with (1) social disapproval and guilt feeling, (2) competitive ambition, and (3) her pregnancy and impending trip to the hospital for parturition. Her anxiety was, in general, of the unsystematized, intermittent kind. It was deeply disturbing, but she was able to recover from it quickly. Her chief methods of dealing with anxiety were intellectualizing, "laughing-it-off," denial, and evasion. She is rated with respect to anxiety on the Rorschach: depth 4, width 2, handling 2. This placed her in the *moderately high* category of anxiety in rank with the other girls.[49]

We shall first discuss Helen's anxiety as it focused on her *pregnancy and impending trip to the hospital* for the birth of the baby. Considerable anxiety was shown in six responses of "X rays" and "medical illustrations" on her Rorschach. We may conclude that this is anxiety attached to her anticipation of parturition for several reasons, two of them being: (1) in her second Rorschach after parturition these responses are almost entirely omitted and (2) she herself makes the association of these responses with her pregnancy. She apologized after three of these responses with the phrase, "Sorry, it must be my condition." One such response was associated with an erupting volcano (presumably a birth symbol), which so disturbed her that the following response was markedly distorted. It is to be noted that these anxiety responses are intellectualized—i.e., given a "scientific" content. The responses were regularly accompanied by forced, tense laughter and remarks of evasion and denial ("I shouldn't know about these—I never read medical books").

This focus of anxiety upon the pregnancy and impending parturition, with its related defenses of intellectualizing, laughing-it-off, and evasion, was evidenced in interviews with Helen and in her behavior with the other girls in the house. She regularly refused to discuss her pregnancy with the social worker, insisting, "It just seems to me I'm not pregnant, and until the baby is

---

[49] Her childhood anxiety check-list ranks in the high category with respect to quantity of anxiety, with the chief areas of anxiety being *ambition,* and what *her friends* and *her family* thought of her, in that order.

born I refuse to give it a thought." But it was observed that she spent a great deal of time discussing pregnancy in an intellectualized, quasi-scientific manner with the other girls in the house. She described to them the fetus at various stages in its development as though she were talking from a scientific manual. One day she received a letter from her aunt, telling of the latter's having gone to the hospital for parturition; Helen reacted with a fit of hysterical weeping. It was evident that she displaced much of her own anxiety about parturition on the aunt, but when the social worker pointed this out, Helen still refused to talk about her own pregnancy.

When the psychologist indicated to her that her Rorschach suggested anxiety about going to the hospital, Helen replied:

> No, I haven't the slightest fear. In the event of death or making provision for the baby to be taken care of, I just think, "how dramatic!" But the girls around here are always telling hideous stories of births. They tell of doctors standing over them in the hospital and all the details. They tell terrible stories of women screaming. They tell of Caesarean and forceps births, and they say, "You're just the one to have one." They tell a lot of old wives' tales about every heart-throb giving the baby a mark. They go around feeling each other's stomachs; they want to feel mine but I won't let them. I won't even feel it myself. [Her hands had been folded on her abdomen; at this point she violently jerked them away.] I guess the fact that I'm not afraid shows in the fact that I'm so impatient to go to the hospital. I'm willing to suffer the punishments of the damned to get it over quickly.

It will be agreed, the writer assumes, that this combination of emphases on catastrophe and urgency is the speech of a very frightened person. It suggests the typical picture of one whistling in the dark, putting up a front of dramatic bravado toward the prospect one dreads most.[50] Helen's bravado and laughing-it-off techniques of allaying anxiety were so well developed that

---

[50] The impatience of Helen to get the birth over with reminds us of the observation of R. R. Grinker and S. P. Spiegel that the anxious airman would be the first to get himself into the air and into a situation of danger, the danger itself being less painful than the anticipation of it—*Men under stress* (Philadelphia, 1945).

they carried right up to the parturition itself: on departing for the hospital she left a note for the psychologist, "I'm off to get myself a new figure," and the obstetrician reported that her last words before going under ether were, "This has got to be adoptable material."

With respect to the problem of defining Helen's "fear" of parturition, it might be argued that it was a "real" fear, or normal anxiety, since her anticipated labor might involve suffering. But her apprehension was greatly out of proportion to that of the other girls in a similar situation, and certainly the reports from the girls returning from the hospitals, where parturition was handled with modern expertness, gave no basis for such intense apprehension or for her emphasis on the possible horrors of birth in her speech quoted above.[51] Furthermore, this fear was consciously denied, which removed it from the category of real fears. We here term it a *neurotic fear*. We shall discuss below the evidence for believing that this fear was a focus for neurotic anxiety. What the meaning of this fear was, and why her anxiety should be attached to this particular focal point and not another, are questions which can be answered only on the basis of further understanding of other aspects of Helen's anxiety pattern; they will be discussed below.

The second prominent area of Helen's anxiety was *social disapproval and guilt feeling*. We are immediately struck by her contradictory statements with regard to guilt feeling: her interviews were filled both with indications of strong guilt feeling and with verbal denials of this guilt feeling. She felt that people on the street were looking at her as if to say, "Go home, don't have your baby in public." She would like to "crawl into a hole till after the baby comes." A newspaperman friend wished to visit her at Walnut House, but she couldn't "bear to have him see me in my shame." But at the same time she made strenuous

---

[51] As a matter of actual fact, Helen's labor turned out to be not at all what she had dreaded. After parturition she remarked to the psychologist, "If your wife tells you women suffer in childbirth, just tell her it ain't so." It is impossible, of course, to reason from the fact that her fear actually turned out to be unrealistic to a conclusion that therefore the fear was neurotic. But nevertheless the relief Helen expressed after parturition seemed to be more similar to the "what-was-I-afraid-of?" feeling of people after a neurotic fear has been dispersed than the relief after escaping a real threat: "It was dangerous, but I was fortunate."

efforts to cover up this guilt feeling: this was evidenced in the very first interview, when without the question being raised Helen needed to state emphatically that she had no guilt feelings whatever.[52]   On the Rorschach some of the guilt feeling was connected with sex: on Card VI there was more nervous laughter than usual, and she paused for long periods after each response saying, "It looks like something else I can't get." The final response in this card was a vista of a woman in an idolatrous shrine, which suggests that Helen was not as emancipated from her religious background as she would believe.[53]   But most of her guilt feeling and concomitant anxiety seemed to be connected with what people thought of her: after a response "two old maids pointing and gossiping about the pretty widow," she gave one of her typical anxiety responses related to her pregnancy.   On the childhood anxiety check-list, anxiety related to disapproval by her peers was second, and anxiety related to disapproval by her family was third in quantity.   The same mechanisms which she employed to allay anxiety were used for allaying guilt feelings: a blasé, laugh-it-off attitude and an endeavor to intellectualize and depersonalize the issue of guilt (e.g., "My mother and I are *un*moral, not immoral").

Helen's anxiety about social disapproval and guilt merged into her competitive feelings.   Often her remarks indicated an association between being disapproved of, being guilty, and losing her competitive standing and power with family and friends.   She was adamant that her family not know of her pregnancy, for inasmuch as they had held such high hopes for her, they would be hurt and humiliated (which suggests guilt feelings).   In the next breath, however, she explained that she did not want them to have the "satisfaction of knowing that this had happened to her"; she wanted them to continue thinking she was a big success in New York, and she wished to buy a "splendid outfit" and go home and surprise them (which suggests competitive feelings).   This same significant connection

---

[52] This suggests the mechanism described in Shakespeare's words, "The lady doth protest too much, methinks."

[53] In the second Rorschach there were two responses having to do with religious symbolism.

between guilt and loss of power and prestige was evidenced in her attitudes toward her friends: the father of the baby must not know of her pregnancy, for he would take fiendish delight in telling all her friends and humiliating her. On her childhood anxiety check-list she indicated strong anxiety lest people ridicule or make fun of her. Underlying her fear of ridicule in these varied contexts seems to be a formulation like the following, "If others have cause for disapproving of me, they will humiliate [demote] me and I will lose my power and prestige." A similar merging of guilt and competitive feelings was evidenced in her numerous remarks of self-depreciation in the interviews. At the outset of the Rorschach she coyly warned that she never did well on tests; then she proceeded to throw herself into the endeavor to produce a superior record. On the whole, the many self-deprecatory remarks of Helen were partly an expression of guilt, and partly a way of disarming others and covering up her competitive striving so that her eventual success would be the more noticeable.

We now consider *competitive ambition* as such, the final and in many respects the most pronounced area of Helen's anxiety. In contradistinction to her denial of apprehension in the areas of parturition and guilt feeling, Helen consciously admitted that competitive ambition was a source of pronounced anxiety for her. The highest score on her childhood anxiety check-list was for anxiety in the area of success and failure in school and work. She was unwilling merely to check "often" for her anxiety about "failing a test in school" or "not being a success," but added several exclamation points for special emphasis. Competitive ambition in intellectualized form was evidenced in the Rorschach not only in the "whole compulsion" but also in her straining herself to the limit, which she rationalized by misinterpreting the psychologist's directions ("You told me to give all I could").[54] Helen was aware that her intense anxiety about competitive status inhibited her productivity: "I'm always worried about success," she remarked, "that's why I failed the newspaper typing test last night." Though her competitiveness chiefly as-

---

[54] Another evidence of this competitive ambition is suggested in the social worker's judgment that Helen sought to impress her with the high intellectual talent of the groups in which she moved in the city.

sumed an intellectual expression, it carried over into the area of physical attractiveness. The only girl in the house with whom Helen had difficulty in relationship, a difficulty largely caused by rivalry, was the one girl (Agnes) who by common consent was prettier than Helen. But it is consistent with Helen's pattern that she always hid this rivalry under a façade of casual poise (in itself a subtle way of asserting superiority).

It is not difficult to see why the intellectual sphere had developed in Helen's pattern as the chief area for the exercise of her competitive ambition. As a child she was known as precocious in school; her family had rewarded her with considerable prestige for her academic successes. In periods of emotional insecurity in the family—caused chiefly by violent quarrels between the parents—Helen was able, even as a child, to assume leadership and exercise control over her parents because they recognized her as the "bright one" in the family. Apparently from her early childhood onward her intellectual capacities had been rewarded not only as a method of gaining competitive prestige but also specifically as a means of controlling and ameliorating anxiety-creating situations.[55]

Helen's Relationship with Her Parents.—The chief facts that stood out in Helen's description of her childhood were the violent quarrels of the parents, the frequent periods of upheaval in the family group (parental divorce, conflict with stepparents, etc.), and Helen's testimony to her considerable loneliness as a child. There was evidence for much outright rejection of her, as well as of the other children, by the father: she recalled that his regular practice was to deposit the children at the movies

---

[55] In a person as competitive as Helen, we should expect to find strong needs to remain independent and detached from other people; one has to remain detached in order to triumph *over* others, and to be absorbed in a close relationship would therefore be a threat to a security device. There was evidence that Helen had this need for detachment. She regarded marriage as a "ball and chain," and asked rhetorically, "What is the matter with me that I feel repelled by a man as soon as he proposes marriage?" She felt the present man would interpret the pregnancy, if he should hear of it, as a sign that he had "caught" her and use it as an additional argument for marriage. Another indication of her strong needs to appear independent and unbeholden to anyone is seen in the fact that she refused to accept money from Walnut House for her personal necessities, even though she let it be known that she was in need.

all day while he played golf; he would then come home drunk, and a quarrel between the parents would ensue. Her present attitude toward her mother was one of pity, with resentment at her mother's "disloyalty" toward her. This "disloyalty" had been felt by Helen since she was fifteen, when she and her mother had begun to quarrel violently. Her reasons for thinking her mother disloyal were (a) the mother's ill-considered love affairs, (b) the fact that the mother had served a short prison sentence for involvement in some minor crime,[56] and (c) the fact that the mother now permitted the sister to have more influence over her than Helen. It is difficult to determine with any clarity Helen's attitude toward her mother during early childhood: she speaks of being "excessively devoted" to her mother as a child, but it was the psychologist's impression that the content of this "devotion" was unconvincing and that the phrase was really a construct from the fact that at that age Helen was considered the favorite child by the mother. Definite indications of hostility and resentment toward both parents, and especially the mother, were present in Helen's Rorschach and in the interviews.[57] *In fine*, the above motif of "disloyalty," quite apart from its content, implies strong disappointment with, and resentment toward, her mother; and since the objective data indicate that the mother was a very unstable, inconsistent, and emotionally immature person, the hypothesis is justified that Helen experienced considerable rejection in her early as well as her later relations with her

[56] Another aspect of the contradiction in Helen over guilt feeling and moral standards is shown in the fact that, despite her protest that she and her mother were emancipated from moral standards, she held her mother responsible for infractions which apparently have a moral character.

[57] One such response on the Rorschach was "children scaring their parents to death," and another was "Brownies with round bellies laughing with great pleasure because they have just pulled a hot joke, messing up the housewife's floor." This last response suggests that her pregnancy is associated with aggression against her mother. The hostile, aggressive elements in both these responses were omitted in the Rorschach after parturition, the Brownies now specifically described by Helen as "wistful, not malicious." It would seem that the aggression and hostility toward her parents, especially toward her mother, diminished after parturition. Several hypotheses suggest themselves: (a) she was more anxious before parturition, and therefore felt more hostility and aggression; (b) she employed the pregnancy as a weapon against the parents, and (c) she held them in some way responsible for her being in this difficult state of pregnancy.

mother.[58] Hence we place Helen in the *moderately high* category with respect to rejection by her parents.

Conclusions.—(1) Our over-all ranking for Helen's degree of anxiety was *moderately high*. We have seen that this anxiety arose (a) in the area of social disapproval and guilt, (b) in the area of competitive ambition, and (c) focused particularly on her pregnancy and impending parturition. Her ranking for rejection by her parents was likewise *moderately high*.

(2) The *methods of avoiding anxiety* illustrated in the case of Helen deserve further discussion. We have seen that these methods consisted of (a) laughing-it-off behavior,[59] (b) evasion and outright denial, which might be termed an "ostrich" pattern of behavior toward anxiety, and (c) intellectualizing. If it is correct that these are Helen's methods of avoiding anxiety, two conditions should be demonstrable. First, it should be true that when her anxiety is relatively greater, these avoidance forms of behavior should be more in evidence; and second, when the anxiety subsides, the avoidance behavior mechanisms should abate likewise. In other words, the more the subject experiences anxiety, the more the mechanisms for avoiding anxiety are called into play, and vice versa. Both of these conditions were demonstrable in Helen. We have observed above that at the points in the first Rorschach where Helen showed anxiety, she also exhibited more forced laughter, evasion, and intellectualization. In the second, post-parturition Rorschach, in which there was less anxiety largely because the anxiety responses related to parturition were almost entirely omitted,[60] the behavior mechanisms for avoiding anxiety abate accordingly. The whole compulsion was reduced from 66 per cent to 47 per cent, and the responses to

---

[58] This rejection may have been all the more painful and psychologically significant for Helen because of her having been at the same time the "favorite" child.

[59] Cf. Symonds (1947) for a discussion of laughter as a method of avoiding anxiety and Grinker and Spiegel *op. cit.* for a discussion of jocularity as related to anxiety in combat airmen.

[60] Though the second Rorschach shows less anxiety than the first, there is still a substantial amount of anxiety present. We believe that Helen would have a moderate to moderately high degree of anxiety in any situation in which her subjective conflicts (the presence of which we assume the case presentation has indicated) are cued off.

specific details were considerably increased, indicating less eva-siveness.[61] Likewise the intellectualizing and forced laughter were considerably lessened in this second record.

It is interesting to note that Helen's techniques of denying anxiety and at the same time intellectualizing it were logically contradictory. Helen's pattern, as shown especially in her val-iant endeavor to avoid the anxiety focusing on pregnancy and parturition, might be formulated as follows: "If I deny the anxi-ety, it will not be there," and at the same time, "If I wave the wand of 'scientific' knowledge, the anxiety will vanish." The former was an outright endeavor to repress the anxiety. But on a "deeper" level [62] she was aware of the anxiety, and this level was the base of the intellectualizing method of warding off anxi-ety (such as the "scientific" Rorschach response and the quasi-scientific discussions with the girls). What both the outright denial and the intellectualizing had in common was evasion of an emotional reality.

(3) Helen's methods of avoiding anxiety are *typical of a trend in our culture*. To the present writer Helen's pattern is illustrative of what has previously been discussed in this study as a dominant pattern in modern Western culture with respect to both sources of anxiety and methods of avoiding anxiety.[63] We have noted in Helen a dichotomy between emotion and intellectual functions, with an endeavor to control her emotions intellectually; and when this control was ineffective (e.g., when she became emotionally involved in her Rorschach responses), she became upset. We have earlier discussed the tendency in our culture to deny anxiety because it seems to be "irrational." It is highly significant, in this regard, that the two most important

---

[61] This relaxing of the whole compulsion also may be taken to indicate that she is now less pushed to exercise her intellectual ambition. This suggests that her intellectual ambition takes a compulsive form, that it is used for purposes of allaying anxiety ("If I can be intellectually successful, I will not be anxious"), and therefore it abates when the anxiety does.

[62] As Sullivan has pointed out, individuals have varying levels of awareness, of which conscious awareness is only one, albeit the most complete kind of aware-ness. In studying patients with anxiety, a phenomenon like Helen's is often observable: the patient does not consciously admit the anxiety, but *behaves* in all sorts of ways as though he were aware of it; which must mean he is aware of it on levels other than consciousness.

[63] Chapter 2.

aspects of her emotions—anxiety and guilt feeling—she emphatically denied. The denial and the intellectualizing were both parts of the same pattern with Helen, as we have submitted they are in our culture; if the anxiety and guilt could not be denied, it must be rationalized; and to the extent that it could not be rationalized, it must be denied.[64] The admission of anxiety about parturition would be both a confession of failure for Helen (the scientific "wand" should be able to dispel the anxiety) and would also be a severe threat to a security device. Likewise the admission of guilt feelings about pregnancy would imply to Helen a failure to have become intellectually "emancipated." [65] Again, Helen is typical of a pattern in our culture in that the one area of anxiety which she could consciously and freely admit was that of success and failure; apparently she had learned, in her school experience among other places, that it is acceptable and respectable to compete and to admit one's anxiety about the outcome of that competition.

(4) We now raise the interesting question, why was Helen afraid of parturition? We submit that *this neurotic fear was a focus for anxiety which arose from her repressed guilt feeling about the pregnancy*. Her phrases such as "suffering the punishments of the damned" in childbirth and the association of "dying" with parturition, bring into the picture both her guilt feeling (being "damned") and the anticipation of punishment. It is as though a formulation, "I have done wrong, I will be punished," is in operation. It is well known that repressed guilt feeling gives rise to anxiety, and we believe it is plausible to conclude that it is this anxiety in Helen which emerges in the exaggerated fear of parturition.

But why did her anxiety focus on parturition and not on another focus? We submit that anxiety clustered around parturition because that was the point at which her habitual anxiety

---

[64] It is perhaps needless to emphasize that we are not referring to a genuinely scientific and rational attitude toward anxiety and guilt feelings; we are rather speaking of intellectualizing as a defense; an attitude of rationalization rather than a rational attitude.

[65] The earlier discussions in this study have been concerned with the suppression and denial of anxiety because of its seeming irrationality. We now submit that the suppression of guilt feeling falls in somewhat the same category and is likewise a tendency in our culture. See Mowrer in Chapter 4.

defenses were unavailing. Despite her endeavors to think that she was not even pregnant ("It seems to me I am not pregnant until the baby is born"), pregnancy is a state that cannot be wholly denied short of much more serious psychological deterioration than Helen's state. It was clear, even to her, that her abdomen was enlarged whether she would permit herself to feel it or not. Again, birth is an experience in which there is bound to be feeling and emotion; and hence parturition was a point at which her defense by means of intellectualizing and suppressing feeling would not be effective.

5. AGNES: ANXIETY RELATED TO HOSTILITY AND AGGRESSION

Agnes, age eighteen, had been a night club dancer since leaving her father at the age of fourteen. Her mother had died when she was one year old; she had lived with her father and stepmother (both Catholic) until the latter died when she was thirteen. After keeping house for her father for a year, she left him because of his excessive drinking and his attitude, as she expressed it, of "complete lack of concern for me." There was some doubt in her mind as to whether her father and mother had been her real parents; this doubt was also shared by the social workers, on the basis of the scanty legal birth data available. She had no siblings. Her father and stepmother had adopted a boy when Agnes was eight, but she had objected so strongly that they had returned the boy to the orphanage. Her Wassermann at entrance to Walnut House was +4, the syphilis being considered congenital. It is difficult to place Agnes accurately with respect to socioeconomic class; her father had frequently changed his occupation, at this time being a cook in a restaurant. Her vocational aims at the time of her stay at Walnut House were to leave show business, attend art school, and then become a commercial artist. On the basis of her aims, as well as the socioeconomic status of her friends, we place her in the middle class.

She was pregnant by a married man considerably older than herself, whom she had met as a coperformer in show business. Because she "loved" him, she stated, she had entered willingly into the relationship, which lasted about half a year.

The chief feature of her Rorschach was the large amount of aggression and hostility.[66]   Almost every response having to do with human beings consisted of people fighting or of semihuman monsters. The monsters were seen in sexual contexts; she associated sex with brutal aggression against her. Though her inner promptings of an imaginative sort were given much expression, her instinctual promptings were suppressed, the sexual promptings being suppressed in order for her to avoid becoming the victim of aggression. The Rorschach indicated that she felt driven by her extensive hostile and aggressive tendencies (both potential and actual) and that if these were not at least partially suppressed, they would be uncontrollable for her. There was a good deal of emotional excitability, particularly of a narcissistic form. On the whole, her Rorschach showed a sado-masochistic pattern. She endeavored to avoid her aggression and hostility by retreats into fancy, abstraction, and moralism—e.g., the aggression was seen as a struggle between "good and evil." Her good intellectual capacities were used for purposes of aggressive ambition—gaining control over others. The hostility and aggression in this record involved much anxiety, cued off largely by her expectations of others' aggression and hostility against her, which in turn was to a considerable extent a projection of her aggressive and hostile feelings toward them. Her chief way of trying to manage the anxiety was by retaliatory aggression and hostility. Her rating on anxiety in the Rorschach was: depth $2\frac{1}{2}$, width $4\frac{1}{2}$, handling $4\frac{1}{2}$, which placed her in the *high* category of anxiety in comparison to the other girls. On the childhood anxiety check-list Agnes ranked moderately low, and on the future check-list moderately high. The predominant areas of anxiety were *ambition* and *phobial* apprehension.

In her first interviews both with the social worker and with the psychologist, Agnes seemed in pronounced, though controlled, terror; her eyes were dilated, her gestures were sharp and nervous, and though she occasionally laughed metallically, she

---

[66] Total responses, 13 : 6 *M*, 2 *FM* (5 additional *m*), 2 *F*, 1 *Fc*, 2 *CF*; popular responses 3, originals 7; *W%* 62, *D%* 30; *Dd%* 8; intelligence estimate: potentiality 120, efficiency 110.

never smiled. It appeared in these first interviews that Agnes was expecting, consciously or unconsciously, some attack. This same expectation of aggression against her appeared in forms of phobial anxiety in her behavior at Walnut House; whenever she was given an aspirin by the nurse, she looked at it carefully with the expectation that she was being poisoned. (In reporting these feelings to the psychologist, Agnes realized their irrationality.) She stated that she often had "claustrophobia" in her room at Walnut House and on the subways, which she associated with a traumatic experience as a child when her mother, after "she got tired slapping me, locked me in a closet."

Her relations to the other girls were marked by much open hostility and some contempt on her part, with no effort whatever to be friendly. As a consequence the other girls were hostile toward her and teased her frequently, which Agnes affected to meet with disdain. Her mood at the house was characterized by brooding on one hand and temper-tantrums on the other.

There were many evidences that Agnes was engaged in continual struggles for power—getting the upper hand—with other people. She stated that she greatly admired strength, especially in men. She felt contempt for her father because of what she called his weakness in drinking, and contempt for the men in night clubs who "pulled the line of my-wife-doesn't-understand-me." Her attitude toward the father of her baby was generally aggressive: she would "get a lawyer and ruin him" if he did not support her through her pregnancy. In direct contact with him, however, this aggression was usually masked behind a strategy of feminine weakness; with entirely conscious premeditation, she would weep over the telephone to convince him of her "helplessness" and play what she called her "martyr act" ("look how much I am suffering"). But when he did periodically send her a check, she would be temporarily filled with affectionate feelings toward him and say she had misjudged him. She employed her exotic feminine attractiveness likewise for aggressive purposes: when she was to meet Bob, the man by whom she was pregnant, for lunch (or, for that matter, on the days she was to have interviews with the psychologist) she would spend hours getting herself made up as attractively as possible. After par-

turition, she enjoyed considerable feelings of triumph from creating a "sensation" in stores by her stunning appearance. These
particular evidences of her aggressive struggle to gain power
over other people fit the sado-masochistic pattern which has
already been seen in her Rorschach.

At first Agnes refused to accept her pregnancy as a realistic
fact. Apparently it made her feel weak and victimized, and prevented her from using her attractiveness as a weapon of aggression. But she soon was able to work the expected baby into her
sado-masochistic pattern: she began to talk continually of her
responsibility as a mother. (In this connection the other girls
referred to her sarcastically as the "madonna.") She treated
the baby after its arrival as a "toy," an extension of herself, and
emphasized that now at long last she had some one to belong to.
These attitudes toward the baby were accompanied by a complete
absence of realistic planning for the baby's future. The baby
also now served her as an aggressive weapon against Bob; she
stated after parturition that the baby was something to "fight
for."

It was clear that Agnes felt a high degree of rejection by her
parents. Beyond the doubt as to whether they were her real
parents (which is significant symbolically as well as possibly true
in fact), considerable factual data indicated that she had had a
cold and reciprocally hostile relationship with her stepmother.
Her father's attitude toward her had always been one of indifference to her and to her abilities. Even at the present time, Agnes
was engaged in trying to break down his indifference. After
parturition she made a trip to a near-by city to see him, ostensibly
to get factual data about her birth records but actually to get him
at long last to show some concern for her—expressed in symbolic
terms by her hope that he would give her a little money.[67] She
expressed the conviction before the trip that he would not "materialize"—i.e., give her material proof of his concern. After
the trip she reported that he had enjoyed showing his colleagues
what an attractive daughter he had, but beyond that had, as

---

[67] We say the money was a "symbol" because Agnes was not particularly in
need at the time, and furthermore the sum she suggested (five dollars) would
have made very little realistic difference.

always, exhibited complete indifference to her. In her interviews at Walnut House Agnes continually talked of her loneliness—"I never belonged to anyone." Making allowance for her need to dramatize this loneliness, there is still adequate ground for concluding that she had always been a very isolated person. We place her in the *high* category of rejection by parents.

The interrelation of Agnes' anxiety with her hostility and aggression can be seen in three different ways. First, Agnes' anxiety was a reaction to situations which she interpreted in terms of the threat of outright attack upon her by others. This seemed to be a prominent source of her terror in the first interviews at Walnut House. It is entirely understandable that the anxiety reaction to such threats would be accompanied by counter-hostility and aggression on Agnes' part—which at Walnut House she did not express against the social workers or psychologists, but displaced on the other girls. Second, her anxiety was a reaction to the threat of being rejected, made lonely. Her hostility and aggression connected with this anxiety reaction is the familiar pattern of being angry at those who cause one the pain of isolation and anxiety.

But a third and less common aspect of the interrelationship of anxiety with hostility and aggression is demonstrated in Agnes' case, namely, *she uses hostility and aggression as a method of avoiding the anxiety-creating situation.* This is not the usual behavior: we have seen that other girls try to avoid anxiety by withdrawing or by placating or by being compliant to others and that in most cases the periods when they are anxious are precisely the times when they are least aggressive (in order not to alienate the persons on whom they are dependent). Agnes, however, operates on the formula that by attacking others she can force them not to reject her, not to make her anxious. This can be seen more clearly by inquiring further into her behavior toward the father of her baby. Her general attitude toward him was: "He rejects me, therefore he, like all men, is a welcher." Whenever he did reject her (e.g., fail to send her a check), she reacted with anxiety and great anger, the chief content of which was: "He must not be allowed to welch on me." But when, in response to her determined long-distance telephone calls, he did send her money, she felt relieved of her anxiety and satisfied despite the fact that the sum of money was so paltry as to make very little objective difference. *The issue was not the money itself* (Agnes could have gotten that from Walnut House) *but that he must be made to show concern for her.*[68] The case of Agnes in this connection may throw light on anxiety phenomena in sado-masochistic cases in general: namely, *relief from anxiety comes not only from keeping the other person in a symbiotic relationship, but also in gaining control, triumphing over, or bending the other person to one's own will*. If one cannot gain relief from anxiety except by bending the other to one's own will, one's method of allaying anxiety is bound to be essentially aggressive.

The official judgment at Walnut House was that Agnes' pattern was so firmly crystallized that very little therapy could at that time be accomplished. Her second Rorschach, taken three weeks after parturition, and therefore when she was relieved of the particular feelings of helplessness which attended her inability to use her feminine attractiveness as a source of power, shows some relaxing of the feeling that she is the victim of aggression and hence some relaxing of the stringency of her pattern, but it is still essentially a sado-masochistic character structure characterized by feelings of aggression and hostility. The last we heard of Agnes (from a letter written a month after her leaving Walnut House), she was being supported by a man much older than herself and bringing up her baby on Bach and Beethoven.

Conclusions.—(1) In Agnes' case we have seen a *high degree of anxiety* together with a *high degree of rejection by parents*. The relation of her then present anxiety pattern to her early relations with her parents was shown in a number of ways, two of them being her association of her phobial anxiety with her early relation of reciprocal hostility and aggression with her step-

---

[68] The fact that the symbol of concern, in Agnes' struggles both with her father and the father of her baby, is money is interesting in itself: in her mind "love" consists of giving up something, and her power to make others "concerned" for her consists of taking away something from them.

mother and the fact that the anxiety-creating pattern of relationship with the father of her baby followed very closely her relationship with her own father.   It is to be emphasized that Agnes,
like Nancy and Helen, did not accept rejection by her father as a
realistic fact, but entertained a contradiction between subjective
expectations and what she knew to be the realistic situation in
her relation with her father.   This was shown most clearly in her
journey to see him to force him to show concern for her, despite
the fact that she knew realistically that he would not change.

(2) This case demonstrates *the interrelation of anxiety with
feelings of aggression and hostility.* Agnes was made anxious
by her expectations of others' hostility and aggression against
her (e.g., the phobial crystallizations), which in turn were related through the mechanism of projection with her own hostility
and aggression against others.   The hostility and aggression
were expressions in Agnes of a sado-masochistic character structure, which involved her interpreting anxiety-creating situations
as her being victimized by others.   In corollary, she employed
her own hostility and aggression as a means of avoiding being
victimized.   Thus Agnes' chief defenses against the anxiety-
creating situation were hostility and aggression—a striving to
triumph over the other person, to become the victor rather than
the victimized.   In this respect she interpreted others' rejection
of her as their victory over her and her capacity to keep them in a
symbiotic relationship as her triumph over them, her bending
them to her will.   It is clear that such a pattern would generate
great quantities of anxiety in the respect that she expected other
people were doing to her what she was trying to do to them (the
great quantity of anxiety being illustrated in her terror in the
first interviews, and in her phobia at Walnut House).

(3) A further question arises: *Can any specific genetic elements* be discovered in Agnes' case which determine her use of
aggression and hostility as methods of avoiding the anxiety-
creating situation? We suggest that such methods in Agnes'
case point toward the presence of a *level of overprotection in her
early background.* Her considerable degree of narcissism would
fit such a hypothesis. The hypothesis is likewise supported by
her father's behavior in taking pride in her attractive appearance

but rejecting her in all other respects.[69]   There are evidences
that she did wield power in her family situation as a child: her
objections forced the parents to relinquish the adopted boy.   If
such a hypothesis is true, it would explain why the aggressive
method of forcing others not to reject her and bending them to
her will was to some extent successful, and therefore reinforced,
in her relations with her parents.   This hypothesis would also
explain why Agnes interpreted rejection as an attack upon her,
as though if others did not fulfill her expectations of directing
affect toward her, they were welching on agreements or what
she had learned to expect as her "right," and were therefore
exploiting her.

6. Louise: Rejection by Mother Without Consequent Anxiety

Louise, the twenty-four-year-old daughter of proletarian parents, was a domestic servant, an occupation she had followed
since her mother's death when she was twelve.   Her father, who
had been a laborer in a steel foundry, had died when Louise was
thirteen.   The only sibling, a sister, had died before Louise was
old enough to know her.   Louise was pregnant by a man eleven
years her senior, the only man with whom she had ever felt herself to be in love or with whom she had ever had sexual relations.
When she had been informed by her doctor that she was three
months pregnant, she had had momentary thoughts of suicide
but had later made the adjustment of simply calling a telephone
operator and asking where a girl should go "in a fix like mine."

Her Rorschach indicated a relatively undifferentiated personality, with average intelligence and some originality.[70]   There
were no movement responses in the record, indicating both a

---

[69] It is, of course, not at all uncommon that parents overprotect children and
at the same time reject them, or direct excessive affect toward them on some
levels and reject them on other levels. The overprotection and rejection are sometimes reactions to each other; e.g., if the parent really rejects the child, he may
"spoil" it on a different level in order to make up for his rejection.

[70] Total responses, 22: 1 K, 11 F, 4 Fc, 1 c, 3 FC, 2 CF; $W\%$ 45, $D\%$ 55;
popular responses 2, originals 4; intelligence estimate from Rorschach: potentiality
100, efficiency 100.

meagerness of intratensive activity and a repression of instinctual promptings. She showed an easy, ready adaptation to
stimuli from the outside, but this was a somewhat *pseudo* form
of responsiveness and suggested a superficial adjustment to relations with other people. It is significant that she saw no human
beings in the cards (which is frequently the case with subjects
who have had bad relations with parents). The closest Louise
got to a human being was the "back of a woman's head," which
implied that she felt women turned away from her; and in this
response she placed the woman's head not in the blot itself but in
the space, which suggested her own oppositional tendencies toward women. It is a sound inference that both of these ways of
relating to women referred prototypically to her relations with
her mother. Practically no overt anxiety was shown in the Rorschach. Some underlying anxiety may be inferred from the lack
of movement responses: whereas this absence of inner promptings was partly a mark of an undifferentiated personality in
Louise's case, it was also partly due to a blocking off of instinctual urges, particularly with respect to sexual contact with men,
to make herself less vulnerable. Her rating for anxiety on the
Rorschach was: depth 3, width 2, handling 1. This placed her
in the *moderately low* category of anxiety in relation to the other
girls. Louise was able to avoid personal relationships which
might arouse anxiety, and the avoidance system did not present
her with any deep conflicts.

Louise's childhood history indicated an extreme rejection,
expressed in cruel punishment, at the hands of her mother. In
her words,

> My mother beat me all the time. Even my father would ask
> her why she did it, and then she would beat me all the more. . . .
> She beat me with everything she had. She broke my elbow, she
> broke my back and nose. The neighbors next door used to want
> to call the police, but they didn't want to interfere. My mother
> would say, "Come here, or I'll kill you." Sometimes I was so
> banged up I would feel all right if somebody ran a knife through
> me. . . . My aunt and uncle wanted to take me, but she wouldn't
> let them. I don't understand why, seeing she hated me, that she
> didn't get rid of me.

Louise related these incidents of childhood punishment without much affect or change in expression. The psychologist had the impression that she had probably told the story frequently (possibly to the women for whom she worked as a domestic) and that there may be some exaggeration for effect upon the listener (e.g., the details surrounding the "breaking" of the elbow and back did not sound convincing). But granted this possibility of some exaggeration, there still is every indication that she was subject to severe rejection as a child. While there was obviously great objective trauma in these childhood experiences, the significant fact is that Louise was able to avoid subjective trauma, both as a child and now as an adult. Her relation to her father, toward whom she felt friendly, was apparently a mitigating influence but on a superficial rather than profound level (e.g., she sees no men in the Rorschach). It does not seem a tenable hypothesis that Louise was simply repressing all affect connected with this mother relationship; at other points in the interviews, she did express considerable emotion—she cried when she told of her hatred for her mother. But the hatred was stated as a simple fact, without indication of accompanying psychological conflict and without evidence of pervasive underlying resentment of the mother. As a child Louise's chief concerns—beyond the understandable desire to escape the pain of the punishments— were a fear that other people might hate her because her mother did, and a perplexity as to why her mother was so hostile toward her. In her childhood thoughts she had hypothesized that perhaps she was not really her mother's own daughter. In her behavior toward her mother Louise made no pretense or endeavor to cover up the reality of their relationship; when company was present, the mother would demand that Louise show her affection, but Louise always refused to do this even though she knew she would be punished for it on the morrow. Louise's own subjective attitude toward her childhood rejection and punishment is shown in her lumping of these experiences under the heading of "hard luck." In short, Louise seems to have accepted rejection at the hands of her mother realistically, as an objective and somewhat impersonal fact.

While filling out the childhood anxiety check-list, Louise significantly remarked, "You don't worry as a child. You just take things as they come, you don't suffer." Though the number of items she checked placed her in the *high* category of anxiety on this list, her ranking for anxiety on the present check-list was the *lowest* among all of the girls.[71] She stated while filling out the latter list, "I practically never worry about anything." The chief kinds of anxiety in the check-lists were disapproval by her peers and phobial apprehensions. With respect to anxiety related to competitive ambition, she ranked lowest among all the girls.

Louise's behavior and attitude toward the psychologist and social workers were always deferential, with apologies for taking their time and some indications that she felt it unusual that they should be interested in her. In the interviews she talked freely but gave the impression (particularly in the fact that her facial expression was generally characterized by narrowed eyelids) that she was prepared to be rebuked. She showed considerable desire to please her "superiors" and performed her duties at the house with conspicuous conscientiousness. The opposite side to this compliant behavior seemed to be expressed in some defiance of the other girls: she was critical of them to the housemother and consequently was disliked by the girls. This did not seem to bother her: she stated that when she didn't get along with other people, "I just keep out of their way." Her only amusement was taking long daily walks by herself, which served the purposes, in addition to her enjoyment, of keeping her out of the way of the other girls and helping her to go to sleep at night rather than "lie awake with the blues."

There was never any question in Louise's mind about her wanting to keep her baby, and she made realistic plans about placing it in a foster home until she had earned enough to establish her own home or had married. How much her own baby

---

[71] The quantity of anxiety on the childhood list seems to be a function of Louise's conscientiousness and her considerable desire to please the psychologist, in whose study she wished to cooperate. (See subsequent discussion of her being a deferential, compliant personality with people she considered her "superiors.") The "present anxiety" check-list, filled out in the presence of a social worker, seems to be a fairer indication of her quantity of anxiety.

would have meant to her was shown in her great pleasure in taking care of the other girls' babies before her own parturition. When her own baby was stillborn, Louise was inconsolable, wept profusely the first days in the hospital, and could talk of nothing else during her three weeks of convalescence at Walnut House. She then went to a convalescent home in the country, where she made a good recovery from her depression and grief. The final data concerning Louise were the long, endearment-filled letters which she continued to write to the nurse at Walnut House, with whom she had established a close and affectionate relationship.

Conclusions.—(1) Our over-all rating for Louise was *low* in anxiety and *high* in rejection by her mother. This immediately presents the problem of a person who experienced severe rejection but did not exhibit consequent neurotic anxiety.

(2) *Is this lack of anxiety to be explained by her lack of differentiation as a personality or by suppression of affect?* This question must be answered in its two phases. To some extent it may be said that Louise was a relatively simple, undifferentiated personality in the "normal" sense (i.e., the lack of differentiation not being due to present subjective conflicts). The repression of inner promptings in the Rorschach referred to her sexual promptings toward men and did not in itself explain the lack of neurotic anxiety from her rejection by her mother. To what extent her meagerness in responsiveness to relations with other people was a result of the lack of affection in her relation with her mother it is not possible to state, beyond the obvious point that there would be an important relation between these factors. But her lack of neurotic anxiety could not be explained by a hypothesis of lack or suppression of all affect. This is shown in (a) the fact that she did exhibit affect in talking of her hatred for her mother, (b) she had very great feelings for her hoped-for baby, and (c) she was able to establish an affectionate relationship with the nurse at Walnut House.

(3) *Louise accepted her mother's rejection as a realistic fact rather than as a source of subjective conflict.* To the writer this seems the essential point in her freedom from neurotic anxiety.

Her mother's hatred and punishment of her were taken as objective and relatively impersonal—as "hard luck." Her own statement that children accept things as they come without suffering (in the sense of experiencing neurotic anxiety) seems to be a fairly accurate description of her understanding of herself. That the rejection and punishment caused objective trauma in the respect of great pain is clear, but subjective trauma and conflict with respect to her relations with her mother were not present. Her mother's hatred is met with direct hatred and does not become a reason for persistent resentment in Louise. It is significant that Louise entertained no pretense about her mother: in radical distinction from the case of Nancy, for example, Louise did not live in expectation that her mother could or would change into a "good" mother. Likewise, Louise's behavior toward her mother was not influenced by pretension, as witness her refusal to show hypocritical affection for her mother despite the threat of punishment. In contrast to the cases of a number of other girls in this study (Nancy, Helen, Agnes, etc.), Louise did not have a cleavage between her expectations and the reality situation with respect to the parent.[72] Her case demonstrates that neurotic anxiety is not produced by rejection if the individual is free from subjective contradictions in his attitudes toward his parents.

---

[72] It has been noted that Louise's adaptation to traumatic situations of all sorts was characterized not by neurotic conflict but by seeing the problem as objective and "keeping out of the way." This was seen in her desire to get away from her mother as well as in her adaptation to difficulties with the girls at the house. It is true that this "keeping out of the way" might take pathological forms with Louise if she were confronted with an insupportable trauma; on learning of her pregnancy, though she later made a simple objective adjustment, there were the first thoughts of suicide. There were likewise thoughts of suicide in her childhood as the only way out if the pain of her mother's punishment were to become insupportable. It is the writer's impression, which cannot be substantiated in detail, that an insupportable trauma in Louise's experience would result in psychotic developments rather than deep neurotic conflicts. We believe this point does not, however, qualify our above statements as to her freedom from neurotic anxiety.

Some elements in this case, if they should appear in a more extreme form than we have observed in Louise, would suggest psychopathic developments. The psychopathic personality, produced by such complete rejection in the family that the child has no basis for future relatedness, does not exhibit neurotic anxiety (see footnote re Lauretta Bender's viewpoint, page 343). But we believe it is clear that Louise cannot be classed as psychopathic.

7. BESSIE: REJECTION BY PARENTS WITHOUT CONSEQUENT ANXIETY

Bessie, the one case of incest pregnancy in this study, was a fifteen-year-old daughter in a proletarian family, her father being employed on a river barge. There were eight siblings, four older than Bessie; the living conditions in the home had been poor and crowded. At the time of her pregnancy, Bessie was in the second year of a vocational high school in which she was learning the trade of textile machine operating. She had been impregnated by her father during the preceding summer. It was the mother's practice to insist that the children spend the summer on the barge to lessen her work in the house. Since an older sister had been forced by the father to submit to sexual relations (and was herself pregnant by the father at this time), Bessie protested violently against going on the barge—a protest which went to the extent of her drinking some iodine—but she eventually had to give in to her mother's insistence. On the barge Bessie occupied a bed with a brother and her father, and during the summer was forced three times by the father to submit to intercourse with him, he threatening to kill her if she refused his demands or if she told anyone. When the mother subsequently learned of Bessie's pregnancy by the father, she placed all the blame on Bessie, beat her severely, and threatened to kill her if she remained in the house. Bessie was housed temporarily at the Society for the Prevention of Cruelty to Children and was later removed to Walnut House. During her confinement here, the father was brought to trial on the charge of rape by the older sister and was sentenced to the penitentiary.

Though it was difficult for Bessie to talk of the particular events leading to her pregnancy, she was responsive and open, albeit somewhat restless and bashful, in the interviews and impressed social workers and psychologist alike as an outgoing, cooperative, and responsible girl.

Bessie's Rorschach showed an averagely intelligent, restless, self-assertive (in the constructive sense of "independent") person, but with a meagerness and somewhat emaciated quality of

personality.[73] The term "emaciated" refers to the indications in
the record that her meagerness was not entirely a result of lack
of capacity for differentiation but was also due to her slight tendency to keep herself at a relatively simple level of emotional development in order to avoid difficulties (i.e., complications) in
her relations with other persons. The human beings in the
responses were frequently skeletons or pictures, a fact which,
coupled with the fact that her record showed her able to respond
directly and easily to people, suggests that she sought to keep
her dynamic, vital impulses out of her interpersonal relations.
The only overt anxiety shown in the record was in three vista
(FK) responses; but these, in the relatively balanced proportion
in which they appeared in the record, indicated a fairly adequate
and direct method of handling conflicts. The particular conflicts which arose in the Rorschach, and to which these direct
methods of handling were applied, were sexual and seemed to
refer directly to her problem with her father and indirectly to
her difficulties with her mother. Two of these vista responses
were scenes in parks, a fact which makes sense in view of
Bessie's remark that it had been her practice to escape into a
park near her home when her parents were abusive toward her.
There was some latent schizoid possibility in the record (suggested in the bland use of color), but it was not pronounced and
is significant here chiefly in its indication of the form Bessie's
adjustment would take in the face of insupportable stresses.
While the anxiety in the Rorschach was in general not at all severe, there was an indication of some deeply encapsulated anxiety
which would become overt in Bessie's case only in a very severe
crisis. Her rating was: depth 3, width 2, handling 1, which
placed her in the moderately low category of anxiety in comparison to the other girls.

Both Bessie's *childhood* and *present* check-lists showed very
little anxiety. She ranked lowest of all the girls in quantity on

---

[73] Total responses, 20: 1 *M*, 5 *FM*, 3 *FK*, 7 *F*, 2 *Fc*, 2 *FC*, popular responses
4, originals 2; *W %* 50, *D %* 40; *S %* 10; percentage of responses in last three
cards, 25; intelligence estimate: potentiality 115, efficiency 100. (This accords
with an I.Q. of 101, from the report of psychometric tests given Bessie at the
Children's Court during her stay at Walnut House.)

the former, and third from the lowest on the latter.[74] The areas of anxiety were success or failure in work, what her family thought of her, and what her peers thought of her (though this determination of kinds should not be given much weight because of the small number of items checked in each area).

The mother not only exhibited an attitude of severe rejection toward Bessie, but also she consistently sought to make Bessie's problems in the pregnancy as difficult as possible. At first the mother insisted that she wanted no responsibility whatever for Bessie, but when Bessie had decided to have the baby adopted, the mother began to insist that Bessie keep it and bring it home. Since it was "Bessie's fault," she should be made to take care of the baby; and the mother rationalized her desire to have Bessie and the baby under her control by saying that since her husband was the father, the baby was her own flesh and blood. But it was obvious, as an older sister pointed out to the social worker, that the mother's real motives were punitive; she wished to have Bessie and the baby home in order that she could continually berate Bessie for the pregnancy. Whenever Bessie had decided on a plan of her own, the mother would aggressively attack her with a contrary plan. She strongly opposed Bessie's first decision to make her home with an older sister after parturition and also her later plan to live in a foster home. These indications all form a picture of the mother as definitely sadistic. It was not easy for Bessie to take a stand against her mother, as it was likewise difficult for her to verbalize hostility toward the mother. But the significant point is that in each issue, Bessie arrived at a realistic decision independently of her mother's demands or pressure. Bessie's attitude, in her own words, was "My mother is just that way—I just have to pay no attention to what she says." During her visits to her family, when her mother would begin the familiar berating of her, Bessie would

[74] It will be noted several times in the subsequent cases that the quantity of items checked on these lists seemed to be partly a function of the conforming, compliant tendencies of the girl in question (i.e., her being influenced by the belief that checking a large number would please the psychologist). The fact that Bessie did not check many items is support of this hypothesis in the respect that she was not a conforming type but was relatively self-assertive and was not noticeably influenced by the need to please other people.

simply remark, "I came here on pleasure, not business," and would walk out of the house.

Bessie had warm and affectionate relations with her brothers and sisters.[75] These siblings had had during childhood, and likewise now had, their own constellation of affection quite apart from the parents; there was no competition among them for a love from parents which they apparently knew would not be forthcoming anyway. It seems that these brothers and sisters viewed their parents as the dominating and punitive persons they actually were. That Bessie was able to have these affectionate relations with siblings, in the face of parental rejection, undoubtedly is basically connected with her relative freedom from neurotic anxiety.

Bessie's rejection by her father, already obvious from his treatment of her in the rape, has an illuminating prelude in the stories she related about her childhood. Whenever the father was romping with the other children and Bessie would approach, the father would immediately stop his playing. Bessie had always wondered about his behavior in these instances and had ascribed it to the fact that he had wanted another boy when she was born. But what is significant is that on these occasions Bessie would not withdraw from the group in a pout. "I just went ahead," she remarked, entering into the play with the siblings regardless of the father's withdrawal. Apparently his rejection of her was accepted by Bessie as an objective fact and neither led to subjective conflict and resentment nor changed her behavior.

While at Walnut House the anxiety Bessie exhibited was always connected with realistic situations. She was very much afraid of going to court in the instance of her father's trial, and also in the later instance of the court hearing to permit her to stay at a foster home rather than at her mother's. In the first

[75] Apparently some of Bessie's difficulty in standing against her mother was related to the power the mother derived from the fact that she happened to be the head of a family which—by virtue of the siblings—meant a great deal to Bessie. We wish to make it clear, however, that Bessie's difficulty in standing against her mother was objective and not neurotic; it is to be emphasized that in each issue which occurred during her months at Walnut House and the later foster home, Bessie did not capitulate either subjectively or objectively to her mother's demands.

instance she feared meeting her father; and in the second she was apprehensive about taking the stand before judges to testify.[76] She experienced a realistic conflict about giving up her baby but came to the conclusion that she could take care of her married sister's baby in place of her own. It was the judgment of social workers and psychologist that Bessie's anxiety in these instances was situational rather than neurotic (i.e., was not the result of subjective conflict) and was handled by her with objectivity and responsibility.

Her relations with both girls and personnel at Walnut House were uniformly good. She laughingly spoke of herself as the "house tease," but her teasing was all of the amicable kind and was accepted thus by the other girls. She received much spontaneous pleasure from taking care of the other girls' babies, and apparently was stating a fact when she said, "All the children I've minded in my life like me, and I like them." In her placement in the foster home after leaving Walnut House, she stated that she was very happy and she was described by the foster mother as a dependable girl with a very good disposition.

Conclusions.—(1) Bessie exhibited a *moderately low* degree of anxiety. Her conflicts were chiefly situational, and she handled them with a relatively high degree of realism and responsibility. There was an understandable tendency to withdraw from stresses which could not otherwise be managed. This withdrawal generally took an objective (in this sense "normal") form, e.g., in her going into the park to get away from her parents' abuse. There was the latent possibility of schizoid behavior if stresses should become insupportable. But the fact that no such extreme tendency entered into her behavior in the face of the severe crisis of an incest pregnancy indicated that this latent tendency should not militate against the conclusion that she was prey to relatively little neurotic anxiety and that what anxiety she did have was handled in a relatively healthy way.

(2) Bessie experienced a *high degree of rejection* by both parents. This again presents a problem similar to that in the

---

[76] It turned out not to be necessary that she go to court in the father's trial, and she carried through the second instance successfully when the social worker and foster mother went with her.

case of Louise: why did severe parental rejection not lead to the development of neurotic anxiety? In Bessie's case it seems clear that the parental rejection did not engender internal, subjective conflicts. The problems with her parents were not introjected, either as a source of self-condemnation or as a source of persistent resentment. She accepted her parents' rejection as an objective, realistic fact, an acceptance which was based on her realistic appraisal of her father, and (though the mother still had the power to make decisions difficult for her) her appraisal of the mother was likewise realistic. Thus the rejection was dealt with on the level of conscious awareness; it did not become confused with expectations that the parents might or could be different. The rejection did not basically pervert her own behavior: in the interesting childhood vignette, she continued her plan of playing with the children despite her father's flagrant rejection on her approach, and she was able to develop affectionate relationships with siblings, peers, and other persons of all ages. *The adjustment to her rejection without internal conflict —i.e., without a rift between subjective expectations and objective reality—is the essential element in Bessie's relative freedom from neurotic anxiety.*

8. DOLORES: ANXIETY PANIC WHILE UNDER SEVERE THREAT

Dolores was a fourteen-year-old Puerto Rican, white, Catholic girl who had come to the United States three years before the present interviews. She was proletarian, her father being an unskilled factory laborer in Puerto Rico. Dolores was partially crippled from tuberculosis of the leg bone in childhood. There were four siblings, two older brothers, an older sister, and a younger brother, all in Puerto Rico. When Dolores was five, her mother was taken sick, and Dolores was required to remain home from school for six years to take care of the mother. On the mother's death, Dolores was brought to the United States by an aunt who was childless; the impression given by this aunt in her interviews with the social workers was that she had sought Dolores to fill her own emotional needs. Affectionate toward Dolores for the first few months, the aunt had then abruptly changed to treating the girl with complete coldness, beating her frequently, and ostentatiously rejecting her in favor of the children of a relative who lived near-by.

Dolores was pregnant by her uncle. He had approached her while she was sleeping, and the act had been completed before she could resist. Dolores had told her aunt, who then added continual threats to her punitive behavior, one threat being that if Dolores ever told anyone the truth about the origin of her pregnancy she would be sent to an institution where she would be beaten daily. The aunt had coached Dolores to tell the story that an unknown man had pushed her into a cellar and raped her. For over six weeks, during the preliminary interviews for her entrance to Walnut House and in the first weeks in the house, Dolores had clung tenaciously to the manufactured explanation of her pregnancy, and we knew nothing except that her story was vague and unconvincing. During this period Dolores was very subservient and resigned, answering questions in the manner of one who dutifully obeys authorities but in every other way exhibiting markedly withdrawn behavior. It was observed that she seemed alert when she thought she was unnoticed, but as soon as she felt anyone was watching her she assumed a hunched-over position and an "encased" attitude. This case is significant because it reveals the anxiety panic and psychological immobilization of an individual under strong, persistent threat.

In her first Rorschach she gave only three responses, rejecting seven of the ten cards.[77] Her behavior during the test was marked by silent but very strenuous effort; she would hold on to each card for periods of three to five minutes, studying the card, then looking silently at the tester or up at the ceiling. It was evident that a strong subjective struggle was occurring. The Rorschach clearly shows a very severe disturbance. A diagnosis of psychosis was precluded by the fact that the three responses she did give are the most obvious ones in the test.[78]

---

[77] She had a headache at the time scheduled for her Rorschach but at the last moment decided to take it anyway. Since headaches are often a psychosomatic symptom of conflict, her headache later was seen to fit plausibly into her situation at the time.

[78] Response to Card I: *W-F-A-P;* to Card III: *W-M-H-P;* to Card VIII: *D→ W- FM- A-P.* In the testing-the-limits phase, she revealed she could use the

There was indication in her behavior in the test that she tended to impute great power to authority (one aspect of which was the marked suspicion with which she regarded the tester's taking notes on her responses), but to submit herself to authority at the same time. We could only hypothesize that Dolores was in an exceedingly severe psychological conflict, which resulted in her being psychologically paralyzed on the test. The content of the conflict we could not determine at the time beyond the indications that it had something to do with the above-mentioned power she imputed to authorities. Her anxiety rating on this Rorschach was: depth 5, width 5, handling 3.

During this same first month she was taken three times to a clinic for the routine gynecological examination preparatory to parturition. The first two times, after having made no previous objection, Dolores became immobile at the clinic and refused to permit any examination. When it was later explained to her that the house could take no responsibility unless she cooperated, she finally agreed to go through with the examination, but when she again arrived at the clinic and was on the examination table she became hysterical and so muscularly rigid that the doctors could not proceed. It was then hypothesized that her conflict had to do with the circumstances under which she had become pregnant. In the next two interviews with the social worker, during which Dolores was assured she would be protected from her aunt, she disclosed the whole account of her uncle's rape and her aunt's threats. It was now clear that the extreme block on being examined—apparently Dolores had viewed the Rorschach in the same category as the gynecological examination— was due to the profound terror that the origin of her pregnancy might in some way be discovered and she would then be subject to her aunt's threats. The conflict itself took the form of the authority of the social workers, Rorschach tester, and doctors on one side and the authority of her aunt on the other—with

---

color and also could employ the details of the blots without difficulty. This phase of the test corroborated the above hypothesis that the disturbance was not psychotic or due to organic deterioration but rather to severe psychological conflict. Dolores had a slight handicap in the use of the English language, but it was clear that this did not materially contribute to her block on the Rorschach, since the responses she did give, as well as her answers to the tester, were made entirely intelligibly.

her aunt's authority having the weight of specific punitive threats.[79]

After this conflict was relieved, Dolores' attitudes and behavior underwent a radical change. She became outgoing and friendly in her relations to the other girls as well as to the personnel at Walnut House, and in contrast to the previous severely subservient behavior she now showed considerable independence in initiating projects in the house and developing her own hobbies.[80] The second Rorschach, taken several months after the clarification of the conflict, also exhibits a radical change.[81] The pathological blockage had disappeared.[82] The Rorschach presented the picture not of overwhelming conflict but of an averagely intelligent, relatively undifferentiated personality with a very healthy core. There was some indication of a need to protect herself from emotional involvement with other persons, and of problems in the area of sex. (E.g., she saw no men in the cards; Card IV was termed a "gorilla.") The avoidance of men, and the association of sex with possible aggression, are understandable in view of her own recent traumatic sexual experience. It is interesting that she first rejected Card VI (the card which often elicits sexual responses) but in the inquiry used it as a "parrot which can talk," which may well refer

---

[79] It will have been observed that she readily subjected herself to the "authority" of the psychologist, social workers, and doctors—e.g., she came to take the Rorschach, and she made the trips to the clinic without objection—until her subjection to these "authorities" came into immediate conflict with the power of her aunt.

[80] During the latter part of Dolores' stay at the house, a minor problem began to develop in her defiant and at times aggressive attitude toward some of the girls. We take this behavior to be the opposite side of her compliant, subservient behavior toward authority which was so predominant in the early attitude toward social workers and psychologist. It may be assumed that a compliant-defiant pattern, particularly related to her belief in authority, is a prominent part of Dolores' character structure.

[81] It would have been desirable to take a Rorschach directly after the "confession," but for temporal reasons this was not possible. We assume it is amply demonstrated in her behavior, however, that the radical change occurred at the time of her telling the truth about her pregnancy.

[82] Total responses, 15: 2 M, 4 FM, 8 F, 1 FC; $A\%$ 60; popular responses 4, no originals; $W\%$ 33, $D\%$ 60, $d\%$ 7; total time 14', as compared with 35' on first Rorschach. Intelligence could not be estimated on the first record; on this one it is: potentiality 110, efficiency 90 to 100. (Her intelligence tests in the New York schools—fifth grade—indicated an I.Q. of 80, but this was considered unreliable because of her language handicap.)

to the fact that she had been able to talk about her sexual problem and the origin of her pregnancy. The rating on anxiety in this second Rorschach was: depth 2½, width 2½, handling 2. This places her in the *moderately low* category in relation to the other girls.

Dolores ranked moderately high in quantity of anxiety on the *childhood* check-list, and high on both the *present* and *future* lists. Since the last was taken after the relief from her conflict, the high quantity of anxiety is not to be explained as a result of that conflict. We believe her relatively large number of items checked on these lists was due—as has been pointed out in cases above which represent the same character structure—to her being a compliant type in relation to authority and her feeling that she must diligently check every item which she could conceivably ever have worried about.[83] The phobial forms of anxiety were the predominant area.

With respect to Dolores' rejection by parental figures, we receive different pictures as we consider her relation to her aunt, to her mother, and to her father. It is clear that her aunt subjected her to extreme rejection. But the data concerning the more crucial early relations with her mother are less clear and must be largely inferred. Dolores stated in very general terms that she had had a warm relation with her mother. But the fact that the mother had been sick since Dolores was five, and that it devolved upon Dolores to remain home (at the price of missing schooling which she had greatly desired) to take care of the mother, despite the presence of two older brothers and an older sister in the family, gives a hint that there may have been some discrimination against Dolores and more rejection than she admits. Her rejection at the hands of her father is indicated more clearly in her recital of childhood events. Since the onset of her mother's illness, the father had lived with another woman, returning home only infrequently. On questioning, Dolores

---

[83] It is significant that her first two check-lists, taken when she was in her period of paralyzing conflicts, show a fairly high degree of response (i.e., a large number of items checked), whereas in the same period she refused to respond to the Rorschach. The plausible explanation seems to be that one knows what one is saying on the check-lists; there is no danger of unwittingly revealing her secret; and hence the check-lists would not be a threat to Dolores.

stated that her father had never played with her as a child, though he did play with her younger brother. When Dolores was asked by the psychologist whether as a child she had regretted that her father never played with her, she looked up in considerable surprise, as though such a question had never entered her head. To the writer, her subsequent answer of "no" is even less impressive than the significant phenomenon that her father's not playing with her not only had never occurred to her as a subjective problem but she was amazed that anyone else would raise it as such. We rate Dolores' rejection by her father as *moderately high*. Because of the paucity of data, especially with respect to the mother, we make our over-all rating of *moderately high* rejection tentative for Dolores, with the realization that she might perhaps as plausibly be placed in the *moderately low* category.

Conclusions.—(1) Dolores' case demonstrated severe conflict while under threat, resulting in anxiety which approached the intensity of panic, characterized by extreme withdrawal and partial psychological paralysis. She illustrates how a person can literally be "scared stiff." The conflict was situational and vanished when Dolores, freed from the power of her aunt's threats, was able to disclose the truth about her pregnancy. The conflict carried over to everything she felt might lead to discovering the secret which she must keep hidden; in this respect, it appears that an irrational, "magical" power to reveal the truth about the origin of her pregnancy was imputed to the gynecological examination.[84] While in the conflict, Dolores' anxiety was very high; after the conflict was relieved, her anxiety was rated as *moderately low*.[85]

---

[84] The fact that Dolores' character structure includes a marked attitude of power over her imputed to authorities and a corresponding tendency to subordinate herself to these powers is important for understanding why her conflict was so severe. For example, it could be hypothesized that the conflict would not have been so marked and the manufactured story would not have been clung to so persistently and tenaciously if she had not believed that the aunt had the power to enforce the threats and she herself had no power. And on the other side, the conflict would similarly have been less severe if Dolores had not imputed such power to social workers and the doctors; one could conceive, on this hypothesis, of her holding to the dissimulation about the pregnancy with less feeling of being "trapped."

[85] This rating of *moderately low* anxiety, based on the second Rorschach and her behavior after the relief of the conflict, is taken as our base in comparing Dolores with the other girls in the concluding chapter.

(2) We have tentatively rated Dolores as *moderately high* in rejection. The significant point, however, is that Dolores— like Louise and Bessie—*did not interpret rejection as a subjective problem.* The clearest example of this was her amazement at the question of whether she was sorry her father had never played with her. Rejection was accepted as an objective fact not as a cause of subjective questioning and conflict. On the basis of this reasoning, it is probable that even if there had been a high degree of rejection of her by her mother, Dolores would neither have interpreted it nor reported it as such.

9. Phyllis: Absence of Anxiety in an Impoverished Personality

Phyllis, age twenty-three, was the oldest daughter in a middle-class family; there were two siblings, sisters of seventeen and twelve. Her father was Protestant and her mother Catholic; Phyllis had been brought up in conformity with her mother's religion. At the time of her pregnancy she was employed as a bookkeeper in a bank. In school and business college (as, indeed, in the other phases of her life) she had always been known as quiet, studious, efficient, and meticulous; the last quality was shown at Walnut House in her excessively careful grooming whenever she came for an interview. The father of her baby was a physician in the army, whom she had met when she served as a USO hostess. His profession and rank of major were points of considerable pride to both Phyllis and her mother. Phyllis' relationship with this man was marked by naïveté on her part and much idealization of him, her repeated remarks being that he was "brilliant" and "without flaw."

Phyllis' Rorschach indicated a highly constricted, compartmentalized, "flat" personality, with very little inner activity or use of capacity for emotional relatedness with others.[86] She exhibited excessive caution, confining her responses to details in which she could be meticulously accurate and successfully held

[86] Total responses, 39: 2 *M*, 1 *FM*, 2 *K*, 18 *F*, 13 *Fc*, 1 *c*, 1 *FC*, 1 *CF*; total percentage in *F* area 80; *W*% 15, *D*% 59, *d*% 5, *Dd*% 21; (*H* plus *A*): (*Hd* plus *Ad*) equals 9:14; popular responses 5, originals 3; intelligence estimate: efficiency 110, potentiality 115.

herself aloof from emotional involvements with other people. Practically no conflicts or tensions were shown in the record, and very little anxiety. Evidently the constricted and cautious behavior had been so well ingrained in her that she accepted such impoverished modes of reaction without any particular subjective problems. Her anxiety rating on the Rorschach was: depth 2, width 2, handling 2, which placed her in the low category of anxiety in relation to the other girls. On the childhood anxiety check-list she ranked moderately low in quantity, with anxiety highest in the areas of the attitude of her peers toward her, success or failure in work, and the attitude of her family toward her. On the present anxiety check-list she ranked high, anxiety about the imminent parturition accounting for the increase.[87]

Phyllis described her childhood as one in which she was "never unhappy" and in which she regularly acceded to the advice of her father ("whom we would never go against") and to the will of her mother, who was a very dominating and anxious person. During the interviews at Walnut House at which her mother was present, Phyllis would always sit placidly while her mother endeavored to deliver the decisions for Phyllis concerning the baby. Only once during her childhood could Phyllis remember having talked back to her parents; after her doing so on this occasion—an auto trip when she was eight—her parents had promptly retaliated by putting her out of the car and temporarily leaving her beside the road. Apparently she learned never again to take a stand against her parents. Phyllis had no friends of her own age, but this caused her no regret for, so far as her peers were concerned, she felt she could "have a good time without needing anybody else." She preferred the society of older people; her "ideal of a good time," never yet realized, was to be invited to join the ladies in her mother's bridge club.

---

[87] Though Phyllis did have some anxiety about the prospective parturition (apprehension which focused around the fact that the birth was expected to be Caesarian), there is some suspicion that the markedly higher quantity of anxiety on this check-list represents at least partially her mother's great anxiety about the parturition rather than her own. This hypothesis is in accord with the fact that Phyllis regularly adopted her mother's attitudes in almost everything. In any case, the high quantity of anxiety on this check-list stands alone, all other criteria indicating that Phyllis had very little anxiety.

The great concern of Phyllis and her mother was that she have expert medical care during her pregnancy. She repeatedly emphasized that she was to go to the best women's hospital in the city, and was now under the care of the head obstetrician at this clinic. The experiences at this clinic which Phyllis related to the psychologist illuminate the dynamics underlying her great emphasis on expert medical care. During a visit to this clinic preparatory to parturition, an assistant obstetrician had remarked that a Caesarian section might be necessary. Phyllis reported that the head obstetrician had then taken the assistant aside to caution him "against telling me anything that would make me nervous." Whenever Phyllis had asked the chief obstetrician about her case, she reported that he always remarked, "You're all right; we don't talk to patients." Phyllis *smiled contentedly* when relating this; it seemed clear that being in the hands of an authority and *not knowing anything about her condition herself* seemed to her an ideal situation. This "ostrich policy," or positive valuation placed upon not knowing, has its motivation in the fact that it is a means of obviating any concern, conflict, or anxiety on her part. Once during the week preceding parturition, Phyllis was seized by a momentary anxiety that she might die. She immediately put this out of her mind by saying to herself, "It's all science, there is no need for worry." She emphasized that she believed "implicitly in science, and only in science."

Only the slightest indications of rebellion against her mother ever emerged in the interviews. One was her interest in horseback riding, which prior to her pregnancy she had pursued despite her mother's apprehension and mild disapproval. But in every major matter, such as in the plans for the baby, Phyllis acceded to her mother's will; it was her mother's eventual decision that they should keep the baby and raise it as their own.[88]

---

[88] The question arises as to whether Phyllis' extramarital pregnancy was in some way a rebellion against the mother, specifically a rebellion against the thwarting, suppressive influence of her mother upon her. No data emerged to confirm such a hypothesis. The data available—e.g., Phyllis' naiveté in her sexual relations and her idealization of the man—suggest that the pregnancy was a product of her conforming, compliant pattern (that is, she engaged in sexual relations out of compliance to the desires of the man) rather than a rebellion against this pattern.

Phyllis expressed the desire to go home after parturition and never leave again. Just prior to parturition, the domination of the mother approached the point of cruelty : she made a practice of watching outside Phyllis' door in the evening at Walnut House until ejected by the nurse and vented her extreme anxiety in the form of outbursts of rage at Phyllis. But all of this behavior by the mother was accepted by Phyllis placidly.

Two weeks after parturition Phyllis and her mother took the baby home, where it shortly died of pneumonia. In her subsequent visits to Walnut House Phyllis was always dressed in black. She exhibited a large colored painting she and her mother had had made of the baby in its coffin; but beyond these ways of dramatizing the death of the baby, she exhibited no particular affect. In the follow-up interviews, Phyllis stated that she had given up horseback riding and was refusing dates with men on the pretext that she was married. The social worker reported that Phyllis seemed like a dignified, dependent little girl, operating almost entirely on the theory "mother knows best."

Conclusions.—(1) In Phyllis, a person of a *low* degree of anxiety, we have observed a conforming, compliant personality. She remained free from emotional entanglements by means of affective impoverishment and submitted to her mother without subjective struggle at the price of surrender of her own individual autonomy. She had been "successfully" constricted by a dominating mother. The constriction was "successful" in the mother's sense in that Phyllis did not rebel; and it was "successful" in Phyllis' sense in that by means of capitulating to the mother and curtailing her own development she avoided conflicts, tensions, and anxiety. Phyllis reported no rejection (except the childhood incident, which was to her the exception that proves the rule) ; she never went against her mother enough to elicit outright rejection; and the covert rejection (e.g., in the mother's hostility and rage just before parturition) was not interpreted in that light by Phyllis. Presumably Phyllis' pattern of constriction had its genesis as a strategy in her childhood of avoiding the anxiety-creating situation of conflict with her mother. Phyllis' present practice was to surrender herself to authorities—the mother, the idealized sexual partner, the expert medical care—and thus to avoid concern, conflict, and anxiety. What we have termed the "ostrich policy," the desire not to know about her condition, the irrational faith in "science," and the use of the phrase "it's all science, there is no need for worry" were all integral parts of her constriction.[89]

(2) This case demonstrates that it is possible to avoid anxiety-creating situations by means of impoverishment of personality, but the price for such avoidance is loss of individual autonomy, personal responsibility, and the capacity for meaningful emotional relatedness to other persons. Phyllis is an illuminating demonstration of the varying theories of Kierkegaard, Goldstein, Fromm, and others that since anxiety arises as the person confronts possibilities for individual development and expansion, anxiety-creating situations may be avoided if the individual refuses to confront these possibilities. But the opportunities for psychological growth and expansion are lost at the same time. We may remark psychotherapeutically that the emergence of anxiety would be the most positive prognostic sign in the career of Phyllis.

10. FRANCES: ANXIETY AND UNSUCCESSFUL CONSTRICTION

Frances, a twenty-one-year-old professional tap-dancer, was the adopted only child of a middle-class family. The case is interesting in the respect that Frances tried to constrict her personality in order to avoid anxiety but (in contrast to Phyllis) was not able to effect constriction successfully; and at the points where the constrictive pattern broke down anxiety emerged.

---

[89] We speak of irrational faith in science not with reference to the medical care itself (which in other persons may obviously be related to rational methods of coping with anxiety) but rather to the use Phyllis makes of what she terms "science." With Phyllis belief in "science" is clearly a way of avoiding facing her anxiety, which in the instance of the momentary anxiety about death, might have had any one of many origins quite other than apprehension about death itself. This kind of "faith in science" is a superstition, falling in the same psychological category as a magical incantation or the use of a prayer-wheel, and serves the same psychological function for Phyllis as her submission to her mother's authority.

The Rorschach showed a relatively high degree of rigidity and constriction of personality on the surface, but the variety and originality in the record, the presence of some color shock, and the fact that the constriction often collapsed in the course of the test indicate that the constriction was not the mark of an impoverished personality.[90] The need to constrict herself was particularly called into play when she was confronted by emotional involvement with other people, who she felt were malicious and hostile toward her. There was present hostility within herself toward others, but this was repressed. The chief technique by which she endeavored to constrict herself was a strong effort to keep her reactions on the level of "common sense," "practicality," and "realism." When this device broke down in the Rorschach, as it did several times, anxiety came out. She sought to suppress her sensual promptings, at which again she was only irregularly successful. A very interesting indication in the Rorschach was that her originality tended to destroy her constrictive pattern. *There were indications that when she could suppress her originality, she was able to avoid much of her anxiety; but when her originality did emerge, it broke the pattern of constriction, and anxiety occurred.* This Rorschach presented the general picture of an individual who tried to constrict herself as a protection against anxiety-creating situations, but the constrictive strategy continually broke down, and anxiety, generally of the free-floating variety, then ensued. The Rorschach anxiety rating was: depth 4, width 3½, handling 2, which placed her in the *high* category in relation to the other girls. Her childhood, present, and future anxiety check-lists showed *moderately low, moderately high,* and *high* quantities of anxiety respectively, with ambition being the chief area of anxiety in each case.

Frances was pregnant by a young man whom she had idealized during the four years of their close friendship because he was a "gentleman and very dependable." When, at her preg-

---

[90] Total responses, 37: 2 *M*, 4 *FM*, 1 *k*, 4 *K*, 21 *F*, 3 *Fc*, 1 *c*, 1 *CF*; percentage in *F* area, 65; popular responses 6, originals 7; percentage of responses in Cards VIII, IX, and X, 51; only one *H* response in entire record; succession rigid; *W* % 16, *D* % 68, *d* % 8, *dd* % 8; intelligence estimate: efficiency 110, potentiality 125.

nancy, he did not propose marriage and even refused to contribute to her preparturition support, her attitude toward him abruptly changed to one of hatred. She verbalized this attitude freely, adding that she now "hated all men." Presumably her idealization of the man had served as a defense against the underlying suspicion of, and her own repressed hostility toward, him; the sudden shift to antagonism suggests that this attitude, in repressed form, was there all the time. What both the idealization and complete antagonism have in common was the pattern indicated in the Rorschach, namely that she needed to avoid a realistic appraisal of human relations. After parturition, her attitude toward men (as shown in both the interviews and the second Rorschach) changed from avoiding contact with men to avoiding involvement. She phrased it, "I no longer hate men; I'm afraid of them"; her plan was to renew contacts with men, especially in her church groups, but never to become involved.

In the interviews with both the social workers and the psychologist she always confined her talk to "practical," "realistic" topics and continually refused to deal with underlying emotional problems. It seemed clear that the great emphasis on "realism" was a means of covering up her real feelings. She had a slight awareness of the protective nature of the "practicality," admitting that she felt it was dangerous to express her real feelings or her originality, one of her reasons being that people would think she was "silly." Thus in the interviews, in contrast to the Rorschach, she was able to hold to her constrictive pattern successfully and avoid most topics which entailed anxiety. Her relations with the other girls in the house were characterized by directness and facility in superficial relationship on one hand, but on the other a recurrent suspicion of and hostility toward them, which constituted at times a considerable problem in the house.

Her description of her relationships to her father and mother was also marked by idealization. She stated that her childhood was "completely contented"; her father was "perfect" and her mother was "sweet" and always responded to her needs and wishes. But these references were regularly summed up in some general, evasive remark, such as, "You know how a mother and daughter talk understandingly with each other," and there were no trustworthy indications that the affirmative relationship with her parents was more than superficial. When she was a child her mother had told her about her being adopted in the form of a "fairy-tale," just as she told her other fairy-tales at bedtime. In later years the mother had suggested that Frances inquire into her real parentage through the adoption agency, but Frances had refused this advice because she "wanted to leave it as a fairy-tale." Some indication appeared in dreams she happened to relate during the interviews that, underneath her ostensibly affirmative relation with her parents, she had pronounced feelings of isolation and hostility arising from the fact that she did not have her own parents. It is a sound inference that the fairy-tale motif and the idealization of the parents served, as did the idealization of her boy friend, to cover up her hostility toward her parents.

In rating Frances' feeling of rejection, we confront the difficulty in the contradiction between surface statements—in which she would deny experiencing rejection—and the underlying indications. Since Frances' constrictive pattern and her strategies of avoidance of her problems could not be broken through in the interviews, and since there was ample evidence (e.g., the idealization of her parents and the fairy-tale motif) for assuming that her verbalizations about her relation to her parents were untrustworthy, we based our judgment of her rejection on the underlying indications. From her failure to see people in the Rorschach, her underlying suspicion of and hostility toward other people, and her strong need to avoid contact and involvement with them, we assumed a *moderately high* degree of rejection.

Conclusions.—We find in Frances a *moderately high degree* of anxiety. She is a demonstration of anxiety emerging in a pattern of unsuccessful constriction. She tried to constrict herself as a means of avoiding anxiety-creating situations, particularly situations of involvement with other people. Two prominent mechanisms for this constriction were her endeavor to keep all her reactions on a very "realistic," "practical" level and to idealize the other persons. Since she was actually not an impoverished personality, since considerable hostility toward others underlay the idealization, and since, indeed, the "realism" and idealization were contradictory, her constrictive pattern regularly broke down. It was at these points that Frances exhibited anxiety. The suppression of sexual and hostile impulses, as well as the suppression of originality, was part of the constrictive endeavor. It is highly significant that when originality did come out in the Rorschach, anxiety did also. We have noted in the case of Phyllis that successful constriction obviates anxiety. A demonstration of the same relationship between constriction and avoidance of anxiety is found in this case: when Frances was able to constrict herself, she did not experience anxiety, but when she was unsuccessful in her constrictive endeavors, considerable anxiety emerged.

11. CHARLOTTE: PSYCHOTIC DEVELOPMENTS OBVIATING ANXIETY

Charlotte was a twenty-one-year-old daughter of middle-class parents in an agricultural community, the siblings being a brother a year older than Charlotte and two younger brothers of seventeen and twelve. Her medical examination showed congenital syphilis and recently contracted gonorrhea. Both her Rorschach and her behavior at Walnut House showed distinct, though mild, psychotic trends. The Rorschach contained several rationally distorted responses and was marked by shading shock, a long time average per response, and a great deal of blocking.[91] She made much effort on the test, making frequent apologies with her responses, but her effort was very ineffectual and without much affect. Some blandness was present, though not of the extreme sort characteristic of severe psychosis. During the Rorschach her behavior was marked by frequent ingratiating but vacant smiles at the psychologist, accompanied by an expressionless quality in her eyes. Diagnostically, the Ror-

---

[91] Though the crucial element in Charlotte's Rorschach was the rationally distorted responses, we are including the numerical scoring because that has been our form of presentation with the other cases. Total responses, 36: 9 M, 4 FM, 4 FK, 9 F, 3 Fc, 4 FC, 3 CF; average time per response, 1'45"; popular responses 8, originals 7; $W\%$ 44, $D\%$ 42, $d\%$ 3, $Dd\%$ 11.

schach indicated a mildly schizophrenic state, possibly of a he-bephrenic nature. Very little anxiety was present, though her handling of her anxiety was by definition poor. The rating on the Rorschach was : depth 1½, width 3, handling 4, which placed her in the *low* category of anxiety with relation to the other girls.

At Walnut House Charlotte was generally gracious, bland, and genial, but these attitudes were periodically interrupted by outbursts of intense rage. The fact of pregnancy made very little impression on her, and, correspondingly, she showed a pronounced lack of realistic planning for parturition and the baby.

Her background likewise suggests some severe psychological disturbance. In her community she was known as a person who part of the time was very respectable and faithful in church activities and part of the time was given to impulsive, defiant acts, frequently becoming what was known in the community as "boy-crazy" and socially "wild." At the age of twenty she impulsively married a rigid, overconscientious young man (to "compensate for my lacks," she put it). He subsequently suffered a psycho-neurotic breakdown in the army. She visited him in the army camp at this time; they agreed their marriage had been a mistake and decided to have it annulled. She described herself at this time as being "so mixed up I didn't care about anything." There followed a period of promiscuous sexual activity, during which the pregnancy occurred. The act of intercourse which she assumed accounted for the pregnancy—with an army officer whose last name she did not know—she described as an experience she had not agreed to, but "I couldn't do anything about it." Possibly the behavior surrounding her becoming pregnant represents a mildly schizophrenic state (or the onset of the state) at that time.

Though Charlotte would talk freely about her childhood in the interviews, she would never talk about any present worries. No present problems seemed to exist for her; and when topics referring to possible present sources of anxiety emerged, she would assume a gay attitude or retreat, with vacant facial expression, into long periods of silence. Some minor remarks suggest a great deal of buried guilt feeling—e.g., "I made a mistake and have to pay for it"—but she showed no affect about guilt. Her childhood anxiety check-list showed a *moderately high* quantity of anxiety, with significant emphasis on "fear of the dark" ("because it represents the unknown") and other apprehensions of a phobial character. But her present and future anxiety check-lists showed *moderately low* and *low* quantities of anxiety respectively. To the extent that the quantities of anxiety shown on these check-lists can be taken at face value, they would support the supposition that in her prepsychotic state she experienced a great deal of anxiety, but that the anxiety was now covered over by the mildly schizophrenic condition.

Conclusions.—Charlotte's low degree of anxiety illustrates that psychotic developments of this kind effectually cover up the individual's anxiety. With respect to the problem of anxiety, many forms of psychosis are to be understood as the end result of conflicts and concomitant anxiety which are too great for the individual to bear and at the same time are insoluble on any other level. In such cases great anxiety is generally found just before the onset of the psychotic state; that period might be represented in Charlotte just after she decided to have her marriage annulled. The psychotic development itself may be characterized as a means of obviating otherwise insoluble conflicts and anxiety, at the price, in cases like Charlotte's, of the surrender of some aspect of adjustment to reality. What the genesis of Charlotte's psychotic trend was we do not know; but it is clear in her case that anxiety and conflict are to a considerable extent "covered over" or "lost" in the psychotic state.[92]

12. Hester: Anxiety Related to Defiance and Rebellion

Hester, seventeen years old, was the only girl in a middle-class family; two of her brothers were two and four years older respectively, and one was five years younger than she. Her

---

[92] We are, of course, speaking here only of the forms of psychosis which are psychogenic—i.e., have their origin in subjective, psychological conflict rather than organic deterioration. The general statement that these psychotic states are characterized by a lack of anxiety is not contradicted by the fact that anxiety is present in some forms of paranoia; the latter is a different configuration within the general pattern.

father, an interior decorator, had drowned after a period of excessive drinking when she was seven. She had attended an upper-middle-class private denominational girls' boarding school for her secondary education, where she was known as rebellious, given to temper-tantrums, intellectually well endowed but "lazy." She was pregnant by a sailor with whom she had had only a casual friendship.

Her Rorschach showed a good deal of emotional impulsiveness and infantilism, some tendencies toward exhibitionism, and prominent tendencies to be defiant toward those in authority over her.[93] Her sexual impulses were used largely in the service of this defiance. The only human being seen in the Rorschach was a clown. The anxiety in the Rorschach emerged especially at the points of her guilt feeling, this in turn being a product of her defiance, particularly her use of sexual impulsiveness as a form of defiance. The rating of anxiety in her Rorschach was: depth 3, width 3, handling 3, which placed her in the *moderately high* category in relation to the other girls. On the childhood and present anxiety check-lists she showed a *high* degree of anxiety, her chief areas of anxiety being what her peers thought of her, phobial apprehensions, and anxiety about competitive status in school and work.

The family atmosphere in her childhood had been marked by much teasing, some of it of a sadistic intensity, on the part of the father and brothers. The mother had been particularly the butt of this teasing, although Hester herself had received a considerable share. She felt she had had a fairly close relationship with her father as a small child, but some of the stories she related suggested that his teasing had pained her more than she admitted and that his behavior involved some definite rejection of her.[94] Hester laid her rebellious behavior to the fact that her father died when she was young; "If I had had a father to talk

---

[93] Total responses, 22 : 1 *M*, 6 *FM*, 1 *K*, 3 *FK*, 5 *F*, 1 *Fc*, 1*FC*, 4 *CF;* popular responses 6, originals 4 ; *W%* 50, *D%* 50 ; intelligence estimate: potentiality 120, efficiency 110.

[94] For example, she had been out fishing with him as a child ; on their way back to the car she had gotten caught on the barbed wire of the fence ; he (ostensibly in "teasing") had gotten in the car and driven around the block, leaving her hanging there.

with, all these messes [including the pregnancy] would not have happened." Her mother (interviewed at Walnut House) appeared to be a passive individual. Beyond the fact that she had always regarded Hester as a problem and had been forced to show some concern about Hester's predicaments at school and elsewhere, she seemed never to have shown much interest in or understanding of her daughter.[95] Though Hester felt that she admired her mother, she also stated that her mother was remote and uncompanionable; she had frequently invited her mother, she asserted, to go to games with her, but the mother had always refused. According to Hester's description, the mother would take the part of the boys when, during childhood, there were quarrels between the siblings.

Hester's defiance and rebelliousness seemed covertly and overtly to be directed against her mother, and there were indications in the interviews (bearing out the Rorschach data) that the sexual impulsiveness fell in this category. Her first sexual experience had occurred when, at the age of thirteen, she had run away from home, hitchhiking to a distant city and back again. There were indications that her pregnancy served both as defiance and as a means of forcing her mother to take an interest in her. Hester's most frequent method of allaying anxiety was to laugh it off—a form of behavior which, in this context, may also be viewed as defiance (e.g., "I don't care").

Conclusions.—We have found in Hester a *moderately high* degree of anxiety and a *moderately high* degree of rejection. Her present anxiety arose out of her guilt feelings over her defiant and rebellious behavior, her sexual impulses (and probably

---

[95] An adult relative who apparently had a fairly thorough understanding of the family was interviewed at Walnut House. She stated that the mother had never been authoritative toward the children, but had been so occupied with preserving material and social advantages for them that she had not paid attention to them personally and that she had given attention to Hester only in the girl's most severe predicaments. It is interesting that this relative thought it would have been better if the mother had been more "authoritative"; to the extent that this means her being more responsive to Hester, more of a real and immediate person in Hester's environment, even at the price of occasional punishment of her, there is ground for the hypothesis that Hester would have received some psychological orientation in her family, and that her extensive rebellious behavior, designed, as we shall indicate below, to commandeer her mother's concern, would have been less necessary.

the pregnancy) being employed in the service of such behavior. The rejection consisted centrally of the mother's lack of concern or interest in her, and Hester's defiance and rebelliousness were motivated chiefly by the need to force her mother to show some concern. The genetic source of her anxiety presumably lay in original feelings of isolation from her mother, with the father's death contributing to this isolation in a significant but probably subsidiary form. In Hester, thus, there was a vicious circle: she sought to overcome the original anxiety (isolation) by methods —defiance and rebelliousness—which produced more anxiety.

13. SARAH AND ADA: ABSENCE AND PRESENCE OF ANXIETY IN TWO NEGRO GIRLS

Sarah.—Sarah, a twenty-year-old proletarian Negro girl, had been born in a Southern state, where her father was a miner and her mother a domestic. At the age of four, Sarah went to live with an aunt and paternal uncle (also a miner) in a borderline Southern state, for the reason that they liked children but had none of their own. Of her five siblings, two others had lived with her at the home of the aunt and uncle. After graduation from high school, Sarah had come to New York and at the time of her pregnancy was working as a welder in a factory.

Sarah's Rorschach showed an original, somewhat naive, genuinely extraverted person with higher than average intelligence.[96] There was some compliance and much capacity for caution in her relations with people, but neither of these characteristics was in neurotic form; i.e., the caution and compliance were conscious ways of adapting to situations rather than mechanisms of self-repression. A fairly high degree of independence was shown, with definite indications that she knew what she wanted and did not want. She employed a technique of not taking life too seriously, preserving a somewhat happy-go-lucky attitude, avoiding complications by avoiding depth in her relations; but these traits again did not appear in severe form and did not involve impov-

---

[96] Total responses, 40: 1 M, 6 FM, 1 FK, 14 F, 10 Fc, 2 FC', 6 FC; $W\%$ 20, $D\%$ 70, $Dd\%$ 5, $S\%$ 5; popular responses 5, originals 15; intelligence estimate: potentiality 110, efficiency 110.

erishment of her capacities. On the whole, it was the picture of a differentiated but uncomplicated personality. Almost no conflicts or indications of neurotic problems were present. Her rating on anxiety in the Rorschach was: depth 1, width 1, handling 1, which placed her in the *low* category in relation to the other girls. Correspondingly, her childhood and present anxiety check-lists placed her in the *low* and *moderately low* categories respectively for quantity of anxiety. The chief areas of anxiety were ambition and what her friends and family thought of her.

Sarah impressed social workers and psychologist alike as a stable, well-adjusted, independent person who accepted and dealt with her problems objectively. She planned realistically for the birth and care of her baby (and after its birth eventually succeeded in the relatively difficult task of keeping it and supporting it herself). She was certain she wished not to accept financial assistance from the city welfare department but to pay for her care at Walnut House out of her own savings. She had been very fond of the young man who was the father of her baby, having at one time considered marriage with him. But after her becoming pregnant, his attitude and behavior became increasingly unreliable. At the time of her stay at Walnut House, she wished neither to marry him nor to receive financial assistance from him, but she did make considerable effort to get him to permit his name to be used by the baby. When he consistently refused, Sarah was disappointed but accepted and adjusted to the fact realistically.

Sarah's ambition (cited above in the check-lists) did not take an aggressively competitive form; in fact, while in school, she had worked out an ideal of "not being at the top, nor at the bottom, but somewhere in the middle." [97] She received much satisfaction from her work, and apparently her employers had a very high opinion of her, for they reserved her job for her till after her parturition.

The only situation which presented a problem in Sarah's behavior at Walnut House arose from the fact that her independ-

---

97 The fact that the $W\%$ on the Rorschach was not high is a corroborating datum for the statement that her ambition was not aggressively competitive.

ence sometimes took a defiant form, largely around the racial issue. Since she and Ada were the only two Negroes living in a group of white girls, and since several of the white girls expressed some racial prejudice, Sarah at first made a practice of remaining aloof and staying much of the time in her room. "If you stay away from groups, you avoid trouble" was her formula. She exhibited outright defiance against one of the staff who, she felt, was "bossy." She reported that she had disliked remaining in the South when she visited her parents because there were "too many rules and restrictions, and you have to say ma'am to somebody no older than yourself." Sarah's defiance was sometimes more extreme than the situation warranted (she admitted that she sensed some affronts where none were intended).[98] On the whole, however, it would seem that her special sensitivity and defiant independence are understandable for a Negro girl living in an intimate situation with a group of white girls in a condition (pregnancy) in which many of them were apt to be especially defensive. In this sense, we consider Sarah's defiant tendency as largely a mode of conscious adjustment rather than as the expression of a neurotic pattern.[99]

There were no definite signs of rejection in Sarah's background. She reported a happy childhood in her own family and in her life with the aunt and uncle, and her attitudes toward her aunt and uncle and her siblings were, like her attitudes toward her parents, affectionate.[100] She did not wish her parents or her aunt and uncle to know about the pregnancy until after parturition, for she felt they would want to help her financially even though they could not afford to. Through an accident in social agency channels, Sarah's parents were informed of her pregnancy before parturition; Sarah was angry that this should have

---

[98] But at the same time it was not indiscriminate defiance as is generally the case when defiance arises from unconscious patterns; it arose only where she felt the racial issue was present in the other person's attitudes.

[99] It would seem to be an entirely tenable hypothesis that this conscious defiance served a positive function, i.e., it had been developed by Sarah as a technique for adjusting to the racial issue without the impoverishment of her capacities or the surrender of her psychological freedom.

[100] A report from the social service agency in the home city of the parents reported them to be hard-working, responsible, sympathetic persons, and all that could be deduced was that Sarah had had a relatively healthy background within her two families as a child.

happened against her expressed wish (cf. her defiance, cited above, at people who are "bossy" or go over her head) ; but the ensuing letters from her parents showed understanding and no condemnation of her whatever.

Conclusions Concerning Sarah.—Sarah ranked *low* in degree of anxiety, and at the same time exhibited no discernible experience of rejection. Her problems were objective and realistic, managed without subjective conflict, with the one possible exception of the special sensitivity to racial discrimination and resulting defiance; but this likewise may be termed a "normal" rather than neurotic reaction in view of her realistic cultural situation.[101]

Ada.—The other Negro girl in this study is Ada, age nineteen, Catholic, who had lived most of her life in a suburb of New York. Since her father's death when she was four, she and her brother (two years younger) had been supported by the mother with some help from the department of welfare. Ada had attended a Catholic primary school, but a public high school. After Ada's graduation from high school at seventeen, the mother had had a "nervous breakdown from overwork" and had gone to live with relatives in the South, with Ada and the brother moving to New York to live with an aunt. Ada's original vocational aim was nursing, but with the occurrence of the pregnancy she decided that she would become a factory worker in order to support the baby. It was difficult to place Ada accurately with respect to socioeconomic class : there were proletarian elements in her background, but her original vocational aims and many of her attitudes (discussed below) seemed to be middle-class. We

---

101 It may be concluded that Sarah's relative lack of neurotic anxiety was related to the fact that she did not experience psychological rejection within her family circles, either as a child or in the present situation. But a cultural factor emerged in the case of Sarah (as of the other Negro girl, Ada) : there are reasons for believing that extramarital pregnancy is not as much of an anxiety-creating situation in the Negro communities from which Sarah and Ada came as in the cultural milieux of the white girls. It may be, thus, that we did not have Sarah in a genuinely anxiety-creating situation. This factor, though it could account for *less* presence of anxiety, could not account for the *absence* of neurotic anxiety in Sarah. (E.g., the Rorschach would reveal neurotic anxiety, if it were present, whether the subject were in an objective anxiety-creating situation or not.)

describe her as on the borderline between proletarian and middle-class.

She was pregnant by a boy her own age with whom she had had a close relationship since the middle of her high-school career. According to her description he had always been very "possessive" of her and jealous of her other friends, and she had apparently submitted to his dominating tendencies. Though admitting paternity, he had refused to marry her, at which she reported she had "put him out of my mind." [102]

Ada's Rorschach showed a very stereotyped, acquiescent, compliant person with no originality and with average intelligence.[103] The chief feature of the record was the fact that she set high standards for herself, but the standards were empty of positive content; it was as though she had a great need to measure up but no self-chosen goals or feelings of what she wanted to measure up to. (It was the picture, in conventional terms, of an individual with a strong superego.) The motivation for holding the high standards was that she could thereby comply with others' expectations of her and with her own introjected expectations. As a consequence her spontaneity and inner instinctual promptings (sex and hostility) were almost entirely repressed. There was considerable potentiality for sensual and other forms of responsiveness to other persons, but such responsiveness gave her anxiety because she could not respond in ways that fitted her high standards.[104] When a response occurred (Card VII) associated with vaginal examination at the hospital, a general disturbance was cued off which lasted through all the remaining cards in the test, amounting almost to a confabulatory tendency. This would indicate that if she failed to live up to her standards (the pregnancy being associated

---

[102] Medical diagnosis: syphilis, which she had contracted from this boy.

[103] Total responses, 12: 1 *M*, 5 *F*, 2 *Fc*, 2 *FC*, 1 *CF*, 1 *C*; popular responses 4, no originals; *W*% 67, *D*% 33; intelligence estimate: potentiality 100, efficiency 100 (or less).

[104] Her motivations for the sexual relations were never stated by her. From the Rorschach picture we hypothesized that the motivations were both her own sexual promptings and her *need to comply with the expectations of the boy*. The latter motivation was probably more significant in the respect that it would be necessary for Ada to have her compliant tendencies on the side of the sexual relationship in order to overcome her strong sexual repressions.

with such a failure), she was deeply disoriented in her relation to herself as well as to others, and much anxiety arose. Anxiety rating on the Rorschach was: depth 2½, width 4½, handling 3, which placed her in the *high* category of anxiety in relation to the other girls.

Ada ranked *moderately high* in the childhood anxiety checklist and *moderately low* in both the present and future check-lists. Her chief areas of anxiety were success and failure in work and what her family and parental surrogates thought of her (anxiety about her teacher or mother scolding her being prominent).

In her behavior at Walnut House as well as in the interviews Ada continually exhibited the above-described combination of compliance and high standards. She answered all questions conscientiously but never volunteered spontaneous expression of thoughts or feelings. She could always be depended upon to run errands at the house and to cooperate in other ways which did not require initiative. Since she had neither the independence nor the defiant tendencies of Sarah, she got along well with the white girls. In her school career she had always obtained very high grades. She expressed satisfaction that in her schools "everything was drilled into you—you learn more that way."

The genetic background of Ada's need to hold rigid standards for herself could be seen in her description of her mother and their relationship. Though Ada remarked in blanket terms that her mother had been a "happy" person during Ada's childhood, the fact that the chief symptom of the mother's present "breakdown" was her "worrying about everything" suggested that she was probably a tense and rigid person. A clearer indication of the mother's rigidity was seen in the fact that she was very strict with the children; Ada reported that the mother frequently whipped the son "because he didn't come exactly when she called." Ada herself had not been punished often, according to her reports; in fact, she felt her mother had been too lenient with her.[105] As a child Ada was always obedient, and always conformed to her mother's wishes, with only occasional and

---

[105] This statement that the mother was "too lenient" may have been an expression of Ada's own rigid standards (i.e., she felt she *should* have been punished more often) rather than an objective description of the childhood situation.

slight feelings of hostility toward her mother. Ada reported that she had learned to go off by herself and "get over" this anger. The mother and aunt with whom Ada later lived were faithfully practicing Catholics, as Ada likewise had always been.

Ada described the aunt as also very strict. In an interview at Walnut House, the aunt explained that she had made a conscious effort to inculcate high standards in Ada, that she had been very proud of her, and though she did not feel punitive toward Ada because of the pregnancy as such, she did not wish to accept Ada back into her apartment after she became pregnant because it would be a sign of the relaxing of the standards she had trained in her own two children. If we may take the aunt's attitudes as representative of the family constellation in which Ada was brought up, we have a graphic expression of the formula of the adults which presumably underlay Ada's psychological pattern: (1) these adults sought to inculcate "high standards" in her; (2) they were proud of her to the extent that she complied with these standards; and (3) they threatened her with rejection if she did not comply with these standards.

It was impossible to find overt feelings in Ada of rejection by her mother, with whom Ada felt she had had a friendly, though somewhat distant, relationship, until she was an adolescent. It seemed clear that from childhood onward Ada had so well accepted and complied with the "high standards" of her mother and the environment that the mother was never given cause to reject her overtly. While at Walnut House Ada could never bring herself to let her brother know about her pregnancy, since she was certain he would reject her; and she hesitated for several months before writing her mother about her situation. When she did finally inform her mother, the mother apparently accepted the fact of the baby and suggested plans for their keeping it together.[106]

---

[106] The fact that the mother accepted the expected baby should not be taken as an argument against the mother's potential and covert rejection of Ada. Indeed, the problem of the occasion for rejection must be viewed differently in the cases of these Negro girls from the cases of the white girls. There were numerous indications in the case of Ada, as well as in the case of Sarah, that having a baby out of wedlock was not in itself as serious or opprobrious a situation in the Negro communities from which they came as it was for the white girls. (Corroborating cultural data could be advanced for this point as a general thesis, but the writer

Conclusions Concerning Ada.—In Ada we find a *moderately high* degree of anxiety. Her degree of rejection varied as it was viewed in different aspects: she was rejected in a moderately high degree by her aunt; she expected a high degree of rejection by her brother; and although the rejection was difficult to assess in her relation with her mother because of her previous complete compliance with her mother's wishes, there were indications that Ada had considerable fear of rejection by her mother. We could, therefore, assume that rejection was present potentially in the relationship. But the essential point for the understanding of the dynamics of Ada's anxiety is *the rejection she felt in the face of her "high standards."* These standards were not indigenous, self-chosen values but were introjections of the formal expectations of her mother and the family environment. Hence the significant form of her present rejection was self-rejection, the self having taken over the authoritative function of the parent. When Ada felt that she had not lived up to these internalized expectations, a profound psychological disorientation occurred (most graphically illustrated in the Rorschach), and subjective conflict and much anxiety ensued.

We have pointed out in previous cases in this study that the conflict underlying neurotic anxiety may be described as a hiatus within the subject between expectations with regard to her parents' attitudes and the reality of the parental attitudes. In Ada's case a clear hiatus was present underlying her anxiety, but it took a somewhat different form, i.e., it was a hiatus between her introjected expectations of herself and the reality situation.

---

will not endeavor to go into that problem further.) It does not seem that rejection in Ada's case—e.g., the aunt's not wishing her to stay at her apartment, Ada's fear of her brother's rejection, and Ada's rejection of herself—arose from the fact that she was going to have a baby out of wedlock, but rather from the acts that led up to the pregnancy. What was disapproved of in these acts is again hard to define specifically, since the "standards" that were violated are formal rather than standards with a specific content (as, for example, a prohibition against sexual relations per se). It seems to the writer that the rejection facing Ada, and the psychological disorientation underlying her anxiety, had their source in the fact that Ada complied with an authority and with expectations (i.e., the boy's expectations and her own sexual impulses) other than those of her mother or the mother surrogates. Corroborating data for this statement are suggested by the fact that Ada did not exhibit any pronounced guilt feeling about the sexual relations or the pregnancy as such; the anxiety appeared to come directly out of a psychological disorientation that arose, in turn, out of her not complying with her mother's expectations.

The anxiety in Ada's case did not arise out of guilt feeling because of the sexual relations or pregnancy as such, but rather arose directly out of the psychological disorientation which she experienced because of her having complied with authority and expectations other than those of her mother.[107]

Comparison and Contrast.—A comparison of Sarah and Ada high-lights the above-described dynamic of neurotic anxiety. For both Negro girls, the fact of illegitimate pregnancy did not present as much of an anxiety-creating situation as for the white girls. Both girls showed compliance: in Sarah compliance was a conscious method of adjusting, particularly to the racial issue, but her autonomy and self-feeling were protected by conscious defiance whenever she felt that to comply would threaten her independence. But for Ada compliance was an unconscious pattern as well as conscious, her self-feeling and self-acceptance depending on how well she complied, prototypically with her mother's expectations. In Sarah, there was very little or no feeling of rejection by her parents; in Ada there was considerable feeling of rejection, in the form of rejection of herself in the face of her introjected standards. In Sarah there was very little subjective conflict and very little anxiety; in Ada there was *strong subjective conflict* between her introjected expectations and her reality situation, leading to pronounced psychological disorientation and a moderately high degree of anxiety.

14. IRENE: ANXIETY RELATED TO OVERCONSCIENTIOUSNESS AND SHYNESS

Irene was the nineteen-year-old adopted daughter of relatively old middle-class parents. The family had always lived in the country, and since there were no siblings, Irene's life had been

---

[107] The implication is that Ada could be free of anxiety only so long as she complied with her mother's expectations, albeit in their introjected form. The ineffectualness of such protection from anxiety is amply demonstrated in Ada's case. To gain and preserve freedom from anxiety on this basis she could never follow her own desires, nor could she ever comply with anyone other than the mother; but since her way of relating to all other persons was to comply, her psychological patterns were bound to be frequently jeopardized. The case illustrates the dilemma of the person whose freedom from anxiety depends on compliance with an authority which is not rooted in his own autonomy.

relatively solitary until high school. She was pregnant by her fiancé, with whom she had had a close relationship during her high school years. Her parents had not overtly opposed her engagement but had not approved of her fiancé for the reason, Irene stated, that his parents' business was selling liquor. The several sexual relations she had had with the fiancé occurred after her graduation from high school and just before they planned to become married.

The chief features of Irene's Rorschach were very great conscientiousness, pronounced contact shyness and withdrawal tendencies, overrefined control, and a tendency toward stereotypy of interest (presumably related to her solitary background), with a fairly high degree of originality at the same time.[108] Her very long pauses, during which she studied the cards industriously as though silently considering and rejecting possible responses, seemed to be partly due to her cultural difficulty in self-expression, but also were evidences of her compulsive conscientiousness. This latter compulsion to do well involved so much effort that it markedly inhibited her productivity. Though her intratensive promptings were easily accepted by her, she exhibited very much caution in responding to emotional stimuli in her relations with other people. The shyness, withdrawal, and caution seemed partly to be understood as cultural difficulties in expression and responsiveness—she herself related these traits to the fact that "I'm just a country girl." But on a deeper level the caution was a protection against anxiety-creating emotional involvements, the anxiety showing itself chiefly in her overconscientiousness. It is as though she felt she could not relate to people except by means of the compulsion to be perfect, to fulfill some very high standards. When, however, she was able to break through her shyness and caution and respond to outside stimuli on the Rorschach, both her anxiety and overconscientiousness diminished (which implied that the overconscientiousness was a defense against the anxiety-creating situation).

---

[108] Total responses, 23: 3 M, 6 FM, 5 F, 6 Fc, 3 FC; $A\%$, 70; popular responses 6, originals 6; $W\%$ 39, $D\%$ 61; average reaction time, 2′, 17″; percentage of responses in last three cards, 48; intelligence estimate: potentiality 125, efficiency 110.

Anxiety rating on the Rorschach was: depth 4½, width 2, handling 2, which placed her in the *moderately high* category in relation to the other girls.

Both her childhood and present anxiety check-lists fell in the *low category* in quantity, but this was undoubtedly due to her block in expression as shown on the Rorschach. On the former list, anxiety concerning success and failure in work was the markedly predominant area, with phobial apprehensions second; on the present anxiety list, the chief area of anxiety was again success and failure in work, and the second what her family thought of her.

Apparently Irene's compulsive conscientiousness had been a character trait all through her background. For one example, she related that by dint of very great effort she had graduated at the head of her high school class and then suffered a temporary "nervous breakdown." For another example, she said she had always been very careful not to select her friends from a "lower social class" than her own. In the interviews she also showed cautiousness and a considerable desire to please, but this behavior seemed not so much for the purpose of gaining the psychologist's or social worker's approval as for the purpose of living up to certain standards of behavior of her own.

Her parents were very conservative, religiously and morally, not believing in dancing, smoking, or going to the movies. They had, however, overtly granted her freedom in these respects; Irene had joined a more liberal church and participated in the above-mentioned recreations without overt conflict with her parents but—as will be discussed below—probably with considerable covert conflict. She characterized her mother as having always "worried a good deal." In an interview at Walnut House the mother referred to Irene as "mother's little girl," and it was admitted by both Irene and her that she had always sought to overprotect and "coddle" the daughter. The parents had been hurt and surprised by the pregnancy but had accepted it and cooperated with Irene in her plans. Again, however, their attitude was that of adults taking care of a child.

The home background was characterized overtly by an emotional vacuum: the parents had scruples against quarreling, either between themselves or with Irene. Their practice had been never to spank her but rather, when she committed some infringement as a child, to reason with her and then to make her sit quietly in a chair—"during which I would boil," Irene remarked. It is a sound hypothesis that this lack of emotional give-and-take and the absence of any emotional outlet as a child, together with the parents' belief in rigid standards, set the stage for the development of considerable guilt feelings in Irene. It is also plausible that these guilt feelings were an important motivation in Irene's overconscientiousness. She stated that she had always been very lonely as a child. Apologizing for saying so, she asserted that she had been closer to her two dogs than to her parents. She had never felt any bond of understanding between herself and her mother, and had never been able to talk intimately to her mother.

Her engagement and sexual relations with a boy of whom the parents did not approve seemed to be motivated both by her repressed hostility toward her parents, especially toward her mother, and by her need to compensate for the lack of warmth and understanding in her relationships at home.

In her later interviews at Walnut House, Irene expressed considerable hostility and resentment against her mother, focusing chiefly on the facts that her mother had coddled her and had had so little understanding of and faith in her. Irene was able to use the therapeutic opportunities at Walnut House very constructively. The follow-up data several months later indicated that she was making a very good and enthusiastic adjustment at college.

Conclusions.—Although there was no physical rejection (e.g., punishment) of Irene, there were sound evidences that she experienced a good deal of emotional rejection and very much loneliness; hence we rated her as *moderately high* in rejection by her parents. On the basis of her well-defined symptoms of anxiety—overconscientiousness, withdrawal, cautiousness, and shyness—our over-all rating for her anxiety was also *moderately high*. Though superficially these behavior traits were related to her solitary background, on a deeper level the withdrawal, conscientiousness, and caution represented endeavors to adjust to the anxiety-creating situation of her relation with her parents. The withdrawal and contact shyness were protections against the emotionally cold milieu of the family, and the overconscientiousness was an endeavor to adjust to the fact that she could not be accepted unless she lived up to her parents' rigid standards. The emotional vacuum and unreality in the family likewise gave the context for the subjective conflict which underlay Irene's anxiety. The parents not only patently repressed their own aggression, but likewise gave her no opportunity to react against them (e.g., the "reasoning" with her and placing her in a chair amounting to an authoritative suppression of her resentment and hostility). We have indicated that, though the parents ostensibly permitted her to make her own liberal choices, there were evidences that in making these choices, as well as in her state of suppressed hostility, Irene experienced considerable guilt feelings. The compulsive conscientiousness was, on one side, motivated by this guilt feeling. It may be observed parenthetically that Irene's subjective conflict and guilt feeling would be all the stronger psychologically because she was never permitted—in contrast to Louise and Bessie, who suffered outright punishment at the hands of their parents—to feel consciously her hostility against the parents or to find an objective focus for her guilt feelings.

Chapter 8

CONCLUSIONS FROM THE CASE STUDIES

> . . . it is silly
> To refuse the tasks of time
> And, overlooking our lives,
> Cry—"Miserable wicked me,
> How interesting I am."
> We would rather be ruined than changed,
> We would rather die in our dread
> Than climb the cross of the moment
> And let our illusions die.
> W. H. Auden, *The Age of Anxiety.*

Our purpose in this chapter is not to catalog all the points brought out in the above cases, but to present and summarize some of the crucial issues in the problem of anxiety as illustrated and demonstrated in the foregoing clinical data.

1. RELATION OF NEUROTIC FEARS TO UNDERLYING ANXIETY

It was observed in the first case above that Brown's fear that he had cancer was presented by him as a "realistic" and "rational" fear, with a denial that it was in any way related to underlying anxiety. But we noted that this cancer fear appeared regularly as the first step in a progression toward an anxiety spell, that as long as the cancer fear remained as the focus of the patient's attention conscious anxiety did not appear, but that when anxiety dreams and conscious anxiety did emerge (as they regularly did after several days), the cancer fear vanished. The cancer fear was thus both the first form of an emerging anxiety spell and also a means of covering the underlying anxiety by means of displacement and objectification on a threat which could be called

331

rational and realistic. The anxiety spell, of which, as we have said, the cancer fear was the initial sign, was regularly related to some aspect of the conflict which underlay the patient's neurotic anxiety, namely his conflict with his mother. We observed that if the patient had been able to hold consistently to his cancer fear (or if, to put the matter hypothetically, he really *had* had cancer), his underlying conflict and anxiety would have been obviated. For he would have been able to remain in a hospital and be taken care of without feeling guilty about it, and he would also have gotten even with his mother since she would have had to support him. Thus, despite superficial and apparent differences in content between the cancer fear and the conflict with his mother, it was discovered that a logical and subjectively consistent relationship existed between the former (the neurotic fear) and the latter (the underlying neurotic anxiety).

In the case of Helen we observed that the neurotic fear of parturition was an objectification of her underlying anxiety arising from repressed guilt feeling associated with her pregnancy. So long as her apprehension could be attached to the possible sufferings in childbirth—a focus of fear which could easily be construed by Helen as "rational"—she was not faced with the much more difficult problem of confronting the underlying guilt feelings, even the admission of which would have threatened her central psychological protective strategies and thrown her into profound conflict.

These cases illustrate that *neurotic fears are the objectified, particularized foci of underlying neurotic anxiety.*[1] It is also to be noted that (a) *the content of the particular neurotic fear is not fortuitiously or accidentally selected by the subject, but bears a consistent and subjectively logical relation to that particular subject's pattern of underlying conflict and neurotic anxiety* and (b) *the neurotic fear performs the function of covering up the underlying conflict and anxiety.*

It was hypothesized at the outset of the study of unmarried mothers that neurotic fears would shift, as the practical issues and problems confronting the individual changed, but that the

---

[1] Cf. earlier statement (Chapter 6) that a neurotic fear has its exaggerated quality by virtue of the neurotic anxiety underlying it.

neurotic anxiety would remain relatively constant.[2] Some few data emerged bearing on this hypothesis. In the cases [3] in which it was possible to continue the study and administer a second Rorschach after parturition, the results indicated (in every case except that of Dolores, for reasons indicated in her case discussion) that (a) the neurotic anxiety had decreased slightly, but (b) the particular anxiety pattern remained the same. Some slight change of foci was evidenced: e.g., Helen's focus of anxiety on parturition had largely vanished, and there was a slight increase of anxiety about her relations with men over that in the preparturition Rorschach. In Frances there was a shift from a rigid defense (constriction) against the anxiety-creating situation of relations with men to a greater acceptance of the possibilities of these relations, with more overt signs of anxiety. But the data in the present study bearing on this hypothesis are scanty.

The case of Brown throws some light on why it was not possible in the study of unmarried mothers (in addition to the fact that we could not study a very large number of the girls after parturition) to get more data on the shifts of foci of neurotic anxiety. In his case, studied over a period of two and one-half years, the shifts of foci of neurotic anxiety were very evident, and the above hypothesis could be clearly demonstrated. An interesting phenomenon, however, was noticed: after his severe anxiety attacks, a respite from anxiety often occurred for a week or several weeks, despite the fact that his underlying conflicts were not radically nearer solution than at the time of the anxiety.[4]

---

[2] As stated earlier, one of the purposes of the second Rorschach and the anxiety check-lists after parturition was to determine if possible the shifts in the foci of anxiety after the birth of the baby.

[3] Helen, Agnes, Charlotte, Frances, Dolores.

[4] This phenomenon—that after a period of severe anxiety there is a respite for a time, despite the fact that the underlying conflict is not radically clarified—obviously raises a perplexing problem. This phenomenon may partially explain the slight decrease of anxiety after parturition in the case of the girls (in addition to the fact that the immediate anxiety-creating situation of parturition was past and the disposal of the baby in most cases arranged for). If this phenomenon occurs generally, one explanation which suggests itself is based upon the guilt feeling involved in the neurotic anxiety. It is our observation that there is generally a considerable amount of guilt feeling, often very subtle but generally pervasive, involved in the inner conflict which underlies neurotic anxiety. In Brown's case it was clearly evident that he experienced much guilt toward his mother in the instances when the occasion for his anxiety was his own achievement, and much guilt toward himself when the occasion was his dependency. It may be that this

After this respite period the neurotic anxiety then re-emerged, generally around new foci. It would seem, therefore, that the study of the girls in our group of unmarried mothers did not continue long enough after the parturition to discover the new foci of anxiety which presumably would emerge, let us say, when the girl got into a work situation or initiated relations with a new man friend. *In fine,* the data in the present study point toward an affirmation of the hypothesis that the foci of neurotic anxiety (neurotic fears) will shift while the underlying pattern of neurotic anxiety remains constant, but the data are not definite enough for this hypothesis to be termed demonstrated.

2. CONFLICT UNDERLYING NEUROTIC ANXIETY

Subjective Conflict as the Source of Neurotic Anxiety.— Whenever neurotic anxiety was found in the above cases, subjective conflict was likewise found.[5] In the cases in which neurotic anxiety was not found in any pronounced degree—Bessie, Louise, Sarah, Phyllis, Charlotte—subjective conflict in any pronounced form was not present either. The subjective conflict took many different forms depending on the individual case. To cite three examples, the subjective conflict in the case of Brown was seen to lie in his need to achieve some autonomy and use of his own powers on one hand, but in his conviction at the same time that if he did appropriate his own power he would be killed by his mother. Hence his behavior was characterized by great dependence on his mother (and mother surrogates) and hostility toward her at the same time. Whenever this conflict was activated, profound and extensive feelings of inadequacy, helplessness, and concomitant anxiety occurred, with paralysis of capacity for acting. In Helen, the conflict lay between guilt feelings on one hand and the need (upon the achieving of which her self-esteem depended) to appear amoral and intellectually

---

guilt feeling is temporarily allayed by having endured the painful experience of anxiety. And hence the anxiety which was caused by the guilt feeling (i.e., fear of punishment) would also be temporarily allayed. It was as though the person were saying, "I've paid the price; now I've earned a little peace." Both this problem and the possible explanation are advanced not in definite form, however, but for their suggestive values.

[5] Cases of Brown, Helen, Nancy, Ada, Agnes, Hester, Frances, Irene.

sophisticated. In Nancy the conflict appeared in the need to depend entirely upon others for her security, while at the same time she believed others to be undependable.

The situations which cued off this conflict in the case of each patient—e.g., for Brown, situations of dependency on one hand or occasions of his individual success on the other; for Helen, the guilt associated with her pregnancy; for Nancy, her relation to her fiancé—were the anxiety-creating situations. In these studies *subjective (inner) conflict was always present with neurotic anxiety, and it was the activation of this conflict which cued off the neurotic anxiety.*

The question arises as to the relation between the threat the individual anticipates and the conflict. The commonly accepted statement that anxiety—both normal and neurotic—always involves some anticipated threat is not contradicted by the data in the present study. In normal anxiety and fear, the description of the threat may account relatively inclusively for the existence of the apprehension.[6] But in neurotic anxiety, two conditions are necessary: (1) *the threat must be to a vital value* and (2) *the threat must be present in juxtaposition with another threat,* so that the individual cannot avoid one threat without being confronted by another.[7] If Brown uses his powers, he is threatened with death, but he can remain dependent upon his mother only at the price of continued feelings of worthlessness and complete helplessness, which is a threat almost as serious as being killed.[8] *The essence of the "trapped" feeling in neurotic anxiety is that the individual is threatened whichever way he turns.* Thus an inquiry into the nature of the threat anticipated by an individual in neurotic anxiety reveals the fact that threat is present on both sides of the conflict.

---

[6] The distinction made in Chapter 6 between anxiety and fear will be recalled, i.e., when the threat is to a vital, essential value, the reaction is anxiety, and when the threat is to a peripheral value, the reaction is fear.

[7] Cf. earlier statement (Chapter 6) that in patterns of neurotic anxiety, the values held essential to the individual's existence as a personality are in contradiction with each other.

[8] For another example, Nancy confronted the threat of being rejected by the others (mother and fiancé) whom she believed to be undependable, but her incapacity to exist without the care of these other persons confronted her with an opposite threat.

A corollary problem has also been raised and illustrated in the above cases, namely the distinction between the *occasion* and the *cause* in neurotic anxiety. (The term "occasion" is here used to mean the event which precipitated the anxiety.) It was observed that the occasions of Brown's neurotic anxiety were frequently situations (such as performing his academic assignments) which he could and did handle adequately; thus the occasion in those instances could not be identified with the cause of the anxiety. We also observed that the more severe his anxiety, the more he insisted that the occasion had nothing to do with it, that he was "afraid of everything," "afraid of life." While it is true that the particular occasion which cued off the anxiety spell could in retrospect be shown to have a psychologically consistent relation to the anxiety, there is none the less some logic in his insistence on the distinction between occasion and cause. In neurotic anxiety, *the occasion is significant in the respect that it cues off the underlying conflict, but the cause of the anxiety is the conflict.*[9]

It seems to the writer that a hypothesis may be formulated as follows: *The more nearly normal an experience of anxiety is, the more the occasion (precipitating event) and the cause of the anxiety are identical; but the more neurotic the anxiety, the more the occasion and the cause are to be distinguished.* For example, a passenger on a ship in submarine-infested waters is anxious lest the ship be torpedoed.[10] Such anxiety may be realistic and proportionate to the situation, and the occasion—the threat of being torpedoed—may conceivably be a relatively sufficient explanation of the anxiety. But at the other extreme, persons with severely neurotic anxiety may be precipitated into an anxiety spell by a chance word from an acquaintance, a lack of greeting from someone on the street, or a fleeting memory. Thus the more neurotic the anxiety, the less adequate becomes the objective occasion as an explanation, and the more we are driven to

---

[9] As was demonstrated in this case, the occasions, no matter how insignificant they may seem to be objectively, always bear a subjectively logical relation to the particular inner conflict in the given individual; that is to say, the occasions are significant for the anxiety of the subject because they, and not other occasions, cue off his particular neurotic conflict.

[10] This illustration is from Dr. P. M. Symonds.

subjective factors in the individual to find the adequate cause of the anxiety. This is generally described as anxiety which is disproportionate to the situation; it *is* disproportionate to the occasion, but it is *not* disproportionate to the cause, namely the inner conflict which the occasion has activated. In the writer's experience in cases of the most severe anxiety—borderline psychotics —the occasion, viewed objectively, is almost entirely inadequate as an explanation for the degree of anxiety, and the cause may be almost entirely subjective.

Rejection by Parents and Predisposition to Neurotic Anxiety.—This question is considered in the light of the study of thirteen unmarried mothers, in which particular emphasis was placed on inquiring into the relationship of the degree of rejection the girl experienced at the hands of her parents (especially the mother) and the girl's degree of present neurotic anxiety. The parallel tables of the rankings according to degrees of anxiety and rejection by parents present immediately two phenomena: (1) *For the majority of the girls there is a clear correspondence between rejection and anxiety; but* (2) *for several girls there is no correspondence whatever.*[11]

In nine cases—Nancy, Agnes, Helen, Hester, Frances, Irene, Ada, Phyllis, Sarah—the degree of anxiety falls in the same cate-

[11]	RANKING ACCORDING TO DEGREE OF ANXIETY		RANKING ACCORDING TO DEGREE OF REJECTION	
	Nancy Agnes	}*high*	Nancy Agnes Bessie Louise	}*high*
	Helen Hester Frances Irene Ada	}*moderately high*	Helen Hester Frances Irene Ada * Dolores *	}*moderately high*
	Dolores Bessie	}*moderately low*		
	Louise Phyllis Sarah	}*low*	Phyllis Sarah	}*low*

* The reader will recall the discussion in their case presentations of the difficulties in ranking these girls on rejection and the bases on which the above judgment was made.

Charlotte, the girl with mildly psychotic trends, cannot be ranked for the above purposes, since in her condition it was impossible to determine the degree of rejection with any confidence.

gory as that of rejection. In this group, whenever there was evidenced rejection by parents, there was present neurotic anxiety, and in a roughly corresponding degree. The indications in these cases are on the side of the classical hypothesis: rejection by parents (especially by the mother) predisposes the individual to neurotic anxiety.[12] But in two cases—Louise and Bessie— a radically different picture was presented: these two girls experienced profound and extensive parental rejection, and yet they did not have a corresponding degree of neurotic anxiety.[13]

The key to the problem is to be found by inquiring into the psychological meaning of the rejection.[14] We shall therefore ask, with reference first to the cases of the girls in whom rejection was found with neurotic anxiety and then to the cases in which it was not: *How did the girl subjectively interpret her rejection?* The chief characteristic of the girls who fit the hypothesis is that they always interpreted the rejection against the background of high expectations of their parents. They exhibited what we have termed a *contradiction between expectations and reality* in their attitudes toward their parents. They were never able to accept the rejection as a realistic, objective fact. In one breath Nancy described how the mother flagrantly left her alone, caring "more for going out to bars than for her child," but in the next breath she added, "She *could* have been such a good mother." Similarly, Nancy needed constantly to repeat that the mother was "good" at certain special periods in her childhood, despite the objective indications that the mother was consistently unstable and irresponsible in her relations with the child.[15] Helen spoke of her mother's "disloyalty" to her,

---

[12] The above discussion has to do with neurotic anxiety. Predisposition to anxiety is taken to mean the presence, at least potentially, of neurotic anxiety, anxiety which is discoverable both in terms of quantity (more anxiety than the girls in a lower category) and in terms of the special features of neurotic, as opposed to normal, anxiety.

[13] Dolores falls in this group, though her case is not as extreme as the other two.

[14] The writer believes that this would be the significant question even if the rankings were not to show these distinct differences. In other words, the convincing conclusions in case studies depend upon the meaning of the point at hand in the constellation of each case.

[15] In the case of Nancy, a point was also demonstrated that may presumably hold for the other cases as well: namely, that the idealized expectations on one hand and the feelings of rejection on the other *reinforce* each other. One specific function of the idealization in Nancy's case (as in others) was to cover up the

implying the expectation that the mother could and should have been different. Frances idealized her parents by describing them as "wonderful" and "sweet," preserved the idealization under the "fairy-tale" motif, and endeavored to suppress her considerable feelings of hostility toward them and her feelings of isolation as an adopted child. These girls exhibited, furthermore, what might be termed a nostalgia about their relations with their parents, dwelling on pictures of what "might have been" if their parents had been different; this nostalgia seemed both to be part of the idealized expectations toward the parent and a way of avoiding the reality situation of their relations with their parents. Hester exhibited a nostalgia in a somewhat different form, "If my father had not died, I wouldn't have gotten in these difficulties." Likewise, these girls still carried hopes and expectations of changing the parent: Hester was engaged continually in rebellious behavior designed to force her mother to pay attention to her. Though Agnes knew that her father had never showed genuine concern for her in the past, and that there was no realistic hope of his now changing, she nonetheless at her present age made another trip to see him in some vague hope that he might be different. These girls seemed to be still fighting old battles with their parents.

In fine, in these cases which fit the classical hypothesis, where rejection is present with neurotic anxiety, we found a certain constellation always present: *The rejection was never accepted as an objective fact, but was held in juxtaposition with idealized expectations about the parent; the girl was unable to appraise the parent realistically, but always confused the reality situation with expectations of what the parent should have been or might yet become.*[16]

As has been pointed out above, all of the girls who exhibited neurotic anxiety exhibited subjective conflict at the same time.

reality of the rejection, but in the light of the idealized expectations the feelings of rejection became the more painful.

16 Though the case of Brown is not in this series, it is illuminating to note that he exhibited the same conscious incapacity to see his mother as the tyrannical person she was, but interpreted her dominating acts as "loving" behavior. The conflict this involves is seen clearly in the respect that his dreams revealed that on a deeper level he actually was aware of her as dominating and tyrannical.

It is now our problem to ask, what is the origin of this subjective conflict? We have seen, for example, that Nancy's neurotic anxiety appeared in the form of a conflict between her need to depend utterly on the love of her fiancé and her everpresent doubt as to whether his love was dependable. This is the same conflict which occurred in early years in her relation with her mother. We have seen that Frances viewed her boy friend with the same combination of idealization and repressed hostility which she exhibited in her relations with her parents. Without citing more examples here, we note in these cases that *the conflict which appeared in later neurotic anxiety was the same general conflict which was and is existent in the subject's relation with her parents.*[17] In these cases the original conflict with parents became introjected, internalized (i.e., became *subjective conflict*), resulting in inner trauma and a fundamental *psychological disorientation of the girl in her attitude toward herself and toward other people.* It not only remained as the source of persistent resentment toward the parents, but was the source likewise of persistent self-condemnation. This is not to say merely that it is the original conflict with parents which is reactivated in the subject's later neurotic anxiety. It is to say, more inclusively and more accurately, that the original conflict in relating to the parents sets the character structure of the individual with regard to interpersonal relations and that the individual meets future situations on the basis of the same character structure. For example, it is clear that a confusion of reality and expectations in relating to the parents would render the individual unprepared to appraise his future relations with other people realistically and that he would therefore be subject to recurrent subjective conflict and concomitant anxiety.

A sharply contrasting constellation is seen in those girls who experienced rejection but did not exhibit any pronounced neu-

---

[17] This is the ground for assuming a causal relationship between the rejection by parents, which generally occurs significantly in the early years, with present predisposition to neurotic anxiety. The *a priori* rationale behind such an assumption of causality has been given in previous chapters (along with the clinical data supporting the assumption) in the discussion of the viewpoints of Sullivan, Horney, Fromm, and in fact practically every psychoanalytic writer from Freud onward. All the above reasoning presupposes a continuity in individual character structure.

rotic anxiety, namely Bessie, Louise, and in some respects Dolores.[18] These girls did not entertain idealized expectations about their parents; they appraised their parents realistically, Louise and Bessie accepting their mothers as the punitive, hating persons they actually were. Neither girl cherished any illusions that the parent had been "good" at some particular date, or that the parent might become loving the next day. Louise and Bessie accepted rejection as an objective fact; Louise impersonally termed it "hard luck," and Bessie took steps to obtain her affection in relations with persons other than her parents. Neither girl permitted the parental rejection to change her behavior: Bessie went ahead playing with the siblings, in the childhood example, despite her father's flagrant rejection at her approach, and Louise refused to engage in hypocritical expressions of affection to a mother she did not love. In these girls *there was no cleavage, no contradiction between expectation and reality* in their relations with their parents. The conflicts these girls experienced in their relations to others as well as their parents were on a conscious, objective basis. *The essential point in their freedom from neurotic anxiety was that their rejection was not internalized; it was not made a source of subjective conflict, and it therefore did not psychologically disorient them in their self-appraisal or appraisal of others.*

While the present study supports the hypothesis that the conflict underlying neurotic anxiety has its origin in the individual's relation to his parents, it does not support the statement that rejection as such predisposes to neurotic anxiety. Rather, *the origin of the predisposition to neurotic anxiety lies in that particular constellation in the child's relation to the parent in which the child cannot appraise the parent's attitude realistically and cannot accept the rejection objectively.* Neurotic anxiety arises not out of the fact of having had a "bad" mother, to use Sullivan's

---

18 The difference between the reactions of these girls to rejection and those of the former group is shown graphically in Dolores' surprise that the psychologist would raise the question of whether she had regretted as a child that her father never played with her. For any of the girls in the first group, such a question would have made entire sense, and would in most cases have been used by the girl as a springboard for getting out a good deal of her resentment toward the parent; for Dolores, however, such a question had apparently never entered her head.

phrase, but out of the fact that the child is never sure whether the mother is "good" or "bad." What causes the conflict underlying neurotic anxiety, looking at the problem from the viewpoint of the parent's behavior toward the child, is *rejection covered over with pretenses of love and concern.* In the cases of Louise and Bessie, the parents—punitive and cruel as they were —at least did not endeavor to cover up their hatred for their children.[19] Louise and Bessie could therefore accept the rejection at face value—and, in Bessie's case, seek love and affirmative relations elsewhere. Thus, when the mothers of Louise and Bessie rejected them in later childhood and adolescence, *no vital value was threatened;* they had not expected anything better from the parents anyway. Louise's statement, "As a child you don't suffer, you take things as they come," may be taken to mean that you don't suffer in the most basic way—i.e., experiencing a threat to vital values—if you can, as she did, call the attitude of the mother by its right name. But in the cases of the girls with subjective conflict, the rejection tended to be covered over by idealized expectations (presumably existent in the parent's earlier pretenses to the child), and hence the child never could adjust to it as a reality.[20] In the light of these observations, one could roughly differentiate three types of parental relationships: (a) the parent rejects the child but the rejection is in the open and admitted on both sides; (b) the parent rejects the child, but covers up the rejection with pretenses of love; and (c) the parent loves the child and behaves toward him on that

[19] Melitta Schmideberg asks why it is that children of modern parents, who obviously are more lenient toward them, still have as much or more anxiety than children of the stern, severe, Victorian parents. She believes the reason is that modern parents do not permit the child to be afraid of them, and therefore the child must displace his fear and hostility and suffer consequent anxiety. If parents cannot refrain from punishing the child, she adds, at least they should give the child the right to be afraid of them (see her Anxiety states, *Psychoanal. Rev.,* 1940, 27 : 4, 439-49). Without going into the historical question of the relative anxiety in these different periods or the complicated reasons for it, we nonetheless feel that Dr. Schmideberg's emphasis on permitting the child to appraise the relation realistically is sound.

[20] Cf. Kardiner's point that the stage is set for the development of neurotic anxiety in Western man's psychological growth pattern by, among other things, the inconsistency in the parental training of the children (Chapter 5 above).

basis. The data in this study affirm that it is the *second* kind of relationship which predisposes to neurotic anxiety.[21]

The point we are here discussing is so significant that we wish to quote some remarkably similar findings from the studies of children by Anna Hartoch Schachtel. Describing one child whose mother rejected her but pretended love and exhibited possessive jealousy of the child's love for the grandmother, Mrs. Schachtel states, "This child lives in a make-believe situation; she has to avoid facing the real situation of not being loved; she lives in a wishful expectancy and bases her whole interests, fears, expectations and wishes on this shaky basis." This child corresponds very closely to the girls in the first group we have been describing. Mrs. Schachtel describes another child who was fatherless, was frequently beaten at home and told what a nuisance she was. "To her it is a fact that she is not loved, but this in no way impairs her own capacity to love." She was an independent, rather tough, aggressive, cooperative, and reliable child who "does not minimize or beautify inhuman and hostile things that happen to her." This child seems to the writer remarkably like Bessie. As was the case with Bessie, this child found love in friends and siblings despite the parental rejection. Mrs. Schachtel points out that *"not being loved is better than the experience of pseudo-love for a child."* The findings of the present study would indicate that this is very true with respect to the predisposition to neurotic anxiety.[22]

Can neurotic anxiety in general be described in the form in which we have discovered it in the relations of these girls to their parents, namely as a *subjective disorientation arising from a fundamental contradiction between expectations and reality?* This question would lead beyond the scope of this immediate

---

21 If the rejection is complete—if, that is, the child in its infant months has no experience of relatedness, even of a hostile nature, with parents or parent surrogates—the result is the psychopathic personality. This type is also characterized by a lack of neurotic anxiety. For an excellent discussion of this point, see Lauretta Bender, Anxiety in disturbed children, paper delivered at the American Psychopathological Association symposium on anxiety, June 4, 1949 (to be published).

22 These findings are contained in a summary of an unpublished paper, "Some Conditions of Love in Childhood," by Anna Hartoch Schachtel, March, 1943.

discussion, but the author suggests the above definition as a hypothesis having both psychological and philosophical promise.[23]

3. Socioeconomic Class and Neurotic Anxiety

A final question arises from the fact that the girls in the first group, i.e., with neurotic anxiety, *were all middle-class girls,* and those in the second group, who were rejected but accepted it without neurotic anxiety, *were all from the proletarian class.*[24] Indeed, of the four proletarian girls in this study—Bessie, Louise, Sarah, and Dolores—not one exhibits any pronounced neurotic anxiety. This raises the important problem of whether, in our culture, the contradiction between expectations and reality underlying the predisposition to neurotic anxiety is especially a characteristic of the middle class and likewise whether neurotic anxiety is predominantly a middle-class phenomenon. The classical hypothesis concerning rejection and predisposition to neurotic anxiety is based upon clinical and psychoanalytic work with subjects who are almost exclusively of the middle or upper middle class.[25] Perhaps the hypothesis is true for the middle classes but not for other classes. There is much *a priori* reason, and there are some *a posteriori* data, for the contention that neurotic anxiety is especially a middle-class phenomenon in our culture. The cleavage between reality and expectations is particularly in evidence, psychologically as well as economically, in the

---

[23] MacKinnon has presented a description of anxiety which, apart from its topological features (which may be open to question), is similar to the above hypothesis. "A person troubled by anxiety . . . simultaneously sees things as both *better* and *worse* than they are. . . . His positive irreality distorts the structure of his level of reality in accordance with his *hopes,* while at the same time his negative irreality distorts it in accordance with his *fears.* . . . This means that psychologically the individual stands on unfirm ground, for the level of reality of his life space lacks clear cognitive structure since it has simultaneously the conflicting meanings of probable success and probable failure."—Donald W. MacKinnon, A topical analysis of anxiety, *Character & Pers.,* 1944, 12: 3, 163-76.

[24] The only difficulty in classification was in the case of Ada. It may be noted that the child Mrs. Schachtel described as accepting rejection as a realistic fact was also proletarian.

[25] This is true of the patients of Freud and of most all the patients of psychoanalysts in private practice since.

middle class.[26] It has earlier been indicated (Chapter 4) that individual competitive ambition, a trait in our culture intimately associated with contemporaneous anxiety, is chiefly a middle-class trait.[27] Fascism, a prominent cultural anxiety symptom in our day, begins as a lower-middle-class movement. Willoughby makes the conjecture that "the anxiety burden lies heaviest upon the 'middle class,' who remain bound by difficult standards without important material support." [28] This paragraph is not intended to advance a conclusion, but rather to raise, as an inquiry worthy of further investigation, the problem of the relation of neurotic anxiety to the situation of the middle class.

4. Interrelation of Anxiety and Hostility

It has been illustrated in the cases in this study that *anxiety and hostility (covert or overt) rise and fall together.* When the subjects (e.g., Brown, Agnes) were relatively more anxious, more covert or overt hostility was evidenced, and when the anxiety abated, the hostility did likewise. We have seen that one reason for this interrelation is that the intense pain and helplessness of the experience of anxiety arouses hostility toward those other persons whom the individual holds responsible for placing him in such a state. We have observed that another reason underlying this interrelation is that hostility (particularly repressed hostility) leads to anxiety: e.g., Brown's repressed hostility toward his mother, if expressed, would alienate the very person he is dependent upon, and hence its existence generates more anxiety. Thus, when hostility arises in persons with neurotic anxiety, *the hostility is generally repressed* and may take the reactive form of an increased striving to please and placate other people (e.g., Nancy). One case, however, was presented (Agnes, whose character structure was sado-masochistic) in

---

26 Karl Marx described the proletarian class as the class which had no expectations short of revolution.

27 The proletarian girls in this study showed less competitive ambition than the middle-class girls (see cases of Bessie, Louise). Sarah had worked out an ingenious system by which her ambition would not be competitive, "I arrange to be not on the top, or not on the bottom, but in the middle."

28 R. R. Willoughby, Magic and cognate phenomena: an hypothesis, in Carl Murchison (ed.), *Handbook of social psychology* (Worcester, Mass., 1935), p. 502.

which hostility and aggression were employed as defenses against the anxiety-creating situation; e.g., by hostile and aggressive behavior she endeavored to force her boy friend not to make her more anxious by abandoning her.

5. Methods of Avoiding the Anxiety-Creating Situation

Many different behavior patterns by means of which the individual sought to avoid the anxiety-creating situation have been shown in the above cases, varying from relatively realistic behavior, like Bessie's escaping into the park to avoid her mother's abuse, to behavior traits like Irene's shyness and the more complex subjective methods of repression and symptom-formation. Without endeavoring to catalog these protective behavior patterns, we wish to summarize some of their common features.

It has been shown that these behavior patterns were called into play when the individual was confronted by an anxiety-creating situation. In Helen's case, for example, it was noted that the more anxiety was present in certain responses in her Rorschach, the more she exhibited her particular defenses of forced laughter, denial, and intellectualization; and in the case of Agnes, the more she was made anxious by her boy friend's inattention, the more she exhibited her particular protective behavior, namely aggression and hostility. It has been shown, moreover, that when the anxiety abated, the defensive behavior likewise abated. The rationale behind these phenomena is obvious: when an anxiety-creating situation confronts the individual, the defenses against it are called into action. Thus there was a *direct relation between the presence of anxiety and the presence of behavioral mechanisms for the avoiding of the anxiety-creating situation.* But when the behavioral mechanism had been structured in the form of a psychological symptom, the anxiety-creating conflict was overcome before it reached the level of conscious awareness.[29] In the case of Brown, for example, so long as the fear of cancer and the preoccupation with the psychosomatic

---

[29] In this connection, a symptom may be defined as an inner, structuralized defense mechanism which obviates the conflict by automatic psychological processes.

symptom of dizziness were present, there was no admission of conscious conflict or neurotic anxiety. But when the conflict and anxiety emerged into consciousness, the symptoms vanished. Hence it has also been illustrated (and this is not contradictory to the previous statement), that when symptomatology is present, *there is an inverse relation between conscious anxiety and the presence of the symptoms.*[30]

It follows, therefore, that in neurotic anxiety the purpose of the defense mechanisms, symptoms, etc., is to keep the inner conflict from being activated.[31] It has been noted that to the extent these mechanisms are successful, the individual is able to avoid confronting his conflict. To cite several examples: If Nancy could keep everyone in her environment benevolently disposed toward her, the conflict involved in her needing to depend en-

---

[30] This is in accord with previous statements in this study (Chapter 3).

[31] It will be noted that the above point, namely that these behavioral patterns and symptoms are defenses against the anxiety-creating situation, is in contrast to the usual statement in psychoanalytic writing that these patterns are "defenses against anxiety." Accurately speaking, the defense is not against anxiety, but against the situation which creates the anxiety. Sometimes the phrase "defense against anxiety" is used simply for stylistic purposes, as a shortened form of the accurate but more bulky statement (this is the case when the phrase is used in this present study). But sometimes it is mistakenly used to mean what it says, namely that the individual carries a certain quantity of anxiety in the form of unrelieved excitation, and this is what he needs to defend himself against. Freud expressed this view explicitly in his first theory of anxiety as undischarged libido. Willoughby carries this theory to its logical conclusion, describing anxiety as a generalization of nervous excitation, . . . "as if a general nervous irradiation or overflow were in process. . . ." (*Op. cit.,* p. 466.) Abnormal anxiety he describes as excitation which has been generated without relief in action until a considerable "head" has been attained. If this were the case, it would indeed be true that the subject would have to defend himself against this "head" of excitation. The writer believes this description arises from a confusion of neurological and physiological modes of anxiety with anxiety itself. The inaccuracy of the concept of carrying a "head" of excitation can be demonstrated in many therapeutic sessions, when severe anxiety may be relieved without any pronounced expression or abreaction of affect, perhaps with no more affect than quiet relief. The relief occurs when the threat is removed, or, in neurotic anxiety, when the conflict is clarified. It is important for clarity of thinking on this issue to emphasize that there would be no anxiety unless the individual were confronted with some threat; the anxiety continues not because a "head" has been generated, but because the threat continues. People who exhibit inordinate amounts of anxiety are not to be accurately described as carrying a considerable "head" of excitation, but rather as persons who are inordinately vulnerable to threats and therefore are often and perhaps even continuously in situations of threat. What the subject seeks to defend himself against is not the anxiety itself (or the "head" of excitation), but the situation which causes the anxiety—the threat, or in neurotic cases, the conflict involving threats. (See also footnote 45, p. 66.)

tirely on others but believing at the same time that they are undependable would never arise. If Helen could successfully deny
or intellectualize her guilt feelings, her conflict would be obviated. In the complicated symptoms of Brown, this same purpose
can be discerned: If he really had cancer or a neurological brain
damage (or could successfully believe he had them), he could
(a) enter a hospital, submit himself to authorities, and be taken
care of without guilt feeling, (b) be relieved of the necessity of
trying to do responsible work for which he felt inadequate, and
(c) get even with his mother by virtue of the fact that she would
be forced to support him in his illness. Thus the three main elements in his conflict would be obviated.

Inasmuch as the conflict in neurotic anxiety is subjective, the
mechanism for obviating it *always involves some form of repression,* or *dissociation* of some reality of feeling or attitude.
In contrast to Bessie's objective behavior in running into the
park, the individual with neurotic anxiety endeavors to run away
from some elements within himself, and this can be accomplished
only by dissociating these elements, which sets up inner contradictions. For example, while Helen attempts on one hand to
deny outright the existence of her guilt feelings, at the same time
she goes to considerable lengths to intellectualize these feelings.
These two methods of obviating the guilt feelings are contradictory: [32] If she really believed she had no guilt feeling, she would
not need to intellectualize it. (It is as though a general were to
declare on one hand that there is no war going on, and on the
other hand be simultaneously calling up his reserves and rushing'
them into battle.) The dissociation which is necessary in the
endeavor to obviate a subjective conflict, involving the setting
up of inner contradictions, is one explanation of the fact that the
defense mechanisms in neurotic anxiety yield a security which is
continually in jeopardy and are never lastingly successful (as was
seen in every case of neurotic anxiety above) at obviating the
conflict.

---

[32] Specifically, the pattern involved is outright endeavor to repress a real feeling
(the denial); on a deeper level she is aware of the deception involved in the repression, so another mechanism is called into play, namely intellectualization.

One behavioral pattern for protecting the individual from anxiety-creating situations has been discussed in the above cases which, so far as the writer knows, has not yet been dealt with in the literature on anxiety. This is the use of *anxiety itself as a defense,* a mechanism best seen in the case of Nancy. This subject had no effective defenses against anxiety except to be continually cautious and alert—in other words, to behave anxiously and to show others that she was anxious. Her endeavor to keep others always benevolently disposed toward her (which would obviate her conflict) was implemented by showing others how much she needed them, how much she would be hurt if they were unfriendly to her. This behavior may be summed up as a method of saying to others, "See how anxious I am—do not make me more anxious." In cases in which being anxious and showing anxiety is a defense against more anxiety, the individual often seeks to avoid conflict by assuming an appearance of weakness, as though he believed that others would not attack him, forsake him, or expect too much of him if they saw that he was anxious. We here term the anxiety which is employed defensively as *pseudo-anxiety.*[33] But it is highly doubtful whether such a defensive use of anxiety would have developed except as the subject was considerably vulnerable to genuine neurotic anxiety on a deeper level. The distinguishing of anxiety which is used as a defense from genuine anxiety is particularly important in psychotherapy, for the defensive pseudo-anxiety constitutes an exception to the generally accepted principle that anxiety must be relieved before the defenses against it can be relinquished by the patient.[34]

---

[33] Adler saw this method of using anxiety, but instead of describing it as a defense or as pseudo-anxiety, he places all anxiety in this category.

[34] When such anxiety is honored or taken at its face value in psychotherapy, the underlying conflict is not clarified, for the anxiety (like any other defense) serves to cover up the conflict. Wilhelm Reich's discussion of the necessity in therapy for attacking the patient's defenses despite the eruption of his anxiety is significant at this point. See his *Character analysis: principles and technique for psychoanalysts in practice and in training,* trans. T. P. Wolfe (New York, 1945).

6. Relation Between Anxiety and Impoverishment of Personality

Whereas the defenses and symptoms discussed in the preceding section were noted to be only partially successful as means of avoiding anxiety-creating situations, there is another means which may serve successfully for the avoidance of subjective conflict and neurotic anxiety. This is impoverishment of personality. This complex and important problem will be discussed from several aspects.

Anxiety Impoverishes Personality.—It was noted that Brown's first Rorschach, taken while he was in a relatively severe anxiety state, exhibited a low degree of productivity, no originality, very little use of either feeling or thinking capacities, a predominance of vagueness of response, and a lack of capacity for relating to concrete realities. It was in general the picture of one whose relation to himself and to his environment is "blurred." But the second Rorschach, taken when he was not in anxiety, showed in marked contrast much greater productivity, some originality, marked increase in the use of thinking and feeling capacities, and much greater capacity to deal with concrete, specific realities. The vagueness and blurred relation to reality had entirely vanished. Another example is the case of Dolores, whose anxiety panic literally paralyzed her productivity on the first Rorschach, as well as rendering her in large measure incapable of relating to the other persons at Walnut House. These instances illustrate that anxiety involves a paralyzing in greater or lesser degree of the productive activities of the individual on various fronts—his thinking and feeling capacities as well as his capacity to plan and act.[35] The "blurred" relation to one's self and to others, as well as to other aspects of reality, is an illustra-

---

[35] This impoverishing effect of anxiety underlies the common dictum that "anxiety cancels out work." The fact that many people in our culture throw themselves into frantic work when they are anxious does not contradict the above statement. Their compulsive activism is both an expression of the tension experienced in anxiety and an endeavor to relieve the tension; it is activity of only a pseudo-productive nature, comparable to Brown's very rapid talking when in anxiety.

tion of Goldstein's contention that anxiety destroys the capacity to evaluate stimuli realistically or to distinguish between subject and object—which amounts, in his phrase, to an experience of the "dissolution of the self."

Distortion of Reality.—This is another means of obviating conflict which involves some impoverishment of personality. We noted that in the mildly psychotic state of Charlotte no present problems seemed to exist; if topics arose in the interviews which might touch upon possible conflicts, Charlotte assumed an artificially gay attitude or retreated into periods of vacant silence. In this case the psychotic development covered over any possible conflicts. With respect to those forms of psychosis which are the end result of subjective conflict which is too great to be borne and at the same time insoluble on any other level, the psychotic development represents at one extreme a way out of the conflict and anxiety. In cases like that of Charlotte, this is effected at the price of distortion of her relation to reality (as shown in her attitude toward her pregnancy as well as in the distorted responses in her Rorschach).[36]

Impoverishment of Personality and Absence of Anxiety.— The case of Phyllis has demonstrated that impoverishment of personality may serve successfully as a means of avoiding subjective conflict and neurotic anxiety. Phyllis submitted entirely to the demands of her environment (especially in the person of her mother), accepted the impoverishment of personality this entailed, and exhibited practically no anxiety. We noted in Chapter 7 that Phyllis was glad that the obstetrician would not tell her about her condition, that she placed a positive value on "not knowing," and that she used her irrational "faith in science" as a magical incantation to allay anxiety in the same way superstitious persons in other historical periods would have used a prayer-wheel. Her case illustrates structuralized constriction of personality; she had accepted constriction and had so thoroughly systematized her activity that (in contrast to

---

[36] Cf. Yaskin's remark that the presence of anxiety is an indication that severe deterioration has not yet set in. In terms of the present discussion, the presence of anxiety indicates that the individual has not yet been forced to capitulate in the conflict.

the cases of Dolores and Brown) her capacity for expansion and development was largely atrophied. The price paid for this means of avoidance of conflict and anxiety was the surrender of her autonomy, the impoverishment of her thinking and feeling capacities, and a radical curtailing of her capacity to relate to other people. The same phenomenon is demonstrated in an unsuccessful form in the case of Frances, who attempted to constrict her personality and suppress feelings and originality as means of avoiding anxiety-creating situations. When she was successful in these endeavors, anxiety was not present; but when the constrictive processes were unsuccessful—when, for example, her originality emerged—anxiety likewise emerged.

Thus, *constriction and impoverishment of personality obviate subjective conflict and concomitant anxiety.* But as Kierkegaard, Goldstein, Fromm, and others have pointed out, the person's freedom, originality, capacity for independent love, as well as his other possibilities for expansion and development as an autonomous personality, are renounced in the same process. By accepting impoverishment of personality, one can buy freedom from anxiety, to be sure; but the price for this "bargain" is the loss of those most precious characteristics of the self which distinguish the human being from animals.

Anxiety and Creative Personality.—A final phase of the problem may be stated in a question: *Are more creative personalities more frequently confronted with anxiety-creating situations?* We have seen that impoverished personalities have relatively little neurotic anxiety; is the converse of this true? This thesis was set by Kierkegaard in his contention that since anxiety arises as one confronts possibility in his own development as well as in his communicativeness with others, the more creative persons are the ones who confront more situations of possibility and hence more anxiety-creating situations. In similar vein, Goldstein has held that the more creative person ventures into many situations which expose him to shock and hence is more frequently confronted with anxiety. We shall approach the problem by observing the parallel rankings of the girls in this study according to amount of anxiety on the one hand and potential intelligence, originality, and level of differentiation on the other. We are aware that this method leaves much to be desired; the rankings are necessarily a gross method of judgment, and furthermore it is doubtful whether the factors of potential intelligence, originality, and level of differentiation are very adequate as descriptions of what Kierkegaard, for example, meant by "creative." His term was, in German, *Geist,* by which he meant the capacity of man, as distinguished from animals, to conceive of possibility and actualize possibility (or as Goldstein phrases it in his studies of the brain-injured, the capacity to transcend the immediate, concrete situation in the light of "the possible"). Granted the shortcomings of our method, however, we believe the following approach may yield suggestive, though not definitive, indications.

RANKING ACCORDING TO AMOUNT OF ANXIETY		RANKING ACCORDING TO INTELLIGENCE POTENTIALITY [37]		
Nancy Agnes	} *high*	Helen Nancy	(130) (125)	} *high*
Helen Hester Frances Irene Ada	} *moderately high*	Hester Irene Frances Agnes	(120) (120) (120) (120)	} *moderately high*
Dolores Bessie	} *moderately low*	Phyllis Bessie Sarah Dolores	(115) (115) (110) (110)	} *moderately low*
Louise Phyllis Sarah	} *low*	Ada Louise	(100) (100)	} *low*

A glance at the comparative rankings for anxiety and for intelligence potentiality shows that the girls who are in the *high* or *moderately high* categories according to anxiety are all (except Ada) in either the *high* or *moderately high* categories for intelligence potentiality, and conversely that the girls who are in

---

[37] The intelligence potentiality is based upon the Rorschach and is to be distinguished from efficiency of intelligence. It is very doubtful whether results from tests which measure efficiency of intelligence would be useful in the present problem.

The case of Charlotte is omitted, since the psychotic development brings different elements into the picture.

the lower two categories in one list are likewise in the lower two on the other (again, Ada is the one exception). The suggested indications are, therefore, that the girls with the greater intelligence potentiality have the greater degree of anxiety.[38]

RANKING ACCORDING TO NUMBER OF ORIGINAL RESPONSES ON THE RORSCHACH		RANKING ACCORDING TO LEVEL OF DIFFERENTIATION AS ESTIMATED FROM THE RORSCHACH	
Helen	15 } high	Helen	high
Sarah	15		
		Irene	
		Frances	
Nancy	8	Nancy	moderately
Frances	7 moderately	Sarah	high
Agnes	7 high	Agnes	
Irene	6	Hester	
Hester	4		moderately
Louise	4 moderately	Bessie	low
Phyllis	3 low		
Bessie	2	Louise	
		Phyllis	low
Ada	0 } low	Dolores	
Dolores	0	Ada	

With respect to comparison of number of original responses with degree of anxiety, we note that all of the girls except one in the *high* and *moderately high* categories with respect to number of original responses are in the *high* or *moderately high* categories in anxiety. The one exception is the Negro girl, Sarah.[39] Likewise, all of the girls except one in the *high* or *moderately high* categories according to level of differentiation are in the upper two categories with respect to anxiety, the one exception again being Sarah. We shall not carry an analysis of these comparative rankings beyond the general form suggested above, since we believe that for the present problem, the ranking method should be employed for its suggestive rather than its definitive

---

[38] We do not mean that they will necessarily exhibit *overtly* greater anxiety; more intelligent persons presumably have also developed more effective ways of managing and controlling their anxiety. Some readers would prefer to speak of "potential anxiety," but the insertion of that term would not change the above point; potential anxiety is still anxiety. (See footnote 8, p. 197.)

[39] In the case discussion of Sarah it was pointed out that, for her, extra-marital pregnancy was probably not so much of an anxiety-creating situation as for the white girls and for the other Negro girl, Ada. Hence it is doubtful whether much weight should be given to her as the exception in these comparisons.

values. So far as the present methods go, however, *the results are on the side of the hypothesis that personalities of higher intelligence, originality, and level of differentiation likewise have more anxiety.*

Conclusion.—In the cases in our study impoverishment of personality is related to the absence of anxiety. Anxiety tends to impoverish and constrict the personality, and where impoverishment is accepted and structuralized in the personality, subjective conflicts and neurotic anxiety are obviated. In these respects the theses of Kierkegaard, Goldstein, and Fromm are confirmed. With regard to the converse proposition, presented by Kierkegaard and Goldstein, that the more creative and productive the personality, the more anxiety-creating situations are confronted (and hence the more potential anxiety is present), it may be said that the data in the present study point toward an affirmation of that thesis.

We now wish to sum up the above points in a conceptualization which may draw together some loose ends of the theory of anxiety. We have pointed out in earlier sections of this chapter that neurotic anxiety results from a cleavage or contradiction between expectations and reality, a contradiction which occurred originally in the person's relations with and attitudes toward his parents. It is important to emphasize now that a cleavage between expectations and reality has its normal and healthy form as well as its neurotic; indeed, it is present as one condition of all creative activity. The artist conceives in his imagination a landscape that has more significant form than the actual view before him, and his painting is the result of his capacity to wed his own expectations—in this case his artistic conception—with the reality of the scene before him. The man-created picture then has more beauty than the inanimate nature from which it was painted. Every scientific endeavor consists of the scientist's bringing to bear his own expectations—in this case hypotheses—upon reality, and when this process is successful he uncovers reality which was not known in just that way before. In ethical activity, the person brings to bear expectations—in this case ideals of more desirable relations—upon the reality of his immediate relations with other people, and by this means transforms his interpersonal relations. This capacity to experience a gap between expectations and reality, and with it the capacity to bring one's expectations into reality, are the characteristics of all creative endeavor which Kierkegaard described as conceiving "possibility" and bringing this possibility into actuality. We have also seen this capacity of man described by Goldstein as the capacity to deal with the "possible," and by Liddell as man's ability to "plan." [40]

Now we have noted that this capacity, however it may be defined, is the condition both for anxiety and for creativity. The two are bound together; as Liddell has put it, anxiety is the shadow of intellect. So our discussion now comes full circle: we see that man's creative abilities and his susceptibility to anxiety are two sides of the same capacity, uniquely possessed by the human mammal, to become aware of gaps between expectations and reality. But there is a radical distinction between the neurotic and the healthy manifestations of this capacity. In neurotic anxiety, the cleavage between expectations and reality is in the form of a *contradiction;* expectation and reality cannot be brought together, and since nobody can bear a constant experience of such a cleavage, the individual engages in a neurotic distortion of reality. Though this distortion is undertaken for the purpose of protecting the individual from neurotic anxiety, in the long run it makes the contradiction between the individual's expectations and reality more rigid and hence sets the stage for greater neurotic anxiety. In productive activity, on the other hand, the expectations are not in contradiction to reality, but are used as means of creatively transforming reality; the cleavage is constantly being resolved by the individual's bringing expectations and reality progressively into greater accord. This, as we have endeavored to show at many points throughout this study, is the sound way to overcome neurotic anxiety. Thus man's power to resolve the conflict between expectation and reality—his *creative* power—is at the same time his power to overcome neurotic anxiety.

---

[40] In this context man may be described as the mammal with imagination.

APPENDIX [1]

ANXIETY CHECK-LIST NO. 1

ANXIETIES I HAD IN CHILDHOOD

Every child has some worries, fears, or anxieties. Will you please check the following list as to whether you had each worry "never," "sometimes," or "often" as a child.

	Never	Some-times	Often
1. Failing a test in school			
2. My father losing his job			
3. Being scolded by the teacher			
4. Being in an accident			
5. My mother leaving me			
6. Not having enough to eat			
7. Not having girl friends			
8. Being left behind in my grade at school			
9. My parents being sick			
10. Someone following me at night			
11. My brother or sister leaving me			
12. Not being popular enough			
13. Getting struck by a car			
14. Making a speech before a group in school			
15. Getting sick			
16. My father scolding me			
17. Having bad dreams			
18. Not having boy friends			
19. Not being able to get a job			
20. Dying			
21. Not being a success			
22. My brother or sister picking on me			
23. Having to support my parents some day			
24. My mother scolding me			
25. Not getting enough presents at Christmas			
26. Being in a play in school (stage fright)			
27. The house burning down			
28. Being poor			
29. Being left alone in the dark			

[1] The three check-lists included here were used in studying the foci of anxiety of unmarried mothers as described in the text.

357

	Never	Some-times	Often
30. My sister or brother getting more presents than I at Christmas			
31. My father leaving me			
32. Whether I would get married			
33. My father punishing me			
34. My mother dying			
35. When my menstrual period came			
36. Robbers breaking in the house			
37. Not having an attractive home			
38. My brother or sister dying			
39. Being lonely			
40. Feeling my parents might not care for me			
41. Witches or ghosts coming			
42. My mother punishing me			
43. My father dying			
44. Not being attractive			
45. Not being healthy			
46. Things I saw in movies, like Frankensteins			
47. Being out in lightning and thunder-storm			
48. People picking fights with me			
49. Meeting snakes			
50. Meeting large animals			
51. Having the dentist pull a tooth			
52. Someone ridiculing or making fun of me			
53. Jumping or falling off a high cliff			
54. Being shut in a room by myself			

ANXIETY CHECK-LIST NO. 2

PRESENT ANXIETIES

People worry or have anxiety about different things. Please check this list as to whether you worry or have anxiety about each thing "often," "sometimes," or "never."

	Never	Some-times	Often
1. Being struck by an auto			
2. Not being attractive to men			
3. Going to the hospital			
4. Whether I will be successful at my jobs			
5. Getting old too soon			
6. Whether my mother is disappointed in me			
7. Whether I will be unhappy			
8. Not having enough money to get along			

		Some-	
	Never	times	Often
9. Being operated on	———	———	———
10. Not having men friends	———	———	———
11. Whether my baby will be healthy	———	———	———
12. What people in the hospital will say to me	———	———	———
13. Being discharged from my work	———	———	———
14. What my brother or sister thinks of me	———	———	———
15. The city being bombed by enemy planes	———	———	———
16. Where I will live	———	———	———
17. Nightmares or bad dreams	———	———	———
18. Whether I will get married some day	———	———	———
19. Being held up by a robber	———	———	———
20. What my baby will look like	———	———	———
21. Losing my figure	———	———	———
22. Not having good health	———	———	———
23. What my girl friends think about me	———	———	———
24. Dying	———	———	———
25. The labor pains of birth	———	———	———
26. What my men friends think of me	———	———	———
27. Bad luck	———	———	———
28. Whether I should keep my baby	———	———	———
29. What my father thinks of me	———	———	———
30. What kind of work I should follow	———	———	———
31. Being lonely	———	———	———
32. My father or mother dying	———	———	———
33. People being angry at me	———	———	———
34. Being poisoned	———	———	———
35. Not getting the man I love	———	———	———
36. Friends letting me down	———	———	———
37. Drowning	———	———	———
38. Not getting the approval of the employers I work for	———	———	———

ANXIETY CHECK-LIST NO. 3

FUTURE ANXIETIES

People have different worries or anxieties. Please check this list as to whether you worry or have anxiety about each thing "often," "sometimes," or "never."

		Some-	
	Never	times	Often
1. Friends not sticking by me	———	———	———
2. Where and how I will live	———	———	———
3. Being discharged from my job	———	———	———

	Never	Some-times	Often
4. Being hurt in an air raid	____	____	____
5. Not having men friends	____	____	____
6. What my sister or brother will think of me	____	____	____
7. My apartment building catching fire	____	____	____
8. How my baby will develop	____	____	____
9. Having an operation	____	____	____
10. Whether I will get married some day	____	____	____
11. Bad dreams or nightmares	____	____	____
12. Not getting the man I love	____	____	____
13. Being poisoned	____	____	____
14. My father or mother dying	____	____	____
15. Being lonely	____	____	____
16. What kind of work I should follow	____	____	____
17. What my men friends will think of me	____	____	____
18. Some calamity befalling me	____	____	____
19. Not having a good figure	____	____	____
20. What my father will think of me	____	____	____
21. What future plans I should make for the baby..	____	____	____
22. Dying	____	____	____
23. Not having good health	____	____	____
24. What my girl friends say about me	____	____	____
25. Being run into by a car	____	____	____
26. Getting old too quickly	____	____	____
27. Not being successful at my work	____	____	____
28. What my neighbors will think of me	____	____	____
29. Whether I will be unhappy	____	____	____
30. Whether I will have enough money to get along	____	____	____
31. How my baby's health will be	____	____	____
32. Not being attractive to men	____	____	____
33. Not getting the approval of employers I work for	____	____	____
34. People picking fights with me	____	____	____
35. A robber entering my house	____	____	____
36. What my mother will think of me	____	____	____
37. Having teeth pulled by a dentist	____	____	____
38. Having to go to the hospital again	____	____	____

NOTE.—The above three check-lists are not presented as models for other studies. They were drawn up for the author's study, and the content of the items is specifically related to that study. They are presented here to enable the reader to see more concretely the basis for one approach to the cases in Chapters 7 and 8.

BIBLIOGRAPHY

ADLER, ALFRED. 1917. *The neurotic constitution.* English trans. by Bernard Glueck. New York: Moffatt, Yard & Co.
——. 1927. *Understanding human nature.* Trans. by W. Beran Wolfe. New York: Greenberg: Publisher, Inc.
——. 1930. *The pattern of life,* ed. W. Beran Wolfe. New York: Cosmopolitan Book Corp.
——. 1930. *Problems of neurosis,* ed. Philippe Mairet. New York: Cosmopolitan Book Corp.
ALEXANDER, FRANZ. 1934. The influence of psychologic factors upon gastrointestinal disturbances. *Psychoanal. Quart.* **3**, 501-88.
ALLPORT, G. W. 1942. *The use of personal documents in psychological science.* New York: Social Science Research Council.
ALLPORT, G. W., and VERNON, P. E. 1933. *Studies in expressive movement.* New York: The Macmillan Co.
AUDEN, W. H. 1947. *The age of anxiety: a baroque eclogue.* New York: Random House, Inc.
BAILEY, PEARCE. 1935. *Theory and therapy: an introduction to the psychology of Dr. Otto Rank.* Paris: Jouve et Cie., Editeurs.
BENDER, LAURETTA. 1949. Anxiety in disturbed children. Paper read before the American Psychopathological Association, June 4, 1949 (to be published).
BERNSTEIN, LEONARD. 1949. Notes on *The age of anxiety,* Bernstein's Second Symphony, in *Concert Bulletin.* Boston: Boston Symphony Orchestra.
BINGER, CARL. 1945. *The doctor's job.* New York: W. W. Norton & Co., Inc.
BROCK, WERNER. 1935. *An introduction to contemporary German philosophy.* London: Cambridge University Press.
BROWN, LAWRASON. 1933. The mental aspect in the etiology and treatment of pulmonary tuberculosis. *International Clinics,* **3**:43, 151-62.
BURCKHARDT, JACOB. 1935. *The civilization of the Renaissance in Italy.* Authorized trans. from 15th ed. by S. G. C. Middlemore. ("Bonibooks Series.") New York: Albert and Charles Boni, Inc.
CANNON, W. B. 1927. *Bodily changes in pain, hunger, fear and rage.* (2d ed.) New York: Appleton-Century-Crofts, Inc.
——. 1939. *The wisdom of the body.* (Rev. and enl. ed.) New York: W. W. Norton & Co., Inc.
——. 1942. Voodoo death. *Amer. Anthrop.,* **44**:2, 169-81.
CASSIRER, ERNST. 1944. *An essay on man.* New Haven, Conn.: Yale University Press.
COUSINS, NORMAN. 1945. *Modern man is obsolete.* New York: The Viking Press, Inc.
DOLLARD, JOHN. 1935. *Criteria for the life history.* New Haven: Yale University Press.
——. 1942. *Victory over fear.* New York: Reynal & Hitchcock, Inc.

DOLLARD, JOHN, and HARTEN, DONALD. 1944. *Fear in battle*. (Rev. ed.) Washington, D.C.: *The Infantry Journal*, 1944.

DU BOIS, CORA. 1944. *People of Alor*. (With analyses by Abram Kardiner and Emil Oberholzer.) Minneapolis: University of Minnesota Press.

DUNBAR, HELEN FLANDERS. 1938. *Emotions and bodily changes*. (Rev. ed.) New York: Columbia University Press.

——. 1942. The relationship between anxiety states and organic diseases. *Clinics*, 1:4, 879-907.

——. 1943. *Psychosomatic diagnosis*. New York: Paul B. Hoeber, Inc., Medical Book Dept. of Harper & Bros.

EBON, MARTIN. 1948. *World communism today*. New York: Whittlesey House.

FRANK, L. K. 1936. Society as the patient. *Amer. J. Sociol.*, 42, 335.

——. 1939. Projective methods for the study of personality. *J. Psychol.*, 8, 389-415.

FREUD, SIGMUND. 1920. *A general introduction to psychoanalysis*. New York: Boni & Liveright. (First published in German in 1916.)

——. 1933. *New introductory lectures in psychoanalysis*. New York: W. W. Norton & Co., Inc.

——. 1936. *The problem of anxiety*. Trans. by H. A. Bunker. (American ed.) New York: W. W. Norton & Co., Inc. (Originally published under the title *Inhibition, symptom, and anxiety* by the Psychoanalytic Institute, Stamford, Conn., 1927.)

——. 1949. *An outline of psychoanalysis*. New York: W. W. Norton & Co., Inc.

FROMM, ERICH. 1939. Selfishness and self-love. *Psychiatry*, 2, 507-23.

——. 1941. *Escape from freedom*. New York: Rinehart & Co., Inc.

——. 1947. *Man for himself, an inquiry into the psychology of ethics*. New York: Rinehart & Co., Inc.

GESELL, A. L. 1929. The individual in infancy. In Carl Murchison (ed.), *The foundations of experimental psychology*. Worcester, Mass.: Clark University Press. Pp. 628-60.

GOLDSTEIN, KURT. 1938. A further comparison of the Moro reflex and the startle pattern. *J. Psychol.*, 6, 33-42.

——. 1939. *The organism, a holistic approach to biology*. New York: American Book Co.

——. 1940. *Human nature in the light of psychopathology*. Cambridge, Mass.: Harvard University Press.

GRAY, G. W. 1939. Anxiety and illness. *Harper's Magazine*, May, 1939, pp. 605-16.

GREENACRE, PHYLLIS. 1941. The predisposition to anxiety. *Psychoanal. Quart.*, 10, 66-94, 610-38.

GRINKER, R. R. 1944. Treatment of war neuroses. *J. Amer. med. Ass.*, 126:3, 142-45.

GRINKER, R. R., and SPIEGEL, S. P. 1945. *Men under stress*. Philadelphia: The Blakiston Co.

HAGMAN, R. R. 1932. A study of fears of children of preschool age. *J. exp. Educ.*, 1, 110-30.

HALLIDAY, JAMES L. 1948. *Psychosocial medicine, a study of the sick society*. New York: W. W. Norton & Co., Inc.

HALLOWELL, A. I. 1938. Fear and anxiety as cultural and individual variables in a primitive society. *J. soc. Psychol.*, **9**, 25-47.

———. 1941. The social function of anxiety in a primitive society. *Amer. sociol. Rev.*, **6**:6, 869-87.

HARTZ, JEROME. 1944. Tuberculosis and personality conflicts. *Psychosom. Med.*, **6**:1, 17-22.

HASTINGS, DONALD W. 1945. What fear is—and does—to fighting men. *New York Times Magazine*, July 15, 1945, pp. 11, 31-32.

HEALY, W., BRONNER, A. F., and BOWERS, A. M. 1930. *The meaning and structure of psychoanalysis.* New York: Alfred A. Knopf, Inc.

HERSHEY, LEWIS B. 1942. Fear in war. *New York Times Magazine*, September 27, 1942, pp. 5, 6, 36.

HESSE, HERMAN. 1947. *Steppenwolf.* Trans. by Basil Creighton. New York: Henry Holt & Co., Inc.

HORNEY, KAREN. 1937. *The neurotic personality of our time.* New York: W. W. Norton & Co., Inc.

———. 1939. *New ways in psychoanalysis.* New York: W. W. Norton & Co., Inc.

———. 1945. *Our inner conflicts, a constructive theory of neurosis.* New York: W. W. Norton & Co., Inc.

HUIZINGA, JOHAN. 1924. *The waning of the Middle Ages.* London: Edward Arnold & Co.

HUNT, J. McV. (ed.). 1944. *Personality and the behavior disorders.* New York: The Ronald Press Co.

IBSEN, HENRIK. *Eleven plays of Henrik Ibsen.* New York: Random House, Inc.

JERSILD, A. T. 1933. *Child psychology.* (Rev. ed.) New York: Prentice-Hall, Inc., 1940.

———. 1935. Methods of overcoming children's fears. *J. Psychol.*, **1**, 75-104.

JERSILD, A. T., MARKEY, F. V., and JERSILD, C. D. 1933. *Children's fears, dreams, wishes, daydreams, likes, pleasant and unpleasant memories.* Child Develpm. Monogr. No. 12. New York: Teachers College, Columbia University.

JERSILD, A. T., and HOLMES, F. B. 1935. *Children's fears.* Child Develpm. Monogr. No. 20. New York: Teachers College, Columbia University.

JONES, E. S. 1944. Subjective evaluations of personality. In J. McV. Hunt (ed.), *Personality and the behavior disorders.* New York: The Ronald Press Co. I, 139-70.

JONES, H. E., and JONES, M. C. 1928. A study of fear. *Childhood Education*, **5**, 136-43.

JUNG, C. G. 1916. *Collected papers on analytical psychology.* Authorized trans. by C. E. Long. London: Baillière, Tindall & Cox.

———. 1938. *Psychology and religion.* New Haven, Conn.: Yale University Press.

KAFKA, FRANZ. 1930. *The castle.* Trans. from the German by Edwin and Willa Muir. New York: Alfred A. Knopf, Inc.

———. 1937. *The trial.* Trans. from the German by Edwin and Willa Muir. New York: Alfred A. Knopf, Inc.

KARDINER, ABRAM. 1939. *The individual and his society—the psychodynamics of primitive social organization.* With a foreword and two ethnological reports by Ralph Linton. New York: Columbia University Press.

———. 1945. *The psychological frontiers of society.* New York: Columbia University Press.

KIERKEGAARD, SØREN. 1941. *Sickness unto Death.* Trans. by Walter Lowrie. Princeton, N. J.: Princeton University Press. (Originally published in Danish, 1849.)

———. 1944. *The concept of dread.* Trans. By Walter Lowrie. Princeton, N. J.: Princeton University Press. (Originally published in Danish, 1844.)

KLINEBERG, OTTO. 1940. *Social psychology.* New York: Henry Holt & Co., Inc.

KLOPFER, BRUNO, and KELLEY, DOUGLAS. 1942. *The Rorschach technique, a manual for a projective method of personality diagnosis.* Yonkers, N. Y.: World Book Co.

KUBIE, L. S. 1941. The ontogeny of anxiety. *Psychoanal. Rev.,* 8:1, 78-85.

LANDIS, C., and HUNT, W. A. 1939. *The startle pattern.* New York: Rinehart & Co., Inc.

LEVY, D. M. 1938. Maternal overprotection. *Psychiatry,* 1, 561 ff.

———. 1949. The source of acute anxieties in early childhood. Paper read before the American Psychopathological Association, June 4, 1949 (to be published).

LEWIN, KURT. 1936. *Principles of topological psychology.* New York: McGraw-Hill Book Co., Inc.

LIDDELL, HOWARD S. 1949. The role of vigilance in the development of animal neurosis. Paper read before the American Psychopathological Association, June 4, 1949 (to be published).

LOWRIE, WALTER. 1944. *A short life of Kierkegaard.* Princeton, N. J.: Princeton University Press.

LUDWIG, WALTER. 1920. Beiträge zur Psychologie der Furcht im Kriege. In Stein and Lipmann (eds.), *Beiträge zur Psychologie des Krieges.* Leipzig.

LURIA, A. R. 1932. *The nature of human conflicts.* New York: Liveright Publishing Corp.

LYND, R. S., and LYND, H. M. 1929. *Middletown.* New York: Harcourt, Brace & Co., Inc.

———. 1937. *Middletown in transition.* New York: Harcourt, Brace & Co., Inc.

MACKINNON, DONALD W. 1944. A topological analysis of anxiety. *Character & Pers.,* 12:3, 163-76.

MALLER, J. B. 1944. Personality tests. In J. McV. HUNT (ed.), *Personality and the behavior disorders.* New York: The Ronald Press Co. I, 170-214.

MANN, THOMAS. 1937. *Freud, Goethe, Wagner.* New York: Alfred A. Knopf, Inc.

MANNHEIM, KARL. 1941. *Man and society in an age of reconstruction.* New York: Harcourt, Brace & Co., Inc.

MASLOW, A. H., and MITTELMANN, BÉLA. 1941. *Principles of abnormal psychology: the dynamics of psychic illness.* New York: Harper & Bros.

MATTHEWS, HERBERT L. 1946. *The education of a correspondent.* New York: Harcourt, Brace & Co., Inc.

MAY, MARK A. 1941. *Education in a world of fear.* Cambridge, Mass.: Harvard University Press.

MAY, ROLLO. 1949. Historical roots of modern anxiety theories. Paper read before the American Psychopathological Association, June 3, 1949 (to be published).

MILLER, N. E., and DOLLARD, J. 1941. *Social learning and imitation.* New Haven, Conn.: Yale University Press.

MITTELMANN, B., WOLFF, H. G., and SCHARF, M. P. 1942. Experimental studies on patients with gastritis, duodenitis, and peptic ulcer. *Psychosom. Med.,* 4:1, 5-61.

MOWRER, O. H. 1939. A stimulus-response analysis of anxiety and its role as a reinforcing agent. *Psychol. Rev.,* 46:6, 553-65.

——. 1939. The Freudian theories of anxiety: a reconciliation. New Haven, Conn.: Institute of Human Relations, Yale University (mimeographed).

——. 1940. Anxiety-reduction and learning. *J. exp. Psychol., 27:5,* 497-516.

——. 1940. *Preparatory set (expectancy)—some methods of measurement.* Psychol. Monogr. No. 233.

——. 1950. *Learning theory and personality dynamics.*

——. 1949. Pain, punishment, guilt, and anxiety. Paper read before the American Psychopathological Association, June 3, 1949 (to be published).

MOWRER, O. H., and ULLMAN, A. D. 1945. Time as a determinant in integrative learning. *Psychol. Rev., 52:2,* 61-90.

MUMFORD, LEWIS. 1944. *The condition of man.* New York: Harcourt, Brace & Co., Inc.

MURPHY, GARDNER. 1932. *An historical introduction to modern psychology.* New York: Harcourt, Brace & Co., Inc.

MURPHY, GARDNER, MURPHY, L. B., and NEWCOMB, T. M. 1937. *Experimental social psychology, an interpretation of research upon the socialization of the individual.* (Rev. ed.) New York: Harper & Bros.

MURRAY, H. A., JR., *et al.* 1938. *Explorations in personality.* New York: Oxford University Press.

NATIONAL SOCIETY FOR THE STUDY OF EDUCATION. 1942. *The psychology of learning,* ed. Nelson B. Henry. 41st Yearbook, Pt. 2. Bloomington, Ill.: Public School Publishing Co.

NIEBUHR, REINHOLD. 1941. *The nature and destiny of man.* New York: Chas. Scribner's Sons.

NORTHROP, F. S. C. 1946. *The meeting of East and West, an inquiry concerning world understanding.* New York: The Macmillan Co.

OBERHOLZER, EMIL. 1949. Anxiety in Rorschach's experiment. Paper read before the American Psychopathological Association, June 3, 1949 (to be published).

ORTEGA Y GASSET, JOSÉ. 1946. *Concord and liberty.* Trans. from the Spanish by Helen Wey. New York: W. W. Norton & Co., Inc.

PASCAL, BLAISE. 1825. *Thoughts.* Trans. by E. Craig. New York: Carter, 1825.

PASCAL, BLAISE. 1946. *Pensées*. Ed. and trans. by G. B. Rawlings. Mt. Vernon, N. Y.: Peter Pauper Press.

PFISTER, OSCAR. 1948. *Christianity and fear, a study in history and in the psychology and hygiene of religion*. Trans. by W. H. Johnston. New York: The Macmillan Co.

PINTNER, R., and LEV, J. 1940. Worries of school children. *J. genet. Psychol.* 56, 67-76.

PLANT, J. A. 1937. *Personality and the cultural pattern*. New York: Commonwealth Fund, Division of Publications.

PLAUT, PAUL. 1920. Psychographie des Krieges. In Stein and Lipmann (eds.), *Beiträge zur Psychologie des Krieges*. Leipzig.

PRESCOTT, DANIEL ALFRED. 1938. *Emotion and the educative process*. Washington, D. C.: American Council on Education.

RADO, SANDOR. 1949. Organization of the emergency function at psychological levels. Paper read before the American Psychopathological Association, June 4, 1949 (to be published).

RANK, OTTO. 1929. *The trauma of birth*. New York: Harcourt, Brace & Co., Inc.

———. 1936. *Will therapy*. New York: Alfred A. Knopf, Inc.

REES, J. R. 1946. What war taught us about human nature. *New York Times Magazine*, March 17, 1946, pp. 11, 54-55.

REICH, WILHELM. 1945. *Character analysis: principles and technique for psychoanalysts in practice and training*. Trans. by T. P. Wolfe. New York: Orgone Press. (First published in German in 1935.)

REIK, THEODORE. 1941. Aggression from anxiety. *Int. J. Psycho-Anal.*, 22, 7-16.

RIEZLER, KURT. 1944. The social psychology of fear. *Amer. J. Sociol.*, 46:6, 489-98.

ROLLAND, ROMAIN. 1915. *Michaelangelo*. New York: Albert and Charles Boni, Inc.

RORSCHACH, HERMANN. 1942. *Psychodiagnostics*. New York: Grune and Stratton, Inc.

SAUL, LEON J. 1944. Physiological effects of emotional tension. In J. McV. Hunt (ed.), *Personality and the behavior disorders*. New York: The Ronald Press Co. Pp. 269-306.

SCHICHE, E. 1920. Zur Psychologie der Todesahnungen. In Stein and Lipmann (eds.), *Beiträge zur Psychologie des Krieges*. Leipzig.

SCHLESINGER, ARTHUR M., JR. 1948. Communism: a clear-eyed view (book review), *New York Times Book Review Section*, February 1, 1948, p. 1.

SCHMIDEBERG, MELITTA. 1940. Anxiety states. *Psychoanal. Rev.*, 27:4, 439-49.

SHAFFER, L. F. 1946. Fear and courage in aerial combat. *American Psychologist*, 1, 257.

SPINOZA, BARUCH. 1910. *The ethics of Spinoza and treatise on the correction of the intellect*. London: Everyman Edition.

STEKEL, WILHELM. 1923. *Conditions of nervous anxiety and their treatment*. Authorized trans. by Rosalie Gabler. London: Kegan Paul, Trench, Trubner & Co., Ltd.

SULLIVAN, HARRY STACK. 1947. *Conceptions of modern psychiatry.* Washington, D. C.: William Alanson White Psychiatric Foundation. (Reprinted from *Psychiatry*, 3:1 and 8:2.)

———. 1948. The meaning of anxiety in psychiatry and life. *Psychiatry,* 2:1, 1-15.

———. 1949. The theory of anxiety and the nature of psychotherapy. *Psychiatry,* 12:1, 3-13.

SYMONDS, JOHN ADDINGTON. 1935. *The Italian Renaissance.* New York: Random House, Inc.

SYMONDS, PERCIVAL M. 1946. *The dynamics of human adjustment.* New York: Appleton-Century-Crofts, Inc.

TAWNEY, R. H. 1920. *The acquisitive society.* New York: Harcourt, Brace & Co., Inc.

TILLICH, PAUL. 1944. Existential philosophy. *Journal of the History of Ideas,* 5:1, 44-70.

———. 1947. *The Protestant era.* Chicago: University of Chicago Press.

———. 1949. Anxiety-reducing agencies in our culture. Paper read before the American Psychopathological Association, June 3, 1949 (to be published).

TOYNBEE, ARNOLD J. 1949. How to turn the tables on Russia. *Woman's Home Companion,* August, 1949, pp. 30 ff.

VASARI, GIORGIO. 1946. *Lives of the artists.* Abridged and ed. by Betty Burroughs. New York: Simon & Schuster, Inc.

WATSON, JOHN B. 1924. *Behaviorism.* New York: W. W. Norton & Co., Inc.

WILLOUGHBY, R. R. 1935. Magic and cognate phenomena: an hypothesis. In Carl Murchison, ed., *A Handbook of Social Psychology.* Worcester, Mass.: Clark University Press.

WOLF, STEWART, and WOLFF, H. G. 1943. *Human gastric function.* New York: Oxford University Press.

WOLFE, THOMAS. 1929. *Look homeward, angel.* New York: Chas. Scribner's Sons.

———. 1934. *You can't go home again.* New York: Harper & Bros.

———. 1935. *Of time and the river.* New York: Harper & Bros.

YASKIN, JOSEPH. 1937. The psychobiology of anxiety, a clinical study. *Psychoanal. Rev.,* Supp. to Vols. 23-24, pp. 1-93.

ZELIGS, ROSE. 1939. Children's worries. *Sociology and Social Research,* 24: 22-32.

ZILBOORG, G. 1932. Anxiety without affect. *Psychoanal. Quart.,* 2, 48-67.

ZINN, E. 1940. Anxiety—clinically viewed. Paper presented before the Monday Night Group, season of 1939-40. New Haven, Conn.: Institute of Human Relations, Yale University (mimeographed).

INDEX OF NAMES

(Page numbers in italics are references to bibliography entries only.)

369

INDEX OF SUBJECTS

371